Colombia

Michael Kohn

Robert Landon & Thomas Kohnstamm

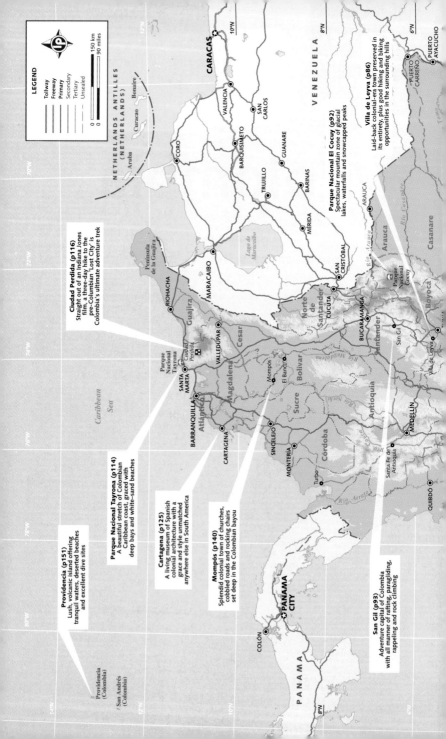

LEGEND

- Tollway
- Freeway
- Primary
- Secondary
- Tertiary
- Unsealed

0 — 150 km
0 — 90 miles

Providencia (p151)
Lush, volcanic island offering tranquil waters, deserted beaches and excellent dive sites

Ciudad Perdida (p116)
Straight out of an Indiana Jones film, a three-day hike to the pre-Columbian 'Lost City' is Colombia's ultimate adventure trek

Parque Nacional Tayrona (p114)
A beautiful stretch of Colombian Caribbean coast, graced with deep bays and white-sand beaches

Parque Nacional El Cocuy (p92)
Spectacular mountain zone of glacial lakes, waterfalls and snowcapped peaks

Villa de Leyva (p86)
Laid-back colonial-era town preserved in its entirety, plus good hiking and biking opportunities in the surrounding hills

Cartagena (p125)
A living museum of Spanish colonial architecture with a grace and style unmatched anywhere else in South America

Mompós (p140)
Splendid colonial town of churches, cobbled roads and rocking chairs set deep in the Colombian bayou

San Gil (p93)
Adventure capital of Colombia with all manner of rafting, paragliding, rappeling and rock climbing

NETHERLANDS ANTILLES (NETHERLANDS)

Aruba Curaçao Bonaire

VENEZUELA

CARACAS

VALENCIA
SAN CARLOS
BARQUISIMETO
CORO
GUANARE
TRUJILLO
BARINAS
MÉRIDA
SAN CRISTOBAL
CÚCUTA
ARAUCA
BUCARAMANGA
San Gil
Villa de Leyva
Parque Nacional Cocuy

MARACAIBO
Lago de Maracaibo

Península de la Guajira
RIOHACHA
VALLEDUPAR
Guajira
Cesar
Magdalena
SANTA MARTA
Ciudad Perdida
Parque Nacional Tayrona

Caribbean Sea

BARRANQUILLA
Atlántico
CARTAGENA
Bolívar
Mompós
El Banco
Sucre
SINCELEJO
MONTERÍA
Córdoba
Turbo
Río Atrato
Antioquia
Santa Fe de Antioquia
MEDELLÍN
QUIBDÓ

Norte de Santander
Santander
Boyacá
Río Arauca
Arauca
Casanare
Río Meta

PANAMA
PANAMA CITY
COLÓN

Providencia (Colombia)
San Andrés (Colombia)

PUERTO CARREÑO
PUERTO AYACUCHO

Río Magdalena

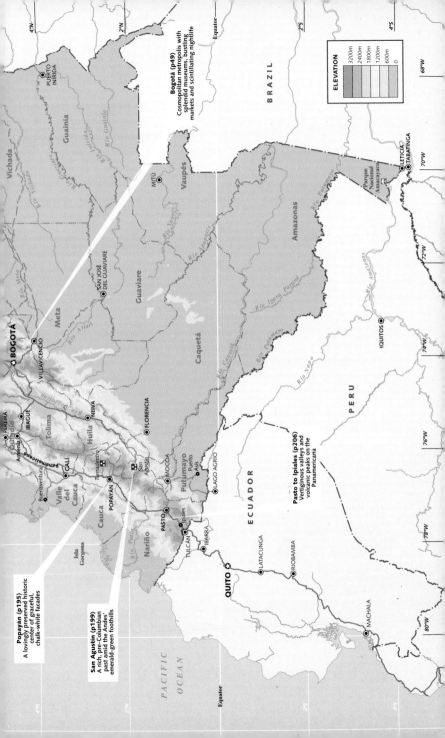

ELEVATION

3200m
2400m
1800m
1200m
600m
0

Bogotá (p49)
Cosmopolitan metropolis with splendid museums, bustling markets and scintillating nightlife

Pasto to Ipiales (p206)
Vertiginous valleys and volcanic peaks on the Panamericana

Popayán (p195)
A lovingly preserved historic center of graceful, chalk-white facades

San Agustín (p199)
A rich, pre-Columbian past amid the Andes' emerald-green foothills

Destination Colombia

Vibrant cities with streaking metros and soaring skyscrapers. Elegant port towns cut by cobbled alleys and graced with bougainvillea-shrouded balconies. Spectacular national parks ranging from Garden-of-Eden-tropical to heavenly-high-alpine. Cruise boats, party buses, late night salsa dancing and shopping glory. Check the cover again – yes, this is Colombia.

Get ready for shattered expectations. While media reports still speak of coca fields, violent crime, rebel shoot-ups and kidnappings, travelers are often left to wonder how so many troubles can plague a country that appears so, well, normal.

Beyond the headlines is a thriving country with a rising middle class, some of the best health care and universities in South America, and an improved level of security. It's true that Colombia also faces massive challenges in dealing with poverty, rebels and the long-standing Drug War, but security improvements have made many tourist destinations accessible to travelers.

Now is the time to go. Costs are low, the welcome is warm and Colombia's sour reputation has kept it off the 'gringo trail.' Many travelers consider Colombia a way station between better known overland destinations, such as Peru and Costa Rica. But once you've explored its wealth of colonial-era towns, swam over its pristine reefs and trekked in its mountains, the land of myths, emeralds and El Dorado may become a highlight of your South American sojourn.

So pack a pair of dancing shoes next to your hiking boots, throw in a mask, snorkel and sunscreen and tell your friends not to worry. They don't know what they're missing!

KRZYSZTOF DYDYNSKI

Natural Wonders

At 5775m, the craggy peaks of Sierra Nevada de Santa Marta (p110) are Colombia's highest

Orchids (p40) grow throughout Colombia; the Spectacular is found only in the Cordillera Oriental

Colombia is a rich source of bird life (p39)

Hike in the Sierra Nevada de Santa Marta (p110), the spiritual home of the Tayronas

OTHER HIGHLIGHTS

- Don't miss a visit to the jungle-covered Parque Nacional Tayrona (p114), on the Caribbean coast (left).
- Spend a little time in paradise at Providencia (p151), a mountainous island of volcanic origin.
- Explore Colombia's portion of the amazing Amazon basin (p209), an area equal in size to California.

6

Colonial & Modern

PATRICIA RINCON MAUTNER

Bogotá's brightly modern people mover, the TransMilenio, passes the 16th-century Iglesia de San Francisco (p61)

OTHER HIGHLIGHTS

- Amble along the streets of Popayán (p195), one of Colombia's most beautiful colonial cities.
- Medellín (p157), a modern city of glass and steel, now has some of the safest streets in Colombia, as well as the friendliest of locals.

Sculptures by Femando Botero, Colombia's most famous artist, stand guard at Medellín's Museo de Antioquia (p159)

KRZYSZTOF DYDYNSKI

Superb sightseeing opportunities abound in Cartagena's picturesque old town (p126)

KRZYSZTOF DYI

Check out Villa de Leyva's colorful market (p90), held in Plaza Mayor every Saturday

Take a crafty turn and visit heavenly Ráquira (p92), home of Colombia's finest-quality pottery and artifacts

Hang out with students in central Bogotá (p55) and experience the vibrancy of this youthful and lively city

Colombian Culture

Be enthralled by the enigmatic statues of
Parque Arqueológico (p200), San Agustín

Catch Colombia's funky beat on the streets of
Bogotá (p49)

KRZYSZTOF DYDYNSKI

OTHER HIGHLIGHTS

- Nightlife captures the irrepressible
  spirit of Colombia's people; check out
  the scene in the big three: Bogotá
  (p71), Medellín (p165) and Cali (p192).
- Carnaval de Barranquilla (p119), is
  Colombia's maddest and most frenzied
  festival, second only to Rio's.

Don't miss a ride on a colourful *chiva* (p242), once Colombia's main means of transport

KRZYSZTOF DYC

Contents

Regional Map Contents

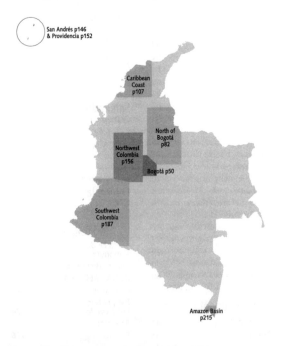

San Andrés p146
& Providencia p152

Caribbean Coast p107

North of Bogotá p82

Northwest Colombia p156

Bogotá p50

Southwest Colombia p187

Amazon Basin p215

The Authors

MICHAEL KOHN
Coordinating Author, Bogotá, North of Bogotá, Caribbean Coast, San Andrés & Providencia

Michael's first forays into Latin America came in 1994 when he traveled by ship from the Bahamas to Venezuela and Brazil. Later Michael made trips to Mexico, Puerto Rico and the Caribbean. For this book, Michael packed a pair of dancing shoes for the anticipated romp through Bogotá's myriad salsa bars, and a sense of adventure for a romp through the Colombian backwaters. Michael has contributed to five other Lonely Planet guidebooks. You can follow his route through Colombia by searching for his author blog on LonelyPlanet.com: www.lonelyplanet.com.

The Coordinating Author's Favorite Trip

The beauty of legendary Cartagena (p125) never fails to impress. One of my favorite things is a sunset stroll through its back streets, when the subsiding heat has a calming effect on its residents and the orange light plays off the church facades. My trip to Cartagena also includes surrounding beaches and sights, including Playa Blanca (p139) and the weird but wonderful Volcán de Lodo El Totumo (p139) for a mud bath. Continuing by bus along the Caribbean coast, I pass through Santa Marta (p108) on my way to the lush surrounds of Parque Nacional Tayrona (p114), a beach-and-jungle paradise. My tour of the coast is only complete once I have spent a few days scuba diving, sunning and lounging in quaint Taganga (p113).

ROBERT LANDON
Northwest Colombia, Southwest Colombia, Amazon Basin

Since earning degrees in literature from Stanford University and the University of California-Irvine, Robert has reported on local news for the *San Jose Mercury News*, written about arts and travel for Beirut's *Aishti* magazine, and made ends meet delivering copy to a long string of tech companies. Robert discovered South America rather late in a life consecrated to travel. He's now traveled to the extremes of the continent, and in 2002 sold everything to move to Rio de Janeiro. For Lonely Planet Robert has written about Lisbon, Florence, Brazil, Cape Verde, Guinea-Bissau and California.

LONELY PLANET AUTHORS

Why is our travel information the best in the world? It's simple: our authors are independent, dedicated travelers. They don't research using just the Internet or phone, and they don't take freebies in exchange for positive coverage. They travel widely, to all the popular spots and off the beaten track. They personally visit thousands of hotels, restaurants, cafés, bars, galleries, palaces, museums and more – and they take pride in getting all the details right, and telling it how it is. For more, see the authors section on www.lonelyplanet.com.

THOMAS KOHNSTAMM   History, Culture, Environment, Food & Drink

Thomas Kohnstamm first visited Colombia in 1999 and finds it to be one of the most intriguing countries in the Americas. He studied Colombian and regional history and politics as a graduate student in Latin American Studies at Stanford University. He currently splits his time between North and South America.

CONTRIBUTING AUTHOR

David Goldberg MD wrote the Health chapter. Dr Goldberg completed his training in internal medicine and infectious diseases at Columbia-Presbyterian Medical Center in New York City, where he has also served as voluntary faculty. At present, he is an infectious diseases specialist in Scarsdale NY and the editor-in-chief of the website MDTravelHealth.com.

PREVIOUS AUTHOR

Krzysztof Dydyński wrote the previous three editions of *Colombia*.

Getting Started

Colombia is a surprisingly easy place to get your travel needs squared away. Soon after stepping off the plane you'll have changed money, booked into your hotel, checked your email and downed a *tinto* (coffee). You may also start wondering about the war going on somewhere in the country. Bogotáns would rather ignore this fact, but it's a good idea to ask about the security situation in other parts of the country, as it does change.

Probably the most important thing you can do before coming to Colombia, besides reading as much as you can about the country, is to brush up on your *español*. There are very few English speakers in Colombia. Even people important to you – hotel receptionists, tour guides and travel agents – will probably only speak Spanish. Bring a phrasebook and memorize a few polite greetings and enough of the basics to find a hotel.

Traveling outside the main cities can be as easy or as hard as you want it to be. There is a range of accommodations suiting everyone, from cheapskates to high rollers. Food is good, plentiful and cheap. Transportation is reasonably efficient, main roads are well maintained and serviced frequently by air-conditioned buses. There's also a range of activities for every age and taste, from candle-lit dinners in romantic Cartagena to hard-core alpine trekking in Parque Nacional El Cocuy. Flexibility is crucial, but making hotel reservations is also a good idea, especially for the first couple of nights after you arrive. Always check the security situation if you plan to visit very remote regions, which are likely to be sensitive military or rebel-held areas.

WHEN TO GO

The most pleasant time to visit Colombia is in the dry season, between December and March or in July and August. This is particularly true if you plan on hiking. The dry season also gives visitors a better chance to savor local cultural events because many festivals and fiestas take place during these periods (see p227).

Apart from the weather, you may also consider Colombian holiday periods. There are basically three high seasons when Colombians rush to travel: from late December to mid-January, during Semana Santa (Holy Week; March or April), and from mid-June to mid-July. Also take note

See Climate Charts (p222) for more information about the weather.

DON'T LEAVE HOME WITHOUT...

- maximum-protection sunscreen, sunglasses and a hat
- a light rain jacket and sweater/fleece jacket for Bogotá and the mountains
- a decent change of clothing and a pair of nice shoes for clubbing
- a mask, snorkel and swimsuit for beach trips
- some paperback books in English (poor availability in Colombia)
- photocopying all your important documents, including credit cards, traveler's checks and your passport (take a set with you and leave a set at home)
- labeling your valuables (camera, MP3 player, mobile phone) in case something goes astray
- checking your passport for validity (make sure it's good for at least six more months)
- a small flashlight (for Tierradentro tombs and dodgy electricity supplies)

of three-day weekends, which send a rush of urban dwellers to rural getaways (eg Villa de Leyva), and regional celebrations (eg Baranquilla de Carnaval). During these periods transport gets more crowded, hotels tend to fill up faster and prices in holiday destinations may rise. If you travel at this time, you will have to plan your trip a little ahead and do more legwork to find a place to stay, but you'll also enjoy more contact with traveling Colombians, who will be in a relaxed, holiday spirit.

IS IT SAFE?

At the time of research, security in Colombia was improving, and all the areas mentioned in this guide were being frequented by travelers. If you didn't know anything about Colombia and just popped in for a tour of the main sights, you would have no idea that a war was being fought elsewhere in the country, which is mostly an indication of the level of security in the cities and on the main roads. That said, the situation is still unpredictable and it's best to confirm the level of security in all areas you wish to visit. Your first point of contact is the Internet, where you can search through recent news results related to the areas you plan to visit. (Search for specific cities and departments rather than just 'Colombia'.) Other good sources of information are tour agencies, guesthouses, the Thorn Tree page on **LonelyPlanet.com** (www.lonelyplanet.com) and your country's government travel advisory (though these advisories can often be overly cautious).

Once on the ground, continue to ask around for the latest security information. However, bear in mind that locals are likely to be ill informed and their information based on rumors and stories about places they themselves have never been. The fighting with Fuerzas Armadas Revolucionarias de Colombia (FARC) gets relatively little media attention, so a lot of information that locals have might be based on incidents that occurred 10 or more years ago. In this case, travelers and guesthouse owners will probably have the freshest information.

For specific tips on how to travel safely in Colombia, see p223. For dedicated regional safety information see the 'Traveling Safely in…' boxed texts in the Bogotá (p51), North of Bogotá (p83), Caribbean Coast (p108), San Andrés & Providencia (p145), Northwest Colombia (p157), Southwest Colombia (p188) and Amazon Basin (p210) chapters.

COSTS & MONEY

Colombia is a reasonably cheap country to travel in, provided you are traveling overland. Backpackers should be prepared to shell out US$15 to US$25 per day on average. If you want a more comfy trip, with midrange hotels, some better restaurants and a flight from time to time, you'll average somewhere between US$25 and US$45 daily. Some resort areas, especially along the Caribbean coast, have all-inclusive resort packages that cost US$100 to US$150 for two people, a good value anywhere. You can save money by going to free days at museums (often the last Sunday of the month), or using a student card when buying plane and museum tickets. Also remember that bus ticket fares are always negotiable. A little haggling can usually knock off around 20% to 30% of the cost, though you may need to shop around at the various bus company windows.

TRAVEL LITERATURE

Most recent literature on Colombia consists of journalists' accounts of the Drug War, its causes and effects. One of the most controversial books on the subject, *America's Other War: Terrorizing Colombia* (2005) by Doug

HOW MUCH?

M&Ms: US$1

Internet café (per hr): US$0.80-2

Toilet paper roll: US$0.40

Laundry (per kg): US$1.60

Postage for a letter to USA: US$2

See also Lonely Planet Index, inside front cover

TOP TENS

CDs

Colombia is rich in music traditions and you'll hear plenty of music at all hours, blaring from cars, nightclubs or the juice stand outside your hotel. Prepare yourself by packing a few of the following CDs onto your MP3 player before hitting the road.

- *El Rock de Mi Pueblo,* Carlos Vives
- *Los Más Grandes Éxitos de El Maestro,* Lucho Bermúdez
- *El Otro Lado de Mi,* Soraya
- *De Nuevo Con Mi Gente,* Diomedes Diaz
- *Laundry Service,* Shakira
- *Fijacion Oral,* Shakira
- *Putumayo Presents,* various artists
- *Romántico,* Carlos Vives
- *Latinismo Dance: Cumbias,* Linda Vera
- *Un Día Normal,* Juanes

Chill-Out Places

Long bus rides, bad hotels and crowded streets can grind down your morale; once in a while you'll just want to kick back in a hammock and stare at the clouds. The following places are the best spots to snooze.

- Aguadulce (p153), Providencia
- Taganga (p113), Magdalena
- Arrecifes (p115), Parque Nacional Tayrona
- San Luis (p148), San Andrés
- Ecotermales San Vicente (p180), Zona Cafetera
- Villa de Leyva (p86), Boyacá
- Playa Blanca (p139), Bolívar
- El Rodadero (p111), Santa Marta
- Río Claro (p162), Antioquia
- Puerto Nariño (p216), Amazon Basin

Festivals & Events

Colombia can party with the best of 'em, and there is no shortage of festivals and events to get your party juices flowing. There are some 200 festivals annually; the following are the best of the best.

- Carnaval de Barranquilla (Carnival at Barranquilla; p119), Barranquilla, February or March
- Carnaval de Blancos y Negros (Carnival of Black and White; p204), Pasto, January
- Festival de la Leyenda Vellenata (p135), Valledupar, April
- Semana Santa (Holy Week; p142), Mompós, March or April
- Semana Santa (Holy Week; p198), Popayán, March or April
- Festival Iberoamericano de Teatro (Latin American Theater Festival; p63), Bogotá, March or April
- Feria de las Flores (Festival of Flowers; p163), Medellín, August
- Festival Latinoamericano de Teatro (Latin American Theater Festival; p173), Manizales, September
- Reinado Nacional de Belleza (National Beauty Pageant; p132), Cartagena, November
- Feria de Cali (Festival of Cali; p191), Cali, December to January

Stokes, is a critical account of US policy in Colombia that gets its message across by using declassified documents. The reading is a little dry and academic, and the tone is unmistakably anti-American (which may appeal to some travelers in this day and age).

Along similar lines, but with a more personal angle, is *More Terrible Than Death: Violence, Drugs and America's War in Colombia* (2003) by Robin Kirk. Kirk spent a dozen years in Colombia working for Human

Rights Watch and recounts some of the most brutal incidents of terror she witnessed during her field work. She does well in summarizing Colombia's woes over the past 50 years and the role that the USA has played in propagating the violence.

A less-biased account can be found in Steven Dudley's book *Walking Ghosts: Murder and Guerrilla Politics in Colombia* (2004). Dudley, a reporter for National Public Radio in the USA, weaves many personal stories into the larger theme of death and war. It's well written and one of the most up-to-date accounts of the war with FARC.

'Pablo Escobar is still a very popular topic'

Although Colombians appear to be less than interested in reading about FARC, Pablo Escobar is still a very popular topic and *Killing Pablo: The Hunt for the World's Greatest Outlaw* (2002) by Mark Bowden is a hot seller.

For a more light-hearted account of traveling in Colombia, try Charles Nicholl's book *The Fruit Palace* (1998), a very funny diary of his wanderings through the country in the 1980s. It's dated, but the personal stories are as relevant today as when they were written.

INTERNET RESOURCES

Colombia in Cyberspace (www.javier.net/colombia) A website filled with pictures and background information, plus a music page with audio files.

El Tiempo (http://eltiempo.terra.com.co) Spanish-language readers will want to browse the website of Colombia's leading newspaper.

Locombia (www.locombia.com) News, comments and opinion on all things Colombian.

LonelyPlanet.com (www.lonelyplanet.com) Lonely Planet's website includes a dedicated Colombia page with photos, travel tips and the ever useful Thorn Tree online forum.

Poor But Happy (www.poorbuthappy.com/colombia) An online forum used mostly by expats living in Colombia, the site is a good place to go for practical information.

Third World Traveller (www.thirdworldtraveler.com) This good alternative source of news has a bank of articles about Colombia, mostly dealing with the American policy.

Itineraries
CLASSIC ROUTES

ESSENTIAL COLOMBIA
Five to Eight Weeks / Bogotá to Bogotá

This itinerary takes in the major sites of the country.

From Bogotá, travel north to **Villa de Leyva** (p86). Explore for two days, then visit **San Gil** (p93) for some hiking and rafting, and make time for historic **Barichara** (p94). Passing through **Bucaramanga** (p97) and **Girón** (p99), continue to quaint **Mompós** (p140). Next is **Cartagena** (p125), the jewel of the Caribbean. You'll need at least a week to explore Cartagena, **Santa Marta** (p108) and other attractions on the Caribbean coast. It's also possible to take a side trip to the islands of **San Andrés** (p145) and **Providencia** (p151).

From the Caribbean, bus your way southwest to **Medellín** (p157), with a side trip to **Santa Fe de Antioquia** (p169). Next jump to **Cali** (p187), visiting regional highlights such as the spectacular 'coffee country' (**Zona Cafetera**, p171).

From Cali, travel south again to **Popayán** (p195), **Tierradentro** (p202) and **San Agustín** (p199). Return to Bogotá by plane or bus, or continue south to Quito in Ecuador. Do the route in reverse if you're heading for Venezuela.

This loop includes Colombia's best colonial cities, beaches and pre-Columbian sites. It encompasses a big area so be prepared for a few long-distance bus trips. You'll need five weeks to travel this route properly, more if you plan on trekking or diving.

SUN, SAND & SEA
Two to Four Weeks / Santa Marta to Bogotá

There's a lot to see and do along the Caribbean coast, which means less arduous travel. Start by flying to **Santa Marta** (p108), which makes a fine base to explore the surrounding area. If you want to do the **Ciudad Perdida trek** (p116) begin making inquiries early, as trips don't run all the time, or they may be booked out.

Once you've sorted out your dates for the trek, take some side trips to **Taganga** (p113), **Parque Nacional Tayrona** (p114) and **El Rodadero** (p111). You may also want to do a dive course – Taganga is one of the cheapest places around to get certified; it's well worth blocking out a week for this. Parque Nacional Tayrona is another place that can take time to see. Plan for at least two days there (although some travelers stay a week or even more).

If it's Carnaval time, make sure you have room in your itinerary for a trip to **Barranquilla** (p117), otherwise, bypass the city and head straight for **Cartagena** (p125). You'll need at least two days to explore its glorious backstreets, plus at least one full day for a trip around the wonderful **Islas del Rosario** (p137).

With more time on your hands, spend extra days in **Playa Blanca** (p139), **Volcán de Lodo El Totumo** (p139) or **Mompós** (p140).

From Cartagena, fly back to Bogotá. If you have more time for rest and relaxation, you could travel on to **San Andrés** (p145) and **Providencia** (p151), or join a sailboat tour to Panama via Archipiélago de San Blas.

This itinerary is ideal for travelers who want to laze on the beach and take in a bit of Colombian culture. You could easily see the main sites in two weeks, but you'll need more time if you plan to scuba dive or tackle some treks.

ROADS LESS TRAVELED

CALI TO ECUADOR   Two Weeks / Cali to Ipiales

Off-the-beaten-track travel in Colombia can mean rougher roads and possible contact with risky areas held by paramilitaries or Fuerzas Armadas Revolucionarias de Colombia (FARC). The following areas are regarded as 'safe' destinations, but it's still a good idea to ferret out the latest travel warnings wherever you go.

Start with a flight to Cali, the jumping-off point for **Isla Gorgona** (p194), a remote, lush island off the Pacific coast, definitely worth visiting, especially if you time it with the whale migration (November). Back on the mainland, make a trip to **San Cipriano** (p194), deep in the tropical forest and only accessible by a unique hand-propelled rail cart. After visiting **Popayán** (p195), spend a few days in **Silvia** (p199) and the Guambiano Indian region. The unique, remote and little-visited pre-Columbian site of **Tierradentro** (p202) is also in the region. The famed **San Agustín** (p199) archeological site, with its monumental statues, is better known but receives few visitors because of past guerrilla presence in the area. Keep your ear to the ground and be ready to alter your travel plans if fighting breaks out.

From Popayán, continue south towards **Pasto** (p204), where you can organize a trip up the still-active **Volcán Galeras** (p206). If you're heading towards Ecuador, visit **Santuario de Las Lajas** (p208), an architectural wonder hovering above the Río Guaitara, just a few kilometers from the border town of **Ipiales** (p206).

Southwest Colombia provides a safe cushion between you and the more touristy areas around central Colombia and the Caribbean coast. It's a culturally and geographically rich area and is still home to large of numbers of indigenous peoples, mainly the Paez and Guambianos.

TAILORED TRIPS

NATIONAL PARKS & PROTECTED AREAS

Colombia has 34 national parks spread across the country, some easily accessible and others so remote that their number of yearly visitors can be counted on two hands.

One of the most frequently visited parks, **Parque Nacional Tayrona** (p114), is popular among aspiring beach bums who have a wide selection of hammocks in which to swing. Also well known on the Caribbean coast is the **Parque Nacional Corales del Rosario** (p137), just off the coast of Cartagena.

Most visitors base themselves at Playa Blanca and take boat trips out to the cays and islets.

Travelers seeking fresh alpine air and glacier-wrapped peaks would do well to head for **Parque Nacional El Cocuy** (p92). Considered off-limits for security reasons a few years ago, the park is now safe for trekkers. Closer to Bogotá, the **Parque Nacional Santuario de Iguaque** (p91) is lower in elevation, but still offers some fine hikes to a group of alpine lakes. **Laguna de Guatavita** (p80) can be reached from the capital in a day trip and offers both beauty and spiritual significance.

Budding vulcanologists will want to visit the **Parque Nacional Los Nevados** (p174), located southeast of Manizales. It contains several volcanic cones, some of them active. If the jungle is more your thing, it's hard to beat the **Parque Nacional Amacayacu** (p216) in Colombia's Amazon Basin.

HERITAGE SITES & ARCHITECTURAL DELIGHTS

Fans of Spanish colonial architecture may well overdose on the wealth on offer in Colombia. Travel anywhere and you'll find perfectly preserved town squares, churches and mansions.

Bogotá (p60) has the most stunning collection of churches, including the monumental Catedral Primada and the incredibly elaborate Iglesia de San

Francisco. In terms of overall beauty, it's hard to beat the walled center of **Cartagena** (p125). It's one of the best preserved historical centers, a Unesco World Heritage site and is particularly noted for its captivating balconies. Another Unesco site, the town of **Mompós** (p140) has a particular style of architecture all its own – *arquitectura momposina*. Other protected towns in northern Colombia include **Villa de Leyva** (p86), **Barichara** (p94) and **Girón** (p99). All contain fine central squares bordered by whitewashed buildings and a church. In particular, Barichara's church, when illuminated at night, is a sight to behold. The oldest town in western Colombia is **Santa Fe de Antioquia** (p169), a quaint and tidy town with narrow streets and four churches. Finally, don't miss **Popayán** (p195), whose architectural wonders include the spectacular Iglesia de San Francisco.

Snapshot

You can love him or hate him, but you can't deny that Colombia's President Álvaro Uribe has created a new environment in Colombia at the start of the 21st century. The statistics tell half the tale. Since Uribe took office in August 2002, homicides are down by more than 40%, acts of terror by 66% and extortive kidnappings by 79%. These are stunning numbers, and they are just a short list of figures that the government hopes will alter Colombia's long-suffering image problem.

Indeed, Colombia does appear to be turning a corner and the proof is in the pudding – the job market is widening and international investment was up by 70% in 2004. For mainstream Colombians living in big cities such as Bogotá, all this means a freer existence where going outside after dark is no longer a high-risk activity.

Equally important, Uribe has sent the rebel Fuerzas Armadas Revolucionarias de Colombia (FARC) running deeper into the jungles. The war continues but the FARC retreat has meant improved security along main roads and population centers.

Uribe has also struck a blow to the illicit drug trade and managed to wrest guns from some paramilitary groups, with hundreds of the right-wing groups laying down their arms in exchange for immunity against prosecution.

While all this may sound wonderful, it is only half the story. Colombia's woes resemble a B-movie monster – cut off one of its heads and a new one grows back. So while the Cali and Medellín drug cartels have been dismantled, and the guerrillas are on the run, the government now finds itself embroiled in new battles.

The biggest threat must be growing paramilitary strength, which has woven a tight web over many urban areas, including Ciudad Bolivar in southern Bogotá. Paramilitaries have infiltrated this district of two million people, organized their own chain of command and carried out a brutal campaign of social cleansing – killing or disappearing thousands of people whose only 'crime' was poverty. Human-rights abuses that rival the Balkans for their barbarity are being carried out with impunity.

In rural areas it is also the paramilitaries who have filled in the void of cocaine production vacated by retreating rebels. The spraying of crops has only forced farmers to look for new land, including national parks where the land (and their crops) is protected.

As for FARC, its retreat has been hailed by the government as progress in its own 'war on terror,' but the 40-year fight still has no foreseeable end. Large swaths of the country still suffer the horror of war and unspeakable violence; in 2005 the southern province of Putumayo saw a surge in guerrilla attacks that forced tens of thousands to flee to Ecuador. Colombia now has three million internally displaced people, second in the world after Sudan.

Uribe, an ultranationalistic right-winger and ally to the Bush regime, now has the chance to upgrade his controversial, hardline campaigns. In October 2005, Colombia's Constitutional Court ruled that presidents could seek a second term in office, allowing Uribe to stand for reelection in 2006.

FAST FACTS

Population: 43 million

GDP growth: 4.5% per capita (US$6600 in 2004)

Leading sectors for foreign investment: mining (US$488 million) and oil (US$188 million)

Unemployment rate: 11.8%

'Plan Colombia' costs American taxpayers US$740 million per year

During Uribe's first three years in office, over 450,000 hectares of coca crops were sprayed and 5000 drug labs destroyed

Oil represents 20% of Colombian exports

History

Colombia's history reads like a romance, a drama and a bad action movie all rolled into one. Just as foreign attraction to oil in Venezuela or silver in Bolivia led to turmoil and upheaval in those countries, international desire for cocaine has pushed existing tensions in Colombia well beyond their boiling point. The country's history is saddening, complex and vastly interesting. To get a fuller understanding of the life of the nation, it is necessary to do significant reading of varying accounts, but the following is a starting point.

The Explorers of South America (1972) by Edward J Goodman brings to life some of the more incredible explorations of the continent, from Columbus to Humboldt, some of which refer to Colombia.

PRE-COLUMBUS COLOMBIA

Colombia is the only overland gateway to South America and is assumed to have been the route pioneered by the continent's first human inhabitants, who migrated from North and Central America. Some tribes, such as the Inca, headed further south and built major civilizations, while smaller groups settled in what is now Colombia and eventually reached a high level of development. These people are little known internationally because they left few enduring monuments.

There are three main archeological sites in Colombia. They are San Agustín (p199), Tierradentro (p202) and Ciudad Perdida (p116). Some communities left behind artifacts – mainly gold and pottery – some of which are now in museums across the country. This art reveals a high degree of skill, and the goldwork is the continent's best, both in techniques and artistic design.

In contrast to the Aztecs or Incas, who dominated vast regions, a dozen independent Colombian groups occupied relatively small areas scattered throughout the Andean region and along the Pacific and Atlantic (Caribbean) coasts. Despite trading, these cultures developed largely independently. Among the most outstanding were the Calima, Muisca, Nariño, Quimbaya, San Agustín, Sinú, Tayrona, Tierradentro, Tolima and Tumaco.

SPANISH CONQUEST

Colombia is named after Christopher Columbus, even though he never set foot on Colombian soil. It was Alonso de Ojeda, one of Columbus' companions on his second voyage, who was the first European to set foot on the land in 1499. He briefly explored the Sierra Nevada de Santa Marta and was astonished by the wealth of the local Indians. Their gold and their stories about fabulous treasures inland gave birth to the myth of El Dorado, a mysterious kingdom abundant in gold. In its most extreme interpretation, El Dorado was believed to be a land of gold mountains littered with emeralds.

A good overview of the period of Spanish colonization is provided by John Hemming's *The Search for El Dorado* (2001). It's a fascinating insight into the conquest of Colombia and Venezuela.

From the moment the Spaniards arrived, their obsession with El Dorado became the principal force driving them into the interior. They did not find El Dorado, but their search resulted in rapid colonization.

The legend of El Dorado became linked to the Muiscas and their famous Laguna de Guatavita. There, the expectations of the Spaniards

TIMELINE

1499	1525
Spaniard Alonso de Ojeda lands at the Cabo de la Vela on the Guajira Peninsula	Rodrigo de Bastidas lays the first stones of Santa Marta

were to some degree confirmed by the rituals of the Indians, who threw gold offerings into the sacred waters, though very little has been found despite numerous efforts; see Laguna de Guatavita (p80).

Attracted by the presumed riches of the Indians, the shores of present-day Colombia became the target of numerous expeditions by the Spaniards. Several short-lived settlements were founded along the coast, but it was not until 1525 that Rodrigo de Bastidas laid the first stones of Santa Marta, the earliest surviving town. In 1533, Pedro de Heredia founded Cartagena, which soon became the principal center of trade.

In 1536 a general advance toward the interior began independently from three different directions, under Jiménez de Quesada, Sebastián de Benalcázar (known in Colombia as Belalcázar) and Nikolaus Federmann. Although all three were drawn by the Indian treasures, none intended to reach Muisca territory, where they finally met.

Quesada set off from Santa Marta, pushed up the Valle del Magdalena, then climbed the Cordillera Oriental, arriving in Muisca territory early in 1537. At the time, the Muiscas were divided into two clans – the southern one ruled by the Zipa from Bacatá (present-day Bogotá), and the northern empire under the Zaque in Hunza (present-day Tunja). The two caciques quarreled over territory and the rivalry considerably helped Quesada conquer the Muiscas without undue difficulty. In August 1538 he founded Santa Fe de Bogotá on the site of Bacatá.

Belalcázar deserted from Francisco Pizarro's army, which was conquering the Inca empire, and mounted an expedition from Ecuador. He subdued the southern part of Colombia, founding Popayán and Cali along the way, and reached Bogotá in 1539. Federmann started from the Venezuelan coast and, after successfully crossing Los Llanos and the Andes, arrived in Bogotá shortly after Belalcázar. Thus, in a short period of time, a large part of the colony was conquered and a number of towns were founded.

The three groups then battled for supremacy, and it was not until 1550 that King Carlos V of Spain established a court of justice in Bogotá and brought the colony under the control of the Viceroyalty of Peru.

Although the conquistador Sebastián de Belalcázar was rewarded for his killing of thousands of indigenous people, the Spanish Crown sentenced him to death for ordering the assassination of one rival landowner.

THE COLONIAL PERIOD

In 1564 the Crown established a new system, the Presidencia del Nuevo Reino de Granada, which had dual military and civil power and greater autonomy. Authority was in the hands of the governor, appointed by the King of Spain. The Nuevo Reino at that time comprised present-day Panama and all of Colombia, except what is today Nariño, Cauca and Valle del Cauca, which were under the jurisdiction of the Presidencia de Quito (present-day Ecuador).

The population of the colony, initially consisting of indigenous communities and the Spanish invaders, diversified with the arrival of Blacks, brought from Africa to serve as the workforce. Cartagena was granted the privilege of being the exclusive slave-trading port in which Blacks were sold as slaves and distributed throughout the colony. Most of them were set to work in mines and plantations, mainly on the Caribbean and Pacific coasts. During the 16th and 17th centuries the Spaniards shipped in so many Africans that they eventually surpassed the indigenous population in number.

1819	1830
Bolívar defeats the Spanish army and the Republic of Gran Colombia is founded	Gran Colombia splits into Colombia, Ecuador and Venezuela

The demographic picture became more complex when the three racial groups began to mix, producing various fusions, including mestizos (people of European-Indian blood), mulatos (of European-African ancestry) and zambos (African-Indian). However, throughout the whole of the colonial period, power was almost exclusively in the hands of the Spaniards.

With the growth of the Spanish empire in the New World, a new territorial division was created in 1717, and Bogotá became the capital of its own viceroyalty, the Virreinato de la Nueva Granada. It comprised the territories of what are today Colombia, Panama, Ecuador and Venezuela.

INDEPENDENCE WARS

As Spanish domination of the continent increased, so too did the discontent of the inhabitants. Slavery, and the monopoly of commerce, taxes and duties – among other factors – slowly gave rise to protests. The first open rebellion against colonial rule was the Revolución Comunera in Socorro in 1781, which broke out against tax rises levied by the Crown, before taking on more pro-independence overtones. When Napoleon put his own brother on the Spanish throne in 1808, the colonies refused to recognize the new monarch. One by one, Colombian towns declared their independence. Unfortunately, political divisions and infighting appeared almost immediately.

'One by one, Columbian towns declared their independence'

In 1812 Simón Bolívar, who was to become the hero of the independence struggle, appeared on the scene. He won six battles against Spanish troops, but was defeated by the next year. Spain recovered its throne from Napoleon and then set about reconquering its colonies. The 'pacifying' Spanish troops reconquered the interior and full colonial rule was reestablished by 1817.

Bolívar retreated to Jamaica after the defeat and took up arms again. He went back to Venezuela, and after assembling an army of horsemen from Los Llanos, strengthened by a British legion, he marched over the Andes into Colombia, claiming victory after victory. The last and most decisive battle took place at Boyacá on August 7, 1819. Three days later he arrived triumphantly in Bogotá. Colombia's independence was won.

THE HIGHS & THE LOWS OF SIMÓN BOLÍVAR

Simón Bolívar was born into a wealthy family in Caracas in 1783. His parents died shortly after his birth. He was sent to study in Europe where he met and married a beautiful woman. She died shortly after the marriage and he returned to his homeland that was still in the colonial headlock of Spain. A combination of Bolívar's education, his time in Spain (which thereby gave him an understanding of both the colonizer and the colony), the growing influence of Napoleon and a visit to the newly independent United States all contributed to his belief in the liberation of South America. After numerous failed attempts to break Spain's grip on the colonies, and with little more than the shirt on his back, Simón Bolívar regrouped from exile in Jamaica and successfully won independence for the entire northwest of South America – today's Venezuela, Colombia, Panama, Ecuador, Peru and Bolivia. He became the single leader of Colombia, Panama, Ecuador and Venezuela, then known as Gran Colombia, but was quickly banished from office and, continuing the roller-coaster that was his life, died abandoned, rejected and penniless. Shortly before he died, Bolívar commented, 'There have been three great fools in history: Jesus, Don Quixote and I.'

1903	1948
The US sneakily orchestrates the secession of Panama from Colombia	The assassination of radical presidential candidate Jorge Eliécer Gaitán sets off the Bogotazo riots in Bogotá

AFTER INDEPENDENCE

With Colombia free, a revolutionary congress was held in Angostura (modern-day Ciudad Bolívar, in Venezuela) in 1819. Still euphoric with victory, the delegates proclaimed the Gran Colombia, a new state uniting Venezuela, Colombia, Panama and Ecuador (although Ecuador and large parts of Venezuela were still technically under Spanish rule).

The Angostura congress was followed by another one, held in Villa del Rosario, near Cúcuta, in 1821. It was there that the two opposing tendencies, centralist and federalist, came to the fore. Bolívar supported a centralized republic, succeeded in imposing his will. The Gran Colombia came into being and Bolívar was elected president. Francisco de Paula Santander, who favored a federal republic of sovereign states, became vice president.

From its inception, however, the vast state began to disintegrate. Bolívar was far away fighting for the independence of Ecuador and Peru, leaving effective power in Santander's hands. It soon became apparent that a central regime was incapable of governing such a vast and diverse territory. The Gran Colombia had split into three separate countries by 1830 and Bolívar's dream of a sacred union of the nations he had freed came to an end even before he died.

Thus began a new inglorious page of Colombia's history. The political currents born in the struggle for independence, centralist and federalist, were formalized in 1849 when two political parties were established: the Conservatives (with centralist tendencies) and the Liberals (with federalist leanings). Fierce rivalry between these two forces resulted in a sequence of insurrections and civil wars and throughout the 19th century, Colombia experienced no fewer than eight civil wars. Between 1863 and 1885 alone there were more than 50 antigovernment insurrections.

In 1899 a Liberal revolt turned into a full-blown civil war, the so-called War of a Thousand Days. That carnage resulted in a Conservative victory and left 100,000 dead. In 1903 the USA took advantage of the country's internal strife and fomented a secessionist movement in Panama, then a Colombian province. By creating an independent republic, the USA was able to build a canal across the Central American isthmus under its control. It wasn't until 1921 that Colombia eventually recognized the sovereignty of Panama and settled its dispute with the USA.

LA VIOLENCIA

After a period of relative peace, the struggle between Liberals and Conservatives broke out again in 1948 with La Violencia, the most destructive of Colombia's many civil wars to that point. With a death toll of some 300,000, La Violencia was one of the bloodiest conflicts in the western hemisphere, comparable only to the Mexican Revolution and the American Revolutionary War. Urban riots, known as El Bogotazo, broke out on April 9, 1948 in Bogotá, following the assassination of Jorge Eliécer Gaitán, a charismatic populist Liberal leader. Liberals soon took up arms throughout the country.

To comprehend the brutality of this period, one must understand that generation after generation of Colombians were raised as either Liberals or Conservatives and imbued with a deep mistrust of the opposition. In

Colombia's red, yellow and blue tricolor flag was adopted in 1861. Yellow represents the land, blue symbolizes the ocean and red is the blood spilled by patriots.

Titles covering Colombia's modern history include *The Politics of Colombia* (1987) by Robert H Dix, *Colombia: Inside the Labyrinth* (1990) by Jenny Pearce and *The Making of Modern Colombia: A Nation in Spite of Itself* (1993) by David Bushnell.

1964	1974
The FARC is founded; the ELN and M-19 follow a year later	President Michelsen launches the first major counterinsurgency against all three main guerrilla groups

THE ABCS OF THE COLOMBIAN CONFLICT

■ FARC (Fuerzas Armadas Revolucionarias de Colombia – The Armed Revolutionary Forces of Colombia) This group was founded in 1964 as a military wing of the pro-Soviet Communist Party of Colombia. The FARC is the largest leftist guerrilla group in the country.

■ ELN (Ejército de Liberación Nacional – The National Liberation Army) Founded in 1965 by urban intellectuals and inspired by Castro, ELN was originally pro-Cuban, but later became a hardline Christian Marxist group headed by former Spanish priests. The ELN is the second largest leftist guerrilla group after the FARC.

■ AUC (Autodefensas Unidas de Colombia – United Self-Defense Forces of Colombia) An umbrella group formed in 1997 by right-wing paramilitary groups. The paramilitaries grew out of the security forces and militias of large land holders and the drug cartels. The AUC is possibly larger than the FARC and opposes the leftist guerrillas.

■ M-19 (Movimiento 19 de Abril – The 19th of April Movement) Founded in 1965, this guerrilla force overtook the Palace of Justice in 1985. Some 35 guerrillas died, as did 11 Supreme Court justices. In 1990 it demilitarized and became a political party under the same name.

the 1940s and 1950s, these 'hereditary hatreds' were the cause of countless atrocities, rapes and murders, particularly in rural areas.

The 1953 coup of General Gustavo Rojas Pinilla was the only military intervention the country experienced in the 20th century. The dictatorship of General Rojas was not to last. In 1957 the leaders of the two parties signed a pact to share power for the next 16 years. The agreement, later approved by plebiscite (in which women were allowed to vote for the first time), became known as the Frente Nacional (National Front). During the life of the accord, the two parties alternated in the presidency every four years. In effect, despite the enormous loss of lives, the same people returned to power. The agreement also disallowed political parties beyond the Liberals and the Conservatives – therefore forcing opposition outside of the normal political system and sowing the seeds for guerrilla insurrection.

The official site of the Colombian embassy is www.colombiaemb.org. It is good for up-to-date information on the country.

AN UNCIVIL CIVIL WAR

The tentacles of the Cold War reached Colombia in the late 1940s and early 1950s. Disillusioned liberals set off to establish their own independent communities – modeled on leftist doctrine – in the countryside. Wealthy landowners began to raise militias and security forces as they feared a breakdown of the status quo. The world was dealing with an ideological struggle between communism and capitalism, and Colombia, with its colonial legacy of poor land distribution, a veritable oligarchy and impoverished mestizo and indigenous underclasses, was ripe for the rise of Marxist guerrilla opposition. By the mid-1960s the political divide hardened into armed conflict. Opposition parties were outlawed from the political process and a new group, the Fuerzas Armadas Revolucionarias de Colombia (FARC), took up arms against what they saw as the corrupt and self-serving government. The security forces, which had grown into paramilitaries, and the government fought back, often taking the offense in the burgeoning conflict. In all, Colombia gave birth to perhaps a dozen different guerrilla groups, each with its own philosophy and its own political and military strategies. The movements that have had the biggest impact include the FARC, the Ejército de Liberación Nacional (ELN) and the Movimiento 19 de Abril (M-19).

Leftist guerrillas battled the government, paramilitaries and even the cocaine cartels for two decades. Tragedy overtook all sides and horrific murders and acts of terrorism were committed. As communism fell around the globe and the political landscape shifted, the FARC and the ELN lost support from Moscow and Havana. They moved on to drugs, extortion, robbery and kidnapping to finance their struggle. The struggle itself became clouded by the cocaine trade. Rambo and Tony Montana replaced Ché Guevara and Leon Trotsky as role models for the conflict. Regardless of the nebulous political goals, the sale of marching powder has kept the soldiers marching well after the end of Cold War conflict in neighboring countries. The guerrillas have controlled large swaths of the countryside – at times estimated up to 40% – and, in 2002, the USA and the EU included the guerrillas on their list of terrorist organizations.

The so-called *paramilitares* or *autodefensas* built by the landholders and cartels flourished into standing armies. In the past, Colombia's military has turned a blind eye and even supported the paramilitaries, who share similar objectives. This was often done with money and weapons from the US. The AUC has committed horrendous massacres of civilians (allegedly guerrilla sympathizers) and terrorized the countryside as much as its opposition. One of its techniques is to simply kill off young people in villages that support the FARC or ELN – eliminating potential future combatants.

Some former AUC leaders suggest that as much as 70% of their funding comes from the drug trade. Many of the paramilitary leaders were former employees of the cartels and took over as the cartels were dismantled. Diego Francisco Murillo, the commander of the AUC and known as Don Berna, once worked under Pablo Escobar and allegedly controls much of what was once Escobar's empire. Although the AUC may still receive indirect assistance from the USA, it has also been included on the above-mentioned list of terrorist organizations.

COKE IS IT

Colombia is the world's largest producer of cocaine, controlling 80% to 90% of the global market. Regional mafias or cartels started small in the early '70s but quickly developed the trade into a big industry, with their own plantations, laboratories, transport services and protection rackets.

The boom years began in the early 1980s. The Medellín Cartel, led by a former car thief named Pablo Escobar, became the principal mafia, and its bosses lived in freedom and luxury. They even founded their own political party, held congressional seats, established two newspapers and financed massive public works and public housing projects. By 1983 Escobar's personal wealth was estimated to be US$2 billion, making him one of the richest criminals in the world.

Concurrently, the government launched a thorough campaign against the drug trade. In response, the cartel bosses disappeared from public life and proposed an unusual 'peace treaty' to then President Belisario Betancur. For immunity from both prosecution and extradition, they offered to

Killing Pablo: The Hunt for the World's Greatest Outlaw (2002) by Mark Bowden is an in-depth exploration of the life and times of Escobar and the operation that brought him down. While the book has some small inaccuracies it is a fun crime read.

1983	**1985**
Justice Minister Rodrigo Lara Bonilla is assassinated because he supports an extradition treaty with the US	Superior Court Judge Tulio Manuel Castro Gil who indicted Escobar for Lara Bonilla's assassination is murdered

invest their capital in national development programs. More tantalizing still, they proposed to pay off Colombia's entire foreign debt, some US$13 billion at that time. The government turned down the proposals and violence escalated between the cocaine mafia and the government.

The war became even bloodier in August 1989, when the drug lords gunned down Luis Carlos Galán, the leading Liberal contender for the

PLAN COLOMBIA

Conceived in 1999 by the administration of President Andrés Pastrana, Plan Colombia is an ambitious and controversial initiative to resolve the 40-plus-year civil conflict and curtail drug trafficking. The most contentious element of the antinarcotic strategy is aerial fumigation to eradicate coca crops – basically dumping tons of Roundup herbicide all over the country. This not only damages legal crops, kills off biodiversity and has adverse health effects on people, but it does little to stop the activities of the cocaine processors and traffickers. It punishes the small farmers and the traffickers get their coca leaves elsewhere. While US senators have called for the use of even stronger herbicides, anyone who has spent time in the Andean region of South America knows that coca grows like apples in the United States – everywhere.

Another dilemma is that sections of the Colombian security forces, who receive aid and training from Plan Colombia, indirectly support or tolerate right-wing paramilitaries guilty of human rights violations and murder. The Plan also permits US soldiers to operate within the sovereign territory of Colombia. In a sinister twist, there are increasing numbers of arrests of American soldiers and officers now involved in the enticing cocaine and heroin trade.

The Clinton administration initially supported the initiative by committing US$1.3 billion in aid, 500 military personnel and 300 civilian contractors. On top of the hundreds of millions of dollars in existing assistance, this move made Colombia the largest recipient of US foreign aid outside of the Middle East; and the third-largest recipient overall. In 2001, and again in 2004, the Bush administration expanded the program by increasing the financing and augmenting the number of military advisors and civilian contractors.

From the perspective of the US and Colombian governments, the results of Plan Colombia have been positive. Plan Colombia has clearly had some success in breaking down the civil conflict or at least improving the security situation. A greater troop presence with access to more helicopters and advanced technology has made the military more efficient and effective.

On the drug front, US government statistics show a significant reduction in coca production, from a peak of 700 metric tons in 2001 to 460 in 2003 and 430 in 2004. However, cocaine retail prices have not changed and there is certainly no shortage of cocaine to be found on the streets of Los Angeles, London or even Leipzig these days.

Critics argue that the Plan does nothing to remedy underlying causes of the drug trade such as decreasing demand or providing a viable alternative for peasants, who turn to coca cultivation due to a lack of other economic possibilities. They also say that simply making coca difficult to grow and transport in one area will lead to the movement of the drug cultivation processes to other areas, both inside and outside Colombia, a consequence also known as the balloon effect.

On November 15, 2005, President Bush signed into law legislation that allows US assistance in disarming and demobilizing former members of groups on the State Department's terrorism list. Former members of FARC, AUC and ELN will be eligible for aid and assistance programs, including job training and education programs. United States Congress approved an initial US$20 million to get the initiative started.

The ELN and representatives of the Colombian government met in Cuba in late 2005 to lay the groundwork for future talks that will hopefully lead to a lasting disarmament and peace.

1985	1989
Carlos Valderrama, the legendary midfielder (with the legendary coiffure), debuts for the Colombian national football (soccer) team	The M-19 demilitarizes; the cartels declare war on the government and the extradition treaty

1990 presidential election. The government retaliated with the confiscation of nearly 1000 cartel-owned properties, and announced a new extradition treaty with the US. The drug traffickers responded by declaring an all-out war on the government and assassinating any politician who supported the extradition treaty. Their campaign of terror included burning the farms of politicians and detonating bombs in banks, newspaper offices, political party headquarters and private homes. In November 1989, the cartels bombed an Avianca flight headed from Bogotá to Cali, killing all 107 on board.

The election of Liberal César Gaviria (1990–94) brought a brief period of hope. Following lengthy negotiations, which included a constitutional amendment to ban the extradition of Colombians, Escobar and the remaining cartel bosses surrendered and the narcoterrorism subsided. However, Escobar escaped from his luxurious house arrest following the government's bumbling attempts to move him to a more secure site. An elite 1500-man special unit sought Escobar for 499 days, until they tracked him down in Medellín and killed him in December 1993.

Despite this, the drug trade continued unabated. While the military concentrated on hunting one man and persecuting one cartel, the other cartels were quick to take advantage of the situation; they also diversified into opium cultivation and heroin trafficking. As those cartels fell in the mid-1990s the guerrillas and paramilitaries filled the void. Meanwhile, the international street prices of cocaine dropped and supply paced with an ever-rising demand.

A NEW HOPE

Álvaro Uribe, an independent hardliner, emerged victorious from a pack of six candidates in the contentious 2002 presidential election. He ran on a strong antiguerrilla ticket swearing also to break the history of governmental cronyism and patronage. His father, a politician, was killed in a botched kidnapping attempt by the FARC, and he specifically promised a more intensive military campaign against the FARC and ELN.

So far, Uribe has delivered and the security situation has drastically improved in Colombia, giving way to a new period of national optimism. The Colombian embassy claims that the armed forces now have 60% more combat-ready soldiers than in 2002. They also have many more helicopters, which allow them to penetrate the rugged territory that the FARC and ELN call home. The government has reclaimed much of the land that was effectively ceded to the guerrillas in the late 1990s.

Uribe's popularity has reached towards 80% during his first term – making him the most popular elected leader in Latin America. This is due not only to his successful campaigns against the FARC and the ELN, but his efforts to demobilize the AUC and the perception of Uribe as a hardnosed workaholic and a model of personal and administrative austerity. While he is a friend to Washington, Uribe has also lined up with other Latin American countries to call for an end to the Cuban embargo and has reached out to regional leftist leaders such as President Luiz Inácio Lula da Silva in Brazil.

Uribe is still faced with a daunting task to secure a lasting peace. He considers the civil conflict to be a terrorist threat from illegal armed

Colin Harding's *In Focus: Colombia – A Guide to the People, Politics and Culture* (1996) is a good, brief introduction to the country's history, economy and society. *Colombia: Portrait of Unity and Diversity* (1983) by Harvey F Kline is a well-balanced overview of Colombian history.

1993	**1998**
Pablo Escobar is killed by a special unit of the Colombian police	President Pastrana pulls troops from a New Jersey–sized area during cease-fire negotiations with the FARC

groups involved in the cocaine trade – making little differentiation therefore between the FARC and the Cali Cartel. The guerrillas want Uribe to first recognize Colombia's internal conflict as a condition before any talks, so that there is a chance that they will be able to leverage their political goals in any negotiations. Both the UN and human-rights groups recognize the conflict as political. Uribe, however, needs to keep his recognition of the status of the conflict as a bargaining chip and has offered that he will revise his view of internal conflict so long as the ELN calls a cease-fire.

The CIA World Factbook website (www.cia.gov) has a breakdown of Colombian government, economy and population issues to keep you in the know.

The AUC is the only group that has offered to stand down; however, they are not in direct opposition to the government and actually share many similar goals. Their purpose is simply defense of the status quo. There are many people concerned – some in the UN, EU and US government – that the AUC are being given unduly generous terms for demobilization. A few heads may roll; the AUC leader Don Berna is wanted in the US on money-laundering and drug-trafficking charges – but the threat of his extradition will likely be used to rein in fringe elements of the paramilitaries and he will probably never leave Colombia. Others will turn in their arms, take amnesty and a slap on the wrist and go on with their lives (and possibly continue the criminal and drug trade networks under a different guise). Some will clearly get away with murder but Uribe is betting that it is worth it in the long run for the good of the country. As of late 2005, some 10,000 AUC members have laid down their weapons but it remains to be seen if they will dismantle their political, economic and drug-trafficking structures.

Arguing that he needs four more years in office to implement his tough policies against terrorists and drug-traffickers, Uribe was able to amend the constitution in October 2005 so that he can stand for a second presidential term in May 2006. Uribe continues to be the strongest South American ally of the USA. Although most other South American nations are currently moving to the political left, it appears likely that Uribe will win reelection.

2000	2006
Plan Colombia is instituted and met with an escalation of violence by the FARC	Colombia agrees to a free trade deal with the United States after two years of talks; opponents vow to fight the agreement

The Culture

Colombian culture gets a bad rap. Just as Chicago is not full of Al Capones, there is hardly a Pablo Escobar lurking around every bend in Colombia. As with most international news, tragedy, violence and gore make headlines, while the positives of Colombia don't pique enough interest to even make the back page. The best antidote to the negative perception is to meet and interact with Colombians in person. You'll find yourself quickly won over by this warm and welcoming culture. Those who have only heard horror stories about Colombia will be surprised to learn that it is a country bursting with music, arts, literature, fashion, fine cuisine and (legitimate) commerce.

THE NATIONAL PSYCHE

Colombians are generally gregarious people who make an effort to demonstrate the opposite of their violence- and crime-stricken stereotype: they are incredibly proud of their country and go out of their way to show foreigners a good time in their beautiful land. The average Colombian could teach people of 'more civilized' North American and European countries a lesson on how to be courteous, polite and hospitable. The exception to the rule seems to be an acrid national sentiment toward Venezuelans, who suffer from being on the wrong side of a neighborly rivalry.

Due to decades of past national insecurity, Colombians have an obvious passion for life in the present and a sense of how to enjoy themselves in the here-and-now. Five minutes of Bogotá or Cartagena nightlife will make that blaringly obvious. However, that does not mean that life is haphazard or careless. Colombians are ambitious and organized, which is reflected in the glassy cities, international restaurants, established democracy and armies of briefcase-wielding businessmen that outnumber the gun-toting guerrillas in the countryside.

The national psyche shifts drastically in the small towns. These range from relaxed spots along the Caribbean coast to war-torn and terrorized populations in the jungle and mountains. One thing that always shines through, though, is the indomitable spirit of the Colombian people who have overcome so much tumult in the past and know that they will prevail, one way or another, over current hardships.

Unlike North Americans, Colombians tend to live at home until they are married or enter their 30s (whichever comes first).

LIFESTYLE

Looking at a flat map of Colombia doesn't do the country justice. Seen in all three dimensions, it is a varied country of highland metropolises, the Andes Mountains, sweltering Caribbean coastlines and the Amazon jungle. As you would assume, the different areas are occupied by diverse cultures and lifestyles.

Bogotá, for example, is on the cusp of being a world business and fashion capital. Locals dress in sleek urban attire, dabble in such pastimes as tennis, golf and bowling, drive foreign cars and keep in touch through their laptops and mobile phones with a barrage of instant messages and text messaging. For better or worse, McDonald's and Kentucky Fried Chicken hold a prominent spot in the urban Colombian lexicon. A night on the town includes hitting up the ATM for pesos and checking out an international film in a multiplex cinema or meeting with friends at a bar and then heading to a nightclub for a night of salsa, cumbia or reggaetón.

There are as many mobile phones as there are normal phone lines in Colombia, and half of all phone-line holders have Internet.

On the other end of the spectrum, some indigenous communities in outlying areas, particularly in the Amazon, are without electricity or running water – and some would prefer to stay that way. A number of populations are ravaged by the ongoing civil war and seem to be a universe away from the stability of the developed urban centers. While there is a fair amount of wealth concentrated in the cities, 55% of the country still falls below the poverty line.

If you want to take a stab at reading in Spanish try *Al diablo la maldita primavera* (2002) by Alonso Sánchez Baute, a Colombian Almodóvar who writes of transvestites, drugs, techno and the underbelly of Bogotá.

POPULATION

The Colombian national population currently hovers around 43 million people, making it the third most populous country in Latin America, after Brazil and Mexico. It is now slightly larger than its former colonizer, Spain.

Colombia has four distinct regional centers, each based around a major city. Bogotá, the capital, has roughly 7.5 million people and is the nucleus of central Colombia; Medellín, the second-largest city, has 2.5 million inhabitants, and dominates the northwest; Cali, the center of the southwest, is only slightly smaller than Medellín; while Barranquilla, the hub of the Caribbean coast has 1.3 million residents. Cartagena, while smaller, is a big draw for national and international tourists.

Colombia's diverse population, an amalgam of three main groups – indigenous, Spanish and African – reflects its colorful history. While 58% of the country claims mestizo (mixed White and indigenous) heritage, other ethnicities include: 20% White, 14% mixed White and Black, 4% Black, 3% mixed Black and indigenous, and only 1% indigenous.

Colombia's greatest pop music export, Shakira, is part Colombian, part Lebanese – showing a new wave of heterogeneity in the country.

Colombia has started to see more immigration from the Middle East, particularly from Turkey and Lebanon, but also from other parts of Latin America including Peru, Ecuador and the Caribbean. Meanwhile the conflict in the southern areas of the country has displaced tens of thousands of Colombians into neighboring Ecuador.

SPORTS

Unfortunately, the most (in)famous moment of Colombian sport came when the national football (soccer) team defender, Andrés Escobar, was shot 12 times after accidentally scoring an auto-goal in the 1994 World Cup. Already having lost to Romania and, then, to the lowly United States, the team was eliminated from the tournament and some fans did not take the loss lightly. Just the same, Colombia's football program moved on and now fields a perennially solid team with a number of players in international league play.

Kings of the Mountains: How Colombia's Cycling Heroes Changed Their Nation's History (2003) by Matt Rendell is a great introduction to cycling culture in Colombia.

The country is also known for its cycling prowess. Colombians regularly take part in the Tour de France, and have recorded some successes. Tennis, boxing, baseball and car racing are other popular sports. Major League Baseball player Edgar Rentería of Barraquilla had the winning hit in the seventh game of the 1997 World Series for the Florida Marlins.

Colombians are passionate about corrida (bullfighting), which was introduced by the Spaniards. Most towns have *plaza de toros* (bullrings). The bullfighting season usually peaks in January, when top-ranking matadors are invited from Spain. Cockfighting is another popular sport. *Galleras* (cockfight rings) can be found in most cities and in smaller towns.

RELIGION

The main thing that you need to know about religion in Colombia is that over 90% of the country is Roman Catholic. The second thing, however, is that the religion is not monolithic and exists in various syncretic forms, with African, indigenous and other regional influences. The melding of faiths can be observed at the Carnaval de Blancos y Negros (p204), which is celebrated in the city of Pasto. While its roots are in the pre-Columbian agrarian rituals and African festivals, it is glossed over with a Catholic veneer.

Catholicism was brought from Spain by the missionaries and introduced rapidly across the colony. After independence, Colombia remained a deeply Catholic nation, a fact that was enshrined in the country's constitution. Although other creeds were officially permitted, their followers were minimal – San Andrés and Providencia islands, which were colonized by the English, remain partly Protestant to this day.

The 1991 constitution marked possibly the most important religious revolution in Colombia's history. References to the 'Sacred Heart of Jesus' were replaced by a universal 'God,' eliminating the concept of a Catholic nation as it had been defined in the previous constitution. As in other Latin American countries, evangelicals, Mormons and other protestants have started to make inroads in recent years, but their influence is still far from a threat to Catholic dominion.

WOMEN IN COLOMBIA

The opportunities for women vary greatly between the more progressive cities and the relatively traditional countryside. While the role of women is tightly proscribed in rural areas, middle-class and upper-class women in the major cities can expect to attend university and major in anything they choose: from medicine to political science. A number of high-ranking politicians, including ambassadors and cabinet ministers, have been women. In fact, a quota law passed in 2000 requires that at least 30% of appointed positions in the executive branch be filled by females.

Considerable progress has been made in terms of equality of the sexes, but Colombia is still a male-dominated country. It is particularly difficult for women to make advances in the hard-nosed world of business and finance because they are excluded from the informal, backroom dealing and good-old-boys networks that are pervasive in Colombian business culture. Also, the emphasis on family obligations make it complicated to forsake a traditional family role for a career.

Modeling and beauty pageants are extremely popular in Colombia and many women try to leverage their good looks as a path to power and self-determination within the confines of the male-dominated system. A number of former beauty queens have gone on to become influential TV personalities and public figures – including the ministers of culture and defense. While that may seem preposterous, the popularity of beauty pageants in Colombia is not unlike the popularity of sports or movies in other countries. Think no further than Schwarzenegger in California.

Colombia is one of three Latin American nations (along with Chile and El Salvador) that prohibit abortions. However, the procedure is widely available in Colombia in underground clinics and through home practitioners. There are an estimated 300,000 to 400,000 illegal abortions annually. Abortion-rights advocates say that bungled abortions are a leading cause of maternal mortality. This issue primarily affects poor women, as the wealthy can go to expensive clinics or fly to Miami for treatment.

In December 2005 the Constitutional Court rejected a controversial lawsuit demanding that abortion be legalized for extenuating circumstances including rape, when having a baby endangers the mother's life or when the fetus is severely deformed. The court rejection will not end the controversy and abortion-rights activists will push for a new legal

The Carnival de Barranquilla (p227) is the largest pre-Lenten celebration in the country. The official site is at www.carnavaldebarranquilla.org (in Spanish).

Colombia ranks highest among South American nations in the percentage of female politicians, with an average of 20% of cabinet posts, congressional seats and mayoralties filled by women.

While the country is considering making divorce an easy 15-minute procedure, abortion can carry a jail term of up to 4½ years.

Gabriel García Márquez'
masterpiece *One Hundred
Years of Solitude* (1967)
takes place in the fictional
Colombian village of
Macondo and tracks the
life of the Buendía family
and Colombian history
over a century.

approach. However, many Colombians support the current ban. According to a Gallup poll released in July by an anti-abortion group, 86% of Colombians remain opposed to legalized abortion. The poll, however, did not address the circumstances outlined in the court case.

ARTS

Colombia surprises and dazzles with its rich visual arts, music, architecture and, increasingly, new wave of cinema that is grabbing international attention. Like other New World countries, the fusion and melding of different ethnic groups have created interesting art forms with their own energies and styles.

Literature

Efraim Medina Reyes
is making a name for
himself as the author of
quirky titles *Masturba-
tion Techniques between
Batman and Robin* (2003)
and *Sexuality of the Pink
Panther* (2004).

Unbeknown to many, there is more to Colombian literature than just Gabriel García Márquez. In fact, the national literary tradition began to form its own characteristics shortly after independence from Spain and gravitated into the sphere of European romanticism. Rafael Pombo (1833–1912) is generally acclaimed as the father of Colombian romantic poetry and Jorge Isaacs (1837–95), another notable author of the period, is particularly remembered for his romantic novel *María*, which can still be spotted in cafés and classrooms around the country.

José Asunción Silva (1865–96), one of Colombia's most remarkable poets, is considered the precursor of modernism in Latin America. He planted the seeds that were later developed by Nicaraguan poet Rubén Darío. Another literary talent, Porfirio Barba Jacob (1883–1942), known as 'the poet of death,' introduced the ideas of irrationalism and the language of the avant-garde.

The phenomenal international success of García Márquez has overshadowed both the accomplishments of his contemporaries and an emerging

GABRIEL GARCÍA MÁRQUEZ – COLOMBIA'S NOBEL LAUREATE

Gabriel García Márquez, or 'Gabo' as he is affectionately known, is the key figure of Colombian literature. Born March 6, 1928 in the town of Aracataca in the department of Magdalena, he has written primarily about Colombia, but lived mostly in Mexico and Europe.

García Márquez began writing as a journalist in the 1950s and worked as a foreign correspondent from where he criticized the Colombian government and basically forced himself into exile. He gained fame through his novels, particularly *One Hundred Years of Solitude*, published in 1967. It mixed myths, dreams and reality, and tantalized readers with a new form of expression dubbed as *realismo mágico* (magic realism) – now so popular that it is invariably the first genre that you will learn about in an introduction to Spanish literature course.

In 1982 García Márquez won the Nobel Prize for literature. Since then, he has created a wealth of fascinating work that extends well beyond magic realism. *Love in the Time of Cholera,* published in 1985, is the story of his parents' courtship. *The General in his Labyrinth,* published in 1989, is a historical novel that recounts the tragic final months of Simón Bolívar's life. *Strange Pilgrims,* published in 1992, is a collection of 12 stories written by the author over the previous 18 years. *Of Love and Other Demons,* from 1994, is the story of a young girl raised by her parents' Black slaves, with the backdrop of Cartagena's inquisition. In 1996, García Márquez returned to journalism with *News of a Kidnapping.* The book relates a series of kidnappings ordered by Medellín cartel boss, Pablo Escobar. Gabo seemed to be tying up his career when he published the first volume of his memoirs, *Living to Tell the Tale,* in October 2002, but didn't fail to surprise when he came back in 2004, at the age of 76, with the novel *Memories of My Melancholy Whores:* the story of a dying old man who falls in love with an adolescent girl who sells her virginity to support her family. And it is doubtful that this is the last we've heard from this literary giant.

group of younger authors. Several talented contemporaries include poet, novelist and painter Héctor Rojas Herazo and Álvaro Mutis, a close friend of Gabo. Of the younger generation, seek out the works of Fernando Vallejo, a highly respected iconoclast who has claimed that García Marquez lacks originality and is a poor writer; popular young expat Santiago Gamboa; and Mario Mendoza and Laura Restrepo, prolific writers who have each cranked out five major works in recent years.

Jorge Franco's 2004 book *Rosario Tijeras*, about a hit woman in Medellín in the 1980s, became one of Colombia's most recent smash films.

Cinema & Television

Much of Colombian art has been forged by the pain and misery of the drug trade and civil war. On one level, TV tends to respond with mindless escapism while cinema increasingly confronts unhealed national wounds by looking frankly at the issues of drugs and war. There is finally enough time and distance from the cocaine cartels of the '80s and '90s so that they can be openly portrayed in Colombian film.

The most internationally famous of recent Colombian films *Maria, llena eres de gracia* (*Maria Full of Grace*; 2004) joined American and Colombian production in a moving film about a pregnant 17-year-old flower-industry employee who leaves her small-town existence to smuggle heroin into the US as a mule. Catalina Sandino Moreno was nominated for an Academy Award for Best Actress for her role in the film.

Two other recent films that looked at Colombian issues of drugs and violence are *Sumas y Restas* (2004) and *Rosario Tijeras* (2005). Though both films were extremely popular in Colombia they lacked international backing and therefore didn't garner the same global attention as *Maria Full of Grace*. *Sumas y Restas* takes a blunt look at an engineer who gets involved in drug trafficking in 1980s Medellín. The story is quirky, looks at the reality of the drug trade and was filmed with gritty and believable amateur actors. *Rosario Tijeras*, on the other hand, won praise for the flawless performance of Colombian actress Flora Martinez in the title role as a hit woman for the Medellín drug cartel in the late 1980s who always gave her victims a kiss before shooting them dead.

Carlos Bernal is an increasingly popular Colombian documentarian. Check out his 2005 short film on Colombian rural life: *1526 metros sobre el nivel del mar*.

Colombian TV has a longer and more moneyed history than its cinematic counterpart and is generally less controversial and less intellectual. Generally, TV has been a way to forget about the hardships at hand. Colombians, like most Latin Americans, are fans of *telenovelas* (soap operas) and the actors and directors achieve major celebrity status in the country. Channels Caracol and RCN battle it out for the top *novelas* in the country. In recent years, RCN's *Yo Soy Betty la Fea* and *Café* and Caracol's *La Saga* have redefined success for Colombian *novelas* (although even the most beloved programs only have a shelf life of a few years). *Los Reyes* is RCN's *telenovela* of the moment, which is dominating national rating with its kitschy blend of drama and comedy.

In the late 1990s, *Yo Soy Betty la Fea* (I'm Ugly Betty) turned *telenovelas* on their head with a rare unattractive (and decidedly comical) protagonist and was a hit not only in Colombia but across Latin America.

Other reality shows take influence from North American TV including *Factor X*, the Colombian version of *American Idol*, and *Cambio Extremo*, the local alteration of *Extreme Makeover*, the plastic surgery extravaganza.

Music

When most people think of Colombian music, salsa, cumbia and Shakira come to mind. While the classic rhythms and, of course, Shakira are not to be overlooked there are many more layers to Colombian music. What about punk-ska fusion in Cali, house DJs in Bogotá or reggaetón in Cartagena?

Salsa spread throughout the Caribbean, hitting Colombia by the late 1960s. Cali and Barranquilla have since become Colombia's bastions of

CUMBIA – THE RHYTHM OF COLOMBIA

Colombia generated many unique rhythms from the fusion of Afro-Caribbean and Spanish influences, including *porro, merecumbe, mapalé, gaita* and cumbia. Of the musical styles, cumbia, a lively 4/4 beat with guitars, accordion, bass, drums and the occasional horn, became the most popular of the musical styles and spread across Colombia and eventually across Latin America. Its name is thought to derive from '*kumb*' or '*cumbe*,' which is a Guinean word meaning 'noise and celebration.'

Cumbia has a rural background and is still most popular in the countryside, where it's played by homebred bands in small villages. It's here that it's at its most authentic and spontaneous. Over recent decades, cumbia has gradually made its way into the city and recording studios. Though it still retains a heavy working-class following, it can be heard in New York, Buenos Aires and Mexico City. Cumbia has also spawned various subgenres including Peruvian *techno-cumbia* and Argentina's *cumbia villera* – South America's closest cousin to gangsta rap and a far cry from the original beats from the Colombian Caribbean.

salsa music, but it's heard all across the country and is the most popular club music in Bogotá. Today, Colombia has innumerable salsa bands and plenty of excellent *salseros*. Considered among the best are Joe Arroyo from the Caribbean coast and Grupo Niche from Cali.

Another popular locally spawned music is vallenato. Born a century ago on the Caribbean coast, vallenato is based on the European accordion. Carlos Vives, one of the best-known modern Latin artists, transformed vallenato into a vibrant pop beat and spread it across the country (see p135).

The music of Los Llanos (The Plains), known as *música llanera,* is usually accompanied by a harp, *cuatro* (a type of four-string guitar) and maracas. It has much in common with the music of the Venezuelan Llanos.

Colombia's most famous musical export is Shakira Mebarak Ripoll, simply known as Shakira, a phenomenally talented singer-songwriter with looks, brains and dance moves to match. She is a global pop superstar, who has recorded in both Spanish and English. With the release of *Fijación Oral Vol 2* in late 2005, she has started to demonstrate a staying power in the music industry not seen since perhaps Madonna.

Not quite as famous, but still with a substantial following, is Colombian guitarist/vocalist Juanes, who won a Grammy in 2002 for his song 'A Dios Le Pido' and was back again in 2005 with the impossibly catchy 'La Camisa Negra.'

Though they have been around for a while, Colombia's most famous rock group is still arguably the duo Los Aterciopelados. Formed in 1990 in Bogotá, they've toured all over the world and won a Grammy in 2001 for the best Latin rock album (entitled *Gozo Poderoso)*. Another top act is the Miami-based Colombian pop/rock/tropical group Bacilos, who fuse smooth vocal harmonies with melodic hooks and pounding guitars for a unique and engaging sound. The have recently taken on issues of social and political importance, including the cocaine wars and immigration.

Moving beyond pop music, Colombia has solid underground musical talent, including a vibrant punk scene in Bogotá, Cali and Medellín. This is nothing new: the skacore flag bearer La Mojiganga has nearly a decade of raw and raucous shows under its belt. Keep an eye out for up-and-coming pop punk bands such as Independiente81 in Bogotá. Colombia also continues to churn out new forms of fusion music, now often combining traditional instruments with electronic overtones. La

Shakira's smash hit 'La Tortura' featuring Alejandro Sanz went as high as number 27 on the US Billboard Top 40 – this was unprecedented as not a single word of the song is in English.

Cartagena, COLOMBIA

Castillo San Felipe, al fondo "La Popa"
San Felipe Castle, at background "La Popa"

COSMOGUIAS
cosmoguias@yahoo.com
GCA 2365

Bogotá Colombia - Photos: Omar Bechara - Graphic Design: Olga Bechara Printed in Colombia

7 707286 251005

Place stamps here

Mojarra Eléctrica is a good example of this trend. As with the rest of Latin America and much of North America, reggaetón is on the move. Influenced by reggae, dancehall and hip-hop, this music has been pouring in from Colombia's Caribbean coast and washing over the country. The global phenomenons of house, techno and trance are to be found in the larger cities, with the largest DJ scene in Bogotá.

The Caribbean coast still vibrates with more classical African-related rhythms, such as the *mapalé* and *porro,* and the Pacific coast has the *currulao,* a more purely African music with heavy use of drums, but tinged with Spanish influences.

Colombian Andean music has been strongly influenced by Spanish rhythms and instruments, and differs noticeably from the indigenous music of the Peruvian and Bolivian highlands. Among typical old genres are the *bambuco, pasillo* and *torbellino,* all of which are instrumental and feature predominantly string instruments.

Check out the site www.musicacol.com (in Spanish) for a sampling of Colombian rhythms and lyrics.

Architecture

Colombia is not known as an architectural paradise, although it is not without its highlights. Modern architectural trends made their way to Colombia after WWII and took the form of boxy, cement buildings that were orderly and efficient, though not particularly attractive. The modernization process accelerated during the 1960s when skyscrapers began to appear in urban centers, most notably in Bogotá and Medellín. These days, the cities have some of the more urbanized skylines in Latin America, full of glass, cement and steel towers.

Cartagena, however, remains the country's architectural jewel, with colonial charm and the old walled city (p126) boasting tiled roofs, pleasantly worn balconies and flower-filled courtyards along twisting, narrow streets. Another highlight is Cali's Iglesia de la Ermita (p190). Spain's strong Catholic tradition left behind loads of churches and convents in the colony – the central areas of Bogotá, Cartagena, Tunja and Popayán also have good examples. The churches built in the early days of the Spanish Conquest were generally small and modest, but in the later period they tended to reach monumental dimensions. Unlike in Mexico or Peru, colonial churches in Colombia have rather austere exteriors, but their interiors are usually richly decorated.

Bogotá is home to a few well-preserved examples of 17th-century mannerist-baroque structures known as *arquitectura santafereña,* Capilla del Sagrario (p60) and the Casa del Marqués de San Jorge (p58).

Painting & Sculpture

The colonial period was dominated by Spanish religious art and although paintings and sculptures of this era were mostly created by local artists, they reflected Spanish trends of the time. Gregorio Vásquez de Arce y Ceballos (1638–1711) was clearly the most remarkable painter of the colonial era. He lived and worked in Bogotá and left behind a collection of more than 500 works, now distributed among churches and museums across the country.

With the arrival of independence, fine arts departed from strictly religious themes, but it was not until the revolution in European painting at the turn of the 19th century that Colombian artists began to experiment and create truly original art.

Many painters and sculptors who started their careers in the 1930s and 1940s developed interesting individual styles. Among the most distinguished are Pedro Nel Gómez, known for his murals, watercolors, oils

---

THE HUGE SUCCESS OF BOTERO

Fernando Botero (b 1932) is the most widely recognized Colombian painter and sculptor. Born in Medellín, he had his first individual painting exhibition in Bogotá at the age of 19 and gradually developed his easily recognizable style characterized by the abnormal fatness of his figures. In 1972 he settled in Paris and began experimenting with sculpture, which resulted in a collection of *gordas* and *gordos*, as Colombians call these creations. Today, his paintings dot the walls of world-class museums and his monumental public sculptures adorn squares and parks in cities around the globe, including Paris, Madrid, Lisbon, Florence and New York.

---

and sculptures; Luis Alberto Acuña, a painter and sculptor who used motifs from pre-Columbian art; Guillermo Wiedemann, a German painter who spent most of his creative period in Colombia and drew inspiration from local themes, though he later turned to abstract art; Alejandro Obregón, a Cartagena painter tending to abstract forms; Edgar Negret, an abstract sculptor; Eduardo Ramírez Villamizar, who expressed himself mostly in geometric forms; and Rodrigo Arenas Betancur, Colombia's most famous monument-maker.

These masters were followed by a slightly younger generation, born mainly in the 1930s, including artists such as Armando Villegas, a Peruvian living in Colombia, whose influences ranged from pre-Columbian motifs to surrealism; Leonel Góngora, noted for his erotic drawings; and the most internationally renowned Colombian artist, Fernando Botero.

Today Colombia is one of Latin America's leading fine-arts representatives. Plenty of exhibitions featuring contemporary art are put on by museums and private commercial art galleries. Bogotá, with university art faculties and loads of art galleries, has the most active cultural life, making it the main center for contemporary art, design and, increasingly, for video and computer arts.

The recent period has been characterized by a proliferation of schools, trends and techniques. The artists to watch out for include Bernardo Salcedo (conceptual sculpture and photography), Miguel Ángel Rojas (painting and installations), Lorenzo Jaramillo (expressionist painting), María de la Paz Jaramillo (painting), María Fernanda Cardozo (installations), Catalina Mejía (abstract painting) and the talented Doris Salcedo (sculpture and installations).

Have a look at www .manzanazeta.com (in Spanish), a portal to cutting-edge Colombian visual arts and design.

The Ibero-American Theater Festival in Bogotá is the largest and most prestigious theater festival in Colombia; check out its website at www .festivaldeteatro.com.co.

Theater & Dance

Although theater first developed in Colombia in the middle of the 19th century, it mainly followed foreign trends and remained insignificant. A genuine national theater emerged in the mid-20th century in Bogotá and Cali. Since then, some 100 theater groups have been founded, most of them small, amateur troupes.

Theater activity is almost exclusively confined to the largest urban centers. Only Bogotá, Medellín and Cali have several groups working permanently in their own theaters. Teatro de la Candelaria (p70) in Bogotá (founded in 1966) and the Teatro Experimental de Cali (TEC; p192) in Cali (1955) are pioneers of Colombian theater and are still interesting and innovative. Several theater schools are now contributing to the development of a national theater, and foreign and local performers gather at the two international theater festivals, in Bogotá and Manizales.

Environment

THE LAND

Colombia may not be the size of Brazil, Canada, the USA or other American heavyweights, but it is no small country. After you head south through the chain of Central American minicountries, it is the first South American behemoth. Colombia covers 1,141,748 sq km, roughly equivalent to the combined area of California and Texas (or France, Spain and Portugal). It is the fourth-largest country in South America, after Brazil, Argentina and Peru.

Colombia is the only South American nation to have coastlines on both the Pacific Ocean and Caribbean Sea.

While most people assume that Colombia is just a tropical land, the country's physical geography is amazingly diverse. The western part, almost half of the total territory, is mountainous, with three Andean chains – Cordillera Occidental, Cordillera Central and Cordillera Oriental – running roughly parallel north–south across most of the country. A number of the peaks are over 5000m, making them higher than anything in the continental United States. Two valleys, the Valle del Cauca and Valle del Magdalena, are sandwiched between the three cordilleras. Both valleys have their own eponymous rivers, which flow northward, unite and eventually empty into the Caribbean near Barranquilla.

Every wonder where all those pretty flowers come from? Check out http://colombianflowers .com for an overview of Colombia's massive flower industry.

Apart from the three Andean chains, Colombia features an independent and relatively small range, the Sierra Nevada de Santa Marta, which rises from the Caribbean coastline to craggy, snowcapped peaks. It is the world's highest coastal mountain range, and its twin summits of Simón Bolívar and Cristóbal Colón (both 5775m) are the country's highest.

More than half of the territory east of the Andes is vast lowland, which is generally divided into two regions: Los Llanos to the north and the Amazon to the south. Los Llanos, roughly 250,000 sq km in area, is a huge open savannah in the Orinoco river basin. The Amazon, stretching over some 400,000 sq km, occupies all of Colombia's southeast and lies in the Amazon basin. Most of this land is covered by a thick rainforest crisscrossed by rivers.

Colombia also has a number of islands. The major ones are the archipelago of San Andrés and Providencia (in the Caribbean Sea, 750km northwest of mainland Colombia), the Islas del Rosario and San Bernardo (near the Caribbean coast), and Gorgona and Malpelo (in the Pacific Ocean).

The famous German geographer and botanist Alexander von Humboldt explored and studied regions of Colombia and describes it all in amazing detail in his three-volume *Personal Narrative of Travels to the Equinoctial Regions of America, 1799–1801.*

WILDLIFE

Colombia claims to have more plant and animal species per square kilometer than any other country in the world. Its variety of flora and fauna is second only to Brazil's, even though Colombia is seven times smaller than its neighbor. This abundance reflects Colombia's varied climatic zones and microclimates, which have created many different habitats and biological islands in which wildlife has evolved independently.

Animals

Colombia is a genuine free-range zoo with more than 350 mammal species, 15% of the world's primates and 18% of the world's birds. Some of the most interesting animals include sleek cats such as the jaguar and the ocelot or the more goofy piglike peccary and tapir (the latter is actually more closely related to the horse and rhinoceros). There are around 1900 recorded species of birds, ranging from the huge Andean condor to the

---

THE ENDANGERED CONDOR – THE SYMBOL OF THE ANDES

Some 24 Colombian bird and mammal species are threatened with extinction, mainly due to deforestation. One of the birds in danger of disappearing is the symbol of the Andes, the great South American condor *(Vultur gryphus)*. This vulturelike giant, which is actually more closely related to the stork, has wingspans reaching toward 2.8m. Its striking dark silhouette, circling in the sky, has intrigued generations of humans and the bird holds a place in local myth and lore similar to that of the bald eagle in North America.

Colombia obviously has a host of other issues that make conservation even more difficult than it is elsewhere. Since 1989, American zoos, especially San Diego and Cincinnati, have raised condors and sent them off to Colombia. The condors are trained to fend for themselves and then released into the wild. As of 2005, 60 condors have been introduced into the country, putting the total number of Colombian condors at around 180 – up one-third from their last generation. While that is a clear improvement, the program won't be considered a success until the population starts to repopulate and grow on its own.

---

tiny hummingbird. More than 140 of these bird species are endemic to Colombia. Unfortunately, many of the more remote natural areas are not safe to visit due to the ongoing civil conflict, although the security situation has improved recently, opening access to a number of parks. For further information, see the national parks chart (opposite).

There is also abundant marine life in the country's extensive river systems and along its two coastlines. The islands of San Andrés and Providencia boast some of the largest and most productive coral reefs in the Americas. In 2000 Unesco declared this area the Seaflower Biosphere Reserve to protect the ecosystem. The reefs are also considered among the most intact in the Caribbean and play an important ecological role in the health of the sea. They provide feeding and nesting grounds for four species of endangered sea turtles and numerous types of fish and lobster. It has been determined that the health of certain fish stocks in the Florida Keys hinges directly on their ability to spawn in the Colombian reefs.

For background reading on birds, look for *A Guide to the Birds of South America* (1970) published by the Academy of Natural Science, Philadelphia. There's also the helpful *Where to Watch Birds in South America* (2000) by Nigel Wheatley.

Plants

Colombia's flora is equally as impressive as its fauna and includes more than 130,000 plants, a third of which are endemic species. This richness does not convey the whole picture: large areas of the country, such as the inaccessible parts of the Amazon, have undiscovered species. It is estimated that, at a minimum, 2000 plant species have yet to be identified and an even greater number have yet to be analyzed for potential medicinal purposes.

For use in the field, grab a copy of *A Guide to the Birds of Colombia* (1986) by Stephen L Hilty & William L Brown. *South American Birds – A Photographic Aid to Identification* (1998) by John S Dunning is a solid second choice.

Orchids are considered among the most intriguing flowers in the country. Although they are the largest flowering plant family, numbering an estimated 30,000 species, they retain an exotic (perhaps erotic) allure. Orchid fans are sure to want to visit Colombia. With its estimated 3000 species (many of which are unique to the country), it holds the most orchid types of any single country. Again, inaccessible parts of the country are sure to hold even more types. Orchids grow in virtually all regions and climatic zones of Colombia, from sandy seaside dunes to the windy highland above the tree line. The greatest diversity, however, is found in mountain cloud forests of the Andean region, between roughly 1000m and 2000m above sea level. The specific area with the widest variety of orchids is Antioquia, partially because much of that region lies in those orchid-favored altitudes.

NATIONAL PARKS & RESERVES

Colombia has some of the most splendid, pristine nature in the Americas, but must fight hard to change its image before it is recognized internationally as an ecotourism destination. In fact, the country has 38 national parks, 12 flora and fauna sanctuaries and four other natural reserve areas. While that is an impressive number of parks and protected areas on paper, it is not necessarily so in the real world. The Colombian government has a fair amount of other priorities, and has never had sufficient funds or personnel to properly guard the parks. Simply decreeing an area as a national park has not eliminated colonization, logging, mining, ranching or poaching, let alone guerrilla activities or an increasing amount of drug cultivation and processing.

Only a dozen or so parks provide accommodations and food; several more offer only camping. The remaining parks have no tourist amenities at all and some, especially those in remote regions, are virtually inaccessible. Many parks can be unsafe for tourists because of the guerrilla or trafficker presence. With all of that said, the parks that are maintained, safe and accessible are positively fantastic.

Any time is a good time to visit the list of Colombia's most accessible parks, although Parque Nacional Los Nevados is best visited in summer (January and February) and Santuario de Iguaque in summer or winter (July and August). It is always a good idea to check ahead of time with tour agencies and the parks department for up-to-date conditions of any park before a visit. As well as those mentioned in the national parks chart (below), the most popular parks include Parque Nacional Corales del Rosario (p137) and Isla Gorgona (p194).

National parks are managed by the Parques Nacionales Naturales de Colombia. As well as their central office in Bogotá (p54), there are regional offices in most large cities and other localities close to the parks. If you plan to visit the parks, you should first visit the park office, check on the status of the park and pay the entrance fee (US$9 per person). Accommodations, when available, cost US$9 per bed. The office

Colombia is the world's largest exporter of cut flowers and the second largest exporter of coffee.

For anything you may need to know about national parks in Colombia go to the government's official site at http://parquesnacionales.gov.co (in Spanish).

NATIONAL PARKS & RESERVES

Protected Area	Features	Activities
Parque Nacional Amacayacu (p216)	accessible Amazon: reptiles, monkeys, fish, birds	canoe trips, trekking, wildlife spotting
Parque Nacional Chicaque (p80)	cloud forest near Bogotá: birds	walking, bird-watching, horseback-riding
Parque Nacional El Cocuy (p92)	spectacular alpine peaks, lakes and valleys	walking, trekking
Laguna de la Cocha (p206)	cloud forest–covered island in a lake	walking
Parque Nacional McBean Lagoon (p153)	coastline and islets: mangroves, crabs, sea life	walking, snorkeling
Parque Nacional Los Nevados (p174)	snowcapped Andean volcanoes and cloud forest	hiking, mountaineering
Parque Nacional Santuario de Iguaque (p91)	mountain lakes: cultural history	walking, historical sites
Parque Nacional Tayrona (p114)	coastal rainforest and beaches: monkeys, corals	walking, trekking, snorkeling
Reserva Natural Puracé (p197)	colorful, mountain park: waterfalls, hot springs	hiking, walking

A Neotropical Companion: An Introduction to the Animals, Plants, and Ecosystems of the New World Tropics (1999) by John Kricher is fascinating reading and the preeminent book of its class.

provides information about national parks, issues permits and books park accommodations.

Growing ecological awareness has led to the creation of privately owned and run nature reserves. They are administered by individual proprietors, rural communities, foundations and other nongovernmental organizations. Most reserves are small but often contain an interesting sample of habitat. They are scattered countrywide, although most are in the Andean region. Some reserves offer accommodations, food and guides.

In 2005 more than 215 of these reserves were affiliated with the **Asociacíon Red Colombiana de Reservas Naturales de la Sociedad Civil** (http://resnatur.org .co), but a number were still closed due to security issues.

ENVIRONMENTAL ISSUES

The issues behind Colombia's environmental problems run deep. Poverty and unequal land distribution, which have their roots back in the colonial era, are much to blame for the ever-advancing human encroachment into virgin forests. Each year settlers cut down nearly 405,000 hectares of forest, converting the land to fields and pastures. Moreover, much like any other country, the rapid push to develop a market-based economy and compete globally has put pressure on Colombia to build on its land and exploit its natural resources. While similar environmental destruction happened in North America and Europe many generations ago, the same thing is happening now in Colombia – before our eyes and video cameras.

Breakfast of Biodiversity: The Truth About Rain Forest Destruction (1995) by John Vandermeer and Ivette Perfecto helps you to understand the underlying roots of deforestation and many of its complexities.

Overall, an estimated 607,000 to 890,000 hectares are deforested each year and, at this rate, Colombia's forests may be depleted in just 40 years. Such deforestation has increased the rate of extinction for many plant and animal species and destabilized soils, leading to the silting of rivers and death of marine species.

This destruction is not just happening in the Amazonian region. Colombia's Pacific coast also finds itself at the crossroads of conservation

GREEN FEVER

Colombia produces the largest percentage of the world's emeralds (50%; Zambia produces 20% and Brazil 15%). Some estimate that the mines inside Colombia may actually contain up to 90% of the world's emerald deposits. This is good news for emerald prospectors and bad news for the local environment – and perhaps Colombia as a whole. The fighting and destruction related to the production of these glamorous gems has had an impact on the country not so different from cocaine or heroin.

There are two sites in Colombia where emeralds are mined, Muzo and Chivor, both in the Boyacá department. Although the Muisca people mined the stones since pre-Columbian times, the Spanish colonialists went crazy for the green stones and greatly expanded the operations. They enslaved the Indians to mine the gems for them and eventually replaced those workers with additional slave labor from Africa. Many of today's miners are the direct descendants of those slaves and live in only slightly better conditions.

The government never managed to gain full control over the mines. Few miners ever heeded the law and rampant digging has torn up the countryside. In an attempt to find new digging sites or to improve their squalid living conditions, miners have continuously pushed further into the forest. Fierce battles were repeatedly fought between rival gangs of miners, claiming lives and ravaging the mines. Between 1984 and 1990 alone, in one of the bloodiest 'emerald wars' in recent history, 3500 people were killed in Muzo. Yet, 'green fever' continues to burn among fortune hunters and adventurers from the four corners of the country and it surely won't stop until the last bewitching green gem is mined.

and development. Under an ambitious arrangement called Plan Pacifico, the area has become a target for the extraction and exportation of natural resources to build and strengthen the regional economy. Under the plan, the forest is mowed down for wood and paper, or to establish crops such as the African palm tree. The coast, with its many Afro-Colombian inhabitants and high poverty levels, has long been marginalized from the seat of power in Hispanic, and relatively wealthy, Bogotá. Who is to say that the region should remain poor for the sake of preservation of biodiversity? Such is the quandary facing many regions of the country.

A less controversial, but equally troubling problem is the more than 40,000 hectares that are deforested each year to grow coca, marijuana and opium poppies. As the Drug War gets more successful in battling growers and producers in their traditional areas, they simply relocate. They move higher up the slopes and to the more remote, virgin forests of the Andes (aided by an increase in opium cultivation, which favors higher altitudes) and deeper into parks and the Amazon. Cocaine processors are definitely not worried about dumping their toxic byproducts and other hazardous materials into streams, nor are they too concerned with following other environmental safety standards. Nearly two-thirds of the Andes, an area that is vital to the conservation of Colombia's water supply, has been deforested as a result of both migration and drug cultivation.

To learn more about pressing environmental issues in Colombia or to see what you can do, see Colombia's Conservation International website: http://conservation.org .co (in Spanish).

Food & Drink

Colombia is famous for many things other than its cuisine, but that is not to say that the food won't delight your taste buds. It is true that those looking for spicy food or exquisite flavors will be disappointed because many dishes are plain. However, Colombian food is good value, with heaping portions of fresh, local ingredients. Dishes are varied and tasty, with regional twists, Latin American staples and a dash of Spanish influence. The country is stocked with countless places to eat, ranging from street stalls to well-appointed restaurants and serving everything from Colombian Creole classics to Chateaubriand with champagne. Even the smallest village will have a place to eat – a restaurant, the market or, at the very least, a private house that serves meals.

The Colorado State Latin American Student Organization has a good online cookbook of Colombian dishes at www.colostate .edu/Orgs/LASO /Colombia/#Cuisine.

STAPLES & SPECIALITIES

Colombian cuisine, referred to as *comida criolla* (Creole food), is varied and boasts a number of regional specialties: lobsters on the Caribbean coast; *ajiaco* (chicken stew with potatoes, served with cream, corn and capers) in Bogotá; and Andean favorites such as *cuy* (guinea pig). Local dishes are hearty and fresh, and can be healthy if you avoid the numerous deep-fried options.

For 199 exceptional photographs and 133 regional recipes try the extraordinary *Taste of Colombia* (1997) by Benjamin Villegas and Antonio Montana.

Overall, there isn't too much variety to the ubiquitous *comida corriente* (set meal), which is the principal diet of the majority of Colombians when dining out. At lunchtime (noon to 8pm), the meal is called *almoners*; at dinnertime (after 8pm), it becomes *comida corriente,* but it is in fact identical to lunch. Lunch is usually the main meal of the day, often followed by a *tinto* (coffee) to get you back on your feet. It is a two-course meal consisting of *soap* (soup) and *bandeau* or *sect* (main course), and usually includes a soft drink. The main course contains a small piece of meat, chicken or fish served with rice, pasta, red beans, lentils or vegetables, sometimes with fried plantains and a small salad. Despite some local additions, it's much the same throughout the country.

Other *comida criolla* specialties include *arepas* (corn pancakes, eaten in place of bread), *sancocho* (a vegetable-based soup with a choice of meat and many regional varieties) and *lechona* (a baked pig stuffed with rice, meat and peas).

Colombia has an amazing variety of fruits, some of which don't have names in English. Try *guanábana, lulo, curuba, zapote, mamoncillo, uchuva, feijoa, granadilla, tomate de árbol, borojó* and *mamey,* to name a few.

DRINKS
Nonalcoholic Drinks

Coffee is Colombia's number-one drink – *tinto* (a small cup of black coffee) is served everywhere. Its quality, however, varies from place to place – don't expect that coffee will always be good just because you are in the land of

---

TRAVEL YOUR TASTE BUDS

If you are out for a culinary adventure, try a *homiga culona* (giant fried ant) or go ahead and get a kilo of the crispy critters. They are unique to Santander and aren't picked at on plates, but purchased by weight in shops. Make sure to go during the prime ant-eating season from March to May.

THE REAL THING

Coca Sek may really hit the spot if you need to quench your thirst, but don't bother looking for it on the supermarket shelves when you return home. Produced by Nasa Indians in southern Colombia, the soft drink is made from coca leaf extract. There's not enough coca in it to get you high, but the bottlers describe it as an 'energizing drink,' lightly stimulating like coffee.

The drink is available domestically, but Coca-Cola and Pepsi corporations can sleep easy at night with the knowledge that Coca Sek will probably never make it to the US, UK or most other countries. Laws prohibiting the importation of raw coca would stop the pop at customs.

Coca Sek (which means Coca of the Sun) looks like apple cider and tastes vaguely like ginger ale. While complete testing has not been performed, it's known that the coca makes up less than one half a percent in the drink itself. Coca Sek is produced and bottled by a staff of around 15 Nasa Indians. A portion of the profits made by the company go to coca farmers.

Juan Valdéz. Other coffee drinks are *perico* or *pintado,* a small milk coffee, and *café con leche,* which is larger and contains more milk.

Tea, of the sort that Brits might expect, is of poor quality and not very popular. On the other hand, *aromáticas* – herbal teas made with various plants such as *cidrón* (citrus leaves), *yerbabuena* (mint) and *manzanilla* (chamomile) – are quite flavorful. *Agua de panela* (unrefined sugar melted in hot water) is tasty with lemon.

In Bogotá, try the famous *chocolate santafereño,* a chocolate drink served with cheese and homemade breads.

Gaseosas (fizzy soft drinks) are cheap and available everywhere. Colombia is one of the world's largest consumers of soft drinks. Apart from locally produced well-known Western drinks, such as Coca-Cola, Pepsi and Sprite, there is a variety of Colombian drinks such as Colombiana, Uva (grape) and Manzana (apple). It is safest to stick to bottled water although the water in the cities is of decent quality.

For anything that you might want to learn about Colombia's coffee industry (the government version of the story, anyway), go to http://juanvaldez.com.

Alcoholic Drinks

Colombians rarely drink alcohol (except for beer) with meals, but are not afraid to imbibe alcohol under most other circumstances. *Aguardiente* is the most popular national spirit and is consumed in large quantities, mostly by the male half of the population. It's basic cane alcohol, often flavored with anise, and is produced throughout the country. Cristal and Néctar are the most popular in the Bogotá region, but Aguardiente Medellín is considered to be the best. A more refined version of *aguardiente* is *mistela,* a homemade sweet liquor, produced by preserving fruit or herbs in *aguardiente* syrup. Beware that *aguardiente* packs a punch and an even heavier hangover.

Ron (rum) is another popular spirit, particularly on the Caribbean coast and in Antioquia. Recommended dark rums are Ron Viejo de Caldas and Ron Medellín; the best white rums are Ron Tres Esquinas and Ron Blanco.

Beer is popular, cheap and decent. Most beers are made in the light, watery and refreshing Latin American style. There are many local brands, including Águila, Poker, Bavaria and Club-Colombia. Colombian wine is poor, not popular and best avoided. Most quality restaurants serve finer Chilean and Argentine vintages, which are on par with European wines and of much better value.

In some regions, mostly in rural areas, you will find *chicha* and *guarapo.* They are homemade alcoholic beverages obtained by the fermentation of fruit or maize in sugar or *panela* water (raw cane sugar dissolved in

Coffee in Colombia, 1850–1970: An Economic, Social and Political History (1980) by Marco Palacios is an academic look at how coffee changed the Colombian economy and played a roll in developing the nation.

Slang for a hangover in Colombia is *guayabo* (wa-ya-bo).

water). Most are low in alcohol, but, if you find the right one, it can put you down for the count.

CELEBRATIONS

Colombians rarely overlook a reason to have a celebration, whether it be a birthday, a going-away party, New Year's or Carnaval. The main Carnaval celebration takes place in Barranquilla, on the Caribbean coast, and is a blur of colorful parades, street parties, Afro-Colombian music and lots of drinking. Other festivals and celebrations run the gamut from the more decidedly religious Semana Santa (Holy Week) in Popayán, to small town parties that may serve tamales or *arepas* en masse accompanied by a healthy dose of *aguardiente,* rum and beer. Enjoying a celebration in Colombia will help you to understand the culture much better and is an experience not to be missed.

For a sobering look at the food production industry in Colombia and its affect on the country, check out Bananas and Business: The United Fruit Company in Colombia, 1899–2000 (2005) by Marcelo Bucheli.

WHERE TO EAT & DRINK

The menu of a basic restaurant may only offer the *comida corriente,* which they serve continuously from noon until they close at night. Restaurants supplement the *comida corriente* with a short list of popular dishes, which almost always includes *carne asada* (roasted or grilled beef) and *arroz con pollo* (rice with chicken). Set meals are also served at the higher-end establishments, where they are more diversified and use finer ingredients; you can usually expect a dessert plate in these places, too.

Roasted- or barbecued-chicken restaurants (there are plenty of them) are an alternative to the *comida.* Half a chicken with potatoes will cost around US$3 to US$4.

Quick Eats

If you're on a tight budget, be prepared to stick to the *comida corriente* in budget restaurants. The way to diversify and enrich your diet is to eat at street stalls and markets. Food stalls are a common part of the urban landscape and every town has a market with food stalls serving fresh snacks and plates that are cooked to order.

While Lonely Planet doesn't recommend frequenting North American fast-food chains, do remember that Colombians love hamburgers as much as their northern neighbors and the occasional (or even frequent) *hamburguesa* will hardly detract from your cultural experience.

VEGETARIANS & VEGANS

More and more vegetarian restaurants are cropping up in the major cities and there is an increasing number of budget vegetarian places, too. In a pinch, it is possible to order a *comida corriente* without meat, but make sure the beans are not made with bacon fat or other animal products. You will also have to remain vigilant about checking that a plate has no animal products in it because some Colombians will assume that no meat *(carne)* simply refers to red meat.

COLOMBIA'S TOP FIVE RESTAURANTS

- Andrés Carne de Res (p68), Chia
- Café Studioa (p154), Providenci
- Salón Versalles (p164), Medellín
- Museo del Tequila (p70), Bogotá
- Platillos Voladores (p192), Cali

HABITS & CUSTOMS

Eating in Colombian restaurants is much the same as eating in North American restaurants except most places allow smoking, the quality of the bathrooms is not to be counted on and you are best to opt for bottled water over a glass of ice water. The major difference is that people dine at a more relaxed pace and meals can go on for hours if other responsibilities do not get in the way. So take your time, enjoy the food and the company.

EAT YOUR WORDS

The following is a list of foods, drinks and other useful words and phrases, their English pronunciations and translations. It should add to your comprehension of Colombian menus.

Secrets of Colombian Cooking (2004) by Patricia McCausland-Gallo is lacking on quality photographs, but has stellar recipes to show you how to make authentic Colombian food with black-belt precision.

Useful Phrases

I'd like ..., please.
kee·*sye*·ra ... por·fa·*vor*   *Quisiera ..., por favor.*
I'd like the set meal, please.
kee·*sye*·ra·la ko·*mee*·da ko·*ryen*·te·por·fa·vor   *Quisiera la comida corriente, por favor.*
What is today's special?
kwal·es·el·*pla*·to·del·*dee*·a   *¿Cuál es el plato del día?*
What do you recommend?
ke·me·re·ko·*myen*·da   *¿Qué me recomienda?*
I'm a vegetarian.
soy·ve·khe·ta·*rya*·no/a   *Soy vegetariano/a* (m/f).
Is service included in the bill?
la·*kwen*·ta·een·*kloo*·ye·el·ser·*vee*·syo   *¿La cuenta incluye el servicio?*
The menu/bill, please.
la·*kar*·ta/*kwen*·ta·por·fa·vor   *La carta/cuenta, por favor.*
Thank you, that was delicious.
moo·chas·*gra*·syas·es·*ta*·ba·bwe·*nee*·see·mo   *Muchas gracias, estaba buenísimo.*

Food Glossary

agua (con/sin gas)	*a*·gwa (kon/seen gas)	water (carbonated/noncarbonated)
agua mineral	*a*·gwa mee·ne·*ral*	mineral water
agua potable	*a*·gwa po·*ta*·ble	drinking water
aguardiente	a·gwar·*dyen*·te	liquor (strong)
ají	a·*khee*	chili condiments
arroz	a·*ros*	rice
azúcar	a·*soo*·kar	sugar
cabro, cabrito	*ka*·bro, ka·*bree*·to	goat
calamares	ka·la·*ma*·res	squid
camarones	ka·ma·*ro*·nes	shrimp
cangrejo	kan·*gre*·kho	crab
carne	*kar*·ne	meat
cerdo, chancho	*ser*·do, *chan*·cho	pork
cerveza	ser·*ve*·sa	beer
ceviche	se·*vee*·che	raw seafood marinated in lemon juice
chicharrones	chee·cha·*ro*·nes	fried chunks of pork or pork skins
choclo	*cho*·klo	corn on the cob
chuzo	*choo*·so	shish kebab
(la) comida corriente	(la) ko·*mee*·da ko·*ryen*·te	set menu
cordero	kor·*de*·ro	mutton
empanadas	em·pa·*na*·das	meat and/or cheese pastries
ensalada	en·sa·*la*·da	salad

estofado	es·to-*fa*·do	stew
frutas	*froo*·tas	fruit
helado	e-*la*·do	ice cream
huevos fritos/revueltos	we·vos *free*·tos/re-*vwel*·tos	fried/scrambled eggs
jamón	kha·*mon*	ham
jugo	*hoo*·go	juice
langosta	lan·*gos*·ta	lobster
leche	*le*·che	milk
lechona	le·*cho*·na	stuffed pig
lomo	*lo*·mo	beef
mantequilla	man·te·*kee*·ya	butter
maracuya	ma·ra·*koo*·ya	passion fruit
mariscos	ma·*rees*·kos	seafood
mate	*ma*·te	herbal tea
mora	*mo*·ra	blackberry
naranja	na·*ran*·ha	orange
palta	*pal*·ta	avocado
pan	pan	bread
papas fritas	*pa*·pas *free*·tas	french fries
parrillada	pa·ree·*ya*·da	grilled meats
pescado	pes·*ka*·do	fish
piña	*pee*·nya	pineapple
pollo, gallina	*po*·lyo, ga·*lee*·na	chicken
postre	*pos*·tre	dessert
queso	*ke*·so	cheese
sopa	*so*·pa	soup
tallarines	ta·ya·*ree*·nes	noodles
toronja	to·*ron*·kha	grapefruit
torta	*tor*·ta	cake
tortilla	tor·*tee*·ya	omelet
trucha	*troo*·cha	trout
verduras	ver·*doo*·ras	vegetables

Bogotá

Bogotá is on the move. Once considered a place to avoid, the capital has cleaned up its act and is fast becoming one of Latin America's urban highlights. Improved security, infrastructure projects and a clean-up campaign have helped bring a new face to the metropolis.

Home to more than seven million people, Colombians still flock to Bogotá in search of opportunities. Many find that the streets are not exactly paved with gold and end up eking out an existence in one of the vast shantytowns that line the southern portion of the city.

Graceful churches, excellent museums, cultural events and a thriving nightlife can keep you busy for several days. Bogotá is also the political, financial and service center for the country, and its geographic heart, making it a useful base from which to explore the country. Despite its massive sprawl, Bogotá is a dotted with parks and leisure spots. Cool air and almost daily rain sweep away residual pollution, and there are several high peaks to the east of town that help you to keep your perspective on the ground.

Most travelers spend their time in or around historic La Candelaria, a pleasant quarter of cafés, churches and museums. Northern Bogotá stands in great contrast to the south, turning up its nose to history and moving forward as a modern district of brash capitalist values.

Bogotá doesn't sweep you off your feet at first glance. But take some time to wander its historical areas, dine in its cafés, and you'll find it offers much more than meets the eye.

HIGHLIGHTS

- Dine in La Candelaria's quaint collection of **cafés** (p69)
- Ride the funicular to the top of magnificent **Cerro de Monserrate** (p61)
- Lace up your dancing shoes and hit Zona Rosa's hottest **clubs** (p72)
- Gaze at the magnificent pieces of gold art in the **Museo del Oro** (p58)
- Tour the city's remarkable collection of colonial-era **churches** (p60)

- TELEPHONE CODE: 1
- POPULATION: 7.5 MILLION
- AREA: 1588 SQ KM

BOGOTÁ

0 — 2 km
0 — 1 mile

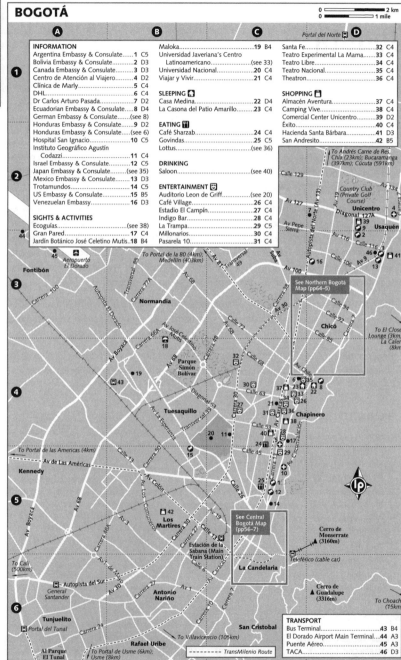

INFORMATION
Argentina Embassy & Consulate......1 C5
Bolivia Embassy & Consulate............2 D3
Canada Embassy & Consulate..........3 D3
Centro de Atención al Viajero.........4 D2
Clínica de Marly..............................5 C4
DHL..6 C4
Dr Carlos Arturo Pasada...................7 D2
Ecuadorian Embassy & Consulate.....8 D4
German Embassy & Consulate......(see 8)
Honduras Embassy & Consulate.......9 D2
Honduras Embassy & Consulate...(see 6)
Hospital San Ignacio......................10 C5
Instituto Geográfico Agustín
    Codazzi...................................11 C4
Israel Embassy & Consulate............12 C5
Japan Embassy & Consulate......(see 35)
Mexico Embassy & Consulate.........13 D3
Trotamundos................................14 C5
US Embassy & Consulate................15 B5
Venezuelan Embassy......................16 D3

SIGHTS & ACTIVITIES
Ecoguías....................................(see 38)
Gran Pared.................................17 C4
Jardín Botánico José Celetino Mutis..18 B4

Maloka...19 B4
Universidad Javeriana's Centro
    Latinoamericano....................(see 33)
Universidad Nacional.....................20 C4
Viajar y Vivir................................21 C4

SLEEPING 🏠
Casa Medina.................................22 D4
La Casona del Patio Amarillo..........23 C4

EATING 🍴
Café Sharzab................................24 C4
Govindas......................................25 C5
Lottus.....................................(see 36)

DRINKING
Saloon.....................................(see 40)

ENTERTAINMENT 🎭
Auditorio Leon de Griff.............(see 20)
Café Village..................................26 C4
Estadio El Campín.........................27 C4
Indigo Bar....................................28 C4
La Trampa....................................29 C5
Millonarios...................................30 C4
Pasarela 10...................................31 C4

Santa Fe......................................32 C4
Teatro Experimental La Mama.......33 C4
Teatro Libre.................................34 C4
Teatro Nacional...........................35 C4
Theatron......................................36 C4

SHOPPING 🛍
Almacén Aventura........................37 C4
Camping Vive...............................38 C4
Comercial Center Unicentro..........39 D2
Éxito...40 C4
Hacienda Santa Bárbara...............41 D3
San Andresito...............................42 B5

To Andrés Carne de Res,
Chía (23km); Bucaramanga
(397km); Cúcuta (591km)

Calle 129

Country Club
(Private Golf
Course)

Unicentro

Usaquén

To El Closet
Lounge (3km);
La Calera
(8km)

See Northern Bogotá
Map (pp64–5)

Chicó

Aeropuerto
El Dorado

Fontibón

Normandia

Parque
Simón
Bolívar

Tuesaquillo

To Portal de la 80 (4km);
Medellín (403km)

Kennedy

To Portal de las Americas (4km)

Av de Las Américas

Chapinero

Los
Martires

Estación de la
Sabana (Main
Train Station)

La Candelaria

See Central
Bogotá Map
(pp56–7)

Cerro de
Monserrate
(3160m)

Teleférico (cable car)

Cerro de
Guadalupe
(3316m)

To Cali
(500km)

To Choachí
(15km)

Antonio
Nariño

San Cristobal

Tunjuelito

Portal del Tunal

Al Parque
El Tunal

Rafael Uribe

To Villavicencio (105km)

To Portal de Usme (6km);
Usme (8km)

General
Santander

Autopista del Sur

TransMilenio Route

TRANSPORT
Bus Terminal................................43 B4
El Dorado Airport Main Terminal....44 A3
Puente Aéreo................................45 A3
TACA...46 D3

HISTORY

Long before the Spanish Conquest, the Sabana de Bogotá, a fertile highland basin which today has been almost entirely taken over by the city, was inhabited by one of the most advanced pre-Columbian Indian groups, the Muisca. The Spanish era began when Gonzalo Jiménez de Quesada and his expedition arrived at the Sabana, founding the town on August 6, 1538 near the Muisca capital, Bacatá.

The town was named Santa Fe de Bogotá, a combination of the traditional name and Quesada's hometown in Spain, Santa Fe. Nonetheless, throughout the colonial period the town was simply referred to as Santa Fe.

At the time of its foundation Santa Fe consisted of 12 huts and a chapel where a mass was held to celebrate the town's birth. The Muisca religious sites were destroyed and replaced by churches.

During the early years Santa Fe was governed from Santo Domingo (on the island of Hispaniola, the present-day Dominican Republic), but in 1550 it fell under the rule of Lima, the capital of the Viceroyalty of Peru and the seat of Spain's power for the conquered territories of South America. In 1717 Santa Fe was made the capital of the Virreynato de la Nueva Granada, the newly created viceroyalty comprising the territories of present-day Colombia, Panama, Venezuela and Ecuador.

Despite the town's political importance, its development was hindered by both the earthquakes, and smallpox and typhoid epidemics that plagued the region throughout the 17th and 18th centuries.

After independence the Congress of Cúcuta shortened the town's name to Bogotá and decreed it the capital of Gran Colombia. The town developed steadily and by the middle of the 19th century it had 30,000 inhabitants and 30 churches. In 1884 the first tramway began to operate in the city and, soon after, railway lines were constructed to La Dorada and Girardot, giving Bogotá access to the ports on the Río Magdalena.

Rapid progress came only in the 1940s with industrialization and the consequent peasant migrations from the countryside. On April 9, 1948, the popular leader Jorge Eliécer Gaitán was assassinated, sparking the uprising known as El Bogotazo. The city was partially destroyed; 136 buildings were burnt to the ground and 2500 people died.

Tranquil life in Bogotá was rocked again on November 6, 1985 when guerrillas of the M-19 Revolutionary Movement invaded the Palace of Justice in Bogotá and made hostages of the 300-plus civilians in the building. By the next day, 115 people were dead, including 11 supreme court justices.

In recent decades the city has continued to expand rapidly to become a vast metropolis.

TRAVELING SAFELY IN BOGOTÁ

Security is improving in Bogotá and it's unlikely you'll experience any trouble, but there are a few things to keep in mind. Be particularly careful about walking at night in poorly lit neighborhoods. The main trouble spots are in La Candelaria, west of Carrera 2, and central Bogotá along Carrera 7.

Cabs are safe, but make sure to lock the doors when you get inside, or risk being taken on a 'millionaire's tour.' This occurs when an unlocked cab stops at a light, an armed miscreant gets in and takes the passenger to a variety of ATMs, maxing out their bank card at each one. Similar stories have grown to urban-legend status, but their frequency of occurrence is actually quite low; be careful anyway.

Northern districts are generally safer, but don't let your guard down. Follow the personal safety rules on p224.

Bogotá's street traffic is fast and wild. Drivers don't obey traffic rules as they usually do in the West and may run red lights or swerve around pedestrians. Be very cautious when crossing the street.

One more tip: avoid local buses marked 'Candelaria.' These do not go to La Candelaria in central Bogotá, but go to Ciudad Bolívar, a slum area on the southern outskirts that is definitely not safe. For central Bogotá areas, take buses marked 'Germania.'

CLIMATE

Bogotá is the third-highest capital in South America, after La Paz and Quito. It sits at an altitude of about 2600m; at this height altitude sickness can occur. You may feel a bit dizzy when you arrive. Take it easy for a day or two – it should soon go away.

The main dry season lasts from December to March, and there is also a second, less dry period with only light rainfall from July to August. The wettest months are April and October. The mean annual rainfall is about 1020mm.

The city's average temperature is 14°C year-round, dropping to about 9°C at night and rising to around 18°C (higher on sunny days) during the day. In the rainy season there is less difference between daytime and nighttime temperatures.

ORIENTATION

Bogotá has grown along its north–south axis and is bordered to the east by a mountain range topped by the two peaks of Monserrate and Guadalupe. Having expanded up the mountain slopes as far as possible, Bogotá is now developing to the west and north.

The city center divides the metropolis into two very different parts. Bogotá's northern sector consists mainly of upmarket residential districts, while the city's southern part is a vast spread of undistinguished lower-income suburbs, culminating in the vast shantytowns on the southernmost outskirts. Western Bogotá is the most heterogeneous and industrial part of the city. This is where the airport and the bus terminal are located.

The central area can be roughly divided into three parts. The southern one (south of Av Jiménez), La Candelaria, is the partly preserved colonial sector, and the heart of the original town. The northern part (north of Calle 26), the Centro Internacional, is a small Manhattan where most of the city's skyscrapers have sprung up. Sandwiched between these two areas is the proper city center, which is full of office buildings, banks, restaurants, shops and cinemas.

Carrera Séptima (Carrera 7) is one of the main streets running parallel to the mountains along the entire length of the city. In the center it links Plaza de Bolívar with the Centro Internacional.

Av Jiménez is now a route for Bogotá's revolutionary new bus service, the Trans-Milenio (p76) and, unusually, it is curved as a result of it having been built over a

---

BOGOTÁ IN...

Two Days

Begin day one at **Plaza de Bolívar** (p55), the historical and cultural heart of the city, and head east into La Candelaria, exploring its wealth of churches and museums, the highlight of which is the **Donación Botero** (p58). Have lunch in La Candelaria before visiting the **Museo del Oro** (p58), perhaps the world's best gold museum. Next take a look at the churches near Parque Santander, including the magnificent **Iglesia de San Francisco** (p61), which is packed at evening mass. Nightlife is best in northern Bogotá, so head for Parque de la 93, a small park surrounded by excellent upscale restaurants. For late-night partying, walk a few blocks south to the **Zona Rosa** (p72), where you can put your salsa steps into motion.

Start day two with a ride to the top of **Cerro de Monserrate** (p61), which is topped with a church and offers spectacular views of the city. Once you are back at the cable car station, take a short walk to the **Quinta de Bolívar** (p59), former home of Simón Bolívar. Have lunch on Av Jiménez and then join the throngs of people for a walk up bustling Carrera 7 to the **Museo Nacional** (p59). For dinner, try out the burgeoning neighborhood of La Macarena, just behind the Museo Nacional.

Three Days

With one extra day you could spend more time in La Candelaria and around the Plaza de Bolívar, visiting some of the museums and churches you missed earlier, and perhaps taking in a theatrical performance at the **Teatro de la Candelaria** (p70). Reserve some time to shop in one of the craft markets or just lounge in one of La Candelaria's cafés, soaking in the bohemian atmosphere. Also consider a trip to Chía for dinner and dancing at **Andrés Carne de Res** (p68).

riverbed. Carrera Décima (Carrera 10) is the busiest traffic artery of the center, crowded with *busetas* (small buses) and countless street vendors. It roughly divides the center into the less dangerous area to the east and the 'heavy' zone to the west. Finally, Av Caracas (Carrera 14) is the major road linking the center with the north and south, the principal TransMilenio route.

INFORMATION
Bookstores
There are plenty of bookstores both in the center and in the northern part of the city. Most of the books are in Spanish; imported books in foreign languages are available but expensive and the choice is limited.

Gaviot @ Libros (Map pp56-7; ☎ 256 5621; Carrera 15 No 82-54) For imported books and magazines.

Pan Americana (Map pp56-7; ☎ 341 7420; Carrera 7A No 14-09) Books, office supplies and electronics. A second central Bogotá location is at Carrera 7 No 18-48.

Taschen Art Books (Map pp56-7; ☎ 342 5337; Calle 26 No 10-18) Has a choice of foreign books.

Cultural Centers
All the listed centers have their own libraries with a selection of books and press in their own language.

Alianza Colombo Francesa (Map pp56-7; ☎ 341 1348; www.alianzafrancesa.org.co in Spanish; Carrera 3 No 18-45)

British Council (Map pp64-5; ☎ 618 7680; www.britishcouncil.org/colombia; Calle 87 No 12-79)

Camarín del Carmen (Map pp56-7; ☎ 283 1780; Calle 9 No 4-96) See p58.

Centro Colombo Americano (Map pp56-7; ☎ 334 7640; www.colombobogota.edu.co; Calle 19 No 2-49; ☺ 7:30am-7pm Mon-Fri, 8:30am-2pm Sat & Sun)

Goethe-Institut (Map pp64-5; ☎ 254 7600; www.goethe.de/hn/bog/deindex.htm; Carrera 7 No 81-57)

Emergency
The services listed below operate 24 hours a day, except for the Tourist Police (7am to 7pm). Don't expect the attendants to speak English, so if your Spanish is not up to scratch, try to get a local to call on your behalf.

Ambulance (☎ 125)

Fire (☎ 119)

Police (☎ 112, 156)

Red Cross (☎ 132)

Tourist Police (☎ 337 4413)

Traffic Police (☎ 127)

Internet Access
There's an Internet café on nearly every block in Bogotá, each costing from about US$0.70 to US$1 per hour. For wi-fi access, visit the Atlantis Plaza (p73) or the Centro Alta Technologia (p73). Most Internet cafés also offer international phone calls for US$0.25 to $US0.75 per minute.

AC&C Internet (Map pp64-5; ☎ 236 8953; Carrera 15 No 94-80; ☺ 8am-8pm Mon-Fri, 8am-4pm Sat)

Café Internet Doble-Click (Map pp56-7; ☎ 286 0725; Carrera 7A No 19-03; ☺ 8am-9pm Mon-Sat, 10am-6pm Sun)

Candelaria Net (Map pp56-7; ☎ 493 5219; Calle 14 No 3-74; ☺ 9am-9pm Mon-Sat)

El Café de Bogotá (Map pp64-5; ☎ 217 5395; Carrera 15 No 72-63) In the northern sector of the city, this is one of the cheapest options.

OfficeNET (Map pp56-7; ☎ 282 6560; Carrera 4 No 19-16, Oficina 112; ☺ 9am-9pm Mon-Sat)

Laundry
Most hotels provide this service for their guests. Budget hotels charge per kilogram or per load, whereas upmarket establishments will probably offer dry cleaning only and will charge by item.

Lavandería Espumas (Map pp56-7; Calle 19 No 3A-37, Local 104) If your hotel doesn't have laundry service, there are several budget *lavanderías* in the center, including this one.

Libraries
Biblioteca Luis Ángel Arango (Map pp56-7; ☎ 343 1212; Calle 11 No 4-14; ☺ 8am-8pm Mon-Sat, 8am-4pm Sun) Library and temporary art exhibits.

Biblioteca Nacional (Map pp56-7; ☎ 243 5969; Calle 24 No 5-60; ☺ 7:45am-5pm Mon-Fri) You will need a library card to visit.

Medical Services
If you're insured, it's preferable to use private clinics rather than government-owned institutions, which are cheaper but may not be as well equipped. Most private clinics carry out laboratory tests and have specialist doctors, some of whom speak English.

Centro de Atención al Viajero (Map p50; ☎ 215 2029, 612 0272; Carrera 7 No 119-14) A travelers' medical center which offers various vaccinations (including yellow fever and hepatitis A and B).

Clínica de Marly (Map p50; ☎ 343 6600; Calle 50 No 9-67) A recommended clinic with doctors covering most specialties.

Dr Carlos Arturo Pasada (Map p50; ☎ 612 3026, 612 3007; Calle 125 No 29-59, oficina 411) Recommended dentist. In the same office, Dr Catalina Mendez specializes in root-canal work.

Dr Miguel Arias (Map pp64-5; ☎ 256 3918; Carrera 10 No 97-41) A recommended English-speaking doctor.

Hospital San Ignacio (Map p50; ☎ 288 8188; Carrera 7 No 40-62) A university hospital with a high level of medical expertise, but long queues.

Money

Bogotá's banks keep different hours than banks elsewhere in the country – they work without a lunch break, 9am to 3pm Monday to Thursday, and 9am to 3:30pm Friday. However, some of them handle foreign-exchange operations only until noon or 1pm. The banks below also change cash, but check the *casas de cambio* (currency-exchange offices) beforehand, which may offer the same rates and do things much more quickly. All banks shown below give cash advances on Visa and/or MasterCard. Most banks have ATMs.

Banco Popular (Map pp56-7; Calle 24) Has an ATM.

Banco Unión Colombiano (Map pp56-7; ☎ 353 5000; Carrera 8 No 14-45) Quickly changes traveler's checks.

Bancolombia (Map pp56-7; Carrera 8 No 13-17) Quickly changes traveler's checks. There is another branch on Carrera 3.

Casa de Cambio Unidas (Map pp56-7; ☎ 341 0537; Carrera 6 No 14-72)

Edificio Emerald Trade Center (Map pp56–7; Av Jiménez No 5-43) There are several exchange offices here.

Expreso Viajes & Turismo (Map pp64-5; ☎ 593 4949; Calle 85 No 20-32) Represents American Express (p230).

Titán Intercontinental (Map pp56-7; ☎ 336 0549; Carrera 7 No 18-42) A *casa de cambio*.

Western Union (Map pp56-7; ☎ 287 1265, 635 3560; Calle 28 No 13-22, local 28) To wire money, you can use Western Union.

Post

Adpostal La Candelaria (Map pp56-7; ☎ 353 5666; cnr Carrera 7 & Calle 13); Centro Internacional (Map pp56-7; Carrera 7 No 27-54) The main office is the La Candelaria branch.

Avianca City Center (Map pp56-7; ☎ 342 7513; Carrera 7 No 16-36); Centro Internacional (Map pp56-7; ☎ 342 6077; Carrera 10 No 26-53) The city center branch has post restante.

DHL (Map p50; ☎ 212 9727; Calle 72 No 10-70)

FedEx (Map pp56-7; ☎ 291 0100; Carrera 7 No 16-50)

Telephone & Fax

Most Internet cafés have reasonably priced international and domestic phone services.

Telecom (Map pp56-7; ☎ 561 1111; Calle 23 No 13-49; ☯ 7am-7pm) The main office is in the city center, but you can make long-distance calls and send faxes from branch offices scattered throughout the city.

Tourist Information

Instituto Distrital de Cultura y Turismo (Map pp56-7; ☎ 327 4916; www.culturayturismo.gov.co in Spanish; Carrera 8 No 9-83; ☯ 8am-6pm) The city tourist office is conveniently located in the western corner of Plaza de Bolívar.

Instituto Information Desks Bus Terminal (Map p50; ☎ 295 4460); El Dorado airport (Map p50; ☎ 413 9053)

THE BULLETPROOF TAILOR OF BOGOTÁ

Miguel Cabellero is the self-styled Armani of bulletproof clothing. Yes, it may be a niche market but with princes, heads of state and diplomats as customers, he has seen profits soar.

Cabellero, who has a shop on Calle 70 in Bogotá, has been making bulletproof clothing for 12 years. His company started with US$10 and a leather jacket; it now earns US$3 million per year and has 80 employees, plus branch stores in Mexico City, Caracas, Quito and Madrid.

The company specializes in suede- and leather-covered jackets and vests, but also sells knife-proof shirts, mine-resistant boots and shrapnel-deflecting blankets. All of it is designed for an increasingly style-conscious public. United States diplomats based in Bogotá have scooped up more than a dozen Cabellero items (which cost from US$200 to US$2000). Other buyers are Venezuelan president Hugo Chavez, Colombian president Álvaro Uribe and the prince of Spain.

The decrease in violence in Colombia over the past three years has been bad for business, the company reports. New buyers, however, are being found in rough neighborhoods from Mexico City to Baghdad.

The 38-year-old Caballero takes pride in one of his marketing techniques – each new employee dons one of his bulletproof jackets and is promptly shot by the boss. The fact that Cabellero has shot his lawyer four times without going to jail seems like a notable selling point.

See Caballero's website at www.miguelcaballero.com.

BOGOTÁ

Parques Nacionales Naturales de Colombia (Map pp56-7; ☎ 243 3003, 341 0676, 341 5331; www .parquesnacionales.gov.co in Spanish; Carrera 10 No 20-30; ⏱ 8am-4pm Mon-Fri) Provides information about national parks, and issues permits and books accommodations in the parks (see p41).

Travel Agencies

Aviatur (Map pp56-7; ☎ 282 8845; www.aviatur.com in Spanish; Av Jiménez No 4-50)

Trotamundos Centro Internacional (Map p50; ☎ 599 6413; www.trotamundos.com.co; Diag 35 No 5-73); La Candelaria (Map pp56-7; ☎ 341 8986; Carrera 6A No 14-43, Oficina 208) Represents STA Travel and may have attractive discounted air fares for students and young people.

Viajes Vela (Map pp64-5; ☎ 635 3827; www.travelstc .com; Calle 100 No 19-61, Oficinas 210 & 211)

Visa Extensions

DAS office (Map pp64-5; ☎ 408 8000; Calle 100 No 11b-27; ⏱ 7:30am-4:30pm Mon-Fri) A 30-day extension can be obtained here. Your passport, two photocopies of your passport (picture page and arrival stamp) and two passport-size photos are required. You may also need to show an air ticket out of the country. You have to pay the US$26 fee at the bank (which does not open until 8:30am, so there's little need to arrive too early). You get the extension on the spot.

SIGHTS
Plaza de Bolívar

The usual place to start discovering Bogotá is Plaza de Bolívar (Map pp56-7), the heart of the original town. In the middle of the square is a bronze statue of Simón Bolívar (cast in 1846), the work of an Italian artist, Pietro Tenerani. This was the first public monument erected in the city.

The square has changed considerably over the centuries and is no longer lined by colonial buildings; only the Capilla del Sagrario (see p60) dates from the Spanish era. Other buildings are more recent and are in different architectural styles. None of the following buildings are open to the public.

On the northern side of the square is the **Palacio de Justicia** (Map pp56-7), a massive, rather styleless edifice serving as the seat of the Supreme Court. The Palace of Justice has had quite a tragic history. The first court building, erected in 1921 on the corner of Calle 11 and Carrera 6, was burnt down by a mob during El Bogotazo in April 1948. A modern building was then constructed on Plaza de Bolívar, but in 1985 it was taken by

M-19 guerrillas and gutted by fire in a fierce 28-hour offensive by the army in an attempt to reclaim it. The new building was designed in a completely different style.

The whole western side of the plaza is taken over by the French-style **Edificio Liévano** (Map pp56-7), which is now home to the Alcaldía (mayor's office). The building was erected between 1902 and 1905.

On the southern side of the plaza stands a monumental stone building in neoclassical style, the **Capitolio Nacional** (Map pp56-7), which is the seat of Congress. It was begun in 1847, but due to numerous political uprisings was not completed until 1926. The facade facing the square was designed by English architect Thomas Reed.

Beyond the Capitolio is the **Casa de Nariño** (Map pp56-7), a neoclassical palacelike building erected at the beginning of the 20th century. It was the official home of presidents from 1908, but in 1948 it was attacked and damaged after the assassination of Jorge Eliécer Gaitán and only restored in 1979.

Between the Capitolio and the Casa are spacious formal grounds where the change of the presidential guard is held at 5pm on Monday, Wednesday, Friday and Sunday. On the western edge of the grounds is the **Observatorio Astronómico** (Map pp56-7); it was commissioned by José Celestino Mutis and constructed in 1803. This is reputedly the first astronomical observatory built on the continent.

La Candelaria

East of Plaza de Bolívar is the colonial barrio of La Candelaria, the oldest part of the city. Some of the houses have been carefully restored, others are in a dilapidated state, but on the whole the neighborhood retains an agreeable old-time appearance, even though a number of modern edifices have replaced the original buildings. Possibly the best-preserved part of the quarter is between Calles 9 and 13 and Carreras 2 and 5. It's a pleasant area for a stroll.

Have a look at the Italian-style **Teatro Colón**, begun in 1885 and opened in 1892 for the fourth centenary of the discovery of America. It was designed by Italian architect Pietro Cantini and is lavishly decorated inside. It is only open for performances. Concerts, opera and ballet are performed here. See p70 for more details.

CENTRAL BOGOTÁ

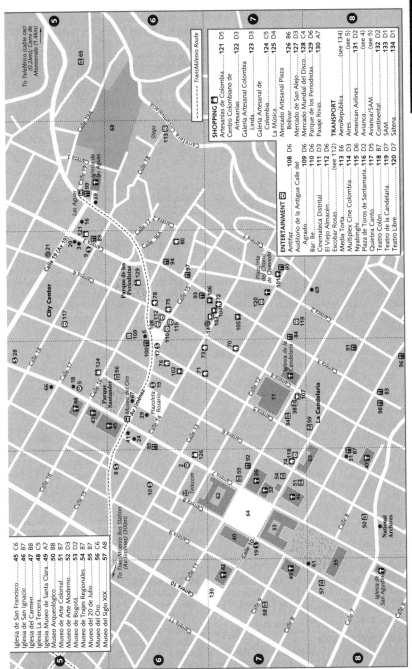

To Teleférico (cable car)
(0.2km); Cerro de
Monserrate (1.4km)

--- TransMilenio Route

Iglesia de San Francisco....................**45** C6
Iglesia de San Ignacio........................**46** B7
Iglesia del Carmen.............................**47** B8
Iglesia La Tercera..............................**48** C5
Iglesia Museo de Santa Clara..............**49** A7
Museo Arqueológico............................**50** B8
Museo de Arte Colonial........................**51** B7
Museo de Arte Moderno.......................**52** D3
Museo de Bogotá................................**53** D2
Museo de Trajes Regionales................**54** B7
Museo del 20 de Julio.........................**55** B7
Museo del Oro...................................**56** C6
Museo del Siglo XIX............................**57** A8

SHOPPING 🛍
Artesanías de Colombia.......................**121** D5
Centro Colombiano de
   Artesanías....................................**122** D3
Galería Artesanal Colombia
   Linda...**123** D3
Galería Artesanal de
   Colombia......................................**124** C5
La Música...**125** D4
Mercado Artesanal Plaza
   Bolívar...**126** B6
Mercado de San Alejo.........................**127** D3
Mercado Mundial del Disco..................**128** C4
Parque de los Periodistas....................**129** D6
Pasaje Rivas.....................................**130** A7

ENTERTAINMENT 🎭
Antifaz..**108** D6
Auditorio de la Antigua Calle del
   Agrado..**109** D6
Bar. Be..**110** D6
Cinemateca Distrital...........................**111** D3
El Viejo Almacén...............................**112** D6
Escobar Rosas..............................(see 112)
Media Torta......................................**113** E6
Multiplex Cine Colombia......................**114** D3
Nyabinghi...**115** D6
Plaza de Toros de Santamaría..............**116** D2
Quiebra Canto...................................**117** D5
Teatro Colón....................................**118** B7
Teatro de la Candelaria.......................**119** D7
Teatro Libre.....................................**120** D7

TRANSPORT
AeroRepública..............................(see 134)
Aires...(see 5)
American Airlines..............................**131** D2
Avianca.....................................(see 4)
Avianca/SAM..............................(see 5)
Continental......................................**132** D2
SAM..**133** D1
Satena..**134** D1

Opposite the theater is the massive edifice of **Palacio de San Carlos** (Map pp56-7; Calle 10 No 5-51), originally a Jesuit college, later the government headquarters, and now the seat of the Ministry of Foreign Affairs (it's not open to the public).

One block south is another fine colonial building, **Camarín del Carmen** (Map pp56-7; ☎ 283 1780; Calle 9 No 4-96), which was originally a Carmelite convent. It's now a cultural center with its own 500-seat auditorium, which features theater, cinema and other performances.

Museums

Bogotá has about 50 museums, most of which are in La Candelaria and within walking distance from each other. The last Sunday of each month is free-admission day, so be prepared for big crowds.

MUSEO DEL ORO

Housed in a modern building facing Plaza de Santander, the **Gold Museum** (Map pp56-7; ☎ 284 7450; www.banrep.gov.co/museo; Calle 16 No 5-41; Tue-Sat US$1, Sun admission free; ⏰ 9am-6pm Tue-Sat, 10am-4pm Sun) contains more than 34,000 gold pieces from all the major pre-Hispanic cultures in Colombia. It is arguably the most important gold museum in the world.

Most of the gold objects are displayed in a strongroom on the top floor – a breathtaking sight (a guard will show you the way). Don't miss the famous Balsa Muisca and ponder the genius of the people who created that mysterious golden world long before Columbus crossed the Atlantic.

Apart from the strongroom, the museum also has a big exhibition on the historical, geographical and social aspects of the pre-Columbian cultures, which are well illustrated by artifacts including objects in stone, bone, clay, gold and textiles.

Guided tours in English are conducted twice daily (at 11am and 3pm). You can also ask about the audio tour in English. Videos featuring various pre-Columbian cultures are shown five times daily (including two with an English soundtrack). Check the program and times when you visit.

DONACIÓN BOTERO

Opened in 2000 in a restored colonial mansion known as Casa Luis López de Mesa, the **Botero collection** (Map pp56-7; ☎ 343 1331; Calle 11 No 4-41; admission free; ⏰ 9am-7pm Mon & Wed-Sat, 10am-5pm Sun) is another Bogotá highlight. It's a permanent exhibition of works of art donated by Fernando Botero, Colombia's most famous artist, to the Banco de la República.

The 208-piece collection contains 123 of Botero's own works, including his paintings, drawings and sculptures, plus 85 works by European artists such as Picasso, Chagall, Dalí, Renoir, Matisse and Monet. For a good overview, take an audio headset for US$2. It's a good idea to familiarize yourself with Botero's rolypoly subjects – you'll see them frequently in bars, restaurants, hotels and public places during your travels across Colombia.

CASA DE LA MONEDA

Next door to Donación Botero, another historic building that served as the **Mint** (Map pp56-7; ☎ 343 1212; Calle 11 No 4-93; admission free; ⏰ 9am-7pm Mon & Wed-Sat, 10am-5pm Sun) gives room to several permanent exhibitions.

Most of the rooms are taken up by a numismatic collection, which includes coins and bills and some related matters such as presses and strong boxes. Other rooms feature paintings by renowned Colombian artists including Guillermo Wiedemann (1905–69) and Luis Caballero (1943–95).

A strongroom at the back of the building shelters a collection of religious objects, which includes two extraordinary *custodias* (monstrances). The larger one, known as La Lechuga, dates from the early 18th century and comes from Bogotá's Iglesia de San Ignacio. It is 4902g of pure gold, encrusted with 1485 emeralds, one sapphire, 13 rubies, 26 diamonds, 168 amethysts, one topaz and 62 pearls. The other one, which has been brought from the Iglesia de Santa Clara La Real of Tunja, dates from a slightly later period and has a marginally shorter list of precious stones.

MUSEO ARQUEOLÓGICO

The **Archeological Museum** (Map pp56-7; ☎ 243 1048; Carrera 6 No 7-43; adult/student US$1.50/0.75; ⏰ 8:30am-5pm Tue-Fri, 9:30am-5pm Sat, 10am-4pm Sun) features an extensive collection of pottery from the country's major pre-Columbian groups, confirming the high technical level and artistic ability achieved by local Indian cultures. The museum is housed in the Casa del Marqués de San Jorge, a beautifully restored 17th-century mansion and an outstanding piece of local colonial architecture known as *arquitectura santafereña*.

MUSEO DE ARTE COLONIAL

The **Museum of Colonial Art** (Map pp56-7; ☎ 341 6017; Carrera 6 No 9-77; adult/student US$1/0.75; ☉ 9am-5pm Tue-Fri, 10am-4pm Sat & Sun) was inaugurated in 1942 in a great 17th-century building, which was originally a Jesuit college. The museum features paintings, carvings, furniture, silverware, books and documents from the colonial era.

The museum's pride and joy is a collection of 76 oil paintings and 106 drawings (not all of which are on display) by Gregorio Vásquez de Arce y Ceballos (1638–1711), the most important painter of the colonial era. This is the largest collection by the artist assembled in one place.

MUSEO HISTORICO POLICIA

The **Museum of Police History** (Map pp56-7; ☎ 233 5911; Calle 9 No 9-27; admission free; ☉ 8am-noon & 2-5pm Tue-Sat) is housed in the former Bogotá police headquarters, built in 1923 but converted into a museum in 1984. The free guided tour shows off all sorts of communication devices and firearms, but the real reason to visit is the basement exhibit focusing on the 499-day hunt for Pablo Escobar. The featured item here is Pablo's bloody jacket worn the day of his death.

MUSEO DEL 20 DE JULIO

In a colonial house that's called the Casa del Florero, the **Museum of Independence** (Map pp56-7; ☎ 282 6647; www.mincultura.gov.co/museo/museo20julio.htm in Spanish; Calle 11 No 6-94; adult/student US$2/1.50; ☉ 9am-5pm Tue-Fri, 10am-4pm Sat & Sun) is on the corner of Plaza de Bolívar. It was here on July 20, 1810 that the Creole rebellion against Spanish rule broke out. The museum has memorabilia (documents, paintings, personal objects etc) recalling that important event, a milestone in the struggle for independence, which was achieved nine years later.

MUSEO DE ARTE MODERNO

Opened in the mid-1980s in a modern, spacious building, the **Museum of Modern Art** (Map pp56-7; ☎ 286 0466; www.mambogota.com in Spanish; Calle 24 No 6-00; adult/student US$1.50/1; ☉ 10am-6pm Tue-Sat, noon-5pm Sun) focuses on various forms of visual arts (painting, sculpture, photography) from the beginning of the 20th century until the present. There are no permanent collections on display; exhibitions by national and sometimes foreign artists change frequently.

MUSEO NACIONAL

The **National Museum** (Map pp56-7; ☎ 334 8366; www.museonacional.gov.co in Spanish; Carrera 7 No 28-66; adult/student US$1.50/1; ☉ 10am-5:30pm Tue-Sun) is in an unusual building known as El Panóptico. It was designed as the city prison by Thomas Reed (the same English architect who planned the Capitolio) and built of stone and brick on a Greek-cross floor plan in the second half of the 19th century. The jail, which housed more than 200 cells for both men and women, was closed in 1946 and after considerable internal reconstruction was transformed into a museum in 1948.

The well-prepared exhibition gives an insight into Colombian history, from the first settlers to the modern times, through a wealth of exhibits including historic objects, photos, maps, artifacts, paintings, documents and weapons, all displayed in several halls over the museum's three floors.

There is also a modern art section that features paintings by some of the best Colombian artists, including Guillermo Wiedemann, Alejandro Obregón and Fernando Botero. The museum also puts on temporary exhibitions.

QUINTA DE BOLÍVAR

The **Quinta** (Map pp56-7; ☎ 336 6419; www.quintadebolivar.gov.co; Calle 20 No 2-91 Este; adult/student US$1.50/1; ☉ 9am-4:30pm Tue-Fri, 10am-3:30pm Sat & Sun) is a country mansion set in a garden at the foot of the Cerro de Monserrate. It was built in 1800 and donated to Simón Bolívar in 1820 in gratitude for his services. Bolívar used it as a retreat on various occasions.

The Quinta was acquired by the government, declared a national monument and turned into a museum. The house has been furnished in the style of Simón Bolívar's day and has been filled with his possessions, documents, weapons, maps, uniforms and medals. Don't miss a stroll in the lovely, sloping garden.

OTHER MUSEUMS

Museo de Trajes Regionales (Map pp56-7; ☎ 282 6531; www.uamerica.edu.co/museo/museo.html in Spanish; Calle 10 No 6-18; admission US$1; ☺ 9:30am-4:30pm Mon-Fri, 10am-4pm Sat) displays costumes from different regions of Colombia, while the **Museo Militar** (Map pp56-7; ☎ 281 3131; Calle 10 No 4-92; admission US$1; ☺ 9:30am-4:30pm Tue-Sun) traces the evolution of Colombia's armed forces.

Culture and art from the 19th century are on display at **Museo del Siglo XIX** (Map pp56-7; ☎ 281 9948; Carrera 8 No 7-93; admission free; ☺ 8:30am-5:30pm Mon-Fri, 9am-1pm Sat), whereas at the **Museo de Bogotá** (Map pp56-7; ☎ 281 4150; in Planetario Distrital, Calle 26 No 6-07; admission US$1; ☺ 10am-4:30pm Tue-Sun) the focus is more modern. This museum has multimedia exhibits that sometimes allow the public to help create the works on display.

In northern Bogotá, you can visit **Museo El Chicó** (Map pp64-5; ☎ 623 1066; www.museodelchico.com in Spanish; Mercedes Sierra de Pérez, Carrera 7A No 93-01; adult/student US$1.50/1; ☺ 8am-1pm & 2-5pm Mon-Fri, 8am-noon Sat), housed in a fine 18th-century *casona* (large, rambling, old house) surrounded by what was once a vast hacienda, now little more than a garden. It features a collection of historic objects of decorative art, mostly from Europe.

Churches

Having been the capital since the early days of Spanish rule, Bogotá boasts a good collection of colonial churches, most dating from the 17th and 18th centuries. Unlike the outwardly ornate churches of the other viceroyalties' capitals, such as Lima or Mexico City, those of Bogotá have usually quite austere exteriors, though internal decoration is often elaborate.

Two elements of decoration are particularly noticeable: the influence of the Spanish-Moorish style known as Mudejar (mainly in the ceiling ornamentation), and paintings by Gregorio Vásquez de Arce Y Ceballos, the best-known painter of the colonial era, who lived and worked in Bogotá.

IGLESIA MUSEO DE SANTA CLARA

Today open as a museum, the **Church of Santa Clara** (Map pp56-7; ☎ 341 1009; Carrera 8 No 8-91; admission US$1; ☺ 9am-5pm Tue-Fri, 10am-4pm Sat & Sun) is probably the most representative of Bogotá's colonial churches. Built between 1629 and 1674 as a part of the Poor Clares Convent, the church is a single-nave construction topped with a barrel vault painted with floral motifs. The walls are entirely covered with paintings (more than 100 of them), statues of saints and altarpieces, all dating from the 17th and 18th centuries.

CATEDRAL PRIMADA

The **cathedral** (Map pp56-7; ☎ 341 1954; Plaza de Bolívar; ☺ 9-10am Mon-Sat, 9am-2pm Sun) is a monumental building in the neoclassical style. It stands on the site where the first mass was celebrated after Bogotá had been founded in 1538. (Some historians argue that the first mass was celebrated on Plazoleta del Chorro de Quevedo, at the corner of Carrera 2 and Calle 13.) Understandably, the original church where the event took place was just a small thatched chapel. A more substantial building was erected in 1556–65, but it collapsed soon after due to poor foundations. In 1572 the third church went up, but the earthquake of 1785 turned it into ruins. Only in 1807 was the massive building – that stands to this day – initiated and it was successfully completed by 1823. Today it's Bogotá's largest church. The interior is spacious and solemn, but has relatively little ornamentation. The tomb of Jiménez de Quesada, the founder of Bogotá, is in the largest chapel off the right-hand aisle.

CAPILLA DEL SAGRARIO

The **Sagrario Chapel** (Map pp56-7; ☎ 341 1954; Plaza de Bolívar; ☺ 8am-noon & 1-4pm Mon-Fri), on the same side of the plaza as the cathedral, was built in the second half of the 17th century and has preserved its mannerist-baroque facade, which is considered to be one of the best examples of *arquitectura santafereña*. The chapel boasts a Mudejar vault and six large paintings by Gregorio Vásquez.

IGLESIA DE SAN IGNACIO

The **Church of San Ignacio** (Map pp56-7; ☎ 342 1639; Calle 10 No 6-35; ☺ 9am-noon & 3-6pm Mon-Fri, 9am-noon Sat & Sun) was begun by the Jesuits in 1610 and, although opened for worship in 1635, it was not completed until their expulsion in 1767. It was the largest church during the colony and perhaps the most magnificent. Today it's one of the most richly decorated churches and houses a wealth of artwork, including numerous colonial paintings.

IGLESIA DE SAN FRANCISCO

Completed in 1556, the **Church of San Francisco** (Map pp56-7; ☎ 341 2357; cnr Av Jiménez & Carrera 7; ⏲ 7am-7pm Mon-Fri, 7am-1pm Sat & Sun) is Bogotá's oldest-surviving church. It is rather sober from the outside, but the interior is elaborately decorated. Of particular interest is the extraordinary 17th-century gilded main altarpiece, which is Bogotá's largest and most elaborate piece of art of its kind. Also of note are the Mudejar ornamentation of the ceiling under the organ loft, and a collection of side altarpieces. The church is always full with worshippers.

IGLESIA DE LA VERACRUZ

The **Veracruz Church** (Map pp56-7; ☎ 342 1343; Calle 16 No 7-19; ⏲ for mass only at 8am, noon & 6pm) is known as the National Pantheon because many of the heroes of the struggle for independence have been buried here. Of the 80 patriots executed by the Spaniards in Bogotá between 1810 and 1819, most have found their resting place in La Veracruz.

The church has a simple interior, topped with a paneled Mudejar vault. There are four decorated altarpieces in the right-hand aisle, of which the impressive Señor de la Buena Esperanza, which has sat at the back of the aisle since colonial times, attracts the major number of faithful. The tomb of the martyrs is in the nave in front of the high altar.

OTHER CHURCHES

There are a dozen other interesting historic churches in the center, including the following.

Iglesia de La Concepción (Map pp56-7; Calle 10 No 9-50) The second-oldest existing church in Bogotá (after San Francisco) is noted for its extraordinary Mudejar vault, brought from Seville and installed in the presbytery.

Iglesia de San Diego (Map pp56-7; Carrera 7 No 26-37) A lovely whitewashed church built as part of a Franciscan monastery at the beginning of the 17th century. It was then well outside the town; today it is surrounded by a forest of high-rise buildings that forms the Centro Internacional.

Iglesia del Carmen (Map pp56-7; Carrera 5 No 8-36) The most recently built church in Bogotá's colonial quarter, this was inaugurated in 1938. It's an impressive piece of architecture, resembling a colorful wedding cake. The interior boasts fine stained-glass windows and a mosaic of the Virgen del Carmen over the high altar.

Iglesia La Tercera (Map pp56-7; Calle 16 No 7-60) Remarkable for its fine stone facade and, inside, for altarpieces carved in walnut and cedar.

Cerro de Monserrate

This is one of the peaks (3160m) in the mountain range flanking the city to the east and overlooking the Sabana de Bogotá. It's easily recognizable by the church crowning its top. Monserrate (Map p50) has become a mecca for pilgrims, due to the statue of the Señor Caído (Fallen Christ), dating from the 1650s, to which many miracles have been attributed. The church was erected after the original chapel was destroyed by an earthquake in 1917.

Several cafés, restaurants and fast-food stalls have sprung up around the church. They get very busy on Sunday, when most pilgrims and tourists visit.

The view of the city from the top is superb. On a clear day you can even spot Los Nevados, the volcanic range in the Cordillera Central, 135km away to the west, noted for a symmetrical cone of the Nevado del Tolima.

There are three ways to get to the top: by *teleférico* (cable car), funicular railway or on foot along a path.

Both the cable car and funicular run from the **lower station** (☎ 284 57 00; Carrera 2E No 21-48) at the foot of Monserrate. It's close to the city center, so you can walk, take a short cab ride or hop on the bus marked 'Funicular.'

The cable car operates every 15 minutes 9:30am to midnight Monday to Saturday, 6am to 5pm Sunday. The funicular normally only operates 6am to 6pm Sunday and public holidays. The return fare by either is US$5. On Sunday the price is US$3.50.

If you want to do the trip on foot (one hour uphill), do it only on Sunday when crowds of pilgrims go; on weekdays you'll be a prime target for thieves who prowl the mountainside.

Mirador Torre Colpatria

For another impressive bird's-eye view of the city, although quite a different one, go to the top of the **Colpatria Tower** (Map pp56-7; ☎ 283 6697; Carrera 7 No 24-89; admission US$1.25; ⏲ 11am-5pm Sat, Sun & holidays). The 360-degree lookout atop this 48-story, 162m-high skyscraper (completed in 1979) provides excellent views in all directions.

Jardín Botánico José Celestino Mutis

The **botanical gardens** (Map p50; ☎ 437 7060; www .jbb.gov.co in Spanish; Calle 57 No 61-13; adult/student

US$1.50/1; 8am-5pm Mon-Fri, 9am-5pm Sat & Sun) has a variety of national flora from different climatic zones, some in gardens and others in greenhouses. To get there take a bus running along the Autopista El Dorado (the bus to the airport will let you off near the gardens).

Maloka
This **interactive centre of science and technology** (Map p50; ☎ 427 2707; www.maloka.org in Spanish; Carrera 68D No 40A-51; adult/student US$3.50/2; 8am-6pm Mon-Thu, 9am-7pm Fri-Sun) is possibly the continent's largest and best. It features a variety of thematic exhibitions such as the universe, human beings, technology, life, water and biodiversity, plus a high-tech Cine-Domo cinema. Set aside at least three hours for your visit.

ACTIVITIES
If you're looking for a place to kick around a football or go for a jog, try the Parque Simón Bolívar, a popular weekend hangout for Bogotáns.

Mountain biking and rock climbing are organized at Suesca (p79), but if you want to hone your skills, there is a climbing wall at **Gran Pared** (Map p50; ☎ 245 7284; www.granpared.com in Spanish; cnr Carrera 7 & Calle 50; per hr with equipment US$5; 2-10pm Mon, 10am-10pm Tue-Sat, 9am-5pm Sun).

For paragliding, contact **Mauricio Eslava** (☎ 599 6413).

Bowling purists simply must visit the **San Francisco Bolo Club** (Map pp56-7; ☎ 342 3232; Av Jiménez No 6-71; per game US$1; 10am-10pm). There's no automatic scorekeeper or even a pin setter – it's all done by hand. Your personal pin setter has one of the most dangerous jobs in Bogotá, so don't forget to tip!

WALKING TOUR
La Candelaria and Plaza de Bolívar are the heart and soul of Bogotá. The area is packed with museums, craft markets, cafés, churches and theaters. It will take more than one visit to see it all, but the following walking tour will get you better acquainted with the neighborhood.

Start from **Plaza de Bolívar** (**1**; p55), where you'll have to duck and dodge squadrons of pigeons as you pop into the various attractions. Begin with the enormous **Catedral**

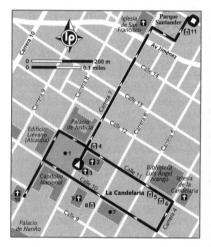

Primada (**2**; p60), arguably the most beautiful piece of colonial architecture in the city, and its smaller neighbor, the **Capilla del Sagrario** (**3**; p60). Next enter the **Museo del 20 de Julio** (**4**; p59), a tribute to the Creole Rebellion of 1810. Just a few steps up the street is La Puerta Falsa (p67), which offers tempting sweet snacks that will keep your energy level on overdrive.

Set an hour aside to poke around the intriguing **Casa de la Moneda** (**5**; p58) and **Donación Botero** (**6**; p58), which are a couple of blocks to the east. The Juan Valdéz coffee shop, outside the museum, is a fine place to enjoy Colombia's second-most famous export.

Turn the corner on Carrera 4 and come back downhill on Calle 10, noting as you go that La Candelaria rooftops are sporadically decorated with oddly dressed human statues (some in a bad state of repair), the remnants of a public art project. Down the street you'll pass the **Palacio de San Carlos** (**7**; p58); it was here that Bolívar once narrowly escaped an assassination attempt. He was bathing in his tub at the time of the incident, and was forced to flee though a window, half naked and covered with soap.

At Carrera 6, take a left to the exquisite **Museo de Arte Colonial** (8; p59) to view its wealth of religious art, and then round the corner to the 350-year-old **Iglesia de San Ignacio** (9; p60).

The other 'must-see' church in this neighborhood is the lavish **Iglesia Museo de Santa Clara** (10; p60), from where you can also have a peek into the gardens behind the Capitolio Nacional. Security is tight along this road – it's guarded by police, the army and the president's special guards decked out in regal uniforms.

From the Central Plaza, head up Carrera 7, a main shopping thoroughfare, across Av Jimenéz to Parque Santander. This is another lively little area, which has craft stalls and street musicians. Finish off the tour with a visit to the enigmatic **Museo del Oro** (11; p58).

COURSES

The best way of finding out about courses is to check the bulletin boards at the guest houses. A couple of years ago two tourists even found a class on coffee making at the **National Federation for Coffee Growers** (www.juan valdez.com). Cooking, yoga and salsa dancing are sometimes occasionally on offer. Language courses are run by universities and language schools. There are also informal classes that are sometimes held at L'Jaim restaurant (p67). Many travelers opt for making informal arrangements with the local tutors. Popular backpacker hotels are usually the best places to ask for information about independent teachers.

Nueva Lengua (☎ 861 5555; www.nuevalengua.com /spanish; Universidad La Sabana, Km 16 Autopista del Norte) Has branches in Bogotá, Medellín and Cartagena.

Universidad de los Andes (Map pp56-7; ☎ 286 9211; Carrera 1 No 18A 10)

Universidad Externado de Colombia (Map pp56-7; ☎ 282 6066; Calle 12 No 1-17)

Universidad Javeriana's Centro Latinoamericano (Map p50; ☎ 320 8320; Carrera 10 No 65-48) Bogotá's best-known school of Spanish language, which offers regular one-year courses and three-week intensive courses.

Universidad Nacional (Map p50; ☎ 316 5335; cnr Carrera 30 & Calle 45)

Universidad Pedagógica Nacional (Map pp64-5; ☎ 594 1894; Calle 72 No 11-86)

TOURS

Most tour companies in Bogotá cater to the domestic market. Therefore language may be a problem if you don't speak Spanish. The following operators have experience with foreign travelers and run trips around Bogotá and across Colombia.

Colombia Ecoturística (Map pp56-7; ☎ 241 0065, 366 3059; Carrera 3 No 21-46, Apt No 802B)

Ecoguías (Map p50; ☎ 347 5736, 212 1423; www.ecoguias.com; Carrera 7 No 57-39, Oficina 501) An adventure-travel company that focuses on ecotourism trips to various regions of the country, including some national parks. It also organizes reasonably priced Sunday walks in the environs of Bogotá.

Sal Si Puedes (Map pp56-7; ☎ 283 3765; Carrera 7 No 17-01, Oficina 639) This is an association of outdoor-minded people who organize weekend walks in the countryside. These excursions are mostly one-day trips to Cundinamarca, though longer excursions to other regions are also arranged during holiday periods and long weekends.

Viajar y Vivir (Map p50; ☎ 368 6139, 211 1368; www.via jaryvivir.com in Spanish; Carrera 13 No 61-47, Local 104)

FESTIVALS & EVENTS

Bogotá hosts a riot of local and national festivals that take place throughout the year. The following is a selection of the best. If none of these fit your time frame, ask around as smaller festivals are held each month.

Feria Taurina (January and February) Bogotá has its bullfighting season when the major corridas take place, with bullfights held on most Sundays. Famous international matadors are invited, mostly from Spain and Mexico. The feria is held at the city's 13,600-seat, Moorish-style bullring, Plaza de Toros de Santamaría.

Festival Iberoamericano de Teatro (March/April) A theater festival featuring groups from all of Latin America and beyond takes place in every evenly numbered year. Many of the local groups present their latest achievements, so it's a good time to taste what's going on in Colombian theater.

Festival de Jazz (September) Organized by the Teatro Libre, this festival features local and national Latin jazz artists, plus an occasional US or European star.

Festival de Cine de Bogotá (October) With a 20-year history, the city's film festival attracts films from all around the world, including a usually strong Latin American selection.

Expoartesanías (December) This crafts fair gathers together artisans and their products from all around the country. Crafts are for sale and it's an excellent place to buy them.

BOGOTÁ

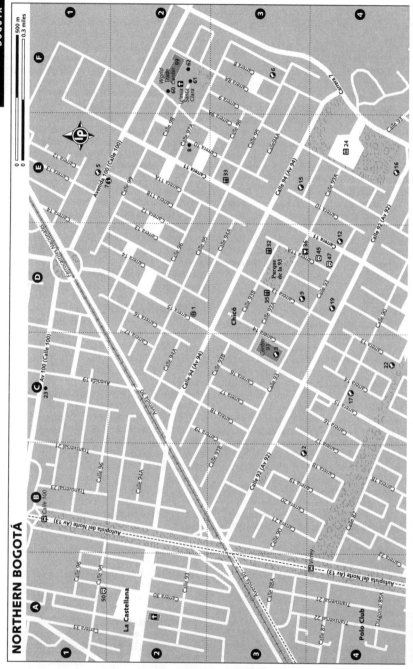

NORTHERN BOGOTÁ

500 m
0.3 miles

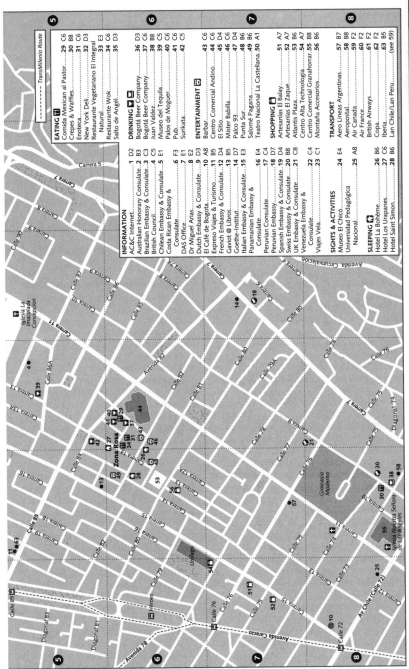

SLEEPING

Bogotá has loads of places to stay in every price bracket. A good share of hotels is concentrated in central Bogotá. This is the most convenient area to stay in, as most tourist attractions are here. The alternative area is northern Bogotá, especially for more upmarket choices. For long-term rentals in La Candelaria, ask at Café del Sol (p69) and Alina (opposite). All places in the midrange category and up have private facilities.

La Candelaria

The historic suburb of La Candelaria is most popular with foreign travelers.

BUDGET

Hotel Aragón (Map pp56-7; ☎ 284 8325; fax 342 6387; Carrera 3 No 14-13; s/d/tr without bathroom US$6.50/12/18) This well-located hotel has 24 private rooms without bathrooms, most with good natural light and city views. It's quiet, the water is always hot and the facilities are clean and well maintained.

Hotel El Dorado (Map pp56-7; ☎ 334 3988; cnr Carrera 4 & Calle 15; d with/without bathroom US$17/13.50) Another convenient option. It has fairly small rooms, but most of them have private bathrooms.

Hotel Internacional (Map pp56-7; ☎ 341 8731; Carrera 5 No 14-45; s/d/tr without bathroom US$5.50/11/16, with bathroom US$6.50/13/16; 🖳) A favorite haunt among Israeli travelers. There's a nice common room with TV, plus use of a kitchen.

Centro Plaza (Map pp56-7; ☎ 243 3818; www.hotel centroplaza.com; Carrera 4 No 13-12; dm/d/tr with bathroom US$6.50/14.50/20; 🖳) Another Israeli hangout, this place has a kosher restaurant and billiards table. Rooms are new and clean, but small and sans view.

MIDRANGE & TOP END

Hotel Ambala (Map pp56-7; ☎ 342 6384; www.hotel ambala.net; Carrera 5 No 13-46; s/d/tr US$20/27/41; ✗) This friendly hotel has 22 immaculate but tiny rooms, each with TV and minibar. A great choice in this category.

Hotel San Sebastián (Map pp56-7; ☎ 480 0503, 337 5031; Av Jiménez No 3-97; s/d/tr US$19/28/36) One of the few reasonable central midrange establishments, San Sebastián provides 35 fairly good, airy rooms (all with TV and private bathroom) and is well situated just a couple of blocks from the Museo del Oro.

THE AUTHOR'S CHOICE

Platypus (Map pp56-7; ☎ 341 2874, 341 3104; www.platypusbogota.com; Calle 16 No 2-43; dm/ s/d without bathroom US$5/10/13.50, s/d/tr with bathroom US$11/16/18; ✗ 🖳) The Platypus is the kind of backpacker mecca you'll hear about long before you arrive in Bogotá. The hostel has three four-bed dorms and several singles and doubles, as well as a triple complete with bathroom and kitchenette. Rooms are simple and the hostel is always busy, but it's safe, reasonably clean and lends great opportunity to meet like-minded travelers. The hostel offers wi-fi access, book exchange, laundry and kitchen facilities, and there's a cozy dining room where you can relax and have a gratis *tinto* (a small cup of black coffee). The star attraction is the friendly owner, Germán (pronounced Hermann), a long-time traveler himself, who speaks several languages and is an excellent source of practical information. Reservations are recommended.

Hotel Dann Colonial (Map pp56-7; ☎ 341 1680; hoteldanncolonial@yahoo.es; Calle 14 No 4-21; s US$33, d US$38-45) Despite its name, Hotel Dann is a modern building, not a colonial one. This 30-year-old, 80-room hotel has seen better days and is in need of refurbishment, but for what it's worth, all rooms have a balcony with views of Monserrate.

Hotel de la Ópera (Map pp56-7; ☎ 336 2066; www .hotelopera.com.co; Calle 10 No 5-72; d/ste US$95/115) The best accommodations option in La Candelaria is housed in two meticulously restored historic buildings right next-door to the Teatro Colón. This five-star hotel has much charm and character, and a rooftop restaurant with views over the red-tiled roofs of the surrounding colonial houses. The atmosphere and service are great, and the place is small enough that you receive personal attention. If you need a classy hotel in the historic center, this is the place to go.

Centro Internacional & City Center
MIDRANGE & TOP END

Hotel La Sabana (Map pp56-7; ☎ 284 4830; www .hotellasabana.com in Spanish; Calle 23 No 5-23; s US$26, d US$34-38, tr US$50; ✗) Large rooms come with couch, TV and minibar, but only a few have a view. There's a generous 4pm checkout.

Residencias Tequendama (Map pp56-7; ☎ 381 3700; Carrera 10 No 27-51; s/d/tr US$62/71/86; ☒) If you need some space to spread out, this monstrous hotel allows you to set up a little 'home away from home.' It has 274 mini-apartments equipped with a bathroom, kitchen and one or two bedrooms. Price includes breakfast and use of the gym and sauna.

Hotel Tequendama InterContinental (Map pp56-7; ☎ 382 0300; bogha@interconti.com; Carrera 10 No 26-20; d US$100-140; ℗ ☒ ▣) This place lures guests with its enormity (578 rooms), facilities (gym and sauna) and location (Centro Internacional). However, readers complain of mediocre service and the decidedly unattractive and noisy setting.

Northern Bogotá
MIDRANGE
La Casona del Patio Amarillo (Map p50; ☎ 212 8805; www.lacasonadelpatio.net; Carrera 8 No 69-24; s/d/tr without bathroom US$12/20/24, with bathroom US$14/24/33; ▣) This place is one of the cheapest options in the area. It is a fine hotel in a quiet residential neighborhood with good transport to the center. The rooms are spotlessly clean and airy, and the place offers various services, including breakfast (US$2) and laundry.

Hotel Saint Simon (Map pp64-5; ☎ 621 8188; hotelsaintsimon@etb.net.co; Carrera 14 No 81-34; s/d US$55/91; ▣) Hotel Saint Simon is the cheapest accommodations in the Zona Rosa, an attractive suburb noted for its nightlife. Rates include breakfast and free Internet access.

TOP END
Casa Medina (Map p50; ☎ 217 0288; www.hoteles-charleston.com in Spanish; Carrera 7 No 69A-22; ste US$160-215) One of Bogotá's finest and most atmospheric places to stay, Casa Medina is housed in a restored historic building and combines old-time charm and beauty with modern facilities. The hotel belongs to the international chain of Charleston Hotels and can be easily booked worldwide.

Hotel Los Urapanes (Map pp64-5; ☎ 218 1188; www.hotellosurapanes.com.co; Carrera 13 No 83-19; d US$100) This boutique hotel has just 32 rooms, but all are well appointed with a modern bathroom. It's one of the quietest in Zona Rosa.

Hotel La Bohème (Map pp64-5; ☎ 644 7132; www.hotelsroyal.com; Calle 82 No 12-35; s/d US$89/103;

℗ ☒ ▣) This top-end choice in the Zona Rosa has a bit of European style and flavor and offers a satisfactory range of facilities, including wi-fi on every floor. Breakfast is included.

EATING
The Bogotá phone directory lists about a thousand restaurants and that's not including markets, food stalls, hotels, supermarkets, transport terminals, universities and clubs. Almost every foreign cuisine is available and, of course, a full range of regional Colombian dishes. On the whole, central Bogotá is better for budget eating while northern Bogotá takes pride in fine dining.

La Candelaria
Restaurante Fulanitos (Map pp56-7; ☎ 352 0173; Carrera 3 No 8-61; mains US$4-7; ☯ noon-4pm Sun-Fri, noon-5pm Sat) This is a beautifully arranged and informal place that offers food typical of the Valle del Cauca in southern Colombia. It has excellent views.

L' Jaim (Map pp56-7; ☎ 281 8635; Carrera 3 No 14-79; meals US$3-5; ☯ noon-9pm Sun-Fri) This little bit of Israel transported to Bogotá serves great *shawarma* (chopped meat and vegies served with pita and hummus) plus felafel and baklava. The twin brothers who run the place provide good travel tips and also organize language classes.

Mora Mora (Map pp56-7; ☎ 400 8466; Carrera 3A No 15-98; smoothies US$1.25; ☯ 7am-8pm Mon-Fri, 9am-4pm Sat) Literally 'Raspberry Raspberry,' this pastel-painted juice shop prepares fruit smoothies, sandwiches and snacks. The muesli and fruit is a good choice for breakfast.

Enchiladas (Map pp56-7; ☎ 286 0312; Calle 10 No 2-12; dishes US$2-4; ☯ noon-5pm Sun-Tue, noon-9pm Wed-Sat) Tacos, quesadillas (cheese and tortilla) and burritos served quickly in an atmospheric restaurant with music provided by an antique jukebox. Desserts are mediocre.

Alina (Map pp56-7; ☎ 341 7208; Calle 9 No 2-81; pizzas US$3-4; ☯ 11.30am-10pm) Reputedly the best pizza place in La Candelaria, Alina has a dozen different pies, plus lasagna. It's run by a Colombian-American named Mario, who also rents out some rooms in his home behind the restaurant.

La Puerta Falsa (Map pp56-7; Calle 11 No 6-50; snacks US$0.50-1.50; ☯ 7am-11pm Mon-Sat) In a 370-year-old house beside the cathedral, La Puerta

Falsa is Bogotá's (and Colombia's, for that matter) oldest operating place to eat. It serves local snacks, including tamales, *chocolate santafereño* (hot chocolate with cheese and local bread) and sweets as it has done since 1816.

Candela Café (Map pp56-7; ☎ 283 1780; Calle 9 No 4-93; mains US$7-9; ⊙ noon-3pm Mon-Sat) This exclusive lunch café is a major hit with the local suit-and-tie set. Try an excellent Mediterranean salmon, a spicy chili con carne or a tasty *gratinado* (cheese and chicken soup).

Andante Ma Non Troppo (Map pp56-7; ☎ 342 3237; Carrera 3A No 10-92; dishes US$1.50-3; ⊙ 8am-8pm) A café and restaurant serving pastas and the best bread in La Candelaria.

El Gato Gris (Map pp56-7; ☎ 342 1716; Carrera 1A No 13-12; crepes US$2; ⊙ noon-10pm) The Salvador Dalí theme and dim lighting lend an air of mystery and romanticism to this pasta-and-crepe place. Live music on weekends.

Pastelería Francesa Peche Mignon (Map pp56-7; ☎ 342 5646; Calle 9 No 1-95; breakfast US$2-3; ⊙ 8am-8pm Tue-Sat, 9am-6pm Sun) This bakery and cake shop has fresh bread and pastries and also provides great breakfasts.

Restaurante Corporación Prodicom (Map pp56-7; Calle 15A No 2-21; set lunches US$1.50-2; ⊙ 7am-4pm Mon-Fri, 8am-4pm Sat) This no-nonsense restaurant attracts office workers looking for a bargain set lunch prepared with healthy ingredients.

City Center

Pastelería Florida (Map pp56-7; ☎ 341 0340; Carrera 7 No 20-82; snacks US$0.50-1.50; ⊙ 6am-10pm Mon-Sat, 7am-8pm Sun) *The* place for the famous *chocolate santafereño*.

Restaurante La Pola (Map pp56-7; ☎ 566 5654; Calle 19 No 1-85; mains US$4-7; ⊙ 11am-5pm Mon-Sat) Another place to go and try some of Bogotá's specialties such as the *ajiaco* (soup with chicken, corn on the cob and three varieties of potato, served with cream and capers) or *puchero sabanero* (soup with lots of different ingredients).

El Chilito (Map pp56-7; ☎ 334 7991; Carrera 3 No 18A-56; dishes US$2-4; ⊙ 9:30am-3:30pm Mon-Thu & Sat, 9:30am-7pm Fri) A burrito and quesadilla joint that caters to the gringo palate. The owner is a musician and can give you tips on the best places to hear live music.

Restaurante Vegetariano Boulevard Sésamo (Map pp56-7; ☎ 341 7123; Av Jiménez No 4-64; set meal US$2-3; ⊙ 8am-4pm) Vegetarian restaurant

where a set lunch includes soup, juice and a plate of mixed vegies.

Autoservicio Luna Nueva (Map pp56-7; ☎ 342 6806; Carrera 7 No 13-55; set lunch US$2; ⊙ 8am-8pm) Budget cafeteria offering a decent and low-priced selection of Colombian foods and desserts.

Centro Internacional

Donostia (Map pp56-7; ☎ 287 3943; Calle 29 BIS No 5-84; dishes US$7-10; ⊙ noon-4pm Mon-Tue, noon-4pm & 7-11pm Wed-Fri, 7pm-11pm Sat) This hip restaurant run by five boyhood friends puts a Mediterranean twist on Colombian food – adding spices to lighten up its meals. Meat lovers will enjoy the *chuleta de cerdo BBQ* (pork ribs grilled with a special recipe native to Mompós). You can hear live music here on Wednesday.

Al Wadi (Map pp56-7; ☎ 334 1434; Calle 27 No 4A-14; dishes US$4-6; ⊙ 10am-9pm) Also located in the neighborhood of La Macarana, this small restaurant is decorated with shisha pipes and scenes from Lebanon. Enjoy a kebab or felafel, finished off with an Arab confectionery. Around the corner, on Carrera 4A, you'll find several other upscale restaurants.

THE AUTHOR'S CHOICE

Andrés Carne de Res (☎ 863 7880; www .andrescarnederes.com in Spanish; Calle 3 No 11A-56, Chía; meals US$12-15; ⊙ Fri-Sun noon-3am) Hang on to your hats: this legendary steakhouse aims to blow you away with its amazing food and a never-say-die party attitude. Located in Chía, well north of Bogotá's city limits, a trip to Andrés Carne de Res is well worth the effort. It serves big steaks in a ranchero atmosphere, with built-in gimmicks such as menus that retract from the rafters. It's also a popular party spot, so bring your dancing shoes (and a thick wallet; it's not cheap). Well-known DJs, occasionally from Europe, have hosted late-night rumbas. To get there, take the TransMilenio from the Portal del Norte and continue by frequent bus to Chía. A taxi from the center will cost around US$15, and if you plan to party late you'll need to take one back as the TransMilenio stops at midnight. You could also visit as part of a trip to Zipaquirá.

Azimos (Map pp56-7; ☎ 400 8058; Carrera 5 No 27-10; snacks US$1-2; 🕑 8am-8pm Mon-Sat) This simple bakery serves homemade bread, cakes and gourmet jams.

Northern Bogotá

Enoteca (Map pp64-5; ☎ 611 0115; Calle 83 No 12-43; meals US$15; 🕑 9am-midnight) This classy Italian restaurant offers 15 types of pizza, plus fish, pasta and chicken dishes. Try the excellent gnocchi. There's plenty of Italian wines, plus a deli with imported Italian cheese, ham and mushrooms.

New York Deli (Map pp64-5; ☎ 616 0203; Calle 93B No 11A-22; sandwiches $4-6; 🕑 8am-10pm) Pinch yourself, but you're not dreaming, though it may seem like it when you're chomping down on an authentic pastrami sandwich or bagel, lox and cream cheese. Corned beef and tuna melts are also available.

Comida Mexican al Pastor (Map pp64-5; ☎ 300 561 2021; Carrera 12 No 83-47; dishes US$2-3; 🕑 noon-11pm) One of the few low-priced restaurants in Zona Rosa, this Mexican place with a bright yellow facade serves up nachos, tacos and quesadillas to hungry partygoers.

Salto de Angél (Map pp64-5; ☎ 236 3139; Carrera 13 No 93A-45; meals US$10-14; 🕑 noon-late Mon-Sat, noon-6pm Sun) Overlooking fashionable Parque 93, this Tex-Mex place is one of the best dining experiences of northern Bogotá. Reservations are required, or you can just come for a drink at the bar, which has swings instead of barstools.

Restaurante Vegetariano El Integral Natural (Map pp64-5; ☎ 256 0899; Carrera 11 No 95-10; meals US$2-4; 🕑 9am-6pm Mon-Fri, noon-6pm Sat) One of the better budget options for vegetarians. This small restaurant offers set lunches and a menu that changes daily.

Café Sharzab (Map p50; ☎ 285 5716; Carrera 16 No 48-79; mains US$3-5; 🕑 noon-10pm Mon-Sat) Run by a friendly Iranian expat, this gem of a restaurant serves excellent, reasonably priced Persian meals.

Restaurante Wok (Map pp64-5; ☎ 218 9040; Carrera 13 No 82-74; mains US$5-10; 🕑 2-11pm) One of the better Asian restaurants in the north.

Govindas (Map p50; ☎ 245 4524; Av Caracas No 32-69; dishes US$1-3; 🕑 noon-3pm) Vegetarian Indian restaurant that specializes in south Indian fare.

Crepes & Waffles (Map pp64-5; ☎ 211 2530; Carrera 9 No 73-33; crepes US$2-5; 🕑 noon-8:30pm Mon-Fri, noon-7pm Sat) This chain of restaurants serves, obviously, crepes and waffles, plus salads and a range of desserts. It's a professional operation with a good philosophy – they only hire single mothers and women in need.

DRINKING

This is no shortage of cafés and bars in Bogotá. Some of the most intimate, character-filled places are in La Candelaria, while upscale watering holes are found in northern Zona Rosa. There are fewer juice bars than you'll find on the coast, but plenty of convenience stores sell bottled juice and water.

La Candelaria

Café Para Dos (Map pp56-7; ☎ 561 3247; Calle 14 No 3-12; 🕑 1:30pm-2am Mon-Sat) Grab a comfortable cushion, adjust your eyes to the candlelight and try the excellent *canelazo de frutas*, the house specialty that mixes juice, fruit and *aguardiente* (Colombia's most popular spirit). It also serves crepes and sandwiches. There are a few tables, but most people sit on the floor of this excellent chill-out bar.

El Corredor De Las Vegonias (Map pp56-7; ☎ 341 9709; Carrera 3 No 14-35; 🕑 4-10:30pm Sun-Thu & Sat, 4pm-3am Fri) This hole-in-the-wall bar is just big enough for a hammock, a few floor cushions and a couple of tables that hold chess boards and candles. Drink menus are glued to old 45 LPs. The friendly English-speaking owner, Mauricio, plays a variety of music and can give tips on other night spots.

Casa De Citas (Map pp56-7; ☎ 282 6368; Carrera 3 No 13-35; 🕑 2pm-3am Mon-Sat) Another good La Candelaria night spot, this place often has live music on weekends.

Café Color Café (Map pp56-7; ☎ 284 7312; Carrera 2 No 13-06; 🕑 noon-11pm) At the Plazoleta del Chorro de Quevedo, this is one of several bohemian bars that features floor seating and cheap beer. This one also has about 50 types of coffee.

Café del Sol (Map pp56-7; ☎ 315 335 8576; Calle 14 No 3-60; 🕑 8am-8:30pm) This coffee shop brews up all manner of cappuccinos, espressos and even Irish coffee. Snacks, sandwiches and breakfast are also available.

Café de la Estacion (Map pp56-7; ☎ 562 4080; Calle 14 No 5-14; 🕑 7am-10pm Mon-Fri, 9am-8pm Sat) A unique address, this is an old train car converted into a tiny café in the middle of the city. Coffee and snacks available.

Northern Bogotá

Museo del Tequila (Map pp64–5; ☎ 256 6614; Carrera 13A No 86A-18; ☿ noon-1am Tue-Sat, noon-6pm Sun) With 1585 bottles of tequila gracing its walls, this is Bogotá's unofficial 'Tequila Museum.' Gracious host Don Alfonso Gonzales personally seats his guests and proudly shows off his collection of booze. The Mexican food comes hot and heavy, served to the sound of mariachi music. Try a quesadilla, *chimichanga* (deep-fried burrito) or platter of tacos, all served with sour cream and gobs of guacamole. This place makes great margaritas, but, not surprisingly, everyone goes for at least one customary shot of tequila. Mind the worm.

Pub (Map pp64–5; ☎ 691 8711; Carrera 12A No 83-48; ☿ noon-late) Zona Rosa wouldn't be complete without a dimly lit Irish drinking den and the Pub fills this role nicely. It has Murphy's on tap (US$4.50 per pint) and also serves burgers and fish and chips.

Palos de Moguer (Map pp64–5; ☎ 218 8038; Calle 84 No 12-09; ☿ noon-3am) This popular pub serves beer made from its own brewery. There's sport on the TVs and American rock blaring from the speakers. It also serves pub grub, including nachos and calamari. Free wi-fi is available for anyone with a beer-proof laptop.

Bogotá Beer Company (Map pp64–5; ☎ 611 1254; Carrera 12 No 83-33; pints US$3.50; ☿ 4am-3am) Brew pub with a second popular branch in Zona Rosa (Carrera 11A No 93-94); both pump out American rock music and pints of beer to Colombian yuppies and the expat crowd.

Surikata (Map pp64–5; ☎ 616 3830; Calle 84 No 13-43; ☿ 6pm-3am Tue-Sat) This intimate bar is about the extent of Zona Rosa's alternative scene. It plays American/British rock from the '80s and '90s, but it's more of a chill-out spot than a place to dance.

Juan Valdéz (Map pp64–5; ☎ 321 0256; cnr Calle 73 & Carrera 9; ☿ 7am-11pm Mon-Sat, 10am-7pm Sun) Caffeine junkies and expats love this chic outlet of the Juan Valdéz chain. Look for the glass and steel structure with the parasols outside. There's a second location at the Donación Botero (p58).

Saloon (Map p50; ☎ 248 4402; Calle 51 No 7-69; ☿ 3pm-2am Mon-Sat) Most popular bar on the Calle 51 'student street.' The US$4.50 cover charge includes vouchers for four beers. Up and down this street you'll find several other student-packed watering holes.

ENTERTAINMENT

Bogotá has far more cultural activities than any other city in Colombia. Check out the Friday edition of local paper *El Tiempo*, which carries a what's-on section, *Eskpe*, listing coming events and short reviews. There is also a what's-on monthly magazine called *Informativo Cultural del Altiplano Quira* (US$0.50). For online coverage, log on to www.terra.com.co/bogota (in Spanish).

Cinema

Bogotá has dozens of cinemas offering the usual Hollywood fare, including the two multiplexes listed below. Major universities have *cineclubes* (film clubs) showing films on campus or using commercial cinemas or auditoriums of some institutions; they are accessible to anybody. Documentaries, and Colombian and foreign films (ie non-Hollywood) are screened at *cinematecas* (art cinemas), as listed below.

Auditorio de la Antigua Calle del Agrado (Map pp56–7; ☎ 281 4671; Calle 16 No 4-75) Art cinema.

Centro Comercial Andino (Map pp64–5; ☎ 404 2463; Carrera 11 No 82-71) In northern Bogotá there is this multiplex in the Zona Rosa.

Cinemateca Distrital (Map pp56–7; ☎ 283 5598; www.cinematecadistrital.gov.co in Spanish; Carrera 7 No 22-79) Art cinema.

Multiplex Cine Colombia (Map pp56–7; ☎ 404 2463; Calle 24 No 6-01) In the city center, try this multiplex.

Museo de Arte Moderno (p59; ☎ 286 0466) Art cinema.

Theater

There are a dozen regular groups with their own theaters, and many more that put on their productions wherever they can.

Teatro de la Candelaria (Map pp56–7; ☎ 281 4814; Calle 12 No 2-59) A small theater that puts on a variety of dramatic productions, ranging from comedies to serious themes that test social boundaries (including gay- and women's-rights issues).

Teatro Experimental La Mama (Map p50; ☎ 211 2709; Calle 63 No 9-60) This is another theater with an alternative bent, which stages performances by amateur groups.

Teatro Colón (Map pp56–7; ☎ 341 0475; www.bogota-dc.com/eventos/teatro/colon.html in Spanish; Calle 10 No 5-32) Large-scale dramatic and operatic productions, mostly by invited foreign groups, can be seen here. The historic auditorium is a piece of art in itself.

Teatro Nacional (Map p50; ☎ 217 4577; Calle 71 No 10-25) Similar in its programming to Teatro Colón.

Teatro Nacional La Castellana (Map pp64-5; ☎ 618 1252; Calle 95 No 30-13) An offshoot of Teatro Nacional.

Teatro Libre (Map pp56-7; ☎ 281 4834; Calle 13 No 2-44) is another venue for small theater, although most of its productions are now presented in the new branch of **Teatro Libre** (Map p50; ☎ 217 1988; Calle 62 No 10-65) in Chapinero.

Music

Biblioteca Luis Ángel Arango (Map pp56-7; ☎ 343 1212; Calle 11 No 4-14) Concerts by international artists are usually presented on Wednesday (tickets are rather expensive) while young local artists are scheduled on Monday (nominal fee).

Auditorio León de Greiff (Map p50; ☎ 316 5562; Universidad Nacional, cnr Carrera 30 & Calle 45) Another regular stage for invited orchestras is the Auditorio León de Greiff in the campus of the university, which usually has concerts on Saturday (tickets cost US$1.50).

Media Torta (Map pp56-7; ☎ 281 7704; cnr Calle 18 & Carretera Circunvalación; ☽ noon-4pm Sun) Live music concerts are staged for free on Sundays at a bandstage above La Candelaria. Take the steps up from the end of Calle 18.

Nightclubs

Bogotá has plenty of nightspots offering a variety of ambience and musical rhythms, such as rock, reggae, rap, tango, samba, techno, hip-hop and salsa. Salsa is perhaps the most popular among hot-blooded city dwellers, and a worthwhile experience for travelers.

Because of its proximity to the guesthouses, most travelers end up in the La Candelaria bars and nightclubs (centered on Carrera 4 and Calle 15), although the night scene here is not well developed and can shut down early. On weekends there may be live music in some places. There's usually no cover charge in this area on weekdays, but there may be on the weekend. Occasionally, the cover charge will include drinks.

If you are seeking out Bogotá's student crowd, check out the clubs on the corner of Carrera 7 and Calle 51.

If you want to eat sushi before you salsa, or down microbrew while watching others boogie, head to ultrachic Zona Rosa in northern Bogotá. Depending on your mood, the nightspots in this part of town may appear sparkling, swank and vibrant or bland, pretentious and artificial. Either way, it's a unique slice of Bogotá, and it's not to be missed. The area sits between Carreras 11 and 15, and Calles 81 and 84, Calle 82 being its main axis. Zona Rosa's clubs, bars and *salsatecas* (nightclubs playing salsa music) really shine on weekend nights (most places only open Wednesday to Saturday). Expect cover charges from US$4 to US$6 in this part of town.

LA CANDELARIA

Escobar Rosas (Map pp56-7; ☎ 341 7903; Calle 15 No 4-02; cover incl 3 drinks US$5; ☽ 8pm-late Thu-Sat) At the time of writing this was La Candelaria's most popular dance place – a gritty and very cramped two-level place spinning '70s and '80s rock. So many people are packed in here that it has to be a fire hazard, but this doesn't seem to bother the throngs, who wait by the door for a chance to squeeze inside.

Bar: Be (Map pp56-7; ☎ 334 4104; Calle 15 No 4-31; ☽ 2pm-3am Fri, 8pm-3am Sat) The most respectable bar on this block, Bar: Be has a swanky upstairs bar and a much better dance floor in the basement. No cover.

El Viejo Almacén (Map pp56-7; ☎ 284 2364; Calle 15 No 4-18; ☽ 7pm-3am Tue-Sat) El Viejo Almacén is a tango bar with a tradition going back to the 1960s. It has 4000 old tango vinyls (many of which are of 78rpm vintage), which provide a nostalgic backdrop to cheap beer. No cover.

Nyabinghi (Map pp56-7; ☎ 480 1437; Calle 15 No 4-15; cover US$1.50; ☽ 7pm-3am Tue-Sat) A small reggae bar sans dance floor; most people find a place to groove between the tables.

Antifaz (Map pp56-7; ☎ 281 0113; Calle 15 No 4-34; cover US$1; ☽ 6pm-2:30am Thu-Sat) This rough-around-the-edges *salsoteca* draws a student crowd that can tolerate its abhorrent sound system. It's the only place in La Candelaria with a reasonably sized dance floor.

CITY CENTER

Quiebra Canto (Map pp56-7; ☎ 243 1630; Carrera 5 No 17-76; ☽ 6:30pm-2:30am Wed-Sat) One of the most popular nighttime hangouts in the center, this pleasant double-level disco features various music beats on different days and

GAY & LESBIAN BOGOTÁ

Bogotá has a large gay scene and there is a variety of clubs to suit different tastes. Travelers can browse www.guiagaycolombia.com/bogota in Spanish for more details. Note that the cover of some of the following places usually includes one or two drinks.

The best places change frequently, but the most consistent is **Theatron** (Map p50; ☎ 249 2092; www.theatrondepelicula.com in Spanish; Calle 58 No 10-34; cover US$7; ☽ 10pm-late), a huge converted movie theater that sports three dance floors, each with a different theme. Right next-door, **Lottus** (Map p50; Calle 58 No 10-42, piso 3; cover US$7; ☽ 10pm-late Thu & Sat) is the newest addition to the gay scene. It has a huge dance floor and a billiards room, but it's open exclusively to male patrons. These are located in Chapinero, affectionately known as the 'gay ghetto.'

Others places to try include **Pasarela 10** (Map p50; ☎ 249 4477; Carrera 13 No 55-42; ☽ 8pm-2am Fri & Sat), which is identifiable from the rainbow flag outside, and **Café Village** (Map p50; ☎ 346 6592; Carrera 8A No 64-29; ☽ 6pm-late).

For something a little more upscale, try **El Closet Lounge** (☎ 520 7126; www.elclosetbogota .com in Spanish; Km5 Via Calera; 10pm-late Fri & Sat), located well east of town towards La Calera. This pleasant bar has a sweeping view of the city and a good sound system. A taxi there will cost around US$14 from the center.

has groups playing on some weekends (expect a US$4 cover for live music).

Indigo Bar (Map p50; Carrera 7 No 51-23; cover US$2; ☽ 3pm-2am Tue-Sat) Lively, two-level disco that attracts students with cheap booze and loud rock and salsa music. There are several other student-oriented discos on this corner.

La Trampa (Map p50; Carrera 7 No 47-61; ☽ 6pm-2am Thu-Sat) Specializing in vallenato music, this colorful dance hall attracts a mostly student crowd who come to dance and drink large quantities of *aguardiente*. No cover.

NORTHERN BOGOTÁ

Salomé Pagana (Map pp64-5; ☎ 218 4076; Carrera 14A No 82-16; cover US$3; ☽ 6pm-3am) Another recommended *salsoteca*, with possibly the best *son cubano* (Cuban music featuring elements of Spanish and African styles) in town, which is not surprising because it's run by the renowned collector and connoisseur of that genre, César Pagano.

Mister Babilla (Map pp64-5; ☎ 617 1110; Calle 82 No 12-15; cover US$5; ☽ 7pm-3am Tue-Sat) This is an over-the-top Cancun-type bar with everything but the kitchen sink nailed to the walls or hanging from the ceiling. Various musical rhythms heard here include rock, merengue and salsa.

Punta Sur (Map pp64-5; Carrera 13 No 81-36; ☽ 4pm-3am Wed-Sat) It seems half the people in this place are either dancing on top of the tables or passed out underneath them. You can join them by first ordering a shot of

booze from one of the waitresses done up in cowgirl outfits. Best of all, there's no cover. Punta Sur is the first in a string of crowded bars just north of the Atlantis Plaza.

El Sitio (Map pp64-5; ☎ 530 5050; Carrera 11A No 93-52; cover US$5; ☽ 10pm-3am) This ultratrendy bar has a large interior lit almost entirely by candlelight. You can expect either live music or a DJ spinning techno and rock.

Barbar (Map pp64-5; ☎ 218 1813; Calle 82 No 12-22; cover US$5; ☽ 9pm-3am Wed-Sat) This three-level discotheque booms out electronic, reggae, salsa and merengue. The upstairs VIP room is all white padding and silver chrome, as if it had been designed by IKEA.

Palco 93 (Map pp64-5; ☎ 617 1278; Carrera 11A No 93-18; cover US$5-15; ☽ 6pm-late Wed-Sat) This live-music venue hosts premier Colombian bands most weekends.

Sports

Football (soccer) is the national sport. The principal venue is the **Estadio El Campín** (Map p50; ☎ 315 8726; Carrera 30 No 57-60). Matches are played on Wednesday night and Sunday afternoon. Tickets can be bought at the stadium before the matches (US$4 to US$40). For local games, tickets can also be bought at **Millonarios** (Map p50; ☎ 347 7080; Carrera 24 No 63-68) and **Santa Fe** (Map p50; ☎ 544 6670; Calle 64A No 38-08). For international matches (and to watch Selección Colombia), you can buy tickets in advance at **Federación Colombiana de Fútbol** (☎ 288 9838; www.colfutbol.org in Spanish; Av 32 No 16-22).

Bullfighting is invariably popular, with fights held at the **Plaza de Toros de Santamaría** (Map pp56-7; cnr Carrera 6 & Calle 27) on most Sundays in January and February. Tickets are available from the bullring's box office (US$10 to US$100). The events bring the area around the bullring to a standstill, whereas the bullring itself invariably fills to capacity, or beyond.

SHOPPING

There are plenty of shopping areas, including the center, Chapinero, the north and beyond, which are all packed with shops, shopping malls and markets. Generally, the center is cheaper than the north.

San Andresito (Map p50; Carrera 38 btwn Calles 8 & 9; 9am-6pm) is a huge shopping area which spreads over several city blocks. It's packed with a couple of thousand stalls that have almost everything that can be bought in Colombia. It is one of the cheapest places to buy video, hi-fi and TV equipment, computers, film and photographic gear, watches, cassettes and CDs, and clothing and footwear. Urban buses and *busetas* go there from the center and you can catch them on Calle 19.

Hypermarkets, huge supermarkets offering food and a wide range of everyday products such as clothing, shoes, toiletries, household appliances and stationery, are located in the outer suburbs and on the city outskirts. The major local player on the market is the Medellín-born chain **Éxito** (Map p50; Calle 52 No 13-70). There is also a convenient branch at the northern terminus of the **TransMilenio** (Calle 170), as well as four others scattered around the city.

Bogotá has many Western-style shopping malls, packed with shops, fast-food outlets, *casa de cambios,* Internet cafés and movie theaters.

Atlantis Plaza (Map pp64-5; Calle 81 No 13-05) New and attractive, this houses Bogotá's most modern cinema complex.

Centro Comercial Andino (Map pp64-5; ☎ 621 3111; Carrera 11 No 82-71) In the Zona Rosa.

Centro Comercial Granahorrar (Map pp64-5; ☎ 312 7077; Calle 72 No 10-34) An older-generation center that is always packed with shoppers.

Hacienda Santa Bárbara (Map p50; ☎ 612 0388; Carrera 7 No 115-60) Built around a colonial *casona,* making the place a fine combination of historic and modern architecture. Recent and stylish.

Unicentro (Map p50; ☎ 213 8800; Av 15 No 123-30) The first large shopping mall in Bogotá; it remains popular and busy.

Crafts & Souvenirs

Artesanías de Colombia (Map pp56-7; Carrera 3 No 18-60) A good place to start. It produces high-quality handicrafts and clothing.

Centro Colombiano de Artesanías (Map pp56-7; Carrera 7 No 22-66/78)

Galería Artesanal Colombia Linda (Map pp56-7; Carrera 7 No 23-49)

Galería Artesanal de Colombia (Map pp56-7; Calle 16 No 5-70) There are several cheap craft and souvenir markets on or just off Carrera 7, the best of which seems to be this one.

Mercado Artesanal Plaza Bolívar (Map pp56-7; Carrera 7 No 12-52/54)

Pasaje Rivas (Map pp56-7; cnr Carrera 10 & Calle 10) Nontouristy craft market, good for cheap buys, particularly for hammocks and *ruanas* (Colombian ponchos).

There are more craft and souvenir shops in the northern districts, several of which are on Carrera 15 between Calles 72 and 85. The following are among the largest and arguably the best craft shops in this area.

Artesanías El Balay (Map pp64-5; Carrera 15 No 75-63)

Artesanías El Zaque (Map pp64-5; Carrera 15 No 74-73)

Bogotá's three flea markets are also good places to shop for crafts and souvenirs:

Mercado de San Alejo (Map pp56-7; Carrera 7 btwn Calles 24 & 26; 9am-5pm Sun) The main one; it's held in a parking lot.

Parque de los Periodistas (Map pp56-7; cnr Av Jiménez & Carrera 3; 9am-5pm Sun) On Sundays a flea market is held in this park in central Bogotá.

Plaza Central de Usaquén (Usaquen; 9am-5pm Sun) In northern Bogotá.

Electronics

Computers, digital cameras and any other digital gizmo you're after can be found at the **Centro Alta Technologia** (Map pp64-5; Carrera 15 No 77-05) or the adjoining Unilago Mall. Both have around a hundred private electronics dealers.

Emeralds

These precious stones can be bought in plenty of *joyerías* (jewelry shops) scattered throughout central Bogotá and the northern districts. In the center, the main emerald area is at Carrera 6 between Calles

12 and 13, where you'll find more than 40 jewelers, plus another 40 in the adjacent streets. Some good (but expensive) jewelers are in the Centro Internacional.

The cheapest place is a flourishing emerald street market at the southwestern corner of Av Jiménez and Carrera 7, where dozens of *negociantes* (traders) buy and sell stones. However, it can be a trap for the uninitiated.

Bear in mind when dealing with emeralds that fakes abound and many stones are bathed in a clear resin that temporarily improves their clarity. Unless you are expert in emeralds it's almost guaranteed you'll be ripped off. Haggle hard and consider purchasing only as a cheap souvenir.

Camping & Outdoor Equipment

While imported camping and trekking gear is increasingly available, it can be expensive. Locally produced gear is cheaper and often of reasonable quality. Gas canisters for common camping stoves (such as Gas Bluet) are available without major problems.

Almacén Aventura (Map p50; ☎ 248 1679; Carrera 13 No 67-26) This shop makes backpacks and also sells sleeping bags, jackets, stoves, tents and other hiking gear.

Camping Vive (Map p50; ☎ 235 7265; Calle 57 No 9-29, Local 301)

Montaña Accesorios (Map pp64-5; ☎ 530 6103; Carrera 13A No 79-46)

Music

All varieties of Colombian music, including salsa, vallenato, cumbia and *música llanera* (plains music, originating from the Río Orinoco basin plains in southeastern Colombia), can be bought in CD stores, which are everywhere. Virtually every shopping mall has at least a few of them. San Andresito has plenty of CD stalls. The following are central and have plenty of branches.

La Música (Map pp56-7; ☎ 281 1188; Carrera 7 No 21-64)

Mercado Mundial del Disco (Map pp56-7; ☎ 342 67 12; Carrera 7 No 21-41/43)

Leathergoods

For quality leathergoods try shops on Calle 19 between Carreras 4 and 7; more shops of that kind are on Carrera 10 in the city center, in the Centro Internacional and further north. Also check the shopping malls.

GETTING THERE & AWAY
Air

Bogotá's airport, Aeropuerto El Dorado, which handles all domestic and international flights, is 13km northwest of the city center and has two terminals. The principal one, **El Dorado** (Map p50; ☎ 413 9053; Av El Dorado), offers plenty of facilities, including snack bars and restaurants, Internet access and money exchange.

In theory, there are two tourist information stands, in the international and domestic arrival areas, where you pick up your luggage. In reality, you can consider yourself lucky if someone is actually staffing one of these desks – both appear on permanent holiday.

Internet access (7am to 7pm daily) is provided by Telecom in its office on the upper floor.

Three *casas de cambio* (Aerocambios, City Exchange and Cambios Country), next to each other on the ground floor (open 24 hours), change cash. The **Banco Popular** (☉ 24hr), next to the *casas*, changes both cash and traveler's checks, but rates for checks are a bit lower than those at banks in the city center. There are a dozen ATMs on the upper level.

The other terminal, **Puente Aéreo** (☎ 413 9511; Av El Dorado), is 1km before El Dorado. It handles some of Avianca's international and domestic flights. Make sure to check which terminal your flight departs from.

Airline offices in Bogotá:

Air Canada (Map pp64-5; ☎ 618 1606; World Trade Center, Calle 100 No 8A-49)

Air France (Map pp64-5; ☎ 650 6000, 326 6030, 800 956 11 11; Carrera 9A No 99-07, torre 1 piso 5)

Aires (Map pp56-7; ☎ 336 6039; www.aires.com.co in Spanish; Carrera 7 No 16-36)

Aero Líneas Argentinas (Map pp64-5; ☎ 313 2853; Calle 76 No 11-17, piso 5)

Aeropostal (Map pp64-5; ☎ 317 2850; Calle 73 No 9-42, piso 1)

AeroRepública (Map pp56-7; ☎ 342 7221; Centro Internacional, Carrera 10 No 27-51, local 165)

American Airlines (Map pp56-7; ☎ 343 2424, 439 8006, 800 522 55; Carrera 7 No 26-20, local 101)

Avianca (Map pp56–7; ☎ 342 6077; Carrera 10 No 26-53)

Avianca/SAM (Map pp56-7; ☎ 404 7862; Carrera 7 No 16-36)

British Airways (Map pp64–5; ☎ 800 934 57 00; Calle 98 No 9-03, oficina 904)

Continental (Map pp56-7; ☎ 800 944 02 19; Carrera 10A No 26-25)
Copa (Map pp64-5; ☎ 800 550 77 00; Citibank Bldg, Carrera 9A No 99-02, local 108)
Iberia (Map pp64-5; ☎ 610 5066; Carrera 20 No 85-11)
Lan Chile/Lan Peru (Map pp64-5; ☎ 611 1533; www .lan.com; World Trade Center, Calle 100 No 8A-49)
SAM (Map pp56-7; Carrera 10)
Satena (Map pp56-7; ☎ 281 7071; Carrera 10A No 26-21)
TACA (Map p50; ☎ 629 5507; Calle 114 No 9-42, local 124)

There are also plenty of domestic flights to destinations all over the country. Some of the major routes are given on p238.

Bus

The **bus terminal** (☎ 428 2424; Calle 33B No 69-13) is situated a long way west of the city center. You can either take a bus or a *colectivo* (shared taxi or minibus) marked 'Terminal' from Carrera 10, or a taxi (US$4).

The bus terminal is large, functional and very well organized. You will find it has restaurants, cafeterias, showers and left-luggage rooms. The tourist information desk appears abandoned.

The terminal has three departure halls: Norte (from which all buses towards the north depart), Oriente & Occidente (handling all buses towards the east and west) and Sur (servicing southbound buses). If one bus company operates buses in various directions, it has separate offices in the relevant halls. The terminal handles buses to just about every corner of the country, except for some short-distance regional buses, which depart from other points of the city.

On the main roads, buses run frequently almost round the clock. For example, for Medellín, Cali or Bucaramanga, you can expect departures every half-hour throughout most of the day, by one or another of several companies that operate these routes. The usual type of bus on long-distance routes is the *climatizado*, which is air-conditioned.

The main destinations, distances, fares and approximate times of journeys are supplied in the following table. All fares are negotiable; if you can't get yourself a discount from one vendor, just try asking at a competitor's window.

Destination	Distance (km)	Fare (US$)	Time (hr)
Armenia	296	15	8
Barranquilla	999	44	18
Bucaramanga	429	24	10
Cali	481	25	12
Cartagena	1127	47	20
Cúcuta	630	32	16
Ipiales	948	36	23
Manizales	292	16	8
Medellín	440	20	9
Neiva	309	10	6
Pasto	865	34	21
Pereira	340	15	9
Popayán	617	29	15
San Agustín	529	17	12
Santa Marta	966	44	16
Tunja	147	4.50	3

GETTING AROUND
To/From the Airport

Both El Dorado and Puente Aéreo terminals are accessible from the center by *busetas* and *colectivos* marked 'Aeropuerto.' In the center you catch them on Calle 19 or Carrera 10. At the airport they park next to the El Dorado terminal. They all pass by Puente Aéreo en route. Urban transport to the airport stops at about 8pm.

If going by taxi (US$6), you pay a *sobre-cargo* (surcharge) of US$1.25.

El Dorado terminal has a special taxi service aimed at protecting passengers from overcharging by taxi drivers. At the exit from the baggage-claim area there's a taxi booth where you get a computer printout indicating the expected fare to your destination. You then take the taxi, which waits at the door, and show the printout to the driver. The fare is paid upon arrival at your destination.

To/From the Bus Terminal

There are both buses and *colectivos* running between the bus terminal and the city center, but the service is relatively infrequent and stops around 9pm. During rush hours the bus trip between the terminal and the city center may take up to an hour.

From the center, take the northbound *colectivo* marked 'Terminal' from Carrera 10 anywhere between Calles 19 and 26. You can also take a bus or *colectivo* from Calle 13 west of Av Caracas.

The best and fastest way is a taxi (US$4). The same applies if you are going from the terminal to the city center; you can take a bus or *colectivo*, but it's best to go by taxi.

The bus terminal has a similar taxi service to the one that is at the airport. Upon arrival, follow the 'Taxi' signs, which will lead you to a taxi booth where you'll get a computer printout indicating the expected fare to your destination.

Bicycle

Bogotá has one of the world's most extensive bike-route networks, with over 300km of bike paths. Most paths, however, are in the north, and central areas still suffer from heavy traffic. If you have a bike, the best day to go for a spin is traffic-free Sunday.

Bus & Buseta

TransMilenio apart, Bogotá's public transport is operated by buses and *busetas*. They all run the length and breadth of the city, usually at full speed if traffic allows.

Except on a few streets, there are no bus stops – you just wave down the bus or *buseta* wherever you happen to be. You board via the front door, pay the driver or the assistant but you don't get a ticket. In buses you get off through the back door, where there's a bell to ring to let the driver know to stop. In *busetas* there's usually only a front door through which all passengers get on and off. When you want to get off tell the driver *'por acá, por favor'* (here, please) or *'la esquina, por favor'* (on the corner, please).

Each bus and *buseta* displays a board on the windscreen indicating the route and number. For locals they are easily recognizable from a distance, but for newcomers it can be difficult to decipher the route description quickly enough to wave down the right bus. It will probably take you several days to learn to recognize *busetas* and buses.

TRAFFIC-FREE SUNDAYS

On Sundays, many main routes are closed to normal traffic and open up only to people using bikes, skates or their feet. The TransMilenio system stays open, as do certain routes (ie the roads to the bus station and airport).

Fares range from US$0.30 to US$0.50 depending on the class and generation of the vehicle, and are slightly higher at night (after 8pm) and on Sunday and holidays. The fare is always posted by the door or on the windscreen. The fare is flat, so you will be charged the same to go one block as to go right across the city.

There are also minibuses called *colectivos*, which operate on major routes. They are faster and cost about US$0.50.

Taxi

Bogotá has an impressive fleet of Korean-made yellow cabs. They all have meters and drivers usually use them, though occasionally the sight of a gringo can make them reluctant to do so. Insist on having the meter running or take another taxi. Taxis also should have stickers displaying day and nighttime fares.

Taxis are a convenient and inexpensive means of getting around. A 10km ride (eg from Plaza de Bolívar to Calle 100 in northern Bogotá) shouldn't cost more than US$4. There's a US$1.25 surcharge on rides to the airport.

You can either wave down a taxi on the street or request one by phone from numerous companies that provide radio service, eg **Taxis Libres** (☎ 311 1111), **Taxi Express** (☎ 411 1111), **Radio Taxi** (☎ 288 8888) or **Taxi Real** (☎ 333 3333). They all have a fixed *sobrecargo* of about US$0.40 for this service, and will usually arrive at the requested address within 15 minutes (this may take longer on weekend nights).

A word of warning: when taxiing from the bus terminal or the airport to a budget hotel, be wary of any driver who insists that your chosen hotel no longer exists, has burned down or suffered some other inglorious fate. They may be trying to steer you to a hotel that pays them a commission.

TransMilenio

TransMilenio has revolutionized Bogotá's public transport. After numerous plans and studies drawn up over 30 years to build a metro, the project was eventually buried and a decision to introduce a fast urban bus service called TransMilenio was taken instead.

It is in essence a bus system masquerading as a subway. TransMilenio has its

BOGOTÁ

BARK ON THE BUS

While the TransMilenio may be a smash hit with humans, canines have discovered an express service all their own. The 'Trans-Miperro' (Transport my Dog) bus service shuttles pampered pooches from the city to a special dog training school in the village of Cajic, 30km north of Bogotá. Once at the school, the shaggy pupils work out on treadmills, play with balls and are read to by the trainers. Owners of the four-legged commuters pay from US$34 to US$106 per month for the transport service and school.

---

own self-contained stations (which keeps things orderly and safe). Buses run on their own lines, which keeps them free from auto traffic. The service is cheap (US$0.40), frequent, and operates from 5am to 11pm. Tickets are bought at the station. Buses get very crowded at rush hour.

TransMilenio moves 950,000 people per day with a fleet of 600 buses. The system is able to accommodate disabled users.

Some buses run on an express schedule, skipping stops on the way. Check the route map in the stations for the best bus to your destination.

The main TransMilenio route is Av Caracas, which links the center to both southern and northern suburbs. There are also lines on Carrera 30, Av 81, Av de Las Americas and a short spur on Av Jiménez to Carrera 3. There are plans to build more lines, including one to the airport. There are three termini, but the only one of real use to travelers is the **northern terminus** (Calle 170).

AROUND BOGOTÁ

Due to its varied topography, Cundinamarca, the department surrounding Bogotá, provides every kind of environment, from hot lowlands in the west to freezing *páramos* (open highlands) in the east. Within a two-hour bus ride from Bogotá you may experience significant differences in temperature and landscape. You will find lakes, waterfalls, forests, mountains and a maze of small towns and villages, many of which have preserved some of their colonial fabric.

The western slopes of the Cordillera Oriental, running gently down to the Río Magdalena, are dotted with old market towns and are very picturesque. The area east of Bogotá, by contrast, where the cordillera reaches its greatest heights, is rugged and sprinkled with tiny lakes, many of which were once sacred ritual centers of the Muisca Indians.

ZIPAQUIRÁ

☎ 1 / pop 70,000 / elevation 2650m / temp 14°C

Zipaquirá, 50km north of Bogotá, is noted for its salt mines, which are in the mountain just to the west of town. The mines date back to the Muisca period and have been intensively exploited, but they still contain vast reserves; they tap into what is virtually a huge mountain of rock salt.

In the heart of the mountain an underground salt cathedral has been carved out and was opened to the public in 1954. It was closed in 1992 for safety reasons, but a new **salt cathedral** (☎ 852 4035, 852 5357; admission US$4, half-price Wed; ☯ 9am-4:30pm Tue-Sun) was scooped out 60m below the old one and opened to visitors in 1995. It is 75m long and 18m high and can accommodate 8400 people.

Visits are by hour-long guided tours. English-speaking guides are sometimes available. The adjacent **salt museum** (admission US$1; ☯ 10am-4pm Tue-Sun) features the history of salt exploitation and a model of the local mine. Further downhill is a small **Museum of Archaeology** (☎ 852 3499; admission US$1.50; Calle 1 No 6-21; ☯ 9:30am-6:30pm), which displays Muisca pottery and artwork.

The salt cathedral and museum apart, you can have a quick glance at Zipaquirá's central plaza with its church and chapel. Founded in 1606, the town still shelters some colonial buildings around the main square.

Getting There & Away

Buses to Zipaquirá (US$0.80, 1¼ hours) run from Bogotá every 10 minutes, departing from the TransMilenio northern terminus, known as Portal del Norte, on Autopista del Norte at Calle 170. From the city center, you can reach Portal del Norte on the TransMilenio in 40 minutes. The mines are a 15-minute walk uphill from Zipaquirá's center.

BOGOTÁ

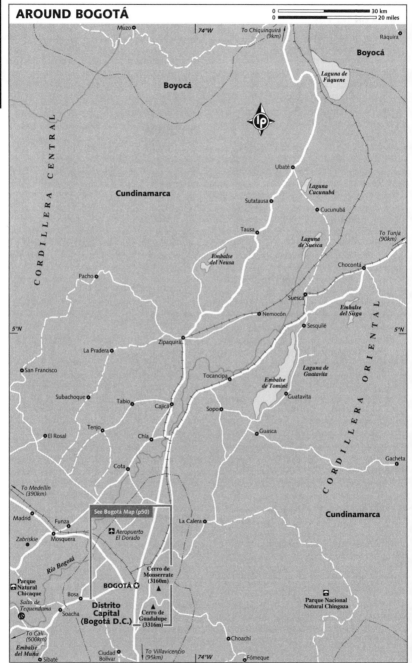

AROUND BOGOTÁ

0 _____ 30 km
0 _____ 20 miles

THE TREASURES OF LAGUNA DE GUATAVITA

Guatavita was formed by a giant meteor, which fell some 2000 years ago and left a huge circular hole shaped like a volcanic crater. The Indians interpreted the phenomenon as the arrival of a golden god who lived thereafter at the bottom of the lake. The lake became an object of worship, where gold pieces, emeralds and food were offered to ensure abundant crops and protection against misfortunes.

When the Spaniards saw the Indians throwing gold into the lake, they believed incalculable treasures were to be found at the bottom and they made numerous attempts to salvage the riches.

One of the best-known early expeditions was directed in the 1560s by a wealthy merchant, Antonio de Sepúlveda, who tried draining the lake by cutting a gap into one side of the crater. The result of this enormous effort was 232 pesos and 10g of fine gold. Sepúlveda died bankrupt.

More operations were conducted in the 19th century. Some explorers tried deepening the gap started by Sepúlveda while others tried siphoning water from the lake with an underground channel. All attempts failed miserably.

By the late 19th century an English company managed to drain the lagoon and even washed out most of the mud from the bottom. However, the 20-odd gold objects plus some emeralds and ceramics found during eight years of exploration didn't compensate for the £40,000 invested in the whole operation. The company went broke.

The rains refilled the muddy basin and peace and quiet returned to the lake. Not for long, however, as new treasure hunters began to search the lake with more determination. In the 1940s, a Colombian miner set about installing a dragline. Soon after, North American divers arrived with sophisticated metal detectors. Yet, like before, very little was found.

Yet another attempt was planned in 1965 by a US–Colombian company. By that time, however, the Colombian authorities decided to ban further excavations in the lake. Thus, after four centuries of digging, draining, dragging, pumping and diving, the lagoon was finally left in peace.

By all rational estimates there couldn't have been much anyway; the Muiscas had emeralds and salt, but no gold mines of their own. Given the number of sacred lakes, the gold offerings are likely to have been distributed over plenty of ritual sites.

It's possible that Guatavita was only a minor ritual site. The Balsa Muisca, considered to be the Muiscas' most elaborate gold object and ultimate proof of their ceremonies, was found (in 1856) in Laguna de Siecha, not in Guatavita. Another Balsa (the one displayed today in Bogotá's Museo del Oro), only found in 1969, doesn't come from Guatavita either, but from a cave near the village of Pasca.

Regardless of whether Laguna de Guatavita contains Muisca treasures, it is certainly full of mystery and beauty.

The alternative is to take the **Turistren** (www .turistren.com.co in Spanish), which runs from Bogotá to Zipaquirá on Sundays and holidays. The train (return US$10) departs **Sabana Station** (☎ 375 0556-8; Calle 13 No 18-24) at 8:30am, stops briefly at **Usaquen Station** (Calle 100 & Carrera 9A) at 9:20am and reaches Zipaquirá at 11:30am. The train departs Zipaquirá 2pm and reaches Usaquen at 5pm. One day advance booking is essential.

SUESCA

☎ 1 / pop 14,000 / elevation 2584m / temp 14°C
Fast becoming a center for adventure activities such as rock climbing, mountain biking and white-water rafting, Suesca makes for

a good day or overnight trip from Bogotá. The town is best visited on weekends, when local outfitters open their doors.

Rock climbers should contact **Hernan Wilke** (☎ 310 216 8119; www.monodedo.com in Spanish; cnr Carrera 7 & Calle 50), who rents out equipment and gives climbing lessons. Full-day climbing trips are also run by **Hugo Rocha** (☎ 315 826 2051; per day US$40).

If you plan to spend the night, most outfitters (including Hernan) will rent rooms for around US$5 per person. The climbing school **Campo Base** (deaventuraporcolombia@yahoo.com) also has a dormitory. Contact Hugo Rocha.

Camping is another option if you have your own gear.

BOGOTÁ

To get to Suesca, take the TransMilenio to its northern terminus at Portal del Norte, and catch a frequent direct bus (US$2, 40 minutes, 67km) to Suesca.

LAGUNA DE GUATAVITA
elevation 3000m / temp 11°C

The Laguna de Guatavita is a small, perfectly circular lake about 50km northeast of Bogotá. It was the sacred lake and ritual center of the Muisca Indians and came to be the cradle of the myth of El Dorado. It was here half a millennium ago that the gold dust–coated Zipa, the Muisca cacique, would throw precious offerings into the lake from his ceremonial raft and then plunge into the waters to obtain godlike power.

The famous golden piece representing the ceremonial raft, Balsa Muisca, is evidence of the elaborate Indian rituals held in the lake. You can see the raft in the Museo del Oro in Bogotá. There are supposedly many other precious gold objects at the bottom of the lake. However, don't bring along scuba gear; instead, enjoy the beauty of this charming lake with its emerald waters, nestled in a craterlike ring covered with greenery.

If you come to see Laguna de Guatavita you may want to visit the town of Guatavita during the same trip from Bogotá, as the lake and town are close to each other. The town was created in the 1960s to provide a home for peoples displaced by the creation of a nearby reservoir, the Embalse de Tominé.

Getting There & Away

Permits are now required to visit the lake and these are given on a very limited basis. Only 20 people are allowed to visit each Saturday and Sunday. For a permit, contact the **Corporacion Autonoma Regional de Cundinamarca** (☎ in Bogotá 1-320 9000; www.car.gov.co in Spanish; Carrera 7 No 36-45, Bogotá).

Permit in hand, take a bus to the town of Guatavita (departing from Portal del Norte, the northern terminus of the TransMilenio) and get off 11km before reaching the town (6km past Sesquilé), where there is a sign directing you to the lake. It's best to ask

the driver and he will let you off at the right place.

From the road, it's a 7km walk uphill to the lake. The first half of the walk follows a partly paved road, until you reach the Escuela Tierra Negra. At this point take a dirt track branching off to the right and leading to the lake. There are several farms around, so ask for directions if in doubt. You will arrive at the lake shore after passing through a deep, V-shaped cut in the lake's bank that is the legacy of ill-fated efforts to drain it. Don't miss the walk around the lake.

PARQUE NATURAL CHICAQUE

This private **nature reserve** (☎ in Bogotá 1-368 3118; www.chicaque.com in Spanish; admission US$2.50; ⏰ 8am-4pm) is about 20km west of Bogotá. Most of its 3-sq-km area is covered with *bosque de niebla* (cloud forest). Walks along the paths of the reserve (about 8km long altogether) give an opportunity to enjoy the forest's flora and fauna, particularly the birds. Horse rental is US$6 per hour. The reserve provides accommodations in a *cabaña* (cabin) for US$23 per dorm bed including three meals. Even better are the huts built for two, though these are pricey at US$73. Camping is expensive inside the park, but you should be able to pitch a tent at the entrance for US$2 per person.

Getting There & Away

The reserve is a few kilometers off the Soacha–La Mesa road. To get there from Bogotá's center, take a bus or *colectivo* to the plaza in Soacha, and negotiate a taxi to the administrative center of the reserve (about US$8 per taxi, up to four passengers). There may be some *colectivos* on weekends.

Ecoguías (see p63) can organize tours to Chicaque on request. The five-hour trip costs about US$10 per person with a minimum of four persons required; the price includes return transport, admission fee to the reserve and guided walks.

From the reserve you can walk along a *camino de herradura* (old Spanish path) to the small village of San Antonio de Tequendama. Ask the management for details.

North of Bogotá

This is Colombia's heartland. The region of deep gorges, fast-flowing rivers and soaring peaks was the first to be settled by the conquistadors, and a number of their colonial towns stand today. It's also the revolutionary heart of the country: it was here that Simón Bolívar took on Spain in the decisive fight for Colombia's independence.

The departments of Boyacá, Santander and Norte de Santander are well set up for the domestic tourist market: they're within easy reach of Bogotá, fixed with a good network of roads and bus services, and there's much to see, including 450-year-old colonial towns, craft markets and spectacular national parks.

Choose between a rafting trip in San Gil or a hike to the sacred Laguna de Iguaque. Dine alfresco at a trendy restaurant in Girón, shop for pottery in Ráquira or hit the fashionable clubs in Bucaramanga. The perfectly preserved town of Villa de Leyva, with its cobbled streets, stone churches and excellent accommodations options, might be the highlight of your trip to Colombia.

The region makes a fine bridge between Bogotá and the Caribbean coast or as a destination in itself. It can also be used as a slow route to Venezuela, jumping off from the hot border town of Cúcuta. You will find travel along the main routes mentioned in this chapter safe and comfortable.

HIGHLIGHTS

- Shop for locally made baskets, trinkets and pottery in the one-street town of **Ráquira** (p92)
- Rappel, paddle or spelunk your way around the ecotourist sites of **San Gil** (p93)
- Take a late-night stroll around the beautifully lit colonial town of **Barichara** (p94)
- Go on a cycle tour of the lovely countryside surrounding quaint **Villa de Leyva** (p90)
- Hike amid the spectacular alpine scenery of **Parque Nacional El Cocuy** (p92)

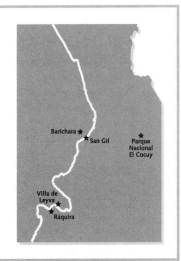

- POPULATION: 4.9 MILLION
- AREA: 75,380 SQ KM

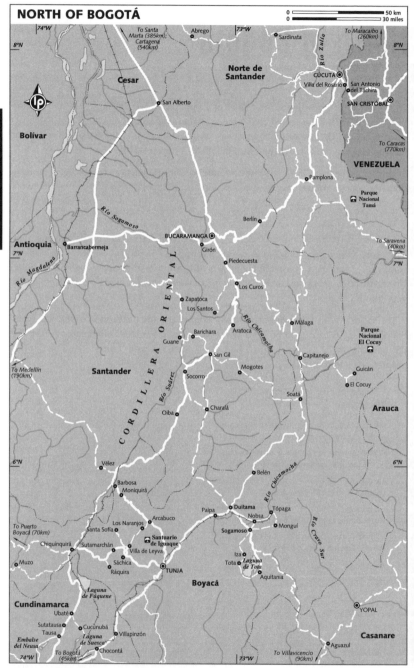

NORTH OF BOGOTÁ

0 — 50 km
0 — 30 miles

74°W
8°N

To Santa
Marta (385km);
Cartagena
(540km)

Abrego

73°W
8°N

Sardinata

To Maracaibo
(260km)

Río Zulia

CÚCUTA
Villa del Rosario · San Antonio
del Táchira
SAN CRISTÓBAL

Cesar

Norte de
Santander

Bolívar

San Alberto

To Caracas
(770km)

VENEZUELA

Pamplona

Parque
Nacional
Tamá

Río Sogamoso

Berlín

To Saravena
(40km)

Antioquia
7°N

Barrancabermeja

BUCARAMANGA
Girón

Piedecuesta

7°N

Río Magdalena

Los Curos

Zapatoca
Los Santos

Baricharа
Aratoca

Guane

C O R D I L L E R A   O R I E N T A L

San Gil

Mogotes

Socorro

Río Suárez

Río Chicamocha

Málaga

Capitanejo

Parque
Nacional
El Cocuy

Guicán

El Cocuy

To Medellín
(190km)

Santander

Soatá

Arauca

Oiba

Charalá

6°N

Vélez

Belén

6°N

Barbosa
Moniquirá

Río Chicamocha

To Puerto
Boyacá (70km)

Los Naranjos
Santa Sofía

Arcabuco

Paipa

Duitama

Tópaga
Nobsa

Mongüí

Río Cravo Sur

Chiquinquirá
Sutamarchán

Muzo

Santuario
de Iguaque
Villa de Leyva

Sáchica
Ráquira

Sogamoso

Iza
Tota · Laguna
de Tota

Aquitania

TUNJA

Boyacá

Laguna
de Fúquene

Cundinamarca

Ubaté

Sutatausa
Tausa

Cucunubá

Villapinzón

YOPAL

Casanare

Embalse
del Neusa

Laguna
de Suesca

Chocontá

74°W

To Bogotá
(45km)

73°W

To Villavicencio
(90km)

Aguazul

TRAVELING SAFELY NORTH OF BOGOTÁ

Roads heading north of Bogotá thread through mountainous terrain, so it's best to travel in daylight hours, both for safety and for the views. Towns in this region are otherwise some of the safest in Colombia, as long as you stick to the main routes.

History

The Muiscas (Boyacá) and the Guane Indians (Santander) once occupied in vast numbers the regions north of what is now Bogotá. Highly developed in agriculture and mining, the Muisca traded with their neighbors and came into frequent contact with Spanish conquistadors. It was their stories of gold and emeralds that helped fuel the myth of El Dorado. The conquistadors' search for the famed city also sparked settlements and the Spanish founded several cities, including Tunja in 1539.

Several generations later, Colombian nationalists first stood up to Spanish rule in Socorro (Santander), stoking the flames of independence for other towns and regions. It was also in here that Simón Bolívar and his upstart army took on Spanish infantry, winning decisive battles at Pantano de Vargas and Puente de Boyacá. Colombia's first constitution was soon after drawn up in Villa del Rosario (Norte de Santander), between the Venezuelan border and Cúcuta.

Climate

Climate varies with the changing altitude. With an elevation of 2820m and an average temperature of 13°C, Tunja is the highest and coldest town in this region; the other extreme is Cúcuta, where hot, muggy weather is the norm and temperatures hover around 27°C. Mountain towns such as Pamplona, San Gil and Barichara are slightly cooler than lower-lying Bucaramanga.

Getting There & Around

The region is easily reached from Bogotá, in the south. Tunja is the first transit point and is connected to the capital by bus in two and half hours (US$4.50). There are also frequent connections between Medellín and Bucaramanga. Cúcuta is a major entrepôt for travelers coming from Venezuela. The road from Barranquilla to Bucaramanga is in good nick but takes around nine hours and costs US$32; unfortunately there are no flights between the two cities.

Within the region, intercity minivans and buses depart every half-hour, so you never have to wait too long. Each bus company runs its own schedule; at bus stations you may need to inquire at a few windows to find out the next bus to your destination. Buses also service smaller towns, but may run only once or twice a day. Taxis are another option when no bus is available. It's possible to hire a bike or a horse in Villa de Leyva; both are a great way to get around the countryside.

BOYACÁ

The department of Boyacá evokes a sense of patriotism among Colombians, as it was here that Colombia won its independence in a decisive battle with Spain. The department is now dotted with quaint colonial towns; you could easily spend a few days bouncing between them. But for all its history, the real highlight is the spectacular Parque Nacional El Cocuy, located 249km northeast of the department capital, Tunja.

TUNJA

☎ 8 / pop 150,000 / elevation 2820m / temp 13°C

Often overlooked by travelers rushing on to illa de Leyva, Tunja, the capital of Boyacá and a bustling student center, has plenty to offer the discerning tourist, with fine colonial architecture, an imposing central square and elegant mansions adorned with some of South America's most unique artwork.

Tunja was founded by Gonzalo Suárez Rendón in 1539 on the site of Hunza, the pre-Hispanic Muisca settlement. Almost nothing is left of the indigenous legacy, but much colonial architecture remains. Tunja is particularly noted for its colonial churches; several imposing examples dating from the 16th century stand almost untouched by time.

Tunja is the highest and coldest departmental capital in Colombia. It has a mountain climate and can be windy or wet any time of the year. If you've forgotten your winter woollies, there are plenty of shops on the lanes north of the main square.

NORTH OF BOGOTÁ

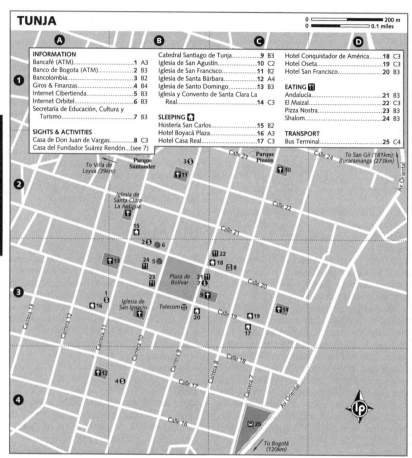

TUNJA

0 ——— 200 m
0 ——— 0.1 miles

INFORMATION
Bancafé (ATM)...............................1 A3
Banco de Bogota (ATM)..................2 B3
Bancolombia...................................3 B2
Giros & Finanzas............................4 B4
Internet Cibertienda.......................5 B3
Internet Orbitel..............................6 B3
Secretaría de Educación, Cultura y
  Turismo.......................................7 B3

SIGHTS & ACTIVITIES
Casa de Don Juan de Vargas............8 C3
Casa del Fundador Suárez Rendón...(see 7)

Catedral Santiago de Tunja..............9 B3
Iglesia de San Agustín...................10 C2
Iglesia de San Francisco................11 B2
Iglesia de Santa Bárbara................12 A4
Iglesia de Santo Domingo.............13 B3
Iglesia y Convento de Santa Clara La
  Real...14 C3

SLEEPING
Hostería San Carlos......................15 B2
Hotel Boyacá Plaza.......................16 A3
Hotel Casa Real...........................17 C3

Hotel Conquistador de América.......18 C3
Hotel Oseta..................................19 C3
Hotel San Francisco......................20 B3

EATING
Andalucía....................................21 B3
El Maizal.....................................22 C3
Pizza Nostra................................23 B3
Shalom.......................................24 B3

TRANSPORT
Bus Terminal................................25 C4

Information

Bancafé (Carrera 11) ATM.

Bancolombia (Carrera 10 No 22-43) Changes traveler's checks and US dollars.

Giros & Finanzas (Carrera 10 No 16-81; 9am-1pm & 2-5:30pm Mon-Fri, 9am-1pm Sat) This *casa de cambio* (currency-exchange office) is at the back of the Supermercado Comfaboy.

Internet Cibertienda (310 563 5665; Carrera 10 No 19-83; per hr US$0.80; 9am-8pm Mon-Fri, 10-noon & 2-7pm Sat) Internet access is on offer as well as CD burning.

Internet Orbitel (743 0955; Calle 20 No 10-26; 9am-7pm) Internet and international phone calls.

Secretaría de Educación, Cultura y Turismo (742 3272; Carrera 9 No 19-68; 8am-noon & 2-6pm) Free maps of Tunja are available here.

Sights

Tunja is a trove of colonial-era churches noted for their Mudejar art, an Islamic-influenced style, developed in Christian Spain between the 12th and 16th centuries. It's particularly visible in the ornamented coffered vaults. As well as churches, some of Tunja's best sights are its historic mansions which have been opened as museums.

CASA DEL FUNDADOR SUÁREZ RENDÓN

One of the finest historic mansions is the **Casa del Fundador Suárez Rendón** (742 3272; Carrera 9 No 19-68; admission US$0.60; 8am-noon & 2-6pm), the original home of the founder of Tunja. Built in the mid-16th century on the eastern side of Plaza de Bolívar (previously called

---

TUNJA'S ENIGMATIC CEILING PAINTINGS

Several colonial mansions in Tunja, including the Casa del Fundador Suárez Rendón and the Casa de Don Juan de Vargas, have their ceilings adorned with unusual paintings featuring a strange mishmash of motifs taken from very different traditions. They include mythological scenes, human figures, animals and plants, coats of arms and architectural details.

You can spot Zeus and Jesus amid tropical plants or an elephant under a Renaissance arcade – you probably haven't seen anything like that before. In fact, there's nothing similar anywhere in Latin America.

The key to the explanation of this bizarre decoration seems to be Juan de Vargas, the owner and resident of one of these mansions. He was a scribe and had a large library with books on European art and architecture, ancient Greece and Rome, religion and natural history. It seems that the illustrations in the books were the source of motifs for the anonymous painters of the ceiling decoration in the houses. Since the original illustrations were in black and white, the color schemes are by the design of the unknown artisans.

Plaza de Suárez Rendón), it's a fine example of a magnificent aristocratic residence from the times of the Spanish Conquest. The most interesting feature is the ceiling which is covered with intriguing painted compositions.

CASA DE DON JUAN DE VARGAS

Once home to Juan de Vargas, **Casa de Don Juan de Vargas** (☎ 742 6611; Calle 20 No 8-52; admission US$1; ⌚ 9am-noon & 2-5pm Tue-Fri, 10am-4pm Sat & Sun) is another splendid 16th-century residence. It also has been converted into a museum and has a collection of colonial artworks on display. However, here again, most captivating are the ceilings, which are also covered with paintings similar to those in the Casa del Fundador, and equally enigmatic.

IGLESIA Y CONVENTO DE SANTA CLARA LA REAL

Founded in 1571, the **Iglesia y Convento de Santa Clara La Real** (☎ 742 5659; Carrera 7 No 19-58; admission US$1; ⌚ 8am-noon & 2-6pm) is thought to be the first convent in Nueva Granada. In 1863 the nuns were expelled and the convent was used for various purposes; among them, a hospital. The church, however, continued to provide religious services. The single-naved church interior shelters a wealth of colonial artwork distributed over the walls, most of which comes from the 16th to 18th centuries. Note the golden sun on the ceiling, a Spanish trick to help the Indians convert to Catholicism (the sun was the principal god of the Muisca people). Next to the choir is the cell where Madre Francisca Josefa, a mystic nun looked upon as Colombia's St Teresa, lived for 53 years (1689–1742).

IGLESIA DE SANTO DOMINGO

Pretty undistinguished from the outside, the mid-16th-century **Iglesia de Santo Domingo** (Carrera 11 No 19-55) has one of the most richly decorated interiors in Colombia. To the left as you enter is the large Capilla del Rosario, dubbed 'La Capilla Sixtina del Arte Neogranadino' (Sistine Chapel of New Granada's Art). Decorated by Fray Pedro Bedón from Quito, the chapel is exuberantly rich in wonderful, gilded woodcarving – a magnificent example of Hispano-American baroque art. The statue of the Virgen del Rosario in the altar niche is encrusted in mother-of-pearl and clad with mirrors, another typical Spanish trick to attract Indians.

OTHER CHURCHES

Located on Plaza de Bolívar, **Catedral Santiago de Tunja** (Carrera 9 No 19-28) is Tunja's largest church and stylistically the most complex. Its construction began in 1554. Completed in 1599, the highlight of **Iglesia de Santa Bárbara** (Carrera 11 No 16-62) is the Capilla de la Epístola with its outstanding Mudejar ceiling. Facing the Parque Pinzón (thought to be the place where the heart of Hunza, the Muisca capital, once was), **Iglesia de San Agustín** (☎ 742 2312; cnr Carrera 8 & Calle 23) is now a library. Built between 1550 and 1572, **Iglesia de San Francisco** (Carrera 10 No 22-23) boasts a splendid main retable framed into an elaborate gilded arch at the entrance to the presbytery. At the beginning of the left-hand aisle is an impressively realistic sculpture of Christ (carved in 1816), *Cristo de los Mártires*.

Festivals & Events

Semana Santa (Easter Week) Boyacá is one of the most traditional departments, so religious celebrations in the countryside and Tunja itself are observed with due solemnity. Processions circle the city streets on Maundy Thursday and Good Friday.

Festival Internacional de la Cultura (September) A cultural event that includes theatre performances, musical concerts (held, among other sites, in the Iglesia de San Ignacio) and art exhibitions.

Aguinaldo Boyacense (December) A religious feast that runs for a week just before Christmas. It features contests, fancy dress, a procession of floats and dances.

Sleeping

Hostería San Carlos (☎ 742 3716; Carrera 11 No 20-12; s/d/tr US$9/13/18; ✗) Located in an atmospheric old home and run by a friendly granny, the San Carlos is a pleasant budget option. There are just five rooms, but one contains five beds and is good for groups.

Hotel Casa Real (☎ 310 852 1636; Calle 19 No 7-65; hotelcasareal@yahoo.es; s/d/tr US$9/13/20; ✗) This new hotel, located between the bus station and the main plaza, is sparsely furnished but painted in colorful pastel designs. All 11 rooms come with private bathroom and hot water.

Hotel Boyacá Plaza (☎ 740 1116; hotelboyacaplaza@hotmail.com; Calle 18 No 11-22; s/d/tr US$30/38/54; P ✗) This small, business-style hotel, with attentive service and smart rooms, is located two blocks from the Plaza de Bolívar. The price includes breakfast.

Hotel Conquistador de América (☎ 742 3534; Calle 20 No 8-92; s/d/tr US$12/15/22; ✗) Colonial-style building at the corner of Plaza de Bolívar; 20 ample rooms, with private bathrooms, hot showers and small TVs. Some rooms are dim and boxy, and the larger doubles (US$23) that face the street suffer from noise pollution, so pick your poison.

Hotel Oseta (☎ 742 2886; Calle 19 No 7-64; s/d/tr US$9/13/20) Bright budget rooms come with TV and bathroom.

Hotel San Francisco (☎ 742 6645; Carrera 9 No 18-90; s/d/tr US$11/18/24) This rambling old place has threadbare furnishings, but mostly clean rooms.

Eating

Andalucía (☎ 300 273 4221; Carrera 9 No 19-92; mains US$11-12) This new restaurant is set inside a colonial mansion on the square. The mostly seafood menu includes lobster thermidor, calamari and grilled fish, while the excellent dessert selection includes chocolate mousse and tiramisu. Ask about concerts; mariachi bands occasionally play here.

El Maizal (☎ Carrera 9 No 20-30; mains US$3-5) This restaurant doesn't look very elegant, but has long been popular with the locals for its tasty food, including regional dishes. It doesn't serve set meals.

There are a number of outlets serving snacks and fast food. For pizza, try **Pizza Nostra** (☎ 740 2040; Calle 19 No 10-36; pizza US$3-8; ☺ noon-11pm), conveniently located just off Plaza de Bolívar.

Every second door around the square seems to lead to a coffee shop, but few places serve a full breakfast. One place to try is **Shalom** (☎ 740 5494; Calle 19A No 10-64, Pasaje de Vargas; breakfast US$2.50; ☺ 7am-6pm), which does scrambled eggs and *arepas* (corn pancakes, eaten in place of bread).

Getting There & Away

The bus terminal is on Av Oriental, a short walk southeast of Plaza de Bolívar. Buses to Bogotá (US$4.50, 2½ to three hours) depart every 10 to 15 minutes. If you're going to central Bogotá, you could get off at the corner of Portal del Norte and Calle 170 and change for the TransMilenio, but during rush hour it's more comfortable to go to the bus terminal and take a taxi.

Buses going to Bucaramanga (US$15, seven hours) run at least every hour. They all travel from Bogotá and pass through San Gil (US$9, 4½ hours).

Minibuses to Villa de Leyva (US$1.80, 45 minutes) depart regularly until about 6pm.

VILLA DE LEYVA

☎ 8 / pop 13,000 / elevation 2140m / temp 18°C
Villa de Leyva is where time stands still. Declared a national monument in 1954, the town has been preserved in its entirety and virtually no modern architecture exists. The result is a colonial town par excellence – a place where the streets are still cobbled and the walls still whitewashed. It's easy to see the place in just a day, but many travelers find themselves caught in its magical grasp and hang on for several more.

The town was founded in 1572 by Hernán Suárez de Villalobos and named Nuestra Señora de la Villa Santa María de Leyva. It enjoys a healthy, mild climate, warmer than Tunja, just 39km away but 700m higher.

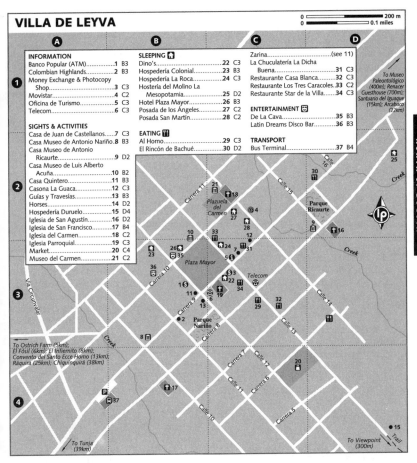

VILLA DE LEYVA

INFORMATION
Banco Popular (ATM)................1 B3
Colombian Highlands................2 B3
Money Exchange & Photocopy
  Shop.................................3 C3
Movistar.................................4 C2
Oficina de Turismo...................5 C3
Telecom.................................6 C3

SIGHTS & ACTIVITIES
Casa de Juan de Castellanos.....7 C3
Casa Museo de Antonio Nariño.8 B3
Casa Museo de Antonio
  Ricaurte.............................9 D2
Casa Museo de Luis Alberto
  Acuña................................10 B2
Casa Quintero........................11 B3
Casona La Guaca....................12 C3
Guías y Travesías...................13 B3
Horses.................................14 D2
Hospedería Duruelo.................15 D4
Iglesia de San Agustín.............16 D2
Iglesia de San Francisco..........17 B4
Iglesia del Carmen..................18 C2
Iglesia Parroquial...................19 C3
Market................................20 C4
Museo del Carmen.................21 C2

SLEEPING
Dino's.................................22 C3
Hospedería Colonial................23 B3
Hospedería La Roca................24 C3
Hostería del Molino La
  Mesopotamia.....................25 D2
Hotel Plaza Mayor...................26 B3
Posada de los Ángeles.............27 C3
Posada San Martín..................28 C3

EATING
Al Horno..............................29 D4
El Rincón de Bachué................30 D2

Zarina..................................(see 11)
La Chuculatería La Dicha
  Buena...............................31 C3
Restaurante Casa Blanca.........32 C3
Restaurante Los Tres Caracoles.33 C2
Restaurante Star de la Villa......34 C3

ENTERTAINMENT
De La Cava...........................35 B3
Latin Dreams Disco Bar...........36 B3

TRANSPORT
Bus Terminal.........................37 B4

To Museo
Paleontológico
(400m); Renacer
Guesthouse (700m);
Santuario del Iguaque
(15km); Arcabuco
(22km)

NORTH OF BOGOTÁ

To Ostrich Farm (5km);
El Fósil (6km); El Infiernito (8km);
Convento del Santo Ecce Homo (13km);
Ráquira (25km); Chiquinquirá (38km)

To Tunja
(39km)

To Viewpoint
(300m)

Villa de Leyva's proximity to Bogotá has made it a popular weekend destination for tourists, a trend that has created a miniboom in hotels, craft shops and tourist-oriented restaurants. You can beat the rush and get a better deal on a hotel if you come early in the week. For more details, check out www.villadeleyva.net (in Spanish).

Information
You can take a virtual tour of Villa de Leyva at www.expovilla.com.
Banco Popular (Plaza Mayor, Calle 12 No 9-43) Has a 24-hour ATM.
Money Exchange & Photocopy Shop (☎ 732 1225; Plaza Mayor, Carrera 9 No 12-36; 9am-6pm) Changes US dollars into pesos, but at a poor rate.

Movistar (Calle 14 No 9-52; per hr US$1.20; 9am-8pm) Internet café.
Oficina de Turismo (☎ 732 0232; cnr Carrera 9 & Calle 13; 8am-1pm & 3-6pm Mon-Sat, 9am-1pm & 3-6pm Sun) Can recommend activities and sells maps (US$1).
Telecom (☎ 732 1040; Plaza Mayor, Carrera 9 No 12-36; per hr US$0.80; 7am-10pm) International phone calls and a fast Internet connection.

Sights
Villa de Leyva is a leisurely place made for wandering around charming stone streets, listening to the sound of church bells and enjoying the lazy rhythm of days gone by. It's still very traditional; locals greet strangers in the street with 'Buenos días' or 'Buenas tardes.' Be sure to return the greeting. Small

as it is, the town has half-a-dozen museums, most of which are in old colonial buildings. For a marvelous bird's-eye view of the town, walk southeast of the market and climb the hill behind the Hospedería Duruelo.

PLAZA MAYOR

You are likely to start your tour from the Plaza Mayor. Measuring nearly 120m by 120m, this is reputedly the largest main square in the country. The vast expanse is interrupted by only a small Mudejar fountain in its middle, which provided water to the village inhabitants for almost four centuries. Unlike all other Colombian cities and towns where the main squares have been named after historic heroes, most often Bolívar, the one in Villa de Leyva is traditionally and firmly called Plaza Mayor.

As you stroll about, pop into the **Casa de Juan de Castellanos** (Carrera 9, No 13-15), **Casona La Guaca** (Carrera 9, No 13-57) and **Casa Quintero** (cnr Carrera 9 & Calle 12), three meticulously restored colonial mansions just off the plaza. They have beautiful patios, cafés and craft shops.

CASA MUSEO DE LUIS ALBERTO ACUÑA

Featuring works by the painter, sculptor, writer and historian who was inspired by influences ranging from Muisca mythology to contemporary art, **Casa Museo de Luis Alberto Acuña** (Plaza Mayor; admission US$0.80; 10am-1pm & 3-5pm Tue-Sun) has been set up in the mansion where Acuña (1904–93) lived for the last 15 years of his life.

CASA MUSEO DE ANTONIO NARIÑO

Antonio Nariño was known as the forefather of Colombia's independence and **Casa Museo de Antonio Nariño** (732 0342; Carrera 9 No 10-19; admission US$1.25; 8am-noon & 2-5pm Thu-Tue) is the house where he lived until his death in 1823. Nariño was a fierce defender of human rights and is also revered for translating Thomas Paine's *Rights of Man* into Spanish. The house has been converted into a museum containing colonial objects and memorabilia related to this great man.

CASA MUSEO DE ANTONIO RICAURTE

Antonio Ricaurte fought under Bolívar and is remembered for his act of self-sacrifice in the battle of San Mateo (near Caracas in Venezuela) in 1814. Defending an armory and closely encircled by the Spaniards, he let

them in, then set fire to the gunpowder kegs and blew up everyone, including himself. The battle was won. **Casa Museo de Antonio Ricaurte** (Calle 15 No 8-16, Parque Ricaurte; admission US$0.80; 9am-noon & 2-5pm Wed-Fri, 9am-1pm & 2-6pm Sat & Sun) is the house where Ricaurte was born in 1786. It's now a museum, which displays period furniture and weapons as well as some related documents.

MUSEO DEL CARMEN

One of the best museums of religious art in the country, **Museo del Carmen** (Plazuela del Carmen; admission US$0.80; 10am-1pm & 2-5pm Sat, Sun & holidays) is housed in the convent of the same name. It contains valuable paintings, carvings, altarpieces and other religious objects dating from the 16th century onward.

MUSEO PALEONTOLÓGICO

About 1km northeast of town on the road to Arcabuco, **Museo Paleontológico** (732 0466; Vía Arcabuco; admission US$0.80; 9am-noon & 2-5pm Tue-Sat, 9am-3pm Sun) has a collection of locally found fossils dating from the period when the area was a seabed (100 to 150 million years ago). It's largely repetitive if you've already been to El Fósil (p90).

CHURCHES

Villa de Leyva has four churches, all dating back to the town's early years. The **Iglesia Parroquial** (Plaza Mayor; 7-8am & 6:30-8pm Mon-Sat, 7-8am, 10-11am, noon-1pm & 6:30-8pm Sun), the parish church facing the main square, was built in 1608 and has hardly changed since. It boasts a marvelous baroque main retable. The only other church in religious service, the **Iglesia del Carmen** (Calle 14 No 10-04; 6:30-8am Mon-Sat, 6:30-8am & 11am-noon Sun), has interesting paintings in the chancel and the wooden structure supporting the roof. The two remaining churches, **Iglesia de San Francisco** (cnr Carrera 8 & Calle 10) and **Iglesia de San Agustín** (Parque Ricaurte), no longer serve religious purposes and are not open to the public (you might be able to cajole the door guard to let you poke your head inside).

Activities

There are **hiking** possibilities all around Villa de Leyva, as well as some longer treks in the Santuario de Iguaque (p91). The region abounds in fossils, so you can combine walking with fossil hunting.

The alternative to foot power is **cycling**; you can hire a bike in Villa de Leyva (see Tours, below).

Horseback-riding is also popular and many locals rent out horses; ask at the tourist office for details on where to rent (the usual place is outside the tourist office). Horse rental costs around US$2.50 per hour plus another US$2.50 for the guide per group.

Tours

Taxis parking in front of the bus terminal offer return taxi trips around the surrounding sights. The standard routes include El Fósil, El Infiernito and Convento del Santo Ecce Homo (US$25), and Ráquira and La Candelaria (US$35). Prices are per taxi for up to four people and include stops at the sights.

Colombian Highlands (☎ 732 1379; colombianhighlan ds@hotmail.com; Carrera 9 No 11-02) Run by biologist Oscar Gilede, this agency has a variety of off-beat tours, including nocturnal hikes, star-gazing using telescopes, rappeling and horse trips. Oscar, who speaks English, also rents bikes and camping equipment, develops film, burns digital photos to CDs and puts up travelers in the Renacer Guesthouse (right).

Guías & Travesías (☎ 732 0742; Calle 12 No 8A-31) This agency rents out bicycles (per hour/half day/full day US$1.50/5/9) and can provide maps and recommended cycling routes. Regional tours and transport are also available. Contact the owner, Enrique Maldanado, for good advice and personal service.

Festivals & Events

Festival de las Cometas (August) Locals and some foreign kite fans compete in this colorful kite festival.

Festival de Luces (December) This fireworks festival is usually on the first or second weekend of the month.

Sleeping

The town has an excellent choice of places to stay, and most hotels, particularly the upmarket ones, are stylish and charming. Note that prices rise on weekends and it may be hard to find a room.

BUDGET

Hospedería La Roca (☎ 732 0331; Plaza Mayor; r per person US$9; ⊠) Located on the main square, this charming *hospedería* (budget hotel) may be the town's best value-for-money hotel. Rambling hallways on two stories lead to a variety of pleasant rooms, all of which have a TV, high ceilings and a modern bathroom. A popular upstairs café overlooks the square.

Dino's (☎ 732 0803; Plaza Mayor; camping per person US$2.50, dm US$7, r per person incl breakfast US$9) Next to the parish church on the main plaza, Dino's has six neat rooms circling a small courtyard restaurant, or you can camp in the garden at the back and use the hotel facilities. Prices are negotiable.

Hospedería Colonial (☎ 732 1364; Calle 12 No 10-81; s/d US$4.50/9) Just a block off the plaza, Hospedería Colonial is another basic, but acceptable, option. It has 20 rooms, some of which have private bathroom.

MIDRANGE & TOP END

Posada de los Ángeles (☎ 732 0562; Carrera 10 No 13-94; r per person incl breakfast US$13.50; ⊠) Excellent midrange option. A pastel-colored affair with modern bathrooms, tile floors and mosquito nets. The historic house, which overlooks Iglesia del Carmen, serves up a morning breakfast of eggs, toast and jam.

Renacer Guesthouse (☎ 732 1379, 311 308 3739; colombianhighlands@hotmail.com; r per person US$9-12, camping per person US$2.50; P ⊠ 🖳) This friendly guesthouse is connected to Colombian Highlands (left) and run by the affable Oscar Gilede. It's located in a private home, about 1km northwest of the main square. The guesthouse contains five double rooms, two with private bathroom.

Posada San Martín (☎ 732 0428; Calle 14 No 9-43; s/d/tr incl breakfast US$13.50/22.50/34; ⊠) Set up in a beautiful old-fashioned house, this quiet and welcoming guesthouse has just five rooms, all with private bathroom.

Hotel Plaza Mayor (☎ 732 0425; Carrera 10 No 12-31; s/d/tr US$36/68/77; ⊠) With a prime location overlooking the square, this 32-room hotel is worth considering for a splurge. English-speaking owner Juan Toro is continually upgrading the facilities and offers little extras, including live music on the rooftop patio. He is also planning to install a Jacuzzi. If you're with a group, there is a three-room suite with fireplace for US$250.

Hostería del Molino La Mesopotamia (☎ 732 0235; Carrera 8 No 15A-265; s/d/tr incl breakfast US$40/48/64; P ⊠) In an old flour mill that was built in 1568, this is the oldest building in town. If you want to sleep in a canopied bed, request the old section. The rooms are a bit dim and the beds are hard, but you are, after all, in a legendary 435-year-old place. Even if you don't stay there, the management will allow you to look around the grounds.

Eating

Restaurante Casa Blanca (☎ 732 0821; Calle 13 No 7-16; set meals US$2.50, mains US$4-5; ☼ 10am-5pm) One of the best budget restaurants in town, Casa Blanca offers a choice of tasty à la carte dishes, as well as set meals.

Restaurante Star de la Villa (Calle 13 No 8-85; set meals US$2.50, mains US$4-5; ☼ 8am-8pm) A good alternative to the Casa Blanca, this one has reasonable food and prices. They also serve breakfast.

Al Horno (☎ 732 1640; Calle 13 No 7-95; mains US$3-6; ☼ 4-10pm) This colorful and atmospheric bistro has a menu stacked with 12 different types of pizza, plus spaghetti, fettuccine, burgers, sandwiches, crepes and great desserts. If you're taken by the artwork on the walls, you're welcome to buy a piece.

Zarina (☎ 732 0735; Casa Quintero; mains US$6-8; ☼ 12:30-9pm) In-the-know locals vote this Lebanese joint the best eatery in town. There's no *shawarma* (kebab), but you can enjoy a genuine felafel with tahini. This is but one of several excellent restaurants in the Casa Quintero.

Entertainment

Latin Dreams Disco Bar (☎ 732 1042; Carrera 10 No 11-24; ☼ 5pm-3am) Don't be fooled by the all the Beatles paraphernalia, this is a dedicated *salsateca* (disco playing salsa music).

De La Cava (Carrera 10 No 12-03; beers US$0.80; ☼ 2pm-2am) If you prefer to just to drink, this small bar on the corner of the plaza has blaring music and freely flowing alcohol.

Don D'Bill (☎ 311 483 9757; Casa Quintero; ☼ 7pm-2am) In most places, Bill Lynn is a trivia question. In Villa de Leyva he is a legend. The elderly drummer, who backed up Elvis Presley for four years, now plays almost nightly in this intimate bar.

Shopping

Go and see the colorful market held on Saturday on the square three blocks southeast of Plaza Mayor. It's best and busiest early in the morning.

Villa de Leyva has a quite a number of handicraft shops noted for fine basketry and good-quality woven items such as sweaters and *ruanas* (ponchos). There are some artisan shops on Plaza Mayor and more in the side streets, particularly on Carrera 9. A number of weavers have settled in town; their work is of excellent quality and their prices are reasonable. Most craft shops open only on weekends for the tourist rush.

The locals and their children offer fossils for sale. Prices are a matter of negotiation and usually drop considerably.

Getting There & Away

The bus terminal is three blocks southwest of the Plaza Mayor, on the road to Tunja. Minibuses run regularly to Tunja (US$1.80, 45 minutes, 39km) until around 6pm. There are only two direct buses daily to Bogotá (US$6, four hours), or go to Tunja and change. For transport information to El Fósil, Convento del Santo Ecce Homo, Santuario de Iguaque and Ráquira, see those entries later in this chapter.

AROUND VILLA DE LEYVA

Don't leave Villa de Leyva without exploring some of the nearby attractions, including archeological relics, colonial monuments, petroglyphs, caves, lakes and waterfalls. It's a great place for fossil hunting.

Security in the area is good, and you can walk to some of the nearest sights, or go by bicycle or on horseback (see Activities, p88). You can also use local buses, go by taxi or arrange a tour with Villa de Leyva's tour operators (p89). If you choose to go by taxi, make sure you confirm with the driver all the sights you want to see and agree on a price before setting off.

Ostrich Farm

Around 5km southwest of Villa de Leyva, in the direction of El Fósil, is a slightly incongruous **Ostrich Farm** (☎ 315 233 5877; admission US$1.80; ☼ 9am-5pm), home to more than 120 ostriches and a handful of llamas, horses and sheep. The farm has a restaurant where you can dine on ostrich meat (US$9) and a small shop that sells ostrich leather shoes and enormous ostrich eggs.

El Fósil

This is a reasonably complete **kronosaurus fossil** (☎ 311 269 4067; admission US$1; ☼ 8am-6pm), a 120-million-year-old prehistoric marine reptile resembling an overgrown crocodile. The fossil is 7m long (the animal was about 12m long but its tail hasn't survived). It's a baby kronosaurus (the adult animals were far larger) and it remains in the place where it was found.

The fossil is off the road to Chiquinquirá, 6km west of Villa de Leyva. You can walk there in a bit more than an hour, or take the Chiquinquirá or Ráquira bus, which will drop you off 1km from the fossil.

Estación Astronómica Muisca (El Infiernito)

The **Muisca observatory** (admission US$1; 9am-noon & 2-5pm Tue-Sun) dates from the early centuries AD and was used by the Indians to determine the seasons, like a sort of Stonehenge. The site contains 30-odd cylindrical stone monoliths sunk vertically into the ground about 1m from each other in two parallel lines 9m apart.

By measuring the length of shadows cast by the stones, the Indians were able to identify the planting seasons. The complete lack of shadow (corresponding to the sun's zenith), which occurred for a short instant twice a year, on a day in March and September, is thought to have been the time for great festivities.

The observatory was also a ritual site, a fact that got in the way of Spanish plans to lure the Indians into church. To prevent the Indians from going to the site, the Spanish renamed it El Infiernito (The Little Hell) and promoted its association with the devil. It's still widely known as El Infiernito, but locals appreciate the reference to the Muisca Observatory.

The site is 2km north of El Fósil. There's no public transport, but you can walk there from the fossil in 25 minutes. Bicycle, horse and taxi are other means of transport.

Convento del Santo Ecce Homo

Founded by the Dominican fathers in 1620, the **convent** (admission US$1; 9am-5pm) is a large stone-and-adobe construction with a lovely courtyard. The floors are paved with stones quarried in the region, so they contain ammonites and fossils, including petrified corn and flowers. There are also fossils in the base of a statue in the chapel.

The chapel boasts a magnificent gilded main retable with a small image of Ecce Homo and the original wooden ceiling. Look out for the drawing of Christ in west cloister – from different angles it appears that the eyes will open and close.

Part of the convent has been turned into an ethnography museum, with displays of agricultural tools and traditional dress worn by the Muisca Indians and the convent members.

The convent is 13km from Villa de Leyva. The morning bus to Santa Sofía will drop you off a 15-minute walk from the convent.

A return taxi trip (for up to four people) from Villa de Leyva to El Fósil, El Infiernito and Ecce Homo will cost about US$20, including waits allowing for visiting the three sights.

SANTUARIO DE IGUAQUE

Iguaque, a 67.5-sq-km national park, is northeast of Villa de Leyva. It covers the highest part of the mountain range that stretches up to Arcabuco. There are eight small mountain lakes in the northern part of the reserve, sitting at an altitude of between 3550m and 3700m. Laguna de Iguaque, which gave its name to the whole reserve, is the most important lake, mostly because it was a sacred lake for the Muiscas.

Considered the 'cradle of humankind,' the lake is the source of the Muisca creation myth. According to the legend, a beautiful woman named Bachué emerged from the lake with a babe in her arms. When the boy became an adult they married, bore children and populated the earth. In old age, the pair transformed themselves into serpents and dove back into the holy lake.

Laguna de Iguaque is not the most beautiful lake you would have seen in your life, but the scenery and the frailejón (a species of plant typical of the highlands) patches on the way certainly justify the trip. You can visit some of the other lakes in the area, most of which are no more than an hour's walk away.

Keep in mind that it can get pretty cold here, so come prepared. The average temperature at these altitudes ranges between 10°C and 12°C. It also rains a lot – the wettest months are April, October and November. However, March and September are not ideal months for hiking, either. It's best to come here between January and February or between July and August.

Sleeping & Eating

The visitors center is at altitude 2950m, 3km off the Villa de Leyva–Arcabuco road. It offers accommodations in dorms (US$9 per person), serves meals (US$8 per three meals) and collects the reserve's entrance fee (US$9). If you plan to stay here overnight, check the availability of the beds in advance at Bogotá's Parques Nacionales Naturales de Colombia park office (p55).

Getting There & Away
The usual starting point for the reserve is Villa de Leyva. Take a bus to Arcabuco (there are four buses a day, at 7am, 10am, 1:30pm and 4pm), get off 12km from Villa at a place known as Los Naranjos, where a rough road branches off to the right and leads uphill to the visitors center (3km). The walk from the center uphill to the Laguna de Iguaque takes around three hours. A leisurely return trip is likely to take five to six hours, unless you plan to visit some other lakes as well.

RÁQUIRA
☎ 8 / pop 1600 / elevation 2150m / temp 18°C
Brightly painted facades, a jumble of craft shops and stacks of freshly fired clay pots make a welcoming sight along the main street of this one horse town. Ráquira, 25km southwest of Villa de Leyva, is well known for its quality pottery – everything from kitchen utensils to copies of indigenous pots. A number of small pottery workshops are in the village itself and on its outskirts, where you can watch the production process and buy some products if you want. Plenty of craft shops around the main square also sell other crafts, such as hammocks, ponchos, baskets, woodcarving and jewelry.

Sleeping & Eating
You shouldn't have any trouble finding accommodations in Ráquira, but food is a different matter. Try the restaurant in Hostería La Candelaria, or bring a picnic.

Hostería Nemqueteba (☎ 735 7083; d/tr with bathroom US$15/20; ✕ ▣) Bright rooms with high ceilings come with desk, TV and a clean bathroom. There's a nice patio and a decent restaurant, but you may want to avoid the swimming pool, which looks like a prime habitat for a kronosaurus.

Hotel Suaya (☎ 735 7029; d/tr with bathroom US$15/20; ✕) A block off the main plaza, Hotel Suaya is set in an old wooden dosshouse. Rooms are clean, have hot water and some have views of the main street.

Hostería La Candelaria (☎ 735 7259; r with bathroom per person US$9) Near the Suaya, this

hostería has 10 rooms that sleep from two to six persons, plus a restaurant.

Getting There & Away
Ráquira is 5km off the Tunja–Chiquinquirá road, down a side road branching off at Tres Esquinas. Four buses per day travel along this road to Ráquira (and continue on to La Candelaria). Both come from Bogotá, one through Tunja, the other through Chiquinquirá.

Four minibuses run daily from Villa de Leyva to Ráquira (US$1.50, 35 minutes) and back, plus the occasional *colectivo* (shared taxi or minibus), if there's demand.

LA CANDELARIA
☎ 8 / pop 300
This tiny hamlet set amid arid hills, 7km beyond Ráquira, is noted for the **Monasterio de La Candelaria** (☻ 9am-5pm). The monastery was founded in 1597 by Augustine monks and completed about 1660. Part of it is open to the public. Monks show you through the chapel (note the 16th-century painting of the Virgen de la Candelaria over the altar), a small museum, the library, and the courtyard flanked by the cloister with a collection of 17th-century canvases hanging on its walls. Some of these artworks were allegedly painted by Gregorio Vásquez de Arce y Ceballos and the Figueroa brothers.

Getting There & Away
Only two buses a day call at La Candelaria, both of which come from Bogotá. Otherwise, walk by a path from Ráquira (one hour). The path begins in Ráquira's main plaza, winds up a hill to a small shrine at the top and then drops down and joins the road to La Candelaria.

You can also go by taxi. A return taxi trip from Villa de Leyva to Ráquira and La Candelaria can be arranged for around US$30 (up to four people), allowing some time in both villages.

PARQUE NACIONAL EL COCUY
With its snowcapped peaks, scintillating alpine lakes, glorious green valleys, waterfalls and glaciers, Parque Nacional El Cocuy ranks as one of Colombia's most spectacular protected areas. In the highest part of the Cordillera Oriental, it tops out at Ritacumba Blanco, a 5330m peak.

The mountain chain is relatively compact and not difficult to reach – the gateway towns are Guicán and El Cocoy in northern Boyacá. It's an ideal place for trekking, although the routes are more suited to experienced walkers. There are no facilities in the park so you'll need to bring all your food and equipment, including sleeping bags, warm clothing and a tent.

Some tour companies run trips this way. For a reliable private guide in Bogotá, contact **Rodrigo Arias** (☎ 310 211 4130; arias_rodrigo@hotmail.com), who can be reached through the Platypus Guesthouse (p66).

SANTANDER

The mountainous department of Santander contains some of the most accessible terrain for hiking and white-water rafting enthusiasts, and crossing it by bus will afford spectacular views of its canyons and rocky peaks. Extreme sports nuts can choose from paragliding, rappeling or kayaking trips, while more sane visitors can enjoy the attractions on foot or in a raft.

While outdoor enthusiasts will get excited about San Gil's adventure trips, travelers seeking out the rustic charm of the colonial era should head straight for Barichara or Girón.

If you're here in March or April, don't miss out on the regional culinary specialty – *hormiga culona* (fried ants).

SAN GIL

☎ 7 / pop 35,000 / elevation 1110m / temp 22°C
For a small city, San Gil packs a lot punch. With the riverside Parque El Gallineral, a quaint 300-year-old town square and a host of ecoadventure tours ranging from rafting to rappeling, there's no shortage of things to do and see.

Information

Bancolombia (Calle 12 No 10-44) 24-hour ATM.
CAI de Turismo (☎ 724 3433; cnr Malecón & Calle 7; ❧ 7:30am-noon & 1-6:30pm) The tourist office is near the entrance to the Parque El Gallineral. More reliable information can be found at one of the nearby ecotour companies.
Foxnet (☎ 724 6659; Carrera 10 No 12-37; per hr US$0.80; ❧ 7am-12:30pm & 2-8pm) Internet access in the Centro Comercial El Edén on the main plaza.

Sights

The town's showpiece is the **Parque El Gallineral** (☎ 724 4372; cnr Malecón & Calle 6; admission US$1.80; ❧ 8am-6pm). The four-hectare park is set on a triangle-shaped island between two arms of the Quebrada Curití and Río Fonce. Almost all of its 1867 trees are covered with barbas de viejo, long silvery fronds of tillandsia that form spectacular transparent curtains of foliage. The park is on the road to Bucaramanga; it's a 10-minute walk from the town center.

San Gil has a rather pleasant main plaza, **Parque La Libertad**, with huge old ceibas and the handsome 18th-century stone **Catedral Santa Cruz** (cnr Carrera 9 & Calle 13). One block downhill from the plaza is the **Casa de Cultura** (☎ 724 6986; Calle 12 No 10-31; ❧ 9-noon & 2-5pm Mon-Sat), an old mansion that has temporary art exhibits and a café.

You could also visit the village of **Curití**, 12km northeast of San Gil, with its 17th-century church and the Pescadarito (aka Quebrada Curití), a mountainlike river with waterfalls and ponds to swim in.

The other highlight in the area is the **Cascadas Juan Curi** (admission US$0.40), a 180m-high waterfall located 25km from San Gil on the road to Charala. Buses (US$1) to Charala depart twice per hour from the east side of the bridge on Calle 10. Ask the driver to let you out at the *cascadas* (waterfall).

Tours

Several tour agencies in San Gil run white-water rafting on local rivers. A standard 10km run on Río Fonce (grades 1 to 3) costs US$12 per person and takes 1½ hours; longer, more adventurous trips on Río Chicamocha (grades up to 4) can be organized on request. Most operators also offer caving, horseback-riding, paragliding, rappeling, rock climbing and ecological walks.
Aventura Total (☎ 723 8888; www.aventuratotal.com.co in Spanish) Located next to the tourist office, this is a reliable outfit with English-speaking staff.
Colombin Rafting Expeditions (☎ 311 283 8647; colombiakayak5@hotmail.com; Carrera 10 No 7-83)
Macondo Adventures (p94) Can organize all manner of tours. It's best to call ahead so they can put groups together (which lowers the cost).
Planeta Azul (☎ 724 0000; planetaazulsg@hotmail.com; Parque El Gallineral)
Ríos y Canoas (☎ 724 7220; riosycanoas@hotmail.com; Parque El Gallineral)

Sleeping & Eating

San Gil has plenty of hotels, predominantly budget ones, all across the center.

Macondo Guesthouse (☎ 724 5646; 311 828 2905; macondohostal@hotmail.com; Calle 10 No 7-66; r per person US$4.50) This Australian-run place is a bit like staying at a friend's house. There is no reception, but it does have a sitting area and three simple rooms that share a single bathroom. It's also a good place for information on adventure trips and tours. Since owner Shaun Clohesy runs the place single-handedly, it's best to call or email ahead.

Centro Real (☎ 724 0387; Calle 10 No 10-41; s/d/tr US$5/9/12; ✗) The Centro Real is a new place with 20 rooms all with private bathroom. It's clean, comfortable, central and in high demand, so try calling ahead.

Hotel Mansión del Parque (☎ 724 5662; Calle 12 No 8-71; s/d/tr with bathroom US$16/21/25) Set in a colonial mansion at the corner of Parque Central, the Mansión del Parque has large rooms, the best of which have balconies overlooking the plaza. Rooms off the plaza are smaller and lack windows, but you might be able to get a discount on these.

Hotel El Viajero (☎ 724 1965; Carrera 11 No 11-07; s/d US$5/8, s/d/tr with bathroom US$8/11/17) This place scores big points for its rustic charm and excellent river views off the back deck, and would be a fine place to stay if the rooms weren't the size of closets.

El Turista (☎ 724 7029; Calle 10 No 10-27; ◷ 7am-8:30pm) 'The Tourist' restaurant is open all day, and you can stop in early for scrambled eggs and *arepas*. At other times you could try Santander specialties such as *cabro al horno* (grilled goat meat served with yuccas).

Cafetería Donde Betty (☎ 724 62978; cnr Carrera 9 & Calle 12; ◷ 7am-midnight) This pleasant café serves breakfast, sandwiches and thirst-quenching fruit shakes.

Getting There & Away

The bus terminal is 2km west of the town center on the road to Bogotá. Urban buses shuttle regularly between the terminal and the center, or take a taxi (US$1). Passengers also wait for buses on the main road near the tourist information booth. This is fine for going north to Bucaramanga, but for points south you're better off at the station.

Frequent buses travel south to Bogotá (US$15, 7½ hours) and north to Bucaramanga (US$5, 2½ hours). There are also half-hourly minibuses going to Bucaramanga (US$5, 2¼ hours). Buses to Barichara (US$1.25, 40 minutes) leave every 45 minutes from the **Cotrasangil bus office** (Carrera 10 No 14-82), in the town center.

BARICHARA

☎ 7 / pop 4000 / elevation 1340m / temp 22°C
Barichara is the kind of town that Hollywood filmmakers dream about. A Spanish colonial town of striking beauty, the whitewashed buildings and stone streets look almost as new as the day they were created some 300 years ago. Granted, the movie-set appearance owes its debt to considerable reconstruction efforts made over the past 25 years, but all rebuilding has been done with taste in mind.

The town, 20km northwest of San Gil and high above the Río Suárez, was founded in 1705 as Villa de San Lorenzo de Barichara. Four stone churches were built, including a massive cathedral. Today it's considered one of the most beautiful small colonial towns in Colombia.

The name Barichara comes from Barachalá, a Guane Indian word (the original inhabitants of this territory) which means 'a good place for a rest' – absolutely true! Whether you are here to sightsee or just to rest, Barichara won't disappoint.

Information

Adpostal (☎ 726 7127; Carrera 6 No 4-90; ◷ 8am-noon & 2-6pm)
Alcaldia & Police (☎ 726 7173; Calle 5)
Hospital (☎ 726 7133; Carrera 2)

Sights

As you stroll about the streets take a look at the churches. The 18th-century sandstone **Catedral de la Inmaculada Concepción** (Parque Principal) is the most elaborate single piece of architecture in town, looking somewhat too big for the town's needs. Its golden stonework (which turns deep orange at sunset) contrasts with the whitewashed houses surrounding it. The building has a clerestory (a second row of windows high up in the nave) which is unusual among Spanish colonial churches.

The **Iglesia de Santa Bárbara** (cnr Carrera 11 & Calle 6), at the northern end of town, has been carefully reconstructed in the 1990s (only the facade survived). The cemetery chapel, the **Capilla de Jesús Resucitado** (cnr Carrera 7 & Calle 3), unfortunately lost a part of its bell tower

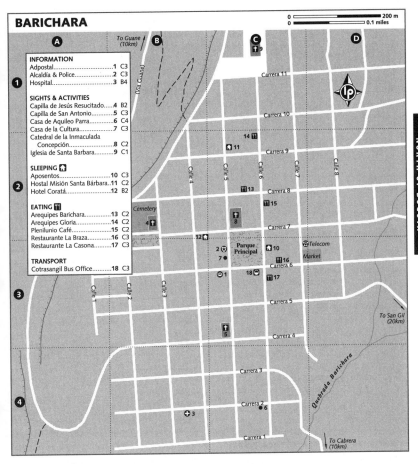

BARICHARA

INFORMATION
Adpostal.....................................1 C3
Alcaldía & Police.......................2 C3
Hospital......................................3 B4

SIGHTS & ACTIVITIES
Capilla de Jesús Resucitado.....4 B2
Capilla de San Antonio.............5 C3
Casa de Aquileo Parra..............6 C4
Casa de la Cultura....................7 C3
Catedral de la Inmaculada
  Concepción..............................8 C2
Iglesia de Santa Bárbara..........9 C1

SLEEPING
Aposentos.................................10 C3
Hostal Misión Santa Bárbara...11 C2
Hotel Coratá.............................12 B2

EATING
Arequipes Barichara.................13 C2
Arequipes Gloria.......................14 C2
Plenilunio Café.........................15 C2
Restaurante La Braza................16 C3
Restaurante La Casona.............17 C3

TRANSPORT
Cotrasangil Bus Office.............18 C3

when it was damaged by lightning. Do visit the cemetery next to the chapel, noted for interesting tombs elaborated in stone. Also have a look at the **Capilla de San Antonio** (cnr Carrera 4 & Calle 5), the youngest of the town's churches, dating from 1831.

The **Casa de la Cultura** (☎ 726 7002; Calle 5 No 6-29; admission US$0.25; ☀ 8am-noon & 2-6pm Mon-Sat, 9am-1pm Sun), a colonial house laid out around a fine patio and situated on the main square, features a small collection of fossils and pottery of the Guane Indians.

The **Casa de Aquileo Parra** (Carrera 2 No 5-60) is a small, humble house where an ex-president lived. Most of the building is now taken up by a weaving cooperative and you can watch the workers make fiber bags. The woman who runs the co-op can give you a tour of the casa, though there is little to see.

Sleeping

Hotel Coratá (☎ 726 7110; Carrera 7 No 4-08; r per person US$10) Any aficionado of historical residences will want to stay at the Coratá, a 280-year-old building decorated with antiques and wood furnishings. Rooms, with some of the highest ceilings you could imagine, have TV and an attached bathroom.

Hostal Misión Santa Bárbara (☎ 726 7163, in Bogotá ☎ 1-288 4949; www.hostalmisionsantabarbara.info in Spanish; Calle 5 No 9-12; s/d/tr incl breakfast US$34/50/65; ☒) Santa Bárbara, set in a meticulously refurbished colonial mansion, has cozy, old-fashioned rooms and a restaurant.

Aposentos (☎ 726 7294; Calle 6 No 6-40; r per person US$9) Aposentos is a small, good-value place, with five rooms set around a courtyard. All rooms have private bathroom and TV. It's right on the main plaza.

Eating

Restaurants are limited and menus brief but ask your waiter about regional specialties, including *cabro* (grilled goat), *mute* (tripe and vegetable soup) and the famous *hormiga culona,* a giant fried ant that appears mainly in March and April. Barichara is also well known for its *arequipe* (thick milk pudding). Breakfast places are almost nonexistent, so your best option is to eat at the Hostal Misión Santa Bárbara where a set breakfast goes for US$3 to US$4.

Plenilunio Café (☎ 726 7485; Calle 6 No 7-74; dishes US$3-4; ⏰ 6.30-11pm) This Italian restaurant serves up several nice dishes; try the crepes and chicken. It's set in a cozy room with just four tables and you can hang out long after you've eaten, enjoying a game of chess.

Restaurante La Braza (Carrera 6 No 6-31; ⏰ noon-6pm) Low-priced Colombian lunches and dinners are served under a thatched roof in this large, open-air restaurant. They specialize in *cabro con pepitoria* (goat meat with blood and organs).

Restaurante La Casona (Calle 6 No 5-68; ⏰ noon-6pm) Run by the friendly Orfelina Calderón, La Casona is another place for cheap set meals and typical regional dishes.

There are a number of *arequipe* shops, including **Arequipes Barichara** (Carrera 8 No 5-51) and **Arequipes Gloria** (Calle 6 No 9-29). The local drink is the *chicha de maíz* (an alcoholic maize drink).

Getting There & Away

Buses shuttle between Barichara and San Gil every 45 minutes (US$1.25, 40 minutes). They depart from the **Cotrasangil bus office** (☎ 726 7132; Carrera 6 No 5-74) on the main plaza.

GUANE

☎ 7 / pop 1500

So little happens in the sleepy town of Guane, 10km northwest of Barichara, that everyone watches when a horse cart trundles past. But the views around the town are spectacular and the handsome main square features a fine rural church, the **Santa Lucía Iglesia**, built in 1720. Across the square is the unique **Museum of Paleontology & Archaeology** (admission US$0.40; ⏰ 8am-noon & 1-5pm), with a well-stocked collection of fossils and Guane artifacts. The curator locks the front door and gives a personal tour whenever someone shows up, so just hang tight.

There are a couple of restaurants in town and one place to stay, the **Hostal Santa Lucía de Mucuruva** (☎ 315 294 2532, 315 854 6109; r per person US$14), a colorful but basic place set in an old colonial home.

Two buses a day (11:30am and 5pm, except Saturday) go to Guane from Barichara

---

WHEN THE COCA PLANT TOOK OVER

The lush national parks north of Bogotá, renowned for their plant and animal diversity, glorious views and pristine habitats, have a new enemy: the coca plant. Recent years have seen increased numbers of coca farmers moving into the parks to plant their highly lucrative crops, and the effects have been devastating.

Farmers use slash and burn technology to wipe out large swaths of virgin forest. They haul in gasoline and hydrochloric acid, which poisons rivers and soil, and they brazenly build semi-permanent structures in sensitive habitats.

The coca planters moved to the protected parks only after being pushed off their own land by the Colombian military, which has spent several years successfully spraying the illegal crops. But strict environmental protection laws prevent the military from spraying in the national parks, giving coca planters a safe haven from which to work.

As of 2005, around 90,000 acres of virgin land in Colombia's 49 national parks had been torn down to make way for the coca fields. The government wants to spray them out but environmentalists and Indians warn that this tactic will kill native plants, animals and people. Their preferred method is to cut down the crops with machetes, but rebels have threatened to kill anyone who gets near the fields. With environmentalists and the army locked in a verbal battle to determine a solution, rebels, for the moment, are reaping the rewards.

and stay for about 20 minutes before going back to Barichara. Alternatively you can walk there by an old Spanish trail in about 1½ hours. The trail was declared a national monument in 1997 and has been extensively restored.

BUCARAMANGA

☎ 7 / pop 560,000 / elevation 960m / temp 23°C

Surrounded by mountains and filled with an air of vibrancy, the rapidly expanding town of Bucaramanga makes for a decent stopover on the long road between Bogotá and the coast. There is little to see in the city itself, but facilities are fine for an overnight stop or as a base to visit Girón, a nearby colonial-era town and legitimate tourist attraction.

Bucaramanga, the capital of Santander, is also noted for its cigars, numerous parks and the famous *hormiga culona,* a large ant that is fried and eaten.

The city was founded in 1622 and developed around what is today the Parque García Rovira, but very little of its colonial architecture remains. Over the centuries, the city center moved eastwards, and today Parque Santander marks the heart of Bucaramanga. Further east are newer districts, peppered with hotels and nightspots.

Information

Bancolombia (☎ 630 4251; Carrera 18 No 35-02)

Click & Play (☎ 642 2882; Calle 34 No 19-46, room 115, Centro Comercial La Triada; per hr US$1; ⏱ 8am-9pm) Internet and international phone calls.

Mundo Divisas (Calle 34 No 19-46, room 120, Centro Comercial La Triada; ⏱ 8am-noon & 2.30-6pm) Money changer.

Police (☎ 633 9015; Calle 41 No 11-44)

Telenet (☎ 670 5850; Calle 36 No 18-03; per hr US$1; ⏱ 7:30am-7:30pm) Internet and international phone call office.

Tourist Police (☎ 633 8342; Parque Santander; ⏱ 24hr) This small police box hands out free city brochures and maps.

Sights

Bucaramanga has several museums. The **Museo Casa de Bolívar** (☎ 630 4258; Calle 37 No 12-15; admission US$0.50; ⏱ 8am-noon & 2-6pm Mon-Fri, 8am-noon Sat) is housed in a colonial mansion with two patios, and is where Bolívar stayed for two months in 1828. The museum displays various historic and archeological exhibits, including weapons, documents, paintings, and mummies and artifacts of the Guane

Indians who inhabited the region before the Spaniards arrived.

Diagonally opposite, the **Casa de la Cultura** (☎ 642 0163; Calle 37 No 12-46; admission free; ⏱ 8am-noon & 2-6pm Mon-Fri, 8am-noon Sat), in another historic building, features a collection of paintings donated by the local artists.

Of the city churches, the **Catedral de la Sagrada Familia** (Calle 36 No 19-56), facing Parque Santander, is the most substantial piece of religious architecture. Constructed for nearly a century (1770–1865), it's a massive, eclectic edifice with fine stained-glass windows and a ceramic cupola brought from Mexico.

The **Capilla de los Dolores** (cnr Carrera 10 & Calle 35), in the Parque García Rovira, is Bucaramanga's oldest surviving church, erected in stone in 1748–50. It's no longer operating as a church and is seldom open.

The pleasant **Jardín Botánico Eloy Valenzuela** (☎ 648 0729; admission US$0.25; ⏱ 8am-5pm) has a small pond and a Japanese tea garden. The gardens are on the old road to Floridablanca, in the suburb of Bucarica. To get there, take the Bucarica bus from Carrera 15 in the city center.

Sleeping

Budget hotels are mostly centered around Parque Centenario, particularly on Calle 31 between Carreras 19 and 22. They're mostly basic, but many have private bathrooms.

Hotel Ruitoque (☎ 633 4567; Carrera 19 No 37-26; s/d/tr US$22/30/38; ⏹ ⏺) Travelers seeking a clean, comfortable and central hotel with air-con should head postehaste to the Ruitoque. Rooms come with TV, fridge and minibar, the management is friendly and prices include a simple breakfast.

Hotel Balmoral (☎ 630 4663; Carrera 21 No 34-75; s/d/tr with fan US$11/13/20; ⏹ ⏺) The Balmoral is one of Bucaramanga's best budget options. Rooms are well maintained, clean and come with TV and private bathroom. For a room with air-con, tack on about US$2 per person. The main drawback is that most rooms face a very noisy street.

Hotel Morgan No 2 (☎ 630 4226; Calle 35 No 18-83; s/d/tr US$13/18/20; ⏹ ⏺) Just off Parque Santander; another reasonable, very central and affordable place. Most rooms are a tad small and have fan only, but better rooms have a fridge and air-con for US$1 extra. Avoid the hot, noisy street-side rooms.

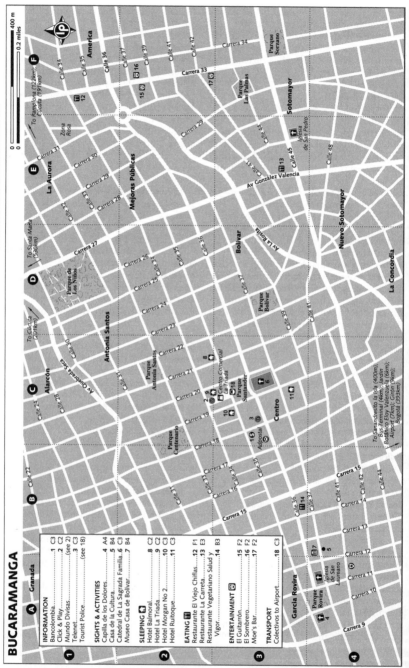

BUCARAMANGA

INFORMATION	
Bancolombia	1 C3
Click & Play	2 C2
Mundo Divisas	(see 2)
Telenet	3 C3
Tourist Police	(see 18)

SIGHTS & ACTIVITIES	
Capilla de los Dolores	4 A4
Casa de la Cultura	5 B4
Catedral de La Sagrada Familia	6 C3
Museo Casa de Bolívar	7 B4

SLEEPING	
Hotel Balmoral	8 C2
Hotel La Triada	9 C2
Hotel Morgan No 2	10 C3
Hotel Ruitoque	11 C3

EATING	
Restaurante El Viejo Chiflas	12 F1
Restaurante La Carreta	13 E3
Restaurante Vegetariano Salud y	
Vigor	14 B3

ENTERTAINMENT	
El Guitarrón	15 F2
El Sombrero	16 F2
Moe's Bar	17 F2

TRANSPORT	
Colectivos to Airport	18 C3

Hotel La Triada (☎ 642 2410; www.hotellatriada
.com in Spanish; Carrera 20 No 34-22; s/d/tr US$60/64/75, ste
US$81-138; P 🅧 🖳) Businesslike rooms, free
Internet, a buffet breakfast and a central lo-
cation makes this a prime top-end choice.
Amenities include a sauna and gym.

Eating
Typical regional dishes include *mute* and
cabro or *cabrito*. The legendary *hormiga
culona* is not ordered in restaurants but is
a snack you buy by weight in shops (about
US$30 per kilogram). The ants appear in
season (March to May) and are sold in deli-
catessens and in the shopping mall of **Sanan-
dresito La Isla** (Diagonal 15 btwn Calles 55 & 56).

Restaurante El Viejo Chiflas (☎ 632 0640; Carrera
33 No 34-10; mains US$3-6; 🕑 11am-midnight) This is
an atmospheric restaurant good for lovers of
meat. Try the *parrillada vieto chiflas* (US$9),
a platter of various meats, designed for two.
Also recommended is the *mute* (US$2.50).

Restaurante La Carreta (☎ 643 6680; Carrera 27 No
42-27; mains US$6-12; 🕑 noon-3:30pm & 6pm-midnight)
Housed in a historic mansion, La Carreta
has a 40-year-old tradition and a good address for a fine dinner.

Restaurante Vegetariano Salud y Vigor (Calle
36 No 14-24; 🕑 7:30am-6:30pm Sun-Fri) Vegetarians
are catered for at this shop and café.

Entertainment
Most of the night entertainment is around
the eastern sector, with the Zona Rosa its
major focus. The Zona Rosa proper is centered on Carrera 31 between Calles 33 and
34, and Calle 33 between Carreras 31 and
33, but bars and discos spread along Carrera
33 up to Calle 45. This area is home to the
city's most famous mariachi venue, **El Guitar-
rón** (Carrera 33 No 37-34), which has live music by
mariachi groups nightly from 10pm to 2am.
Across the road is another mariachi affair,
El Sombrero (Carrera 33 No 37-13).

Die hard fans of *The Simpsons* will also
want to check out **Moe's Bar** (☎ 643 1037; Carrera
33 No 44-12; 🕑 6pm-2am), an over-the-top tribute
to Homer, Bart and the rest of the Simpson
clan (Ay Caramba!).

Getting There & Away
AIR
The Palonegro airport is on a *meseta* (plat-
eau) high above the city, off the road to
Barrancabermeja. The landing here is quite

breathtaking. Local buses marked 'Aeropuerto' link the airport and the city center
every hour or so; you catch them on Carrera 15. It's faster to go by *colectivo* (US$2),
which park in Parque Santander. There are
flights to some major Colombian cities,
including Bogotá (US$70 to US$110) and
Medellín (US$80 to US$130).

BUS
Bucaramanga's bus terminal is situated
southwest of the center, midway to Girón;
frequent city buses marked 'Terminal' go
there from Carrera 15. Buses depart regularly to Bogotá (US$22, 10 hours), Carta-
gena (US$36, 12 hours) and Santa Marta
(US$31, nine hours).

There are also numerous buses to Cúcuta
(US$10, six hours). A scenic road winds up
to the *páramo* (open highland) at 3400m
and then drops down to Cúcuta. If you sit
on the right-hand side of the bus, you will
have a splendid view as you leave Bucaramanga and again when you arrive at Pamplona. Travel by day and take a sweater.

GIRÓN
☎ 7 / pop 45,000 / elevation 780m / temp 24°C
The cobbled streets, horse carts and lazy atmosphere of San Juan de Girón are a world
away in time, but just 9km in distance, from
bustling Bucaramanga. The pleasant town
was founded in 1631 on the banks of the
Río de Oro, and in 1963 it was declared
a national monument. Its central area has
been largely restored.

The town has become a trendy place, and
some artists and intellectuals have settled
here giving it a bit of a bohemian flavor.
Due to its proximity to Bucaramanga, Girón
has become a popular weekend getaway for
city dwellers.

Information
Web surfers can get more info from www
.giron.gov.co (in Spanish).
Banco Popular (Carrera 25) On the eastern side of the
Parque Principal. Has an ATM.
el port@l.net (☎ 646 9878; Carrera 25 No 30-86; per
hr US$0.60; 🕑 8am-11pm Mon-Fri) Internet facilities plus
coffee and snacks.
Secretaría de Cultura y Turismo (☎ 646 1337; Calle
30 No 26-64; 🕑 8am-noon & 2-6pm) Free guided tours
(in Spanish) of the town are available.
Tourist Police (☎ 630 2046; cnr Calle 30 & Carrera 27)

NORTH OF BOGOTÁ

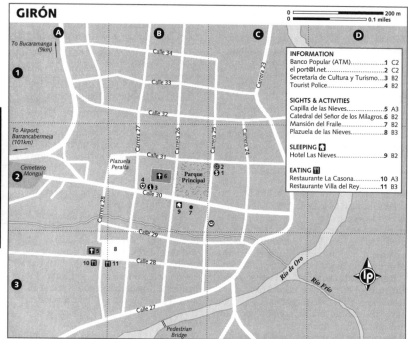

GIRÓN

0		200 m
0		0.1 miles

INFORMATION
Banco Popular (ATM)............................1 C2
el port@l.net.....................................2 C2
Secretaría de Cultura y Turismo...3 B2
Tourist Police....................................4 B2

SIGHTS & ACTIVITIES
Capilla de las Nieves........................5 A3
Catedral del Señor de los Milagros.6 B2
Mansión del Fraile...........................7 B2
Plazuela de las Nieves.....................8 B3

SLEEPING
Hotel Las Nieves..............................9 B2

EATING
Restaurante La Casona....................10 A3
Restaurante Villa del Rey...........11 B3

Sights

Take the time to stroll about Girón's narrow cobbled streets, looking at whitewashed old houses, shaded patios and half-a-dozen small stone bridges, which are reputed to have been built by slaves.

The **Catedral del Señor de los Milagros** on the main plaza was begun in 1646 but not completed until 1876, giving it a stylistically eclectic air.

Also on the main square is the **Mansión del Fraile** (Calle 30 No 25-27), a beautiful 350-year-old colonial mansion that now houses a restaurant and a craft shop.

While wandering around, don't miss the **Plazuela Peralta**, one of the most charming spots in town. Just as enchanting is the **Plazuela de las Nieves**, which features a simple, but noble, 18th-century **Capilla de las Nieves**.

Sleeping & Eating

Hotel Las Nieves (☎ 646 8968; Calle 30 No 25-71; s/d/tr US$11/18/22) Circling a courtyard and overlooking the main plaza is this quaint hotel, featuring large but simple rooms with TV, desk and attached bathroom. Try for one

of the balconied rooms over the plaza. A restaurant downstairs serves budget meals.

A few of Girón's finer restaurants include **Mansión del Fraile** (☎ 646 5408; Calle 30 No 25-27; mains US$4-6; ☐ noon-6pm), **Restaurante Villa del Rey** (☎ 653 2809; Calle 28 No 27-49; mains US$3-6; ☐ 8am-6pm) and **Restaurante La Casona** (☎ 646 7195; Calle 28 No 28-09; mains US$5-8; ☐ noon-6pm). All serve typical hearty food in colonial-style surroundings. And on Sunday, when people from Bucaramanga come, riverside stalls offer a choice of regional dishes.

Getting There & Away

Frequent city buses from Carreras 15 and 33 in Bucaramanga deposit you at the corner of Carrera 26 and Calle 32, one block from Parque Principal (the main plaza).

NORTE DE SANTANDER

Norte de Santander is where the Cordillera Oriental meets the hot, lowland plains that stretch into neighboring Venezuela. The east side of the mountains offer a cool retreat, and colonial-era towns, such as Pamplona, make a pleasant stopover on the overland trail. Cúcuta is a hot market town better known for contraband than its sights, though you may need to stop here if you're crossing the border.

PAMPLONA

☎ 7 / pop 45,000 / elevation 2290m / temp 16°C

Spectacularly set in the deep Valle del Espíritu Santo in the Cordillera Oriental, colonial-era Pamplona is a delightful town of old churches, narrow streets and bustling commerce. If you've just come up from the hot plains of Venezuela, it makes for a nice stopover en route to central Colombia.

Pamplona was founded by Pedro de Orsúa and Ortún Velasco in 1549, making it the oldest town in the region. Soon after its foundation five convents were established and the town swiftly developed into an important religious and political center. A construction boom saw the rise of churches and noble mansions.

Unfortunately, an earthquake occuring in 1875 wiped out a good part of the town. The most representative buildings were restored or reconstructed in their original style, but most of the houses were replaced by new ones. Since then the construction of modern buildings has affected the colonial character of the town even further.

Pamplona was a schooling and catechistic center from its early days, and the traditions have not been lost. Today the town is home to the Universidad de Pamplona, and the large student population is very much in evidence. Pamplona has a distinctly cultured air, and boasts more museums than Cúcuta and Bucaramanga combined.

Information

Adpostal (☎ 568 2405; Calle 6 No 6-36; ⏲ 8am-noon & 2-6pm Mon-Fri)

ATM (cnr Calle 6 & Carrera 6)

Banco de Bogotá (Carrera 6) East of Parque Agueda Gallardo. Has an ATM.

Internet Café (☎ 568 2062; Calle 7 No 5-62; per hr US$0.70; ⏲ 8am-8pm)

Sights

Pamplona has quite a collection of museums and almost all are set in restored colonial houses. **Museo Fotográfico** (Carrera 7 No 2-44) is a curiosity rather than a museum,

but do go in to see hundreds of old photos. **Museo Arquidiocesano de Arte Religioso** (☎ 568 1814; Carrera 5 No 4-53; admission US$0.25; ⏲ 10am-noon & 3-5pm Wed-Sat & Mon, 10am-noon Sun) features religious art, comprising paintings, statues and altarpieces, collected from the region. Have a look at the **Casa de las Cajas Reales** (cnr Carrera 5 & Calle 4), a great colonial mansion, and at **Casa de Mercado** (cnr Carrera 5 & Calle 6), the 19th-century market building, just off the main square. There are some 10 old churches and chapels in town, reflecting Pamplona's religious status in colonial days, though not many have retained their splendor. The **Iglesia del Humilladero**, at the entrance to the cemetery, boasts the famous Cristo del Humilladero, a realistic sculpture of Christ brought from Spain in the 17th century.

MUSEO DE ARTE MODERNO RAMÍREZ VILLAMIZAR

In a 450-year-old mansion, Casa de las Marías, this **museum** (☎ 568 2999; Calle 5 No 5-75; admission US$0.50; ⏲ 9am-noon & 2-6pm Tue-Fri, 9am-6pm Sat & Sun) has about 40 works by Eduardo Ramírez Villamizar, one of Colombia's most outstanding artists, born in Pamplona in 1923. The collection gives an insight into his artistic development from expressionist painting of the 1940s to geometric abstract sculpture in recent decades.

CASA ANZOÁTEGUI

Casa Anzoátegui (Carrera 6 No 7-48; admission free; ⏲ 9am-noon & 2-5:30pm Mon-Sat, 9am-noon Sun) was the home of General José Antonio Anzoátegui, the Venezuelan hero of the independence campaign who fought under Bolívar. His strategic abilities largely contributed to the victory in the Battle of Boyacá of 1819. He died here, three months after the battle, at 30. The house has been turned into a museum witha modest collection of exhibits related to the crucial events of the period.

CASA COLONIAL

One of the oldest buildings in town, **Casa Colonial** (Calle 6 No 2-56; admission by donation; ⏲ 8am-noon & 2-5pm Mon-Sat) dates from the early Spanish days. The collection includes some pre-Columbian pottery, colonial sacred art, artifacts of several indigenous communities including the Motilones and Tunebos (the two Indian groups living in Norte de Santander department), plus antiques.

NORTH OF BOGOTÁ

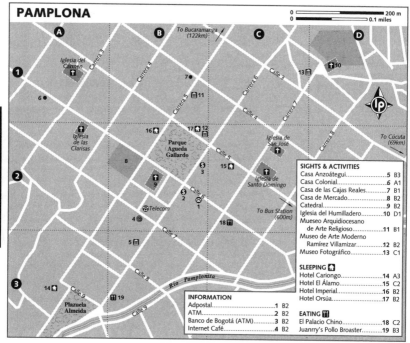

PAMPLONA

0 — 200 m
0 — 0.1 miles

To Bucaramanga
(122km)

To Cúcuta
(69km)

To Bus Station
(600m)

Iglesia del
Carmen

Iglesia
de las
Clarisas

Parque
Águeda
Gallardo

Iglesia de
San José

Iglesia de
Santo Domingo

Telecom

Río Pamplonita

Plazuela
Almeida

SIGHTS & ACTIVITIES

Casa Anzoátegui..............................5	B3
Casa Colonial...................................6	A1
Casa de las Cajas Reales................7	B1
Casa de Mercado.............................8	B2
Catedral...9	B2
Iglesia del Humilladero.................10	D1
Mueseo Arquidiocesano de Arte Religioso...................11	B1
Museo de Arte Moderno Ramírez Villamizar.............12	B2
Museo Fotográfico.........................13	C1

SLEEPING

Hotel Cariongo..............................14	A3
Hotel El Álamo..............................15	C2
Hotel Imperial...............................16	B2
Hotel Orsúa...................................17	B2

EATING

El Palacio Chino............................18	C2
Juanrry's Pollo Broaster................19	B3

INFORMATION

Adpostal..1	B2
ATM..2	B2
Banco de Bogotá (ATM)..................3	B2
Internet Café...................................4	B2

CATEDRAL

The 17th-century Catedral was badly damaged during the earthquake of 1875 and altered in the reconstruction. The five-nave interior (two outer aisles were added at the beginning of the 20th century) is rather austere except for the magnificent main retable that survived the disaster. The central figure of San Pedro was made in Spain in 1618.

Festivals & Events

Semana Santa (Easter Week). The town is known nationwide for its solemn celebrations.

Fiestas del Grito de Independencia (June/July) This is another important annual event, also called the Fiestas de Pamplona. The feast is celebrated for two weeks preceding July 4, and features concerts, bullfights and – never to be missed on such occasions – the beauty pageant.

Sleeping

Hotel Cariongo (☎ 568 1515; cnr Calle 9 & Carrera 5; d US$22) It's clear that the Cariongo has seen better days, and the entire structure appears to be coming apart at the seams, but this place still manages to be the best hotel in town. All rooms come with a TV, but not

all have hot-water showers. It's located three blocks southwest of the plaza.

Hotel El Álamo (☎ 568 2137; Calle 5 No 6-68; s/d/tr US$12/15/18) Rooms with attached bathroom are a bit small but probably the best bet in the budget category. There is a decent restaurant that serves breakfast for US$1.

Hotel Imperial (☎ 568 2571; Carrera 5 No 5-36; s/d US$10/12) Scruffier than El Álamo but still a good budget choice, the Imperial has the advantage of being right on the square, affording nice views from your window.

Hotel Orsúa (☎ 568 2470; Calle 5 No 5-67; s/d/tr US$5/10/14) On the main plaza, this hotel is one of the cheapest places to stay. It's pretty basic and rooms get little natural light, but they do have private bathrooms. A room with a TV costs about US$1 extra.

Eating

Juanrry's Pollo Broaster (Carrera 6 No 8B-49; set meals US$2; ☺ 11am-10pm) Reasonably priced roasted chicken. Check out the various caricatures on walls and you'll see Juanrry the Chicken posing with the likes of Shakira, Michael Jackson and Mick Jagger.

El Palacio Chino (☎ 568 1666; Calle 6 No 7-32; mains US$4-5) While not particularly atmospheric, this Colombian attempt at Oriental cooking produces some fresh and hot dishes of soups, noodles and steamed veggies.

Getting There & Away

Pamplona's new bus terminal is just 600m southwest of the main square. You can walk to town in about 10 minutes, or pay US$1 for a cab.

Pamplona's on the Bucaramanga–Cúcuta road, and buses pass by regularly to both Cúcuta (US$4, 1¾ hours, 72km) and Bucaramanga (US$8, 4½ hours, 124km). Bus and share-taxi companies at the station run sporadic schedules, so if one is not going at the time you want, just ask at another window. For a morning taxi ride, try **Cotranal** (☎ 568 2562).

CÚCUTA

☎ 7 / pop 560,000 / elevation 320m / temp 27°C

Hot, muggy and close to the Venezuelan border, Cúcuta is either the first or last Colombian city that many overland travelers visit. The city has a modern, if rather uninspiring, center and vast poor suburbs. There's little reason to linger, but you may need to stick around for a night if you're crossing the border.

Even if you're coming this way, you may prefer to stay overnight in Pamplona, rather than Cúcuta, as some travelers do.

Information

Adpostal (Calle 8A) North of Parque Nacional.

Bancafé (Calle 10) North of Parque Santander. Has an ATM.

Banco de Bogotá (Av 6) West of Parque Santander. Has an ATM.

Bancolombia (Av 5 No 9-80; ☹ 8am-4pm Mon-Fri, 8am-12:30pm Sat) Changes traveler's checks. There is also a branch at Av 0 No 14-50.

Corporación Mixta de Promoción de Norte de Santander (☎ 571 3395; Calle 10 No 0-30; ☹ 8am-noon & 2-6pm Mon-Fri)

Immigration The Departmento Administrativo de Seguridad (DAS) immigration post (where you have to get an exit/entry stamp in your passport) is just before the border on the Río Táchira, on the left side of the road going towards Venezuela. There's a one hour time difference between Colombia and Venezuela. Move your watch one hour forward when crossing from Colombia into Venezuela. Once in Venezuela, pick up a tourist card – it's issued

directly by the DIEX office in San Antonio del Táchira, on Carrera 9 between Calles 6 and 7.

On-Site (☎ 583 4213; Av 0 No 11-55; per hr US$0.50; ☹ 8am-10pm) Internet café.

SIS Café Internet (☎ 571 0861; Calle 14 No 4-47; per hr US$0.50; ☹ 8am-9pm Mon-Sat, 9:30am-6pm Sun)

Venezuelan consulate (☎ 579 1956; Av Camilo Daza) Located on the road that goes to the airport, about 3km north of the center. You can get there by local buses marked 'Consulado' from the bus terminal or from Calle 13 in the center.

Sights

Visit **Casa de la Cultura** (☎ 571 6689; Calle 13 No 3-67; ☹ 8am-noon & 2-6pm Mon-Fri), noted for its impressive clock tower, which has temporary art exhibitions. **Banco de la República** (☎ 575 0131; cnr Av Diagonal Santander & Calle 11; ☹ 8am-noon & 2-6pm Mon-Fri) also stages temporary exhibitions in its Area Cultural.

You can also take a short trip to Villa del Rosario (p105), 10km from Cúcuta.

Sleeping

Avoid any hotel within six blocks of the bus station; the area is grimy and unsafe at night.

Quinta Avenida (☎ 572 0086; fax 571 9202; Av 5 No 8-32; s/d incl breakfast US$33/47; ℗ ☒ ☒ ☒) One of Cúcuta's best hotels, the Quinta Avenida was recently refurbished and delivers bright, comfortable rooms, each with a modern bathroom and fridge.

Hotel Amaruc (☎ 571 7625; cnr Calle 10 & Av 3; s/d with fan US$18/23, with air-con US$24.50/32; ☒ ☒) The Amaruc overlooks the central square and all rooms come with TV, desk and phone.

Hotel La Bastilla (☎ 571 2576; Av 3 No 9-42; s/d/tr US$7/9/14) This budget option has reasonably clean rooms with private shower, small TV and firm beds. Rooms also have windows, which is rare in this price range.

Hotel Real Cúcuta (☎ 583 2014; Av 4 No 6-51; s/d/tr with fan US$8/11/15, with air-con US$11/14/18; ☒) One of the cheapest options providing aircon, the Real Cúcuta has mostly spacious triple rooms.

Eating

La Mazorca (Av 4 No 9-67; set meals US$2; mains US$5-7) Enjoy Creole meals and a choice of wines in this sunny courtyard, decorated with baskets and saddles.

Punto Cero (☎ 573 0153; Av 0 No 15-60; mains US$4-5; ☹ 24hr) A welcoming restaurant that

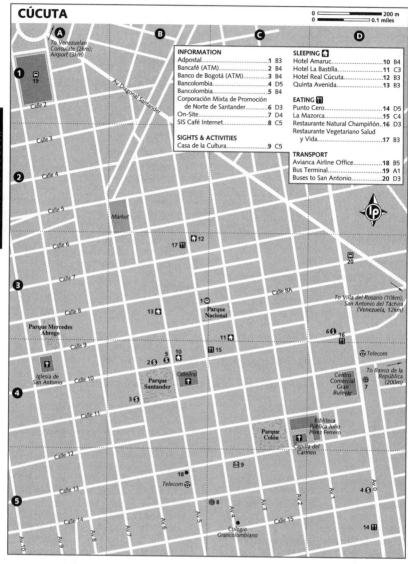

CÚCUTA

0 — 200 m
0 — 0.1 miles

INFORMATION
Adpostal...........................**1** B3
Bancafé (ATM).....................**2** B4
Banco de Bogotá (ATM).............**3** B4
Bancolombia.......................**4** D5
Bancolombia.......................**5** B4
Corporación Mixta de Promoción
de Norte de Santander.........**6** D3
On-Site...........................**7** D4
SIS Café Internet.................**8** C5

SIGHTS & ACTIVITIES
Casa de la Cultura................**9** C5

SLEEPING
Hotel Amaruc......................**10** B4
Hotel La Bastilla.................**11** C3
Hotel Real Cúcuta.................**12** B3
Quinta Avenida....................**13** B3

EATING
Punto Cero........................**14** D5
La Mazorca........................**15** C4
Restaurante Natural Champiñón.....**16** D3
Restaurante Vegetariano Salud
y Vida........................**17** B3

TRANSPORT
Avianca Airline Office............**18** B5
Bus Terminal......................**19** A1
Buses to San Antonio..............**20** D3

offers typical food, such as *bandeja paisa* (a traditional Antioquian dish) and *sancocho* (traditional soup). There are also some more upmarket restaurants further south on Av 0.

Vegetarians can choose between **Restaurante Vegetariano Salud y Vida** (Av 4 No 6-60) and **Restaurante Natural Champiñón** (Calle 10 No 0-05), both of which serve budget set lunches on weekdays.

Getting There & Away
AIR
The airport is 4km north of the city center. Minibuses that are marked 'El Trigal Molinos' (from Av 1 or Av 3 in the center) will

drop you 350m from the terminal. A taxi from the airport to the center costs US$3.

The airport handles flights to most major Colombian cities (direct or with connections), including Bogotá (US$90 to US$120 one way), Medellín (US$80 to US$120), Cali (US$90 to US$140) and Cartagena (US$90 to US$130).

There are no direct flights to Venezuela (you must go to San Antonio del Táchira, the Venezuelan border town, 12km from Cúcuta, from where there are flights to Caracas and other domestic destinations). But the airport does have a DAS post. You can find the airline office for **Avianca** (☎ 571 5161; Av 5 No 13-04) downtown.

BUS
The bus terminal is on the corner of Av 7 and Calle 1 and is very dirty and very busy – one of the most chaotic in Colombia. Watch your belongings closely. If you are arriving from Venezuela, you might be approached by some English-speaking individuals who will kindly offer their help in buying bus tickets and insuring your money. Ignore them – they are con men. Buy tickets directly from bus company offices.

There are frequent buses servicing Bucaramanga (US$13, six hours). At least two dozen buses daily run to Bogotá (US$32, 16 hours).

If you are traveling on a Berlinas bus you'll be taken to a private bus terminal a few blocks south of the center.

To Venezuela, take one of the frequent buses or shared taxis running from Cúcuta's bus terminal to San Antonio del Táchira (around US$0.50, in either pesos or bolívares). You can catch *colectivos* and buses to San Antonio from the corner of Av Diagonal Santander and Calle 8, in the center. From San Antonio's bus terminal you can go further into Venezuela. There are half-a-dozen departures daily direct to Caracas, all departing late afternoon or early evening for an overnight trip. There are no direct buses to Mérida; go to San Cristóbal and change. *Colectivos* to San Cristóbal leave frequently.

VILLA DEL ROSARIO
☎ 7 / pop 52,000 / elevation 280m / temp 27°C
Villa del Rosario, 10km southeast of Cúcuta on the road to the Venezuelan border, is the town where the constitution of Gran Colom-

bia was drawn up and passed in 1821. Gran Colombia, the union of Venezuela, Colombia, Panama and Ecuador, was brought to life in Angostura (today Ciudad Bolívar in Venezuela) in 1819. It was largely a concept of Simón Bolívar, who insisted on creating a strong, centralized republic made up of the provinces he was liberating.

In practice, this didn't happen; Gran Colombia was, since its birth, a weak, vast state incapable of being governed by a central regime. It gradually disintegrated before splitting into separate countries in 1830. Bolívar's dream came to an end before he died.

Sights
The site of this important event in Colombia's history has been converted into a park, the **Parque de la Gran Colombia**. The park's central feature is the ruin of **Templo del Congreso**, the church (built in 1802) where the sessions of the congress were held. The congress debated in the sacristy of the church from May to October, before agreeing on the final version of the bill. Then the inauguration ceremony of Bolívar and Santander as president and vice president of Gran Colombia took place in the church.

The church was almost completely destroyed by the 1875 earthquake and although some efforts were made to reconstruct it, only the dome was rebuilt (in quite a different style from the original). A marble statue of Bolívar has been placed in the rebuilt part of the church.

The park's other major sight is the **Casa Natal de Santander** (☎ 570 0741; admission US$0.80; 🕑 9am-11:30am & 2-5:30pm Mon-Fri), a large country mansion, which was the birthplace of Francisco de Paula Santander and his home for the first 13 years of his life. The house was also damaged by the earthquake of 1875 and restored in a partly altered style. It now houses a modest exhibition of documents and photos relating to Santander's life and to the congress.

Getting There & Away
To get to the Parque de la Gran Colombia from Cúcuta, take the bus to San Antonio del Táchira, which passes next to the park on the way to the border. Don't take buses marked 'Villa del Rosario' – they won't bring you anywhere near the park.

Caribbean Coast

Soaked with sunshine and steeped in history, the Caribbean coast offers a wealth of attractions that make it Colombia's biggest draw for both domestic and international visitors.

Ticking off a list 'must sees' along the coast could take several weeks, so be sure to budget accordingly. Mud volcanoes, lost cities, desert isles, impregnable fortresses and steamy nightlife can hold you captive longer than expected. Throw in superb tourist facilities, welcoming locals and dazzling festivals and you may end up a permanent resident.

The crown jewel along the coast is Cartagena, a colonial city with a beauty and romance unrivaled anywhere else in the country. Santa Marta, the last stop for the legendary liberator Simón Bolívar, also offers a sense of history, but the real reason to visit is nearby Parque Nacional Tayrona, a spectacular stretch of deserted beach and virgin rainforest.

By contrast, Ciudad Perdida (Lost City) is no picnic to reach, but the exhausting three-day trek has become a rite of passage for many travelers. Recovery from the long haul into the jungle is easy – just wander into tranquil Taganga and enjoy the sea, sand and fruit drinks.

The 1760km coast covers a range of ecosystems, from the dense jungles of Darién Gap on the border with Panama in the west, to the desert of La Guajira near Venezuela in the east.

Local inhabitants, the *costenos*, are easy-going folks of mainly African descent. Their quiet lifestyle is interrupted by raucous festivals, including the most colorful and wild of Colombian feasts, the Carnaval de Barranquilla; the Carnaval de Cartagena is only marginally less mad.

CARIBBEAN COAST

HIGHLIGHTS

- Lose yourself in **Cartagena** (p125), a magnificent colonial town and once a favorite of pirate pillagers
- Kick back in a hammock at a quiet bungalow in **Parque Nacional Tayrona** (p114)
- Trek through the jungle to mysterious **Ciudad Perdida** (p116), a great pre-Columbian city of the Tayronas
- Visit the town of **Mompós** (p140), famed for its rocking chairs and colonial architecture
- Frolic in a mud volcano at **Volcán de Lodo El Totumo** (p139)

Parque Nacional Tayrona ★

★ Ciudad Perdida

★ Volcán de Lodo El Totumo

★ Cartagena

Mompós ★

- POPULATION: 5.6 MILLION
- AREA: 85,103 SQ KM

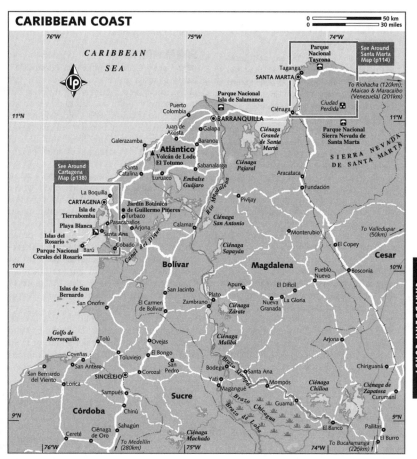

History

The Caribbean coast was inhabited by various Indian communities long before the arrival of the Spaniards. Two of these groups evolved into highly developed cultures: the Tayrona in the Sierra Nevada de Santa Marta, and the Sinú in what are now the Córdoba and Sucre departments. The technological prowess of these people is best demonstrated in the construction of several villages, including Ciudad Perdida (p116).

The coast was the first region conquered by the Spaniards. Santa Marta (founded in 1525) and Cartagena (1533) are the oldest surviving Colombian cities. Both proved valuable to the Spanish as staging posts for missions to the interior and port towns from which plundered riches were sent back to the Old World. Inevitable wealth was accompanied by pirate raids and the entire coast, especially Cartagena, was under siege for most of its early settled existence.

Postindependence, the Caribbean coast continued to thrive economically, helped by the rise of industrial Barranquilla. The newest cash cow is, surprisingly, coal. Latin America's largest coal-mining operation is the El Cerrejón coal mine on the Guajira Peninsula.

Climate

In a word: hot. Temperatures usually hover around 28°C, but the sopping wet humidity is the real killer. To beat the heat, do as

---

TRAVELING SAFELY ALONG THE CARIBBEAN COAST

Traveling along the Caribbean coast poses few hassles or dangers, but it's worth noting a few handy tips. The major problem faced by travelers is staying healthy in the face of brutal heat, humidity and the presence of tropical diseases. Stay well hydrated, keep out of the sun around midday, and protect yourself from mosquitoes and sandflies. Note that Parque Nacional Tayrona has seen cases of dengue fever and yellow fever.

---

the locals do and siesta from noon to 2pm, saving your strength for early-morning and evening activities. October brings much rain, while December and January offer cool winds that make travel more pleasant.

Getting There & Away

There are several ways to approach the Caribbean coast. The easiest option is to fly to one of the main cities – there are even some direct flights to Cartagena from North America and Europe, negating the need to fly via Bogotá. You could also approach by land from Venezuela, Medellín or Bucaramanga – the main routes are paved and there are frequent bus connections. Another option is to travel via Mompós, although minor roads are not paved and travel often requires a river crossing.

Getting Around

With some time on your hands and a sense of adventure, it's possible to travel up and down the Río Magdalena on passenger and cargo ships. Boats ply its murky waters from Barranquilla to El Banco and beyond. From El Banco, it's a 7½-hour trip upstream to Barrancbermeja (Baranca) from where you can catch a bus to Bucaramanga.

MAGDALENA

Magdalena, one of Colombia's most beautiful departments, is renowned for its coastal attractions, namely Taganga and Parque Nacional Tayrona. Its interior is less easily visited, and attractions such as Ciudad Perdida require trekking through thick jungle. If you have time, the slow boats plying the

Río Magdalena are one alternative way to explore the region.

SANTA MARTA

☎ 5 / pop 410,000 / elevation 2m / temp 28°C

Santa Marta's grace as a colonial city has faded under newer concrete buildings, but its proximity to the sea still makes it an attractive destination. For Colombians, this is one of the most popular tourist towns in the country, offering liberal amounts of sun, rum and long stretches of sandy beachfront property.

Among the city's attractions are an aquarium and the grand hacienda where Simón Bolívar died. But most travelers simply use Santa Marta as a jumping-off point for nearby attractions. El Rodadero, just to the south, is a fashionable beach resort. North of Santa Marta is the attractive fishing village of Taganga and, further northeast, the beautiful Parque Nacional Tayrona. Santa Marta is also the place to organize a trip to Ciudad Perdida, Tayrona's great pre-Hispanic city.

The climate is hot, but the sea breeze, especially in the evening, cools the city and makes it pleasant to wander about, or to sit over a beer or juice in any of the numerous open-air waterfront cafés.

History

Santa Marta lays claim to being the oldest surviving colonial town in Colombia. It was Rodrigo de Bastidas who planted a Spanish flag here in 1525, deliberately choosing a site at the foot of the Sierra Nevada de Santa Marta to serve as a convenient base for the reputedly incalculable gold treasures of the Tayronas. Bastidas had previously briefly explored the area and was aware of the Indian riches to be found.

As soon as the plundering of the Sierra began, so did the natives' resistance, and clashes followed. By the end of the 16th century the Tayronas had been wiped out and many of their extraordinary gold objects (melted down for rough material by the Spaniards) were in the Crown's coffers.

Santa Marta was also one of the early gateways to the interior of the colony. It was from here that Jiménez de Quesada set off in 1536 for his strenuous march up the Magdalena Valley, to found Bogotá two years later.

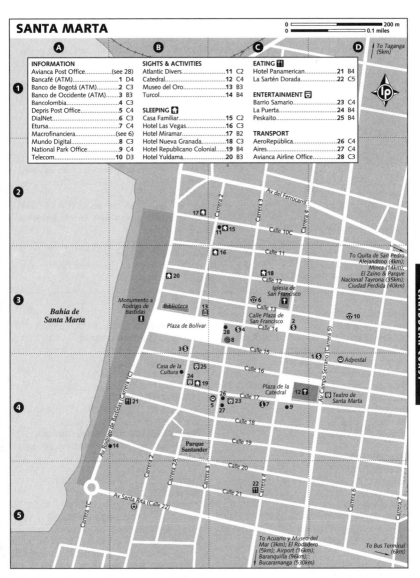

SANTA MARTA

0 ————— 200 m
0 ————— 0.1 miles

INFORMATION
Avianca Post Office.............(see 28)
Bancafé (ATM)..............................**1** D4
Banco de Bogotá (ATM)...........**2** C3
Banco de Occidente (ATM)......**3** B3
Bancolombia.................................**4** C3
Depris Post Office.......................**5** C4
DialNet..**6** C3
Etursa..**7** C4
Macrofinanciera......................(see 6)
Mundo Digital.............................**8** C3
National Park Office...................**9** C4
Telecom......................................**10** D3

SIGHTS & ACTIVITIES
Atlantic Divers..........................**11** C2
Catedral.....................................**12** C4
Museo del Oro...........................**13** B3
Turcol...**14** B4

SLEEPING
Casa Familiar.............................**15** C2
Hotel Las Vegas........................**16** C3
Hotel Miramar...........................**17** B2
Hotel Nueva Granada...............**18** C3
Hotel Republicano Colonial.....**19** B4
Hotel Yuldama...........................**20** B3

EATING
Hotel Panamerican....................**21** B4
La Sartén Dorada.......................**22** C5

ENTERTAINMENT
Barrio Samario...........................**23** C4
La Puerta....................................**24** B4
Peskaito......................................**25** B4

TRANSPORT
AeroRepública...........................**26** C4
Aires..**27** C4
Avianca Airline Office...............**28** C3

To Taganga
(5km)

Av del Ferrocarril

Calle 10C

Calle 11

To Quita de San Pedro
Alejandrino (4km);
Minca (14km);
El Zaino & Parque
Nacional Tayrona (35km);
Ciudad Perdida (40km)

Calle 12

Iglesia de
San Francisco

Monumento a
Rodrigo de
Bastidas

Biblioteca

Calle 13

Calle Plaza de
San Francisco

Plaza de Bolívar

*Bahia de
Santa Marta*

Calle 14

Calle 15

Adpostal

Casa de la
Cultura

Calle 16

Plaza de la
Catedral

Calle 17

Teatro de
Santa Marta

Calle 18

Calle 19

Parque
Santander

Calle 20

Carrera 2
Carrera 2A
Carrera 3
Carrera 4
Carrera 5
Carrera 6
Carrera 7

Av Campo Serrano (Carrera 5)

Av Rodrigo de Bastidas (Carrera 1C)

Calle 21

Av Santa Rita (Calle 22)

To Acuario y Museo del
Mar (3km); El Rodadero
(5km); Airport (16km);
Baranquilla (96km);
Bucaramanga (530km)

To Bus Terminal
(6km)

CARIBBEAN COAST

Engaged in the war with the Tayronas and repeatedly ransacked by pirates, Santa Marta didn't have many glorious moments in its colonial history and was soon over-shadowed by its younger, more progressive neighbor, Cartagena. An important date remembered nationwide in Santa Marta's history is December 17, 1830, when Simón Bolívar died here, after bringing independence to six Latin American countries.

Orientation

In Santa Marta's center, Av Rodrigo de Bastidas (Carrera 1C), which lines the beach is the principal tourist boulevard, alive until late at night. It provides a nice view over the

---

THE LOST CIVILIZATION

In pre-Columbian times, the Sierra Nevada de Santa Marta on the Caribbean coast was home to various indigenous communities, of which the Tayronas, belonging to the Chibcha linguistic family, were the dominant and most developed group. The Tayronas (also spelt Taironas) are believed to have evolved into a distinctive culture since about the 5th century AD. A millennium later, shortly before the Spaniards came, the Tayronas had developed into an outstanding civilization, based on a complex social and political organization and advanced engineering.

The Tayronas lived on the northern slopes of the Sierra Nevada where they constructed hundreds of settlements, all of a similar pattern. Due to the rugged topography, a large number of stone terraces supported by high walls had to be built as bases for their thatched wooden houses. Groups of terraces were linked by a network of stone-slab paths and stairways.

Recent surveys have pinpointed the location of about 300 Tayrona settlements scattered over the slopes, once linked by stone-paved roads. Of all these, the Ciudad Perdida (Lost City), discovered in 1975, is the largest and is thought to have been the Tayrona 'capital.'

Tayrona was the first advanced indigenous culture encountered by the Spaniards in the New World, in 1499. It was here, in the Sierra Nevada, that the conquerors were for the first time astonished by Indian gold, and the myth of El Dorado was born.

The Spaniards crisscrossed the Sierra Nevada, but met with brave resistance from the Indians. The Tayronas defended themselves fiercely, but were almost totally decimated in the course of 75 years of uninterrupted war. A handful of survivors abandoned their homes and fled into the upper reaches of the Sierra. Their traces have been lost forever.

---

bay with a small rocky island, El Morro, in the background.

Most tourist activity occurs between the waterfront and Av Campo Serrano (Carrera 5), the main commercial street.

Another hub of tourist activity, principally for Colombian holidaymakers, is the beach resort of El Rodadero, 5km south of the center. Buses shuttle frequently between the center and El Rodadero and the trip takes just 15 minutes.

Information

INTERNET ACCESS
DialNet (☎ 431 5496; Calle 13 No 3-13, San Francisco Plaza, Local 205; per hr US$0.80; ⏰ 8am-8pm Mon-Sat, 9:30am-5pm Sun) Internet café.
Mundo Digital (☎ 431 9418; Calle 15 No 2B-19, Local 108; per hr US$1.20; ⏰ 7am-8pm Mon-Fri, 8am-8pm Sat, 9am-5pm Sun) Internet café.

MONEY
Bancafé (Calle 15) ATM only.
Banco de Bogotá (cnr Calle 14 & Carrera 4) ATM only.
Banco de Occidente (Carrera 2) ATM only.
Bancolombia (☎ 421 0185; Carrera 3 No 14-10) Changes traveler's checks.
Macrofinanciera (Calle 13 No 3-13, San Francisco Plaza, Local 206) Private money changer. Other *casas de cambio* (currency-exchange offices) are located on Calle 14 between Carreras 3 and 5.

POST
Depris Post Office (Carrera 3 No 17-26; ⏰ 8am-noon & 2-6pm Mon-Fri, 8am-1pm Sat)

TELEPHONE
Telecom (☎ 421 1977; Calle 13 No 5-23)

TOURIST INFORMATION
Etursa (☎ 421 1833; Calle 17 No 3-120; ⏰ 8am-noon & 2-6pm Mon-Fri) The city tourist office.
Parques Nacionales Naturales de Colombia (☎ 423 0704; www.parquesnacionales.gov.co in Spanish; Calle 17 No 4-06)

Sights

MUSEO DEL ORO
The **Gold Museum** (☎ 421 0953; Calle 14 No 2-07; admission free; ⏰ 8-11:45am & 2-5:45pm Mon-Fri) is in the fine colonial mansion known as the Casa de la Aduana (Customs House). It has an interesting collection of Tayrona objects, mainly pottery and gold, as well as artifacts of the Kogi and Arhuaco Indians. Don't miss the impressive model of Ciudad Perdida, especially if you plan on visiting the real thing.

CATEDRAL
This massive whitewashed **cathedral** (cnr Carrera 4 & Calle 17) claims to be Colombia's oldest church, but work wasn't actually completed until the end of the 18th century, and thus

reflects the influences of various architectural styles. It holds the ashes of the town's founder, Rodrigo de Bastidas (just to the left as you enter the church). Simón Bolívar was buried here in 1830, but in 1842 his remains were taken to Caracas, his birthplace.

QUINTA DE SAN PEDRO ALEJANDRINO

This is the **hacienda** (☎ 433 0589, 433 2994; admission US$4; ☁ 9:30am-4:30pm) where Simón Bolívar spent his last days and died. The hacienda was established at the beginning of the 17th century and was engaged in cultivating and processing sugarcane. It had its own *trapiche* (sugarcane mill) and a *destilería* (distillery).

During the Bolívar era, the hacienda was owned by a Spaniard, Joaquín de Mier, a devoted supporter of Colombia's independence cause. He invited Bolívar to stay and take a rest at his home before his intended journey to Europe.

Several monuments have been built on the grounds in remembrance of Bolívar, the most imposing of which is a massive central structure called the Altar de la Patria. Just to the right of this is the Museo Bolivariano, which features works of art donated by Latin American artists, particularly those from Colombia, Venezuela, Panama, Ecuador, Peru and Bolivia, the countries liberated by Bolívar.

The quinta is in the far eastern suburb of Mamatoco, about 4km from the city center. To get there, take the Mamatoco bus from the waterfront (Carrera 1C); it's a 20-minute trip to the hacienda. The quinta may be closed on Monday and/or Tuesday in the off season – call before setting off.

EL RODADERO

Quiet resort town of El Rodadero has sun, sand, sea and little else. Popular with Colombian tourists, the town has a wide beach lined with high-rise apartment blocks and upmarket hotels, plus a collection of restaurants, bars and discos. It gets very crowded during Colombian holiday periods, when prices can skyrocket. El Rodadero is some 5km south of Santa Marta's center and is linked by frequent bus service.

ACUARIO Y MUSEO DEL MAR

The **aquarium** and **museum** (☎ 422 7222; admission US$5; ☁ 9am-4pm) are on the seashore 2km northwest of El Rodadero. The aquarium has sharks, dolphins, turtles, seals and other marine species, and a dolphin show is held when tourists come. The attached museum displays an odd variety of objects, ranging from copies of Inca ceramics to the propeller of an airplane that crashed nearby.

Transport to the aquarium is provided by boats operated from the beach in El Rodadero; tickets can be bought from the stands on the beach (US$3 return).

Activities

Santa Marta is an important center of scuba diving. Most dive schools have settled in nearby Taganga (p113), but there are also some operators in the city center, including **Atlantic Divers** (☎ 421 4883; Calle 10C No 2-08).

There's some good **hiking** around Santa Marta, including walks in the Parque Nacional Tayrona, though if you're after some longer and more adventurous trekking, the hike to Ciudad Perdida (p116) is the region's showpiece.

Tours

Santa Marta's tour market mainly revolves around Ciudad Perdida (p116). Tours are organized by **Turcol** (☎ 421 2256, 433 3737; turcol24@hotmail.com; Carrera 1C No 20-15). You can book and pay for the tour through some hotels (eg the Hotel Miramar or Casa Familiar), which will then transfer your application and payment to Turcol.

Sleeping

Santa Marta *centro* (center) is jam packed with small hotels and family-run residencies, most of them cheap and fairly laid back. If the following are full, there are more options just a few steps away. If you prefer to stay outside town, other options include El Rodadero, Minca and Taganga.

CENTRO

Hotel Nueva Granada (☎ 421 1337; hotelnuevagranada.com; Calle 12 No 3-17; s/d US$11/16, with air-con US$16/23; ☒ 🖥 🖨) Value for money; probably the best midrange place in town. Well maintained (rare in Santa Marta); there's a pretty courtyard with a small swimming pool. The downside is the smallish rooms.

Casa Familiar (☎ 421 1697; www.hospederiacasafamiliar.freeservers.com; Calle 10C No 2-14; dm/s/d/tr US$4/5/8/10) This friendly and clean high-rise hotel is a popular backpacker hangout, with both private rooms and dorms. The upper floors offer a view and there's a nice rooftop terrace.

Hotel Miramar (☎ 423 3276; elmiramar_santama rta@yahoo.com; Calle 10C No 1C-59; dm/s/d US$4/4.50/9; 🖳) Hotel Miramar has long been the archetypal gringo hotel, with a noisy, hippie-type atmosphere, but it's very basic and unkempt. It has a café serving budget meals, snacks, soft drinks and beer. This is also the place to come to inquire about treks and excursions around the area.

Hotel Las Vegas (☎ 421 5094; Calle 11 No 2-08; s/d US$5.50/10, with air-con US$9.50/13.50; 🖳) Small but functional, Las Vegas has some of the cheapest air-con rooms in town. Streetside rooms have a window and balcony but do get noisy.

Hotel Republicano Colonial (☎ 421 2942; Calle 17 No 2-43; s/d US$10.50/15, with air-con US$16/18; 🖳) This reasonable option is just a couple of blocks from the beach. Rooms are boxy and dim but do have air-con.

Hotel Yuldama (☎ 421 0063; hotelyuldama@reserv ashoteleras.com.co; Carrera 1C No 12-19; s/d with air-con & breakfast US$32/40; 🖳) The best among several hotels that offer a sea view.

EL RODADERO

Hotel La Sierra (☎ 422 7960; lasierra@germanmoral esehijos.com; Carrera Primera No 90-47; s/d incl breakfast US$53/68; 🖳 🖳) With its beachside location, sweeping views of the sea from the balconies and well-appointed rooms, this is one of El Rodadero's best sleeping options.

Hotel Becoma (☎ 422 7340, 422 7112; hotelbet oma@etb.net.co; Calle 8 No 1-58; s/d/ste US$18/30/36; 🖳) Just one block from the beach, this reasonably priced dinosaur is a good budget choice. Suites are a bit larger and have better views.

MINCA

Should you want to escape the heat and people, the village of Minca is located at 600m, high on the slopes of the Sierra Nevada de Santa Marta. Minca is reached by hourly pick-up truck from Santa Marta's market (US$1.25, 40 minutes), or take a taxi (US$8).

Sans Souci (☎ 310-710 8563; sanssouciminca@yahoo .com; r US$11-13) Sans Souci is a German-run place offering simple rooms plus meals and the use of the kitchen. It's a good place to relax, walk, rent a mountain bike or ride horses or mules. You can get a small discount by working on the farm.

Eating

There are a lot of cheap restaurants around the budget hotels, particularly on Calles 11 and 12 near the waterfront, where you can get an unsophisticated set meal for at most US$2. **La Sartén Dorada** (☎ 431 0415; cnr Carrera 4 & Calle 21; mains US$4-7; 🕒 11:15am- 3:30pm) is one of the cheaper restaurants that does good seafood.

The Hotel Miramar restaurant serves reasonable budget breakfasts, lunches and dinners. For something more upscale, try the restaurant at **Hotel Panamerican** (☎ 423 3276; Carrera 1C; dishes US$2-3) considered one of the best in town.

Entertainment

Santa Marta's nightlife really heats up on weekends and you'll have no trouble finding a place to dance.

La Puerta (Calle 17 No 2-29; 🕒 6pm-3am Tue-Sat) There's no sign outside, but it's still easy to find La Puerta: just look for the throng of people trying to get through its doors on a weekend night. It's a lively student place offering a mix of rock and salsa music, and it gets very crowded.

La Escollera (☎ 422 9590; Calle 5 No 4-107, El Roda- dero; cover US$13; 🕒 9pm-4am Wed-Sun) This trendy and expensive disco is on a small islet in the northern end of El Rodadero.

El Garaje (☎ 421 9003; Taganga; 🕒 10pm-late Wed- Sat) Well worth visiting on a Wednesday when the rest of Santa Marta is quiet, El Garaje is a fun, open-air bar at the back end of Taganga. It's best after midnight.

Other options:

Barrio Samario (☎ 310 710 9649; Calle 17 No 3-36; 🕒 6pm-3am) This Belgian-run salsa bar reels in a slightly more mature crowd.

Peskaito (☎ 315 729 4818; Calle 16 No 2-08; 🕒 4pm- 3am) Open-air dance bar.

Getting There & Away

AIR

The airport is 16km south of the city on the Barranquilla–Bogotá road. City buses marked 'El Rodadero Aeropuerto' will take you there in 45 minutes from Carrera 1C. **Avianca** (☎ 421 4018; Carrera 2A No 14-47), **AeroRe- pública** (cnr Carrera 3 & Calle 17) and **Aires** (Carrera 3) service Santa Marta. Flights include Bogotá (US$80 to US$130 one way) and Medellín (US$80 to US$130).

BUS
The terminal is on the southeastern outskirts of the city. Frequent minibuses go there from Carrera 1C in the center.

Half-a-dozen buses run daily to Bogotá (US$41, 16 hours) and roughly the same number travel to Bucaramanga (US$28, nine hours). Buses travelling to Barranquilla (US$4, 1¾ hours) depart every 15 to 30 minutes. Some of these buses go direct to Cartagena (US$10, four hours), but if not, there are immediate connections in Barranquilla.

Half-hourly buses head off to Maicao (US$10, four hours), where you change for a *colectivo* (shared taxi or minibus) to Maracaibo (Venezuela). *Colectivos* depart regularly from about 5am to 3pm (US$10, 2½ hours) and go as far as Maracaibo's bus terminal. Note that Maicao is widely and justifiably known as a lawless town and can be unsafe – stay there as briefly as possible and don't move outside the bus terminal. Security in this area has improved in recent years, though it's still a good idea to take precautions.

There are also three buses daily from Santa Marta direct to Maracaibo (US$29, seven hours), operated by Expreso Brasilia, Expresos Amerlujo and Unitransco/Bus Ven. They arrive from Cartagena, go to Maracaibo and continue to Caracas. All passport formalities are done in Paraguachón on the border. Change money here, expect a bag search and wind your clock forward one hour when crossing from Colombia to Venezuela.

TAGANGA
☎ 5 / pop 2500 / elevation 2m / temp 28°C
Taganga is a small fishing village set in a beautiful, deep, horseshoe-shaped bay, 5km northeast of Santa Marta. The beach here is packed with boats, open-air restaurants and bars blasting out music at full volume. Its reputation as a backpacker hangout is growing and there are now several places to stay and eat.

Don't miss Playa Grande, a magnificent bay northwest of the village. Walk there (20 minutes) or take a boat from Taganga

(US$1). The beach is lined with palm-thatched restaurants serving fried fish.

Activities
Taganga is a popular **scuba-diving** center, with half-a-dozen dive schools offering dives and courses. Local services here are among the cheapest you can find in Colombia. A four-day open-water PADI/NAUI course including six dives is advertised for US$200 and a minicourse with two dives for US$45. The best local schools include:
Calipso Dive Center (☎ 421 9146; www.calipsodive center.com in Spanish; Calle 12 No 1-40) Reliable and specializes in multiday 'dive safaris.' All-inclusive dive safaris include food, two or three dives per day and accommodations on the boat or on a secluded beach.
Centro de Buceo Poseidon (☎ 421 9224; www .poseidondivecenter.com; Calle 18 No 1-69)
Centro de Buceo Tayrona (☎ 421 9195; Calle 18 No 1-39)

Sleeping & Eating
Casa de Felipe (☎ 421 9120; www.lacasadefelipe.com; Carrera 5A No 19-13; dm/s/d/tr US$4/10/13/18; 💻) Run by a friendly Frenchman, Jean-Philippe, this quiet and pleasant place offers four rooms with bathrooms and three suites with bathrooms and kitchenettes, and you can have breakfast if you want for an extra US$2. It's located a few blocks uphill from the beach, past the soccer pitch.
Casa Blanca (☎ 421 9232; barbus85@latinmail.com; Carrera 1 No 18-161; r per person US$6; 💻) If beachfront property is a priority, you can't get much closer than Casa Blanca. Each of its 10 rooms has a private bathroom and a balcony with a hammock overlooking the bay. Guests can use the kitchen, fridge and washing machine free of charge. It's not as clean as La Casa de Felipe and is always crowded.
Techos Azules (Blue Roofs ☎ 421 9141; cacabelo freddy@yahoo.com.mx; r per person US$6.50) Many travelers recommend this new hotel, located uphill from the Casa Blanca, between the sea and the road into town. Rooms come with private bathroom and are clean and comfortable,. It also has good beach access. Kitchen and laundry facilities are available too.
Pelikan Hostal (☎ 423 3736; Carrera 2 No 17-04; r per person US$6) Pelikan is reasonably close to the beach and is fairly clean, but is short on atmosphere.

CARIBBEAN COAST

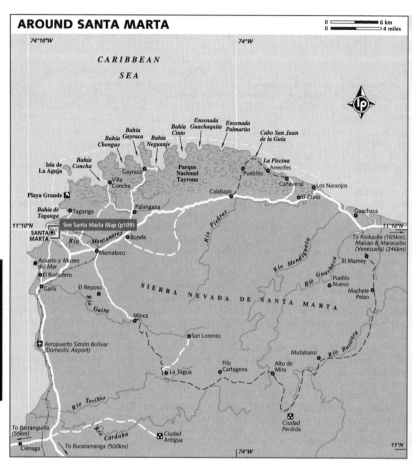

AROUND SANTA MARTA

There are a string of open-air budget **restaurants** along the waterfront, where a fresh fried fish with rice and salad shouldn't cost more than US$5. For entertainment, check out El Garaje (p112).

Getting There & Away
Taganga is easily accessible; there are frequent minibuses (US$0.25, 15 minutes) from Carrera 1C in Santa Marta.

PARQUE NACIONAL TAYRONA
One of Colombia's most popular national parks, Tayrona is set on the jungle-covered coast at the foot of the Sierra Nevada de Santa Marta. The park stretches along the coast from the Bahía de Taganga near Santa Marta to the mouth of the Río Piedras, 35km to the east.

The scenery varies from sandy beaches along the coast in the north to rainforest at an altitude of 600m on the southern limits of the park. The extreme western part is arid, with light-brown hills and xerophytic plant species, such as cacti. The central and eastern parts of the park are wetter and more verdant, largely covered by rainforest. May to June and September to November are the wettest periods. Many animals live in the park but most stay out of sight, deep in the forest.

The region was once the territory of the Tayrona Indians, and some archeological remains have been found in the park. The most important of these are the ruins of the pre-Hispanic town of Pueblito (called Chairama in the indigenous language), considered to have been one of Tayrona's major settlements.

For many travelers, the park's biggest attraction is its beaches, set in deep bays and shaded with coconut palms. In fact, Tayrona beaches are among the loveliest and most picturesque on Colombia's coast. Some of the beaches are bordered by coral reefs providing reasonable snorkeling and scuba-diving opportunities. Bring all your own snorkeling gear from Santa Marta – there is nowhere to rent equipment in the park. Mosquito repellent is also essential.

Orientation

Tayrona's eastern part features most of the park's attractions and tourist facilities, and is by far the most popular and visited area of the park. Its main gateway is El Zaíno, 34km east of Santa Marta on the coastal road to Riohacha, where you pay the US$9 park admission fee.

From El Zaíno, a 4km paved side road goes northwest to Cañaveral, on the seaside. Here is the park's administrative center, a campground, *cabañas* (cabins), a restaurant and the small Museo Arqueológico Chairama, which displays some archeological finds excavated in Pueblito. The beaches in Cañaveral are good, but there is no shade, and swimming can be dangerous because of treacherous offshore currents.

From Cañaveral, most visitors take a 45-minute walk west along a trail to Arrecifes, where there are budget lodging and eating facilities. Bear in mind that sea currents here are just as dangerous as those in Cañaveral.

From Arrecifes, a 20-minute walk northwest along the beach will bring you to La Piscina, a deep bay with quiet waters, making it reasonably safe for swimming and snorkeling.

Another 20-minute walk by path will take you to the Cabo San Juan de la Guía, a beautiful cape with good beaches.

From the cape, a scenic path goes inland uphill to Pueblito, providing some splendid tropical forest scenery. It will get you to Pueblito in a bit more than an hour. Not much of Pueblito's urban tissue has survived, apart from small fragments of the

stone paths and foundations of houses, but it's worth seeing, especially if you aren't planning a trip to Ciudad Perdida.

From Pueblito, a path continues southwest to Calabazo on the main road, but it may be safer not to walk this way – some cases of robbery have been reported here. Check the current safety situation with the park rangers if you want to do this trip.

There are two other tourist areas in Tayrona – Bahía Concha in the western part of the park and Bahía Neguanje in the central sector – but they are nowhere near as popular or visited as the Cañaveral-Arrecifes area. They are accessible by separate roads from Santa Marta, but there's no road or path linking the two bays within the park. Both bays have snorkeling and scuba-diving sites. Tourist facilities are scarce on both beaches.

Sleeping & Eating

In Cañaveral, the park's management operates **Ecohabs** (2-bed/4-bed cabins US$31/46) – a colony of *cabañas*. They are made in the style of Tayrona huts and are spectacularly set on a coastal hill. There are 11 six-bed *cabañas* and three three-bed *cabañas*. Rates rise in the tourist season by about 20%. Another larger cabin at the foot of the hill houses a restaurant.

The park's authorities also run a **camp site** (per person US$5) in Cañaveral during the tourist season, but it's run-down, unkempt and largely overrated. You need to book both cabins and tent sites through the Parques Nacionales Naturales de Colombia (p110) in Santa Marta. You can also do it through the office in Bogotá (p54).

In Arrecifes, there are two places to stay and eat. **Rancho Lindo** (camp sites per person US$1.50, hammocks US$2.50, 2-bed/4-bed cabins US$31/46) is located to your right as you walk into Arrecifes. It has accommodations as well as a restaurant (meals US$4 to US$6). **Finca El Paraíso** (☎ 310 691 3626; camp sites US$4.50, hammocks US$2.50, cabins per person US$9) is closer to the beach, and offers cabins, under-cover hammocks, camp sites and a restaurant (meals US$5 to US$7).

A 10-minute walk further west along the beach is **Bucarú**, an offspring of El Paraíso. It offers similar facilities for marginally less.

Both Finca El Paraíso and Bucarú can be booked through their **Santa Marta office**

(☎ 431 3130; Carrera 7B No 28a-103), or you could just turn up.

Most backpackers end up at Cabo San Juan de la Guía, where there is cheap accommodations in hammocks (US$2).

Getting There & Away

Cañaveral is easy to get to on your own from Santa Marta. Take a minibus to Palomino and get off in El Zaíno (US$2.50, one hour); Palomino minibuses depart every 20 to 30 minutes from Santa Marta's market (at the corner of Carrera 11 and Calle 11). From El Zaíno, walk for 50 minutes to Cañaveral or catch the jeep that shuttles regularly between the two towns (US$0.60, 10 minutes). Alternatively, a tourist bus departs most days from outside the Hotel Miramar at 10am, driving direct to Cañaveral.

Bahía Concha and Bahía Neguanje are accessible by unsurfaced roads, but there's no public transport on these roads. In the tourist season, jeeps go to both bays from Santa Marta; they park on Carrera 1C near Turcol. Inquire at the tourist office and backpackers hotels (Hotel Miramar, Casa Familiar), which may know about other options.

When there is demand, a boat may take tourists to the park from Taganga for US$11 each. Ask around the boat dock so that something can be prearranged.

CIUDAD PERDIDA

Ciudad Perdida (literally 'Lost City') is one of the largest pre-Columbian towns discovered in the Americas. Known by its indigenous name of Teyuna, it was built by the Tayrona Indians on the northern slopes of the Sierra Nevada de Santa Marta, and was most probably their biggest urban center.

The city was built between the 11th and 14th centuries, though its origins are much older, going back to perhaps the 7th century. Spreading over an area of about 2 sq km, it is the largest Tayrona city found so far, and it appears to be their major political and economic center. Some 2000 to 4000 people are believed to have lived here.

During the Conquest, the Spaniards wiped out the Tayronas, and their settlements disappeared without a trace under lush tropical vegetation. So did Ciudad Perdida for four centuries, until its discovery by *guaqueros* (treasure hunters) in 1975.

It was a local man, Florentino Sepúlveda, and his two sons Julio César and Jacobo, who stumbled upon this city in one of their grave robbing expeditions.

Word spread like wildfire and soon other *guaqueros* came to Ciudad Perdida. Fighting broke out between rival gangs, and Julio César was one of the casualties. In 1976 the government sent in troops and archeologists to protect the site and learn its secrets, but sporadic fighting and looting continued for several years.

Ciudad Perdida lies on the steep slopes of the upper Río Buritaca valley at an altitude between 950m and 1300m. The central part of the city is set on a ridge from which various stone paths lead down to other sectors on the slopes. Although the wooden houses of the Tayronas are long gone, the stone structures, including terraces and stairways, remain in remarkably good shape.

There are about 150 terraces, most of which once served as foundations for the houses. The largest terraces are set on the central ridge and these were used for ritual ceremonies. Today, the city is quite overgrown, which gives it a somewhat mysterious air.

Archeological digs have uncovered Tayrona objects (fortunately, the *guaqueros* didn't manage to take everything), mainly various kinds of pottery (both ceremonial and utensil), goldwork and unique necklaces made of semiprecious stones. Some of these objects are on display in the Museo del Oro in Santa Marta and Bogotá. It's a good idea to visit the museum in Santa Marta before going to Ciudad Perdida.

Getting There & Away

Ciudad Perdida lies about 40km southeast of Santa Marta as the crow flies. It's hidden deep in the thick forest amid rugged mountains, far away from any human settlement, and without access roads. The way to get there is by foot and the return trip takes six days. The trail begins in El Mamey, which is reached by vehicle.

Access to Ciudad Perdida is by tour only, organized by Turcol (p111) in Santa Marta. You cannot do the trip on your own or hire an independent guide. The price is around US$180 per person for the all-inclusive six-day tour. This includes transport, food, accommodations (hammocks), porters, guides and all necessary permits. You carry your own personal belongings. Take a flashlight, water container and insect repellent.

Tours are in groups of four to 12 people, and depart year-round as soon as a group is assembled. In the high season, expect a tour to set off every few days. In the off season, there may be just one tour a week.

The trip takes three days uphill to Ciudad Perdida, one day at the site and two days back down. The hike may be tiring due to the heat, and if it's wet (as it is most of the year) the paths are pretty muddy. The driest period is from late December to February or early March. There are several creeks to cross on the way; be prepared to get your shoes wet and carry a spare pair.

ATLÁNTICO

Economically diverse, Atlántico is dominated by Barranquilla's port traffic and large-scale agriculture further inland. The state is also well known for its festivals – events take place every month, culminating in the largest party of them all, Carnaval in Barranquilla.

BARRANQUILLA

☎ 5 / pop 1.3 million / elevation 10m / temp 28°C
A maze of concrete blocks and dusty streets, Barranquilla is an industrial giant that now ranks as Colombia's fourth biggest city. There are few tourist attractions and little reason to visit, unless you happen to be around during Barranquilla's explosive four-day Carnaval, one of the biggest and best fiestas in Colombia.

History
The town was founded in 1629, but did not gain importance until the middle of the 19th century. Despite its potential as a port on the country's main fluvial artery, navigation problems at the mouth of the Río Magdalena hindered development. Most of the merchandise moving up and down the Magdalena passed through Cartagena, using Canal del Dique which joins the river about 100km upstream from its mouth.

Only at the end of the 19th century did progress really begin. The opening of Puerto Colombia, Barranquilla's port built

on the coastline 15km west of the town, boosted the development of the city, both as a fluvial and sea port.

By the early 20th century, Barranquilla was one of the major ports from which local goods, primarily coffee, were shipped overseas.

Progress attracted both Colombians from other regions and foreigners, mainly from the USA, Germany, Italy and the Middle East. This, in turn, gave the city an injection of foreign capital and accelerated its growth. It also brought about the city's cosmopolitan character.

Orientation
Barranquilla's limits are marked by a ring road, Vía Circunvalación. The city center (where the town was originally settled) is along the Paseo Bolívar, close to the river. Most of this sector, especially the area between the Paseo and the river, is inhabited by wild street commerce – it's actually one vast market.

About 3km to the northwest is El Prado, Barranquilla's new center, and the most pleasant district of the city.

The bus terminal is about 1km off the southern edge of the city, beyond Vía Circunvalación. The airport is still further south.

Information
Avianca Post Office (☎ 330 2255; Calle 72 & Carrera 58)
Bancolombia (Carrera 53 No 68-69)
Call Center (☎ 368 9351; Carrera 48 No 70-218; ☽ 7:30am-8pm Mon-Sat, 8:30am-3:30pm Sun)
Chat Net (☎ 369 2600; Carrera 54 No 72-111; per hr US$0.80; ☽ 8am-8:30pm Mon-Sat) Internet café.
Comité Mixto de Promoción Turística del Atlántico (☎ 330 3862; Vía Cuarenta No 36-135; ☽ 8am-noon & 2-6pm Mon-Fri) The tourist office is in the Antiguo Edificio de Aduana, reasonable walking distance southeast of El Prado.
Giros & Finanzas (Carrera 54 No 72-80, Locales 22-24) Changes cash, traveler's checks and represents Western Union.
Prado Web Place (☎ 358 4577; Calle 70 No 53-33; per hr US$0.80; ☽ 9am-7pm Mon-Fri, 9am-2pm Sat) Internet café.

Sights
The two areas you might want to visit are the city center and El Prado. They are just a few kilometres apart, but a world away from each other.

CARIBBEAN COAST

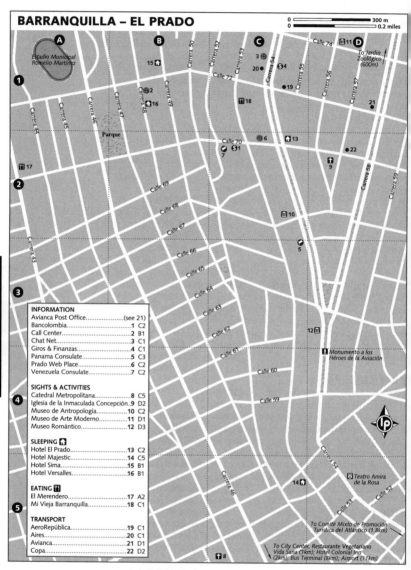

BARRANQUILLA – EL PRADO

The city center is cut in two by Paseo Bolívar. Halfway along is the mock-Gothic **Iglesia de San Nicolás** (cnr Paseo Bolívar & Carrera 42), worth entering for its main altarpiece and pulpit. To the east of the church is the sprawling market that spreads down to the river. Contraband items, presumably coming here from Maicao, are plentiful.

El Prado is cleaner, greener and safer than the center. Calle 72 is the district's principal shopping street, lined with restaurants, shops and supermarkets.

Strolling around, you'll find some architectural relics from the late 19th and early 20th centuries, the time when El Prado began to develop. Note the buildings in the

LA GRAN CARNAVAL

Every year, bustling Barranquilla takes off four days to fire up its famous Carnaval, one of the biggest and best that Colombia can offer. With a century-long official history (but with traditions dating back much further), the festival preceding Ash Wednesday (February or March) paralyses all normal city activities, such as urban transport and commerce, as the streets are taken over by dancers, musicians, parades and masquerades.

The Carnaval begins on Saturday with La Batalla de Flores (the Battle of Flowers), a float parade. It continues on Sunday with La Gran Parada, when thousands of party-goers put on costumes and file through the streets. On Monday there is El Festival de Orquestas, a marathon concert of Caribbean music groups. The Carnaval concludes on Tuesday with a symbolic burial of Joselito Carnaval.

Apart from the official program, it is a round-the-clock party, fueled by large quantities of spirits. An estimated 100,000 cases of rum and *aguardiente* (anise-flavored liquor) are sold. Although it is getting more commercialized and lacks some of the spontaneity of years ago, it is still the most colorful and maddest of all of Colombia's festivals.

Unfortunately, as at all such crowded events, it's a focus for all sorts of local and visiting thieves and robbers. Be on guard, especially if you plan to photograph or film the event. Think twice before accepting drinks or smokes from strangers or new 'friends.'

The last factor to consider is accommodations. Unless you have booked a room well in advance you can almost forget about finding a place to stay. Furthermore, room rates tend to rise by at least 20%.

Islamic-influenced Moorish style – you'll find some of them on and just off Carrera 54. Include in your trip the following attractions, most of which are in El Prado or its vicinity.

CATEDRAL METROPOLITANA

The modern **cathedral** (cnr Calle 53 & Carrera 46) was completed in 1982. Don't be put off by its squat, heavy, somewhat bunkerlike exterior – go inside. The interior features a number of large stained-glass windows in the side walls and over the main entrance. There are two mosaics on the side walls: of María Reyna y Auxiliadora (patron saint of the cathedral) and of San José. Each mosaic is composed of about 400,000 pieces of colored glass imported from Germany.

Over the high altar is a 16m-high bronze sculpture of Cristo Libertador, a 16-ton work by Rodrigo Arenas Betancur, Colombia's preeminent monument designer.

MUSEO ROMÁNTICO

Confusingly named, the **Romantic Museum** (☎ 344 4591; Carrera 54 No 59-199; adult/student US$2/1; 🕑 8:30-11:30am & 2-5:30pm Mon-Fri, 9am-3pm Sat) is actually a museum of the city's history, featuring exhibits related to Barranquilla's past. Some rooms are dedicated to migrant communities – German and Jewish among others – that have influenced the region.

MUSEO DE ANTROPOLOGÍA

The **Museum of Anthropology** (☎ 358 8488; Calle 68 No 53-45; admission free; 🕑 8am-noon & 2:30-5pm Mon-Fri), on the 1st floor of the building of the Universidad del Atlántico, displays a small collection of pre-Columbian pottery from different regions, including pieces from the Calima, Tumaco and Nariño cultures.

MUSEO DE ARTE MODERNO

The **Museum of Modern Art** (☎ 360 9952; Carrera 56 No 74-22; admission free; 🕑 3-7pm Mon, 9am-1pm & 3-7pm Tue-Sat) shows the works of several local artists, as well as some nationally renowned painters, including Ferdinand Botero.

JARDÍN ZOOLÓGICO

The **zoo** (☎ 353 0605; Calle 76 No 68-40; admission US$2.50; 🕑 9am-5:30pm) has some 2000 animals from about 300 species, including birds and several ligers (cross between a lion and a Bengal tiger, first bred in Colombia). Some cages look far too small for their inhabitants. A small Museo de Historia Natural is within the zoo grounds. To get to the zoo from the city center, take the bus marked 'Vía Cuarenta' from Plaza de Bolívar. From El Prado, it's a 10- to 15-minute walk.

Sleeping

The center of budget accommodations is on and around Paseo Bolívar (Calle 34). This area is not that safe at night, so limit your evening stroll and keep your eyes open. If you would like to be safer and in a more pleasant environment, stay in El Prado; it is a rather upper-class district so you will pay for the privilege.

Hotel El Prado (☎ 369 7777; www.hotelelprado .com in Spanish; Carrera 54 No 70-10; s/d/ste with air-con US$72/95/118; P ⊠ ⊞ ⊞ ⊠) A great place with spacious rooms, palm trees and a tropical atmosphere. Built in 1928, it came to be Barranquilla's poshest and trendiest place to stay, and remains so today.

Hotel Colonial Inn (☎ 379 0241; Calle 42 No 43-131; s/d/tr US$11/16/18; ⊠) Located in the city center, the Colonial Inn has fairly comfortable rooms with TV and private bathroom.

Hotel Sima (☎ 358 4600; hotelsima@enred.com; Carrera 49 No 72-19; s/d US$30/36; ⊠) Sima is about as cheap as they come in El Prado. The price includes breakfast, but if you forego the option, the receptionist has been known to give a discount.

Hotel Majestic (☎ 349 1010, 349 2002; www.cotelco .org/hotelmajestic/index.html in Spanish; Carrera 53 No 54-41; s/d/tr US$41/52/63; ⊠ ⊞) With its Moorish air, the Majestic stands out as one of the most stylish places to stay. The hotel has a charming restaurant and breakfast is included.

Hotel Versalles (☎ 368 6970; www.hotelversalles inn.com in Spanish; Carrera 48 No 70-188; s/d US$38/60; ⊠ ⊞) Modern hotel with 41 comfortable rooms and a sauna. Breakfast is included.

Eating

The central city area, along and off Paseo Bolívar, is full of cheap restaurants which offer set meals for US$1 to US$2. Many street stalls sell delicious *arepas de huevo* (a fried maize dough with an egg inside), the local specialty. Vegetarians can have tasty lunches at **Restaurante Vegetariano Vida Sana** (Carrera 44 No 44-74).

El Prado is for finer dining, but there are a number of budget eateries to choose from as well, many of which are on Calle 70.

Mi Vieja Barranquilla (Carrera 53 No 70-150; mains US$5-7; ⊗ 11am-3pm & 6-10pm Mon-Thu, 11am-3pm & 6pm-3am Fri & Sat, 11am-4pm Sun) One of the more unusual places, set in a spacious open-air courtyard painted and decorated to look like a plaza of some imaginary colonial town. It serves typical local food and has live folk music on some evenings.

El Merendero (☎ 345 0956; Carrera 43 No 70-48; ⊗ 11am-midnight) Bring your appetite or a friend because the portions of food at this steakhouse are enormous. It's an open-air place and meals are served in atmospheric thatched huts.

Getting There & Away

AIR

The airport is about 10km south of the city center and is accessible by urban buses. Almost all main Colombian carriers service Barranquilla. Main destinations include Bogotá (US$85 to US$125 one way), Medellín (US$90 to US$135), Cali (US$90 to US$140) and San Andrés (US$100 to US$140). El Prado has airline ticketing offices for **Copa** (☎ 358 8463; cnr Carrera 57 & Calle 72), **Aires** (Carrera 54), **AeroRepública** (☎ 368 4040; Calle 72 No 54-49) and **Avianca** (☎ 330 2255; cnr Calle 72 & Carrera 58).

BUS

The bus terminal is located 7km from the city center. It's not convenient, and it may take up to an hour to get to the terminal by urban bus. It's much faster to go by taxi (US$4, 20 minutes).

A dozen buses travel daily to Bogotá (US$36, 18 hours), Bucaramanga (US$28, 10 hours) and Medellín (US$32, 14 hours). Buses to Cartagena (US$5, two hours) depart every 10 to 15 minutes, as do the buses to Santa Marta (US$4, 1¾ hours).

There are three buses daily operating direct to Maracaibo and on to Caracas (both in Venezuela).

BOLÍVAR

With Cartagena as its major port and the Islas del Rosario just offshore, this department is one of the most visited in Colombia. It's also a major center for commerce, thanks to the Canal del Dique, an important waterway that connects Cartagena with ports down the Río Magdalena. Mompós, located 248km south of Cartagena, was a historic refuge for the famed port city when it was under siege by pirates. It's also well worth visiting for its time warp atmosphere.

(Continued on page 125)

CARIBBEAN COAST

Iglesia del Carmen (p61), La Candelaria, Bogotá

Craft work (p231), Bogotá

Change of the president´s guard at Plaza de Bolívar (p55), Bogotá

KRZYSZTOF DYDYNSKI

La Piscinita (p148), San Andrés

Parque El Gallineral (p93), San Gil

KRZYSZTOF DYDYNSKI

KRZYSZTOF DYDYNSKI

Mud bath, Volcán de Lodo El Totumo (p139)

A trip in a fisherman's boat around Bocagrande and El Laguito, Cartagena (p125)

PATRICIA RINCON M

KRZYSZTOF DYDYNSKI

Craft shop, Medellín (p157)

One of the 23 large, bronze sculptures by Colombia's most famous artist, Fernando Botero, in front of Medellín's Museo de Antioquia (p159)

KRZYSZTOF DYDYNSKI

Santuario de Las Lajas (p208), a neo-
Gothic castle spanning the Río Guaitara

A Guambiano Indian woman from the Silvia
region (p199)

Stone statue, Parque Arqueológico (p200), San Agustín

(Continued from page 120)

CARTAGENA

☎ 5 / pop 1.1 million / elevation 5m / temp 28°C
A fairy-tale city of romance, legends and sheer beauty, Cartagena de Indias is an addictive place that can be hard to escape. This is the place to drop all sightseeing routines. Instead, just stroll through Cartagena's maze of cobbled alleys, where enormous balconies are shrouded in bougainvilla and massive churches cast their shadows across leafy plazas. Take time out to relax at one of Cartagena's many open-air cafés, prime viewing spots to watch the parade of horse-drawn carriages, fashionable locals and mystified tourists. When the bustling city gets too much, you can always escape to the nearby Islas de Rosario.

Cartagena offers a variety of restaurants and accommodations to suit all tastes and budgets. If you've got pesos burning a hole in your pocket, this is the city to splurge on a pricey historic hotel or flashy restaurant.

Listed as a Unesco World Heritage site, Cartagena draws legions of tourists and thus, inevitably, aggressive touts and money changers. You are more likely to get hassled in Cartagena than in any other Colombian city, but this is a small price to pay to enjoy one of the continent's greatest cultural treasures.

History

Cartagena was founded in 1533 by Pedro de Heredia on the site of the Carib Indian settlement of Calamari. It quickly grew into a rich town, but in 1552 an extensive fire destroyed a large number of its wooden buildings. Since that time, only stone, brick and tile have been permitted as building materials.

Within a short time the town blossomed into the main Spanish port on the Caribbean coast and the major northern gateway to South America. It came to be the storehouse for the treasure plundered from the Indians until the galleons could ship it back to Spain. As such, it became a tempting target for all sorts of buccaneers operating on the Caribbean Sea.

In the 16th century alone, Cartagena suffered five dreadful sieges by pirates, the most famous (or infamous) of which was that led by Sir Francis Drake. He sacked the port in 1586 and 'mercifully' agreed not to level the town once he was presented with a huge ransom of 10 million pesos, which he shipped back to England.

It was in response to pirate attacks that the Spaniards built up a series of forts around the town, saving it from subsequent sieges, particularly from the biggest attack of all, led by Edward Vernon in 1741. The successful defense was commanded by Blas de Lezo, a Spanish officer who had already lost an arm, a leg and an eye in previous battles. With only 2500 poorly trained and ill-equipped men, Don Blas managed to fend off 25,000 English soldiers and their fleet of 186 ships. The Spaniard lost his other leg in the fighting and died soon after, but is now regarded as the savior of Cartagena – you can see his statue outside the San Felipe Fortress.

In spite of the high price it had to pay for the pirate attacks, Cartagena continued to flourish. The Canal del Dique, constructed in 1650 to connect Cartagena Bay with the Río Magdalena, made the town the main gateway for ships heading to ports upriver, and a large part of the merchandise shipped inland passed through Cartagena. During the colonial period, Cartagena was the most important bastion of the Spanish overseas empire and influenced much of Colombia's history.

The indomitable spirit of the inhabitants was rekindled again at the time of the independence movement. Cartagena was one of the first towns to proclaim independence from Spain, early in 1810, which prompted Bogotá and other cities to do the same. The declaration was signed on November 11, 1811, but the city paid dearly for it. Spanish forces under Pablo Morillo were sent in 1815 to reconquer and 'pacify' the town and took it after a four-month siege. More than 6000 inhabitants died of starvation and disease.

In August 1819, Simón Bolívar's troops defeated the Spaniards at Boyacá, bringing freedom to Bogotá. However, Cartagena had to wait for its liberation until October 1821, when the patriot forces eventually took the city by sea. It was Bolívar who gave Cartagena its well-deserved name of 'La Heroica,' the Heroic City.

Cartagena began to recover and was shortly once again an important trading and shipping center. The city's prosperity attracted foreign immigrants, and many

CARIBBEAN COAST

Jews, Italians, French, Turks, Lebanese and Syrians settled here. Today their descendants own many businesses, including hotels and restaurants.

Over the past decades, Cartagena has expanded dramatically and is now surrounded by vast suburbs. It now is Colombia's largest port and an important industrial center specializing in petrochemicals, but the old walled town has changed little.

Climate

Cartagena's climate is typically Caribbean; its average annual temperature of 28°C changes very little. Although the days are hot, a fresh breeze blows in the evening, making this a pleasant time to stroll around the city. Theoretically, the driest period is from December to April, while October and November are the wettest months.

Orientation

The heart of the city is the old town, built in two sections, an inner and outer town. Both were surrounded by walls and separated from each other by a channel, the Caño de San Anastasio. The channel was filled up to make way for the construction of the sharp, wedge-shaped, modern district, La Matuna.

The inner walled town consists of El Centro in the west, where traditionally the upper classes lived, and San Diego in the northeast, previously occupied by the middle classes. The outer walled town, Getsemaní, is smaller and poorer, with more modest architecture. Outside the walled town are several monumental fortresses.

Stretching south of the old town is an unusual, L-shaped peninsula, occupied by three districts: Bocagrande, Castillo Grande and El Laguito. This area is packed with top-class hotels, restaurants and nightspots, and is the main destination for moneyed Colombians and international charter tours. Backpackers, however, prefer to stay in the historic part of town.

Information

BOOKSHOPS & LIBRARIES

Biblioteca Bartolomé Calvo (☎ 660 0778; Calle de la Inquisición; ☺ 8:30am-6pm Mon-Fri, 9am-1pm Sat) City library.

Forum Bookshop (☎ 664 8290; Esquina Calles de la Iglesia y Mantilla No 3-86; ☺ 9am-8:30pm Mon-Sat,

4-8pm Sun) Good selection of books on Cartagena. They also serve coffee and snacks.

CONSULATES

Panamanian consulate (☎ 664 1433; Plaza de San Pedro Claver No 30-14)

Venezuelan consulate (☎ 665 0382; Carrera 3 No 8-129) In Edificio Centro Ejecutivo in Bocagrande.

INTERNET ACCESS

Most of the listed places are open seven days a week. A good place to visit is the 2nd floor of Centro Uno, which has several small Internet cafés.

Café Internet (☎ 664 3003; Calle Roman No 34-02; per hr US$1.20; ☺ 8am-7:30pm Mon-Sat, 9am-2pm Sun)

Intranet (☎ 660 0005; Av Daniel Lemaitre; ☺ 8am-6pm Mon-Sat)

Micronet (☎ 664 8409; Calle de la Estrella No 4-47; per hr US$0.80; ☺ 8:30am-7:30pm Mon-Fri, 9am-4pm Sat)

MONEY

Cartagena is the only city in Colombia where you are likely to be propositioned (sometimes persistently) by street moneychangers offering fantastic rates. Don't be fooled. They are con artists and are very skilled at stealing your money. There are plenty of *casas de cambio* in the historic center, many of which are around Plaza de los Coches.

Banco Union Colombiano (☎ 660 1052; Av Venezuela; ☺ 8-11:45am & 2-4:30pm Mon-Fri)

Bancolombia (☎ 664 0401; Av Venezuela, Edificio Sur Americana; ☺ 8am-4:30pm Mon-Fri)

Davivienda (cnr Av Venezuela & Carrera 9) This downtown branch has the only ATM where you can extract up to 500,000 pesos.

Giros & Finanzas (Av Venezuela No 8A-87) This *casa de cambio* in the old town represents Western Union.

POST

Adpostal (☎ 664 3173; Av Concolón; ☺ 8am-noon & 2-6pm)

TOURIST INFORMATION

Turismo Cartagena de Indias (☎ 655 0211; www .turismocartagena.com in Spanish; Av Blas de Lezo; ☺ 8am-noon & 2-6pm Mon-Fri, 8am-noon Sat) The tourist office is situated in the Muelle Turístico.

Sights

OLD TOWN

Without doubt, Cartagena's old city is its principal attraction, particularly the inner walled town, consisting of the historical districts of El Centro and San Diego. It is a real gem of colonial architecture, packed with churches, monasteries, plazas, palaces and mansions with their overhanging balconies and shady patios.

Getsemaní, the outer walled town, is less impressive but has some charming places and is worth exploring. It is less tourist-oriented, but not as safe – be sure to take extra precautions, especially at night.

The old town is surrounded by **Las Murallas**, the thick walls built to protect it against enemies. Construction began towards the end of the 16th century, after the attack by Francis Drake; until that time Cartagena was almost completely unprotected. The project took two centuries to complete due to repeated damage from both storms and pirate attacks. Only in 1796 was it finally finished, just 25 years before the Spaniards were eventually expelled.

Las Murallas are an outstanding piece of military engineering preserved in remarkably good shape, except for a part of the walls facing La Matuna, which were unfortunately demolished by 'progressive' city authorities in the mid-20th century.

The best approach to experiencing the Old Town is to wander leisurely, savoring the architectural details, street life and local snacks along the way. Don't just seek out the sights detailed here – there are many other interesting places that you will find while walking around.

The following attractions have been listed in sequence to conveniently connect them in a walking tour.

Puerta del Reloj

Originally called the Boca del Puente, this was the main gateway to the inner walled town and was linked to Getsemaní by a drawbridge over the moat. The side arches of the gate, which are now open as walkways, were previously used as a chapel and armory. The republican-style tower, complete with a four-sided clock, was added in 1888.

Plaza de los Coches

Previously known as Plaza de la Yerba, the triangular square just behind Puerta del Reloj was once used as a slave market. It is lined with old balconied houses with colonial arches at ground level. The arcaded

walkway, known as El Portal de los Dulces, is today lined with confectionery stands selling local sweets. The statue of the city's founder, Pedro de Heredia, is in the middle of the plaza.

Plaza de la Aduana

This is the largest and oldest square in the old town and was used as a parade ground. In colonial times all the important governmental and administrative buildings were here. The old Royal Customs House was restored and is now the City Hall. A statue of Christopher Columbus stands in the center of the square.

Museo de Arte Moderno

The **Museum of Modern Art** (☎ 664 5815; Plaza de San Pedro Claver; admission US$0.50; 🕑 9am-noon & 3-6pm Mon-Fri, 10am-1pm Sat), housed in a part of the former Royal Customs House, presents temporary exhibitions from its own collection, including works by Alejandro Obregón, one of Colombia's most remarkable painters, who was born in Cartagena.

Convento de San Pedro Claver

The convent was founded by Jesuits in the first half of the 17th century, originally as San Ignacio de Loyola. The name was later changed in honor of Spanish-born monk Pedro Claver (1580–1654), who lived and died in the convent. Called the 'Apostle of the Blacks' or the 'Slave of the Slaves,' he spent all his life ministering to the slaves brought from Africa. He was the first person to be canonized in the New World (in 1888).

The convent is a monumental three-story building surrounding a tree-filled courtyard, and part of it is open as a **museum** (☎ 664 4991; Plaza de San Pedro Claver; admission US$2; 🕑 8am-5pm Mon-Sat, 8am-4pm Sun). Exhibits include religious art and pre-Columbian ceramics. You can visit the cell where San Pedro Claver lived and died, and also climb a narrow staircase to the choir loft of the adjacent church. Guides, should you need one, are waiting by the ticket office and charge US$4/5 for a Spanish/English tour for a group of up to seven people.

Iglesia de San Pedro Claver

The **Iglesia de San Pedro Claver** (☎ 664 7256; 🕑 6:45-7:15am Mon-Sat, 10am-7pm Sun), located

CARTAGENA – OLD TOWN

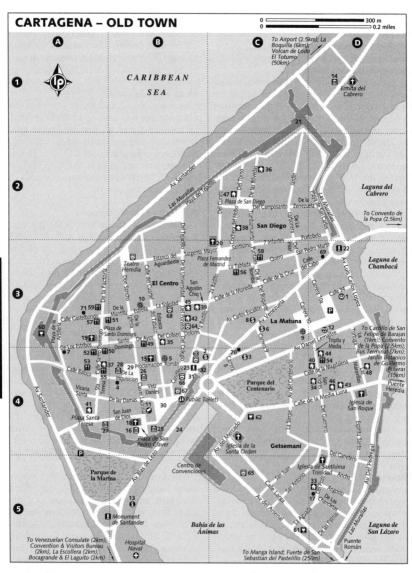

alongside the convent of the same name, was completed in the first half of the 18th century. The church has an imposing stone facade and inside, there are fine stained-glass windows and a high altar made of Italian marble. The remains of San Pedro Claver are kept in a glass coffin in the altar.

Museo Naval del Caribe

Opened in 1992 on the 500th anniversary of Columbus' discovery, the **Naval Museum** (☎ 664 7381; Calle San Juan de Dios; admission US$3.50; ☼ 9am-7pm) occupies a great colonial building, once a Jesuit college. It features a collection of objects related to the maritime history of Cartagena and the Caribbean.

Plaza de Bolívar

Formerly the Plaza de Inquisición, this plaza, or rather a tiny park, is surrounded by some of the city's most elegant balconied colonial buildings. As expected, a statue of Simón Bolívar stands in the middle of the plaza.

Palacio de la Inquisición

The Palace of the Inquisition is one of the finest buildings in the town. Although the site was the seat of the Punishment Tribunal of the Holy Office from 1610, the palace wasn't completed until 1776. It is a good example of late colonial architecture, noted particularly for its magnificent baroque stone gateway topped by the Spanish coat of arms, and the long balconies on the facade.

On the side wall, just around the corner from the entrance, you'll find a small window with a cross on top. Heretics were denounced here, and the Holy Office would then instigate proceedings. The principal 'crimes' were magic, witchcraft and blasphemy. When culprits were found guilty they were sentenced to death in a public auto-da-fé. Five autos-da-fé took place during the Inquisition until independence in 1821. About 800 folk were condemned to death and executed. The Inquisition did not judge the Indians.

The palace is today a **museum** (☎ 664 4113; Plaza de Bolívar; admission US$1.60; ☼ 9am-7pm), which displays Inquisitors' instruments of torture, pre-Columbian pottery and historical objects dating from both colonial and independence times, including arms, paintings, furniture and church bells. There is also a good model of Cartagena from the beginning of the 19th century as well as an interesting collection of old maps of the Nuevo Reino de Granada from various periods.

Museo del Oro y Arqueología

The **Cartagena Gold Museum** (☎ 660 0778, 660 0808; Plaza de Bolívar; admission free; ☼ 10am-1pm & 3-6pm Tue-Fri, 10am-1pm & 2-5pm Sat) has a collection of gold and pottery of the Sinú (also known as Zenú) Indians, who inhabited the region of the present-day departments of Bolívar, Córdoba, Sucre and northern Antioquia before the Spanish Conquest. There is also a model of a hut, complete with household utensils and artifacts, representing a dwelling of the Indians living in the region today.

Catedral

The cathedral was begun in 1575, but in 1586, while still under construction, it was

CARIBBEAN COAST

partially destroyed by the cannons of Francis Drake, and not completed until 1612. Alterations were made between 1912 and 1923 by the first archbishop of Cartagena, who covered the church with stucco and painted it to look like marble. He commissioned the dome on the tower. Recent restoration has uncovered the lovely limestone on the building's exterior. Apart from the tower's top, the church has basically preserved its original form. It has a fortlike appearance and a simply decorated interior with three naves and semicircular archways supported on high stone columns. The main retable, worked in gold leaf, dates from the 18th century.

Iglesia de Santo Domingo

The Santo Domingo Church, built towards the end of the 16th century, is reputedly the oldest in the city. Its builders gave it a particularly wide central nave and covered it with a heavy roof, but it seems they were not too good at their calculations and the vault began to crack. Massive buttresses had to be added to the walls to support the structure and prevent it from collapsing. The builders also had problems with the bell tower, which is distinctly crooked. However, legend has it that it was the work of a devil who knocked the tower.

The interior is spacious and lofty. The legendary figure of Christ carved in wood is set in the baroque altar at the head of the right-hand aisle. The floor in front of the high altar and in the two aisles is paved with old tombstones dating mostly from the 19th century.

Iglesia de Santo Toribio de Mangrovejo

Compared with the others, this church is relatively small. It was erected between 1666 and 1732 and its ceiling is covered with Mudejar paneling. During Vernon's attack on the city, a cannon ball went through a window into the church when it was filled with worshipers, but fortunately there were no casualties. The ball is now on display in a glassed niche in the left wall.

Las Bóvedas

These are 23 dungeons built between 1792 and 1796 in the city walls, which are more than 15m thick in this part. These dungeons were the last major construction carried out in colonial times and were destined for

military purposes. The vaults were used by the Spaniards as storerooms for munitions and provisions. Later, during the republican era, they were turned into a jail. Today they house tourist craft and souvenir shops.

Casa de Rafael Núñez

This mansion, just outside the walls of Las Bóvedas, was the home of the former president, lawyer and poet. He wrote the words of Colombia's national anthem and was one of the authors of the constitution of 1886, which was in force (with some later changes) until 1991. The wooden mansion is now a **museum** (☎ 664 5305; admission US$1.70; ✆ 8am-noon & 2-6pm) featuring some of Núñez' documents and personal possessions. The chapel opposite the house, known as the Ermita del Cabrero, holds his ashes.

Monumento a la India Catalina

The monument at the main entrance to the old town from the mainland is a tribute to the Carib Indians, the group that inhabited this land before the Spanish Conquest. The lovely bronze statue depicts Catalina, a beautiful Carib Indian woman who served as interpreter to Pedro de Heredia upon the arrival of the Spaniards. The statue was forged in 1974 by Eladio Gil, a Spanish sculptor living in Cartagena.

Muelle de los Pegasos

Back at the point from where you began your tour, Muelle de los Pegasos is the lovely old port of Cartagena on the Bahía de las Ánimas. It is invariably full of fishing, cargo and tourist boats. Sip a fruit juice from any of the stalls while watching easy-going port life. The new harbor where big ships dock is on Manga Island.

SPANISH FORTS

The old city is a fortress in itself, yet there are more fortifications built at strategic points outside the city. Some of the more important ones are included following.

Castillo de San Felipe de Barajas

The **castillo** (☎ 656 0590, 666 4790; Av Arévalo; admission US$3; ✆ 8am-6pm) is the greatest and strongest fortress ever built by the Spaniards in their colonies. The original fort was constructed between 1639 and 1657 on top of the 40m-high San Lázaro hill, and was quite small. In

1762, an extensive enlargement was undertaken, which resulted in the entire hill being covered over with this powerful bastion. It was truly impregnable and was never taken, despite numerous attempts to storm it.

A complex system of tunnels connected strategic points of the fortress to distribute provisions and to facilitate evacuation. The tunnels were constructed in such a way that sounds reverberate all the way along them, making it possible to hear the slightest sound of the approaching enemy's feet, and also making it easy for internal communication.

Some of the tunnels are lit and are open to visitors – a walk not to be missed. Take a guide if you want to learn more about the curious inventions of Antonio de Arévalo, the military engineer who directed the fortress's construction.

The fortress is just a 20-minute walk from the old town, or take a local bus from the Parque del Centenario. There is a statue of Blas de Lezo in front of the fortress.

Fuerte de San Sebastián del Pastelillo

This fort, on the western end of Manga Island, was constructed in the middle of the 16th century as one of the town's first defense posts. It's quite small and not particularly inspiring, but it's quite close to the old town – just across the bridge from Getsemaní. Today the fort is home to the Club de Pesca which has a marina where local and foreign boats anchor.

CONVENTO DE LA POPA

On a 150m-high hill, the highest point in the city, about 1.5km beyond Castillo de San Felipe de Barajashe is this **convent** (☎ 666 2331; admission US$2.50; ☑ 9am-5pm). Its name literally means the Convent of the Stern, after the hill's apparent similarity to a ship's back end, but it's actually the Convento de Nuestra Señora de la Candelaria, founded by the Augustine fathers in 1607. Initially it was just a small wooden chapel, which was replaced by a stouter construction when the hill was fortified two centuries later, just before Pablo Morillo's siege.

A beautiful image of La Virgen de la Candelaria, the patroness of the city, is in the convent's chapel, and there's a charming flower-filled patio. The views stretch all over the city. The patron saint's day is February 2 (see Festivals & Events, p132).

There is a zigzagging access road leading to the convent on the hilltop (no public transport) and paths cutting the bends of the road. It takes half an hour to walk to the top, but it's not recommended for safety reasons – there have been cases of armed robbery. Instead go by taxi (US$2.50).

MANGA ISLAND

While Cartagena is principally noted for its Spanish colonial architecture, other styles have also left their mark. Walk around the residential sector on Manga Island to see some interesting houses, mainly from the late-19th to early-20th centuries – a real hotchpotch of styles. The most noticeable feature is the Islamic influence brought by immigrants from the Middle East. You can also visit Manga's Cementerio de la Cruz, noted for many ornate old graves.

Activities

Cartagena has grown into an important scuba-diving center, taking advantage of the extensive coral reefs along its coast. Most local dive schools are in Bocagrande and El Laguito.

Caribe Dive Shop (☎ 665 3517; www.caribediveshop .com; Hotel Caribe, Bocagrande)

Cultura del Mar (☎ 664 9312; Calle del Pozo 25-95, Getsemaní)

Dolphin Dive School (☎ 660 0814; www.dolphindive school.com; Edificio Costamar, Av San Martín No 6-105, Bocagrande)

Eco Buzos (☎ 655 5449; Edificio Alonso de Ojeda, Av Almirante Brion, El Laguito)

Tours

City tours in a *chiva* (a colorful, traditional bus) depart daily at 2pm from Av San Martín between Calles 4 and 5 in Bocagrande. The four-hour tour includes rides around Bocagrande, Castillo Grande and the walled city, plus visits to the Convento de la Popa and Castillo de San Felipe.

You can also take a city tour in a horse-drawn carriage, which gives a glance of Bocagrande and the walled city. The carriages depart from the corner of Av San Martín and Calle 4 in Bocagrande and go along the waterfront to the old town. After a run around the main streets of the walled city they return via either Av San Martín or the waterfront, whichever you prefer. They operate daily from 5pm until midnight. The tour takes one hour and costs US$15 per coach for up to four people. There are also nighttime tours (p136), which are more a party parade than a sightseeing tour.

For tours to Islas del Rosario and Volcán de Lodo El Totumo, see p137 and p139.

Festivals & Events

Feria Taurina (January) The bullfighting season takes place at the bullring on Av Pedro de Heredia during the first week of the year.

Fiesta de Nuestra Señora de la Candelaria (February 2) The day of Cartagena's patron saint. A solemn procession is held on that day at the Convento de la Popa, during which the faithful carry lit candles. Celebrations begin nine days earlier, the so-called Novenas, when pilgrims flock to the convent.

Festival Internacional de Cine (March/April) Cartagena hosts an international film festival, usually a week before Easter. Winners are presented with statues of India Catalina.

Reinado Nacional de Belleza (November) The national beauty pageant celebrates Cartagena's independence day. Miss Colombia, the beauty queen, is elected on November 11, the high point of the event. The fiesta, which includes street dancing, music and fancy-dress parades, strikes up several days before the pageant and the city goes wild. The event, also known as the Carnaval de Cartagena or Fiestas del 11 de Noviembre, is the city's most important annual bash.

Sleeping

Cartagena has a reasonable choice of accommodations and, despite its touristy status, the prices of its hotels are not higher than in other large cities. The tourist peak is from late December to late January but, even then, it's relatively easy to find a room.

Most travelers stay within the walled city. In this area, Getsemaní is the principal area of budget accommodations, whereas El Centro and San Diego shelter the city's top-end hotels.

Other areas that are well dotted with tourist facilities are the modern and rather charmless districts of Bocagrande and El Laguito. These are mainly destinations for Colombian holidaymakers and occasional international charter packages. Very few independent foreign travelers stay here.

GETSEMANÍ

Budget travelers will find several choices in the Getsemaní area, especially on Calle de la Media Luna. Many are dives that double as love hotels or brothels, but there are a few clean and safe options. Getsemaní is a bit dodgy at night; keep your late-night wandering to a minimum.

Casa Relax B&B (☎ 664 1117; www.cartagenarelax .com; Calle de Pozo No 20-105; s/d US$36/45; 🞵 🖵 🞵) The best place to stay in Getsemaní, this French-run B&B has 10 well-appointed rooms with TV and modern bathroom. A French breakfast is served around a communal table, allowing you to get to know the other guests.

Hotel Behique (☎ 664 3511; Calle Tripita y Media No 31-29; s/d without air-con US$9/16, with air-con US$16/23; 🞵 🖵) This 38-room hotel offers simply furnished and comfortable rooms, some of the best in the neighborhood. But the atmosphere is a little staid.

Hotel Villa Colonial (☎ 664 4996; daniela.akel@ gmail.com; Calle del las Maravillas No 30-60; s/d without air-con US$9/16, with air-con US$16/21; 🞵 🖵) A family-run operation, the Villa Colonial offers well-maintained rooms painted in pastel colors. Try for one with a balcony over the street.

Hotel La Casona (☎ 664 1301; Calle Tripita y Media No 31-32; s/d without air-con US$7/12, with air-con US$12/16.50; 🞵) This family-run hotel consists of several boxy rooms with private bathroom. There's a friendly monkey in residence, as well as some tropical birds. It's just opposite the Hotel Behique.

Casa Viena (☎ 664 6242; www.casaviena.com; Calle San Andrés No 30-53; dm with air-con US$3, d with/without bathroom US$10/5; 🞵 🖵) Run by a helpful Austrian named Hans, Casa Viena is a long-time backpacker hangout. It has a variety of simple rooms, most with shared facilities. The hotel offers the usual range of Western facilities, including laundry service, book exchange, individual strongboxes, cooking facilities and tours. It's also one of the best places in the city for practical tourist information and overland trips.

Hotel Marlin (☎ 664 3507; Calle 30 No 10-35; s/d US$7/12) This small backpacker shelter is one of the best of several cheap hostels in the area. Some rooms have a window and others are cell-like. Rooms come with private bathroom.

Hotel Holiday (☎ 664 0948; Calle de la Media Luna No 10-47; s/d with bathroom US$4.50/9) Travelers who can't get into the Casa Viena often end up in this small hotel sporting several fan-cooled rooms around a courtyard.

THE AUTHOR'S CHOICE

Hotel Sofitel Santa Clara (☎ 664 6070; www
.hotelsantaclara.com; Calle del Torno, San Diego;
d US$300, ste US$360-400; P ✗ ✗ 🖳 🖵)
Stay at the Santa Clara for a night or two
and you'll start to feel like royalty. The
sumptuous hotel shows little of its bland
past – it used to be a the Convento de
Santa Clara (dating from 1621), and was
later a charity hospital. Now the essence
of luxury, it has 162 rooms and 18 suites, a
gym, business center, and two restaurants
(French and Italian). As the premier place
in town, it has seen its share of famous
faces – even President Clinton had lunch
here in 2000. Even if you can't afford to
stay here, it's still worth coming in for a
drink; try atmospheric El Coro bar, which is
dressed up like an antiquarian library.

EL CENTRO & SAN DIEGO

Hotels in El Centro and San Diego, the
heart of the old town, are on the whole
more expensive and not always as good
value as those in Getsemaní, but there
are some reasonable options here as well.
There is also a good supply of classier accommodations, which includes some of
Cartagena's poshest hotels. The sector is
safer than Getsemaní and you'll feel more
relaxed here while walking at night.

Hotel Charleston Cartagena (☎ 664 9494; www
.hoteles-charleston.com; Plaza Santa Teresa; d US$215, ste
US$235-484; ✗ ✗ 🖳 🖵) The former Con-
vento de Santa Teresa has 91 rooms and
22 suites distributed around two amazing
historic courtyards straight out of a picture
postcard. Amenities include a rooftop pool,
gym and three restaurants, but the price
does not include breakfast.

Centro Hotel (☎ 664 0461; www.centrohotelcarta
gena.com; Calle del Arzobispado No 34-80; s/d incl breakfast
US$50/60; ✗) The old-style Centro Hotel is
a good bet in this range. Well-maintained
rooms are arranged around an open courtyard, and it is just a few steps from the
Plaza de Bolívar.

Hostal Tres Banderas (☎ 660 0160; www.hotel3
banderas.com; Calle Cochera del Hobo No 38-66; d incl
breakfast US$50-57; ✗ ✗ 🖳) This French-
Canadian hotel is decorated with lively
pastel colors, a faux waterfall and scattered
coconut trees. Rooms are small but the

slightly more expensive 2nd-floor rooms
have a nice balcony. House rules that prevent drinking and smoking draw an older,
more conservative crowd.

Hostal San Diego (☎ 660 0986; hostalsandiego@
enred.com; Calle de las Bóvedas No 39-120; s/d/tr incl breakfast US$41/60/76; ✗) In the quiet northern end
of San Diego is this pleasant mock-colonial
place offering 27 simply furnished rooms
arranged around a sunny courtyard.

Hotel El Viajero (☎ 664 3289; Calle del Porvenir No
35-68; s/d with bathroom US$16/21; ✗) One of the
best budget bets in the area, this recently
renovated 14-room hotel has a spacious
courtyard and free use of the kitchen.

Hotel Las Vegas (☎ 664 5619; Calle San Agustín
No 6-08; s/d/tr with bathroom US$14/19/23; ✗) Just
round the corner from El Viajero, Las Vegas
is another decent choice in this central area.
Rooms are clean and come with TV. But
those that face the street are noisy day and
night.

Hostal Santo Domingo (☎ 664 2268; Calle Santo
Domingo No 33-46; s/d/tr with bathroom US$20/28/34;
✗) On a lovely street in El Centro, this
one offers few amenities for the price. For
air-con, tack on another US$6 per person.

Hotel Arthur (☎ 664 2633; Calle San Agustín No 6-
44; d with bathroom & fan/air-con US$14/18; ✗)
Scruffy Hotel Arthur is another reasonably
priced option on this corner, but mediocre
compared to nearby Las Vegas and El Viajero. Rooms off the street are quieter.

Eating

Plenty of snack bars all across the old town
serve typical local snacks such as *arepas
de huevo* (fried maize dough with an egg
inside), *dedos de queso* (deep-fried cheese
sticks), empanadas and *buñuelos* (deep-
fried maize and cheese balls).

Very characteristic of Cartagena are *bu-
tifarras* (small smoked meatballs), only sold
on the street by *butifarreros*, who walk along
with big pots, striking them with a knife to
get your attention. The *peto* is a sort of milk
soup made of maize, similar to Antioquian
mazamorra, sweetened with *panela* (unrefined sugar) and served hot. It, too, is only
sold by street vendors.

Try typical local sweets at confectionery
stands at El Portal de los Dulces on the
Plaza de los Coches (p127).

Plaza Santo de Domingo is home to six
open-air cafés that serve a varied menu of

mains, snacks, sweets and drinks. It's a popular place for people-watching, although prices are a little higher than they should be (dishes US$7 to US$10).

Restaurante Pelíkanos (☎ 660 0086; cnr Calle Santo Domingo & Calle Gastelbondo; set meals US$10; ☼ 11am-11pm Mon-Sat, 5-11pm Sun) This arty, bohemian two-level restaurant is different from any other. It has just one set menu daily, consisting of six Caribbean-style courses (four entrées, main course and dessert); plus there is unlimited Chilean wine included in the price.

Restaurante Vesuvio (☎ 664 2249; Calle de la Factoria No 36-11; mains US$5-8; ☼ 11am-3pm & 6pm-1am Mon-Sat, 6pm-1am Sun) Run by a friendly Napolitano named Mariano, this place serves authentic Italian meals and desserts. It's a favorite among Italian expats living in Cartagena, so there is always a lively crowd dining at its streetside tables.

El Burlador de Sevilla (☎ 660 0866; Calle Santo Domingo No 33-88; mains US$7-12; ☼ noon-midnight) Giant bulls' heads mounted to the wall stare down at you as you dine on some excellent Spanish treats, including paellas, tapas and *jamónes* (hams).

Parrilla Argentina Quebracho (☎ 664 1300; Calle de Baloco No 2-69; mains US$8-12; ☼ noon-3pm & 7pm-midnight Mon-Thu, noon-midnight Fri & Sat) The gutted pig slowly roasting inside the giant glass oven may not be too appetizing, but this place does offer some great steaks cooked in the pampa style, and a long list of Argentine wines and champagnes. It's easy to spot, thanks to a big bull at the door.

Restaurante Donde Olano (☎ 664 7099; Calle Santo Domingo No 33-08; mains US$6-8; ☼ noon-11pm Mon-Sat) This cozy place offers fine French and Creole specialties, plus a nice brownie and ice-cream concoction for dessert.

La Bodeguita del Medio (☎ 660 1993; Calle Santo Domingo No 33-81; mains US$6-9; ☼ noon-midnight) Eat and drink under the watchful eyes of Che Guevara and Fidel Castro in this hardcore Cuban *café de la revolución.*

El Rincón de la Mantilla (☎ 660 1436; Calle de la Mantilla No 3-32; mains US$6-9; ☼ 8am-10pm Mon-Sat) Decorated with baskets and seashells that gently wave from the rafters, this atmospheric Colombian place serves meals both hot and fast. To cool off, try their excellent *sapote,* an addictive milk and fruit shake.

El Bistro (☎ 664 1799; Calle de Ayos No 4-42; sandwiches US$2.50; ☼ 8am-11pm Mon-Sat) Sandwiches,

juice, pastas, desserts and mountains of German-language magazines feature prominently in this welcoming bistro. It's run by a pair of Germans who offer useful travel tips as well as serving up budget lunches and excellent dinners.

Dozens of simple restaurants in the walled city serve set meals for less than US$2. They include **Restaurante Coroncoro** (Calle Tripita y Media No 31-28; ☼ 8am-8pm) in Getsemaní and **Restaurante Mesón Caribe** (Calle La Tablada No 7-62; ☼ 7am-8pm Mon-Sat, 7am-3pm Sun) in San Diego. And at **Restaurante Vegetariano Girasoles** (☎ 664 5239; Calle de los Puntales No 37-01; ☼ 11:30am-5pm) in San Diego vegetarians will get tasty meals at budget prices.

Drinking

A dozen stalls on the Muelle de los Pegasos (p130) operate around the clock and have an unbelievable selection of fruit juices. Apart from pineapple, banana and mandarin, they'll have plenty of exotic local fruit including *níspero, maracuyá, lulo, zapote* and *guanábana,* all of which make for delicious juices. These stalls also have local snacks.

Cartagena's bar scene is centered on the Plaza de los Coches in El Centro and along Calle del Arsenal in Getsemaní. Weekends are best and the action doesn't really heat up until after midnight.

Leon de Baviera (☎ 664 4450; Av del Arsenal No 10B-65; ☼ 4pm-3am Tue-Sat) Run by an expat German named Stefan, this intimate bar serves Edinger, a German beer, and harder booze. The German touch is furthered by the pork pie hats and lederhosen that hang from the walls, and waitresses dressed up like the Saint Pauli girl. Stefan plays '80s and '90s rock music, with videos projected on a large screen.

Café del Mar (☎ 664 6513; Baluarte de Santo Domingo; cocktails US$6; ☼ 4pm-2:30am) A popular spot for long-term visitors, the café is actually a bar located on the western ramparts of the old city. Drinks and food are available and the music options are often house or salsa. The spectacular views are free.

Via Apia (☎ 664 9175; Calle Santo Domingo No 33-46; ☼ 4pm-2am) This lively tapas bar is one of the best places in the center for evening drinks and good music. They also have a big-screen TV projecting either football matches or music videos.

Entertainment

A number of bars, taverns, discos and other venues stay open late. Plenty of them are on Av del Arsenal in Getsemaní, Cartagena's Zona Rosa.

NIGHTCLUBS

Mister Babilla (☎ 664 7005; Av del Arsenal No 8B-137; cover US$6; ☿ 9pm-4am) One of the most popular discos; consists of two rooms, a dance floor and a large bar. It's a colorful and atmospheric place that plays mostly salsa music, but might not get going till quite late. Its crowd tends to be a bit more businesslike and highbrow than other clubs, many of which don't have a cover charge.

Tu Candela (☎ 664 8484; Portal de los Dulces No 32-25; cover US$4; ☿ 8pm-4am) A smaller, less formal version of Mister Babilla, this place is decorated with tribal masks, sea shells, old transistor radios and bongo drums. The upstairs section is great for dancing, but the downstairs bar is pretty quiet. The cover includes one drink.

Ritmo Caribe (☎ 660 0780; Portal de los Dulces No 32-79; ☿ 9:30pm-4am) Ritmo Caribe is a small techno place with a bombing base that doesn't allow for much conversation. However, it's great if you just want to dance. It's free on weekdays but charges a US$4 cover on weekends.

Casablanca (☎ 664 7568; Plaza de las Coches; cover US$4; ☿ 10pm-4am Mon-Sat) Another very loud disco bar, but this one has a nice balcony overlooking the square, just in case you need a break from the dance floor.

VALLENATO – THE INESCAPABLE BEAT

Once you arrive on the Caribbean coast, you will quickly learn that vallenato is everywhere – in bars, restaurants, discos, hotels and buses, on the street and on the beach. You may love it or hate it, but you can't escape it.

Vallenato is a typical musical genre of the coast. A classical vallenato ensemble includes the accordion, *guacharaca* and *caja*. The *guacharaca* is a percussion instrument of indigenous origins. It consists of a sticklike wooden body with a row of cuts, and a metal fork. The sound is produced by rubbing the stick with the fork. The *caja* is a bucket-shaped wooden drum which is played by hand. It has clear African roots. The accordionist is usually also the principal vocalist of the band.

Vallenato has four major musical forms: the paseo, merengue, *puya* and *son*. Generally speaking, the paseo and *son* are slower and gentler than the *puya* and merengue. The paseo is the youngest and most varied of all the four forms, and it has come to be the most common vallenato species over recent decades.

Vallenato was reputedly born in the Valle de Upar, somewhere around the town of Valledupar, on the present-day borderland of the Cesar and La Guajira departments. It evolved into a distinct musical genre during colonial times, though back then it was quite different to what it is today. Its melodic line was initially led by the *gaita*, a sort of simple vertical flute. This changed when the accordion arrived in the region in the mid-1800s.

Vallenato began to spread beyond its native region from around the 1930s, helped largely by the record industry, radio and TV. The Festival de la Leyenda Vallenata, held in Valledupar annually since 1968, has become one of Colombia's major musical events.

However, it wasn't actually until the 1990s that vallenato made the move to become a national, not just regional, musical genre, and it is now making inroads into neighboring Venezuela. Incidentally, vallenato fits snugly as a musical symbol of the country as it features the three instruments representing the three races that compose the majority of Colombia's population.

Until the 1950s, vallenato was essentially a folk rhythm of the countryside, created largely by anonymous authors. Today it boasts famous composers, interpreters, vocalists and accordionists, and has entered concert halls. Yet it sounds more authentic and natural in the seedy, smoky taverns of popular suburbs on the Caribbean coast, where it was born.

Vallenato's great composers include Rafael Escalona and Leandro Díaz. One of the vallenato's most remarkable innovators of recent years is Carlos Vives, who has used elements of traditional vallenato to create an attractive pop rhythm. He is largely credited with bringing vallenato to a younger audience and spreading it beyond national borders.

You can also go on a night trip aboard a *chiva*, a typical Colombian bus, with a band playing vallenato. *Chivas* depart around 8pm from Av San Martín between Calles 4 and 5 in Bocagrande for a three- to four-hour trip, and leave you at the end of the tour in a discotheque – a good point to continue your party for the rest of the night.

GAY & LESBIAN BARS

Lincoln Road (☎ 660 2790; cover US$4; Centro Calle del Porvenir No 35-18; ☺ 10:30pm-3am Thu-Sat) Open on weekends, this ultra-flash gay club has fiery lasers, strobe lights and pumping music, plus the occasional strip tease.

Via Libre (☎ 664 8886; cover US$4; Centro Calle de la Soledad No 5-52; ☺ 10pm-4am Sat) Only open one night a week, this discotheque also plays loud thumping music, but is more casual than Lincoln Road.

Shopping

Cartagena has a wide choice of shops selling crafts and souvenirs, and the quality of the goods is usually high. The biggest tourist shopping center in the walled city is Las Bóvedas (p130), offering handicrafts, clothes, souvenirs and the like. Artisans appear during the afternoon at the Plaza de Santo Domingo and sell a variety of crafts.

Getting There & Away

AIR

The airport is in Crespo, 3km northeast of the old city, and is serviced by frequent local buses. Also, there are *colectivos* to Crespo, which depart from Monumento a la India Catalina. By taxi, there's a surcharge of US$1.50 on airport trips. It's US$3 from the center to the airport, but it'll be only US$1.50 if you ask the driver to leave you on the corner of Av 4 and Calle 70, just 100m before the airport. The terminal has two ATMs and the Casa de Cambio América (in domestic arrivals), which changes cash and traveler's checks.

All major Colombian carriers operate flights to and from Cartagena. There are flights to Bogotá (US$90 to US$120 one way), Cali (US$120 to US$150), Cúcuta (US$90 to US$130), Medellín (US$80 to US$125), San Andrés (US$270 to US$300 return) and other major cities.

Avianca (☎ 664 5650; Edificio Caja Agraria) flies to Miami via Bogotá. **Copa** (☎ 664 1018; Calle

Gastelbondo No 2-107) has daily flights to Panama City for US$280. **AeroRepública** (☎ 664 9079; Centro, Av Venezuela, Centro Comercial invercredito) has flights to Bogota (US$100 one way), Cali (US$143 one way), Medellín (US$107 one way) and San Andrés (US$272 return).

BOAT

There is no ferry service between Cartagena and Colón in Panama, and there are very few cargo boats. More boats operate between Colón and Barranquilla, some of which will take passengers, motorcycles and even cars, but these services are irregular and infrequent.

A far more pleasant way of getting to Panama is by sailboat. There are various boats, mostly foreign yachts, that take travelers from Cartagena to Colón via San Blas Archipelago (Panama) and vice versa, but this is not a regular service. The trip takes four to six days and normally includes a couple of days at San Blas for snorkeling and spear fishing. It costs US$220 to US$270, plus about US$30 for food. It can also be organized as a return trip from Cartagena, in which case the boat doesn't go as far as Colón, but only to San Blas (about US$250, 10 days).

Check the advertising boards at Casa Viena and Hotel Holiday in Cartagena for contact details. Boats include the **Golden Eagle** (☎ 311 419 0428) and the **Melody** (☎ 315 756 2818; freshaircharters@yahoo.com); both have semiregular departures.

Beware of any con men attempting to lure you into 'amazing' Caribbean boat trips. The most reliable boats trips will be organized via Casa Viena (p132).

BUS

The bus terminal is on the eastern outskirts of the city, far away from the center. Large green-and-white Metrocar buses shuttle between the city and the terminal every 10 minutes (US$0.50, 40 minutes). In the center, you can catch them on Av Daniel Lemaitre. Catch one with the red letters on the board, which goes by a more direct route and is faster. Avoid slower local buses.

Half-a-dozen buses go daily to Bogotá (US$43, 20 hours) and another half a dozen to Medellín (US$40, 13 hours). Buses to Barranquilla run every 15 minutes or so (US$4, two hours), and some continue on to Santa Marta; if not, just change in Barranquilla. Unitransco has one bus to Mompós at 7am (US$15, eight hours); see Mompós (p143) for more details.

Three bus companies – **Expreso Brasilia** (☎ 663 2119), **Expresos Amerlujo** (☎ 653 2536) and **Unitransco/Bus Ven** (☎ 663 2065) – operate buses to Caracas, Venezuela (US$68, 20 hours) via Maracaibo (US$37, 10 hours). Unitransco is a bit cheaper than the other two, but you have to change buses on the border in Paraguachón. Each company has one departure daily. All buses go via Barranquilla, Santa Marta and Maicao. While the service is fast and comfortable, it's not that cheap. You'll save quite a bit if you do the trip to Caracas in stages by local transport, with a change in Maicao and Maracaibo.

AROUND CARTAGENA
Fuerte de San Fernando & Batería de San José
On the southern tip of the Isla de Tierrabomba, at the entrance to the Bahía de Cartagena through the Bocachica strait, is **Fuerte de San Fernando**. On the opposite side of the strait is another fort, **Batería de San José**, and together they guarded the access to the bay. A heavy chain was strung between them to prevent surprise attacks.

Originally, there were two gateways to Cartagena Bay, Bocachica and Bocagrande. Bocagrande was partially blocked by a sandbank and two ships that sank there. An undersea wall was constructed after Vernon's attack in order to strengthen the natural barrage and to make the channel impassable to ships. It is still impassable today and all ships and boats have to go through Bocachica.

The fort of San Fernando was built between 1753 and 1760 and was designed to withstand any siege. It had its own docks, barracks, sanitary services, kitchen, infirmary, storerooms for provisions and arms, two wells, a chapel and even a jail, much of which can still be seen today.

The fortress can be reached only by water. Boats leave daily from the Muelle Turístico in Cartagena between 8am and 10am, and return in the afternoon. The tour is US$9, including lunch and entrance to the fort. Some boats charge US$4 for the journey only, but you must pay the US$2 admission to the fort. Boats leave from launch No 2.

Islas del Rosario
This archipelago, about 35km southwest of Cartagena, consists of 27 small coral islands, including some tiny islets only big enough for a single house. The archipelago is surrounded by coral reefs, where the color of the sea ranges from turquoise to purple. The whole area has been decreed a national park, the Corales del Rosario. The park is going to be expanded southward to cover the Islas de San Bernardo as well.

Sadly, recent warm water currents have eroded the reefs around Islas del Rosario, and the diving is not as good as it once was. But water sports are still popular and the two largest islands, Isla Grande and Isla del Rosario, have inland lagoons and some tourist facilities. An oceanario (aquarium) has been established on the tiny Isla de San Martín de Pajarales.

TOURS
The usual way to visit the park is a one-day tour, and the cruise through the islands has become an established business. Tours depart year-round from the Muelle Turístico in Cartagena. Boats leave between 8am and 9am daily and return about 4pm to 6pm. The cruise office at the Muelle sells tours in big boats (US$18 per person), whereas the independent operators hanging around offer tours in smaller vessels (US$16). Popular backpacker hotels sell these tours too, and may offer lower prices. Tours usually include lunch, but not the entrance fee to the aquarium (US$5), Fuerte de San Fernando (US$2), port tax (US$2), and national park entrance fee (US$2).

The route is roughly similar with most operators, though it may differ a little between small and large boats. They all go through the Bahía de Cartagena and into the open sea through the Bocachica strait, passing between two Spanish forts: the Batería de San José and, directly opposite, the Fuerte de San Fernando.

The boats then cruise among the islands and get as far as the aquarium, where they stop for about an hour. As the admission fee is not included in the tour, you may decide to pay and visit it or just hang around waiting for the trip to continue. The aquarium has various marine species, including sharks, turtles and rays, and runs a dolphin show for tourists. The boats then take you

AROUND CARTAGENA

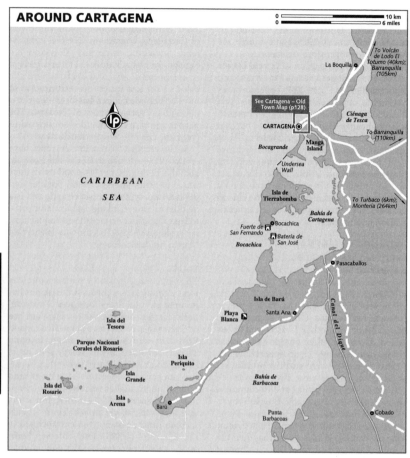

to Playa Blanca on the Isla de Barú to let you rest and bathe for about two hours.

The main choice you have to make is whether or not you want to travel by the bigger, slower boats or the smaller, faster boats. There advantages and disadvantages to both. The most popular large boat, the *Alcatraz*, can accommodate 150 people. There is food on board, music and room to move around. On the small boats, you are confined to your seat, but you get around quicker and can see more. Reviews are mixed, but overall, travelers prefer the big boats for their quality of service. Readers report that pilots of small boats rush around too quickly and have little concern for your personal safety – some of these

small boats have sunk. Travel companies will try to sway you one way or the other, so the best bet is to talk with other travelers or ask at Casa Viena.

SLEEPING & EATING
The islands have some tourist infrastructure, so you can stay longer, go sunbathing, swimming, diving, snorkeling or just take it easy in a hammock. Apart from a collection of hotels, some folk rent out their houses or bungalows on the islands and provide their own transport or have arrangements with boat owners.

Hotel Kokomo (☎ 673 4072; hotelkokomo@hotmail .com; hammocks/beds US$10/20) The Isla Grande has half-a-dozen accommodations options, including Hotel Kokomo. It's run by a Norwegian and offers *cabañas* and budget meals. Breakfast is included in the bed (but not hammock) rates. Diving gear can be rented on the island.

Playa Blanca

Playa Blanca is one of the finest beaches around Cartagena. It's about 20km southwest of the city, on the Isla de Barú. It's the usual stop for the boat tours to the Islas del Rosario, so the beach may be crowded with tour participants in the early afternoon; at other times it's pretty quiet. It's also good for snorkeling as the coral reef begins just off the beach (take snorkel gear).

SLEEPING & EATING

The beach has some rustic places to stay and eat.

Campamento Wittenberg (☎ 311 436 6215; hammocks with mosquito net US$3) This place is the most popular with travelers. It's run by a Frenchman, Gilbert, who offers hammocks under a thatched roof, plus meals.

La Sirena (☎ 310 661 1964; www.playa-blanca.net; s/d without bathroom US$9/14) Another foreign-run place with rustic accommodations, it's located next to Wittenberg.

GETTING THERE & AWAY

The easiest way of getting to the beach is with Gilbert, who comes to Casa Viena in Cartagena once a week (call to ask which day) and takes travelers in his boat (US$6, 45 minutes). If his schedule does not match yours, go to Cartagena's main market, Mercado Bazurto, and go by boat or bus. Boats depart from about 8am to 10:30am daily except Sunday. On Sunday, there's an early morning bus direct to the beach.

La Boquilla

This is a small fishing village 7km north of Cartagena. It sits at the northern tip of a narrow peninsula, bordered by the sea on one side and the Ciénaga de Tesca on the other. You can see locals at the *ciénaga* (lake/lagoon) working with their famous *atarrayas,* round fishing nets that are common in Colombia, particularly on the Caribbean coast.

There's a pleasant place known as El Paraíso, a five-minute walk from the bus terminus, where you can enjoy a day on the beach. You can also arrange a boat trip with the locals along the narrow water channels cutting through the mangrove woods to the north of the village. Negotiate the price and pay upon return.

There is a collection of palm-thatched shack restaurants on the beach, which attract people from Cartagena on weekends; most are closed at other times. Fish is usually accompanied by *arroz con coco* (rice prepared with coconut milk) and *patacones* (fried plantain).

Frequent city buses run to La Boquilla from India Catalina in Cartagena (US$0.40, 30 minutes).

Volcán de Lodo El Totumo

About 50km northeast of Cartagena, a few kilometers off the coast, is an intriguing 15m mound, looking like a miniature volcano. It's indeed a volcano, but instead of lava and ashes it spews forth mud.

Legend has it that the volcano once belched fire but the local priest, seeing it as the work of the devil, frequently sprinkled it with holy water. He not only succeeded in extinguishing the fire, but also in turning the insides into mud to drown the devil.

The crater is filled with lukewarm mud with the consistency of cream. Go down into the crater and have a refreshing mud bath. It certainly is a unique experience – surely you haven't already tried volcano-dipping! The mud contains minerals acclaimed for their therapeutic properties. Once you've finished your session, go and wash the mud off in the lagoon, just 50m away.

The volcano is open from dawn to dusk and you pay a US$0.50 fee to have a bath.

GETTING THERE & AWAY

El Totumo is on the border of the Atlántico and Bolívar departments, roughly equidistant between Barranquilla and Cartagena, now linked by a new coastal highway (buses are not allowed on this road). Cartagena is a far more popular jumping-off point for the volcano and has better public transport, and numerous tours.

The volcano is 52km northeast of Cartagena by the highway, plus 1km by a dirt side road branching off inland. To get to the volcano, go to main bus terminal, and take an hourly bus bound for Galerazamba. Get off before Galerazamba at Lomita Arena

CARIBBEAN COAST

(US$1.50, 1½ hours). Ask the driver to let you off by the petrol station and walk along the highway 2.5km towards Barranquilla (30 minutes), then to the right 1km to the volcano (another 15 minutes). The last direct bus from Lomita Arena back to Cartagena departs at around 5pm.

A tour is a far more convenient and faster way of visiting El Totumo, and not much more expensive than doing it on your own. Several tour operators in Cartagena organize minibus trips to the volcano (US$11 transport only, US$14 with lunch in La Boquilla), which can be bought through popular backpacker hotels, including Casa Viena and Hotel Holiday.

Jardín Botánico de Guillermo Piñeres

A pleasant half-day escape from the city rush, these **botanical gardens** (admission US$4; ☼ 9am-4pm Tue-Sun) are on the outskirts of the town of Turbaco, 15km southeast of Cartagena. Take the Turbaco bus departing regularly from next to the Castillo de San Felipe and ask the driver to drop you at the turnoff to the gardens (US$0.75, 45 minutes). From there it's a 20-minute stroll down the largely unpaved side road.

The 8-hectare gardens feature plants typical of the coast, including two varieties of coca plant. While buying your entry ticket you get a leaflet which lists 250 plants identified in the gardens.

MOMPÓS

☎ 5 / pop 28,000 / elevation 33m / temp 28°C
In the evenings, when residents of Mompós rock calmly in their rocking chairs and the bats flutter through the eaves, you may feel like you've stepped into the pages of *Huckleberry Finn* or *Gone With the Wind.*

The atmosphere evoked in the Mompós environs is certainly unique in Colombia (it may feel more like Mississippi), and is well worth experiencing, despite the hardships of getting there. Surrounded by muddy rivers and thick vegetation, Mompós is 200km southeast of Cartagena, and reached by a combination of bus, boat and car.

Mompós has a long tradition in hand-worked filigree gold jewelry, which is of outstanding quality. Nowadays both gold and silver is used. The town's other specialty is its furniture. Despite the scarcity of timber in the region, several workshops

still continue the tradition, making *muebles momposinos,* particularly rocking chairs, which are renowned nationwide.

Mompós also has a tradition in literature and was the setting for *Chronicle of a Death Foretold* by Gabriel García Márquez.

History

Traditionally known as Santa Cruz de Mompox, the town was founded in 1537 on the eastern branch of the Río Magdalena, which in this part has two arms, Brazo Mompós and Brazo de Loba. The town's name comes from Mompoj, the name of the last cacique (tribal head) of the Kimbay Indians, who inhabited the region before the Spanish Conquest.

Mompós soon became an important trading center and active port, through which all merchandise from Cartagena passed via the Canal del Dique and the Río Magdalena to the interior of the colony. When Cartagena was attacked by pirates, Mompós served as a refuge for the families of the city's defenders.

The town flourished and several fair-sized churches and luxurious mansions were built. In 1810 Mompós proclaimed its independence from the Virreynato de la Nueva Granada; it was the first town to do so. Simón Bolívar, who stayed here for a short time during his liberation campaign, said: 'While to Caracas I owe my life, to Mompós I owe my glory.'

Towards the end of the 19th century, shipping on the Magdalena was diverted to the other branch of the river, the Brazo de Loba, bringing the town's prosperity to an end. Mompós has been left in isolation, living on memories of times gone by. Little has changed since. The town's colonial character is very much in evidence, as are the airs of a bygone era. It's fun to wander aimlessly about this tranquil town, discovering its rich architectural legacy and absorbing the old-time atmosphere.

Information

Adpostal (Calle de Atrás)
ATM (BBVA) (Plaza de Bolívar)
Club Net (☎ 685 5915; Carrera 1 No 16-53; per hr US$0.80; ☼ 6am-9:30pm) Internet café.
Hospital (Calle 19)
Money Changer (Plaza de Bolívar; ☼ 8am-noon & 2-5pm) May change your US dollars at a very poor rate.

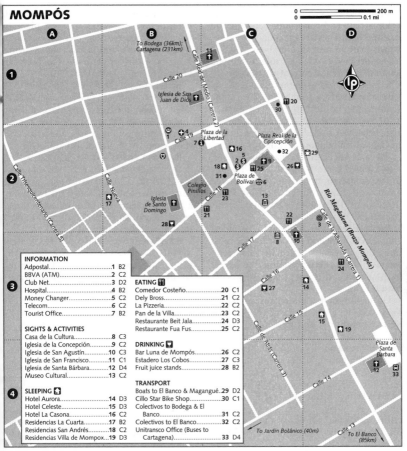

MOMPÓS

CARIBBEAN COAST

Telecom (☎ 685 5138; Plaza de Bolívar; ⏰ 8am-8pm Mon-Sat)

Tourist office (☎ 685 5738; Plaza de la Libertad; ⏰ 8am-noon & 2-6pm Mon-Fri) Located in the Alcaldía building. Ask where to find artisans' workshops where you can see and buy local jewelry.

Sights

Mompós' colonial architecture, which is in remarkable shape, has its own distinctive style known as the *arquitectura momposina*. Central streets, and particularly the main thoroughfare, Calle Real del Medio, are lined with fine whitewashed colonial houses. Their characteristic feature is the elaborate wrought-iron grilles based on pedestals and topped with narrow,

tiled roofs, that cover the windows. Some of the houses boast imposing carved doorways – a mark of the town's former glory and the wealth of its dwellers. The best way to get a feel for the local architecture and atmosphere is to wander through the streets.

Visit the two museums in the town, both set in colonial houses on Calle Real del Medio: **Casa de la Cultura** (admission US$0.50; ⏰ 8am-5pm Mon-Fri), displays memorabilia that relates to the town's history, and **Museo Cultural** (admission US$1.50; ⏰ 9am-noon Mon-Sat), which is situated in the house where Simón Bolívar once stayed and features a small collection of religious art plus some objects related to Bolívar.

Mompós has six churches, all dating from colonial days and fairly similar in style and construction. They are open only for mass, which may be just once or twice a week. The tourist office may be able to tell you about the churches' current opening hours. The most interesting and unusual is the **Iglesia de Santa Bárbara**, facing the square of the same name and next to the river. Built in 1630, the church has an octagonal Moorish-style bell tower circled by a balcony, unique in Colombian religious architecture.

Iglesia de San Agustín houses the famous, richly gilded Santo Sepulcro, which is one of the most prominent objects carried around the streets during the Holy Week processions. The statues of the saints in this church are paraded as well.

Iglesia de San Francisco is one of the oldest churches in town and has possibly the most interesting interior, particularly the lateral retables. **Iglesia de la Concepción** is the largest local church and is open more frequently than the others.

Go to the market which spreads along the waterfront to the north of the Plaza Real de la Concepción, and visit the cemetery with its collection of old tombstones. And don't miss the small Jardín Botánico, with it's many hummingbirds and butterflies.

In the evening, when the baking heat of day has slightly cooled, you'll see many locals relaxing in front of their homes, sitting in – of course – Mompós-made rocking chairs. At certain periods of the year there may be mosquitoes around, so have insect repellent at hand.

Festivals & Events
Semana Santa, or Holy Week, is taken seriously in Mompós. The celebrations are very elaborate, comparable only to those in Popayán. The solemn processions circle the streets for several hours on Maundy Thursday and Good Friday nights. Many images of the saints from the town's churches are involved.

Sleeping
Except for Holy Week, you won't have problems finding accommodations. There are a dozen *residencias* (budget hotels) in town, most of them pleasant and friendly.

Hostal Doña Manuela (☎ 685 5621; mabe642@ hotmail.com; Calle Real del Medio No 17-41; s/d with fan

US$26/33, with air-con US$30/39; 🚻 🖭) Although overpriced, this is still the best place in town, set in a restored colonial mansion with two ample courtyards, plus a swimming pool and a restaurant. The pool can be used by nonguests (US$2.50).

Hotel La Casona (☎ 685 5307; Calle Real del Medio No 18-58; s/d with fan US$8/13.50, with air-con US$13.50/23; 🚻) Probably the best-value place in town, this *residencia* has well-appointed rooms, a welcoming common area and a friendly staff. Laundry service is also available.

Hotel San Andrés (☎ 685 5886; Calle Real del Medio No 18-23; s/d with fan US$9/13.50, with air-con US$13.50/23; 🚻) Close to La Casona, this place has a similar setup, although the rooms are a bit more bland. The atmosphere is somewhat livened up by parakeets and parrots that inhabit the courtyard.

Hotel Celeste (☎ 685 5875; Calle Real del Medio No 14-174; s/d with fan US$7/13.50) Notable for its nanna atmosphere, this is a welcoming, family-run place with good service. Rooms are a tad small.

Other recommendations:

Hotel Aurora (☎ 684 0102; Calle Real del Medio No 15-65; r per person US$6.80) Atmospheric, but a bit moldy.

Residencias Villa de Mompox (☎ 685 5208; Calle Real del Medio No 14-108; s/d with fan US$7/13.50, with air-con US$10/19; 🚻) Low-priced air-con rooms.

Eating
Comedor Costeño (☎ 685 5263; Calle de la Albarrada No 18-45; ⏰ 5:30am-4:30pm) One of several rustic, riverfront restaurants in the market area to provide cheap meals. This one serves good bocachico fish and has views over the river.

Pan de la Villa (☎ 685 6761; Calle 18 No 2-53; ⏰ 7am-10pm) A welcome sight for travelers with a sweet tooth, this place specializes in ice cream, cakes and baked goods, and also serves crepes.

Dely Bross (☎ 685 5644; Calle 18 2-37; ⏰ noon-9pm) A reasonably priced chicken restaurant with both indoor and outdoor seating.

La Pizzeria (Calle Real del Medio; No 16-02; pizza US$6-9; ⏰ 5-10pm) In the evenings you can sit at tables set in the middle of the street and enjoy a cold drink or a pizza.

Drinking
In the evenings you'll find fruit juice stands on the plaza outside the Iglesia de Santo Domingo.

Bar Luna de Mompós (☎ 311 412 2843; Calle de la Albarrada; ☽ 6pm-late) A great place for a drink; also organizes tours.

Estadero los Cobos (Calle 16 No 2-133; ☽ 8pm-late Tue-Sun) This atmospheric open-air bar serves up cheap beer and plays good music till the wee hours.

Getting There & Away
AIR
Mompós has an airport, but it has been years since any commercial airliner has used it.

BUS & BOAT
Mompós is well off the main routes, but can be reached relatively easily from different directions by road and river. Whichever way you come, however, the journey is time consuming. As Mompós lies between two unbridged rivers, any trip involves a ferry or boat crossing.

Most travelers come to Mompós from Cartagena. Unitransco has a direct bus daily, leaving Cartagena at 7:30am (US$15, eight hours). It's faster to take a bus to Magangué

(US$11, four hours; half-a-dozen departures per day with Brasilia), change to a *chalupa* (boat) to Bodega (US$2, 20 minutes, frequent departures until about 3pm) and continue by *colectivo* to Mompós (US$2.50, 40 minutes). There may also be direct *chalupas* from Magangué to Mompós.

If you depart from Bucaramanga, take a bus to El Banco (US$13.50, seven hours) and continue to Mompós by jeep or boat (either costs US$9 and takes about two hours); jeep is a bit faster but the trip is bumpy.

In Mompós, a Unitransco bus to Cartagena (US$13.50) departs at 6:30am from near Iglesia de Santa Bárbara. *Colectivos* to Bodega and El Banco park on Calle 18 just off the Plaza de Bolívar. Boats to Magangué and El Banco anchor just off the Plaza Real de la Concepción.

Getting Around
The best way to see Mompós is by bike. These can be rented from **Cillo Star Bike Shop** (☎ 684 0636; Carrera 1A No 18-81) for about US$2 per hour.

CARIBBEAN COAST

San Andrés & Providencia

Geographically near Nicaragua, historically tied to England and politically part of Colombia, the islands of San Andrés and Providencia may at first glance seem a little schizophrenic. But after experiencing its isolated beaches, pristine coral reefs and unique island flavor, there is no doubting the reasons to visit the far-flung archipelago.

The lure of sun and sand (and duty-free imports) has been attracting tourists and mainland Colombians for several decades, and the principal town on San Andrés has grown into a bustling center of shopping malls and holiday resorts. The crowds, however, are not difficult to escape, and you could easily take up a Robinson Crusoe lifestyle on any number of isolated beaches.

In 2000 the archipelago was declared the Unesco Seaflower Biosphere Reserve. The reserve includes the islands proper and a vast surrounding marine area of 300,000 sq km, which is equal to about 10% of the Caribbean Sea. The objective is to encourage the conservation and environmental protection of an ecosystem of enormous biological diversity, and to foster sustainable development of the archipelago.

The islands, especially Providencia, provide a good opportunity to experience the unique Caribbean ambience. The turquoise sea, extensive coral reefs and rich underwater life are a paradise for snorkelers and scuba divers. The easygoing pace, friendly locals, relaxed lifestyle, developed tourist facilities and general safety are other factors that make the islands an attractive destination.

HIGHLIGHTS

- Sit back and enjoy the reggae rhythms at **Roland Roots Bar** (p154)
- Pack a lunch and spend the day on the beautiful **Johnny Cay** (p148)
- Dig your feet into the sand and while away the days in lovely **Aguadulce** (p153)
- Go scuba diving at some of Colombia's best coral reefs such as **Nirvana** (p148)
- Take a relaxing **bike ride** (p153) around either San Andrés or Providencia

★ Aguadulce

★ Roland Roots Bar

approximate distance 90km

★ Johnny Cay

★ Nirvana

- POPULATION: 80,000
- AREA: 45 SQ KM

TRAVELING SAFELY IN SAN ANDRÉS & PROVIDENCIA

San Andrés and Providencia are safe holiday destinations where the worst things you'll need to worry about are petty theft and sunburn. Be especially careful on the beaches of Providencia; the friendly nature of the place leads many travelers into a false sense of security, and this has made them easy targets for thieves.

History

The first inhabitants of the islands were probably a group of Dutch colonists who made their home on Providencia toward the end of the 16th century. In 1631 they were expelled by the English who effectively colonized the islands. They brought in black slaves from Jamaica and began to cultivate tobacco and cotton. The Spanish, irate at the English success on the islands, unsuccessfully invaded the archipelago in 1635.

Because of their strategic location, the islands provided convenient shelter for pirates waiting to sack Spanish galleons bound for home laden with gold and riches. In 1670 legendary pirate Henry Morgan established his base on Providencia and from here he raided both Panama and Santa Marta. Legend has it that his treasures are still hidden on the island.

Shortly after independence, Colombia laid claim to the islands, although Nicaragua fiercely disputed its right to do so. The issue was eventually settled by a treaty in 1928, which confirmed Colombia's sovereignty over the islands.

Geographic isolation kept the unique English character virtually intact, though things started to change when a flight service connected the islands to the mainland in the 1950s. In 1954, a government plan to make the islands a duty-free zone brought with it tourism, commerce, and entrepreneurs.

In the early 1990s, the local government introduced restrictions on migration to the islands in order to slow the rampant influx of people and preserve the local culture and identity. Yet, Colombian mainlanders account for two-thirds of San Andrés' population.

The tourist and commercial boom has caused San Andrés to lose much of its original character; it's now a blend of Latin American and English-Caribbean culture. Providencia has preserved much more of its colonial culture, even though tourism is making inroads into the local lifestyle.

Although the political status of San Andrés and Providencia are unlikely to change, Nicaragua continues to press the issue of its sovereignty over the islands at the International Court of Justice in the Hague. The latest chapter in this saga saw Bogotá threatening military action if Nicaragua's oil prospectors crept into Colombian maritime space. In 2004 a Colombian frigate and submarine were sent to patrol the maritime borders, but analysts put the naval exercises down to mere 'saber-rattling.'

Climate

The climate is typical of the Caribbean islands, with average temperatures of 26° to 29°C, but humidity can be uncomfortably high. The rainy period is September to December and (a less wet period) May to June. Tourist season peaks are from late December to late January, during the Easter week and from mid-June to mid-July.

SAN ANDRÉS

☎ 8 / pop 75,000 / temp 27°C

Covered in coconut palms and cut by sharp ravines that turn into rivers after rain, the seahorse-shaped San Andrés is the largest island in the archipelago, covering 27 sq km. It's the main commercial and administrative center of the archipelago. As the only transport hub to the mainland, it's the first and last place you are likely to see.

The town of San Andrés (known locally as El Centro), at the northern end of the island, is a hideous agglomeration of fero-concrete blocks that look as if they were thrown together with a pitchfork. Fortunately, new zoning laws prevent its expansion and a recently constructed brick promenade along the waterfront will somewhat ease any sore eyes.

San Andrés Town is packed with hotels, restaurants and shops; it has more than two-thirds of the island's population. There are two other small towns: La Loma in the central hilly region and San Luis on the eastern coast, both far less tourist-oriented than

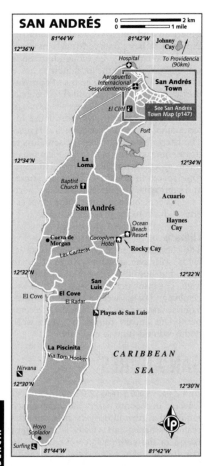

SAN ANDRÉS & PROVIDENCIA

just opposite San Andrés Town, though it gets very crowded in the high season.

The commercial aspect of San Andrés has been another magnet for Colombian visitors. But measures to liberalize the economy have caused San Andrés to lose a lot of its commercial attractiveness. Today many products can be bought at competitive or lower prices on the Colombian mainland. With the duty-free heyday over, the main focus of local government now is tourism.

In the past, San Andrés was used by foreign travelers as a bridge between Central America and Colombia, but connections and airfares have changed. It's no longer a popular transit point, but it still draws in foreign visitors seeking a taste of the Caribbean.

Information

Bancolombia (Map p147; ☎ 512 4195; Av Atlantico, San Andrés Town) Changes traveler's checks and cash.

Café Internet Sol (Map p147; ☎ 512 2250; Av Duarte Blum, San Andrés Town; ☼ 8am-10pm)

Costa Rican consulate (Map p147; ☎ 512 4938; Av Colombia, Novedades Regina Shop, San Andrés Town) Next to the Calypso Beach Hotel.

Creative Shop (Map p147; ☎ 512 3416; Av Las Américas, San Andrés Town) Internet café located below the Hotel Hernando Henry on the stretch of Av Las Américas known as Calle 4.

Depris (Map p147; ☎ 512 9405; Av Colón, San Andrés Town) Post office.

Giros & Finanzas (Map p147; Centro Comercial San Andrés, Local 12, Av Costa Rica, San Andrés Town) The local agent of Western Union.

Honduran consulate (Map p147; ☎ 512 3235; Av Colombia, Hotel Tiuna, San Andrés Town)

Macro Financiera (Map p147; Edificio Leda, Av Providencia No 2-47) Changes US dollars.

Secretaría de Turismo Departamental (Map p147; ☎ 512 5058; www.sanandres.gov.co; Av Newball, San Andrés Town; ☼ 8am-noon & 2-6pm Mon-Fri) In the building of the Gobernación, Piso 3. At the time of research it had a temporary office across from the Restaurante La Regatta.

Sights
CUEVA DE MORGAN

This is the cave where Welsh pirate Henry Morgan is said to have buried some of his treasure. The **cave** (Map p147; admission US$1) is 120m long, but it's filled with water, so you see only its mouth. You can't enter the cave and there's not much to see here anyway, yet the magic of alleged riches draws in plenty of tourists.

San Andrés Town. Both have fine English-Caribbean wooden architecture.

A 30km scenic paved road circles the island, and several minor roads cross inland, providing sufficient infrastructure to get around. It's relatively flat, with a small, low range crossing the island from north to south, reaching an altitude of 85m at the highest point.

San Andrés offers excellent scuba diving opportunities all around the island, but sunbathers should note that beaches are limited to the eastern coast. There's a pleasant beach at the northern end of the island, in San Andrés Town, but it can be crowded in the tourist season. Possibly the best beach is on the islet of Johnny Cay,

SAN ANDRÉS TOWN

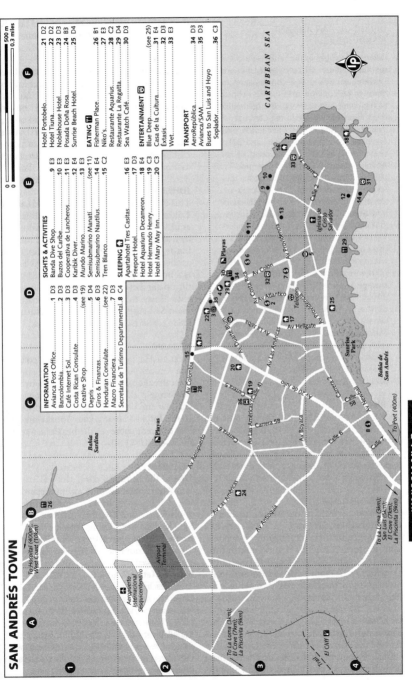

INFORMATION		
Avianca Post Office	1	D3
Bancolombia	2	D3
Café Internet Sol	3	D3
Costa Rican Consulate	4	D3
Creative Shop	(see 19)	
Depris	5	D4
Giros & Finanzas	6	D3
Honduran Consulate	(see 22)	
Macro Financiera	7	D3
Secretaría de Turismo Departamental	8	C4

SIGHTS & ACTIVITIES		
Banda Dive Shop	9	D3
Buzos del Caribe	10	E3
Cooperativa de Lancheros	11	E3
Karibik Diver	12	E4
Mundo Marino	13	D3
Semisubmarino Manatí	(see 11)	
Semisubmarino Nautilus	14	E4
Tren Blanco	15	C3

SLEEPING		
Apartahotel Tres Casitas	16	E3
Freeport Hotel	17	D3
Hotel Aquarium Decameron	18	E4
Hotel Hernando Henry	19	C3
Hotel Mary May Inn	20	C3

Hotel Portobelo	21	D2
Hotel Tiuna	22	D2
Noblehouse Hotel	23	D3
Posada Doña Rosa	24	B3
Sunrise Beach Hotel	25	D4

EATING		
Fisherman Place	26	B1
Niko's	27	E3
Restaurante Aquarius	28	C2
Restaurante La Regatta	29	D4
Sea Watch Café	30	D3

ENTERTAINMENT		
Blue Deep	(see 25)	
Casa de la Cultura	31	E4
Éxtasis	32	D3
Wet	33	E3

TRANSPORT		
AeroRepública	34	D3
Avianca/SAM	35	D3
Buses to San Luis and Hoyo		
Soplador	36	C3

DIVING ON SAN ANDRÉS & PROVIDENCIA

Divers will delight in the underwater viewing opportunities off both San Andrés and Providencia. While the courses may be cheaper at Taganga (p113), the richness of the corals and variety of the marine life rivals almost any place in the Caribbean.

Both San Andrés and Providencia have extensive coral reefs – 15km and 32km respectively. Nirvana off the coast of San Andrés is a particularly good dive spot. The reefs on both islands are notable for their sponges, which appear in an amazing variety of forms, sizes and colors. Other aquatic inhabitants include barracudas, turtles, lobsters, rays, groupers and red snappers. Wreck divers will want to check out the two sunken ships, the *Blue Diamond* and *Nicaraguense*, off the coast of San Andrés.

Underwater visibility is remarkable, on average between 25m and 30m of sight throughout the year; at some places it can be up to 45m or even 60m. This is largely due to the lack of currents and minimal erosion. The surface is generally calm, particularly on the west side of the islands. Water temperature is admirably pleasant, ranging from 26°C to 28°C.

LA PISCINITA

Also known as West View, shortly past El Cove, La Piscinita (Map p146) is a good site for snorkeling, with calm water, plenty of fish (which will eat bread out of your hand) and some facilities, including a restaurant with traditional local food and snorkel rental.

HOYO SOPLADOR

At the southern tip of the island, the Hoyo Soplador (Map p146) is a small geyser where sea water spouts into the air (up to 20m at times) through a natural hole in the coral rock. This phenomenon occurs only at certain times, when the winds and tide are right. An international surf contest is held nearby in January.

LA LOMA

This small town (Map p146), in the inner part of the island, is one of the most traditional places here. It is noted for its Baptist church, the first established on the island

(in 1847). In 1896, the church was largely rebuilt in pine brought from Alabama.

SAN LUIS

Located on the island's east coast, San Luis (Map p146) still boasts white-sand beaches and some fine traditional wooden houses. The sea here is good for snorkeling, though it can be a little rough. San Luis has no center and is really just a 3km string of houses along the coast, but there are some tourist facilities and some travelers are discovering it as a quiet alternative to San Andrés Town.

JOHNNY CAY

This is a small coral islet (Map p146) about 1.5km north of San Andrés Town. It is covered with coconut groves and surrounded by a lovely, white-sand beach. The sunbathing is good, but be careful swimming here as there are dangerous currents. The island is a popular picnic spot and at times it can fill up far beyond capacity. Food is available. Boats to Johnny Cay leave from the main San Andrés Town beach (return trip US$3). The last boat back is at 4pm.

ACUARIO

Next to Haynes Cay, off the east coast of San Andrés, Acuario (Map p146) is another place frequently visited by tourists by boat (return trip US$4). The surrounding sea is shallow and calm and good for snorkeling. If you forget to bring your snorkeling gear you can rent some on the beach in Acuario for about US$1.50.

Activities

Due to the beautiful coral reefs all around, San Andrés has become an important diving center, with more than 35 different spots for diving. The following are some of San Andrés' best diving schools:

Banda Dive Shop (Map p147; ☎ 512 2507; www .bandadiveshop.com; Hotel Lord Pierre, Av Colombia, San Andrés Town)

Buzos del Caribe (Map p147; ☎ 512 8931; www .buzosdelcaribe.com in Spanish; Av Colombia No 1-212, San Andrés Town) The oldest and largest facility. It has good equipment and a fine reputation, but it's expensive (US$250 for the open-water PADI or NAUI course).

Karibik Diver (Map p147; ☎ 512 0101; www.karibik diver.com; Av Newball No 1-248, San Andrés Town) This small school is also expensive (US$300), but provides quality equipment, personalized service and long dives.

Tours

Cooperativa de Lancheros (Map p147) On the town's beach, provides trips to Johnny Cay (US$3) and Acuario (US$4), plus a combined tour to both cays (US$5). The Cooperativa also offers tours to the outlying islands, including Cayo Bolívar. These longer tours can also be organized through some of the diving schools.

Mundo Marino (Map p147; ☎ 512 1749; munmarino@hotmail.com; Centro Comercial New Point Plaza, Local 234, San Andrés Town; tickets US$13.50; ☻ 8.30pm Tue, Thu & Sat) Operates the Morgan party boat, a two-hour evening boat ride with live music.

Semisubmarino Manatí (Map p147; 1½hr tour per person US$13.50) A specially designed boat with large windows in its hull. It departs once or twice daily (depending on demand) for a tour around the nearby reefs northeast of town. If you are not planning on scuba diving or snorkeling, this trip is probably the next best option for viewing the rich marine wildlife. Tickets for the trip can be bought from the office of the Cooperativa de Lancheros.

Semisubmarino Nautilus (Map p147; 2hr tour US$13.50) Does similar trips from the wharf just west of the Casa de la Cultura. Tickets can be bought from Mundo Marino or from the operator's desk at the wharf.

Tren Blanco (Map p147; cnr Avs Colombia & 20 de Julio; tickets US$3) A sort of road train pulled by a tractor dressed up like a locomotive, it departs every morning to circle the island, stopping at several sights along the way (three hours). The same route can be done, by up to four people, in a taxi (US$18).

Sleeping

The overwhelming majority of the island's accommodations can be found in San Andrés Town, which has loads of hotels. Outside San Andrés Town, there are some hotels in San Luis, but elsewhere there are few places to stay.

San Andrés' hotels may fill up during short tourist peaks, but most of the year there are likely to be plenty of vacancies. On the whole, accommodation on the island is more expensive than on the mainland. Rates rise during holiday seasons.

SAN ANDRÉS TOWN

Posada Doña Rosa (Map p147; ☎ 512 3649; Av Las Américas; s/d US$9/18) The low prices make this the obvious choice for solo budget travelers. The Doña Rosa has eight rooms, all of which have bathrooms and fans.

Hotel Mary May Inn (Map p147; ☎ 512 5669; ketlenan@yahoo.com; Av 20 de Julio No 3-74; s/d US$16/20; ☒) This small and friendly place offers eight, well-appointed rooms with attached bathroom. The double is a good deal, but solo travelers may want to bargain for a more reasonable price.

Hotel Hernando Henry (Map p147; ☎ 512 3416; Av Las Américas No 4-84; s/d with fan US$12/20, with air-con US$14/23; ☒) It may not look like much, but this is one of the best-value options in town. Clean, antiquated rooms come with TV, fridge, private bathroom and balcony. On the Calle 4 stretch of Av Las Américas.

Freeport Hotel (Map p147; ☎ 513 1212; freeport90@ yahoo.com; Av Las Américas No 2A-101; s/d/tr US$13.50/ 23/34; ☒) This clean and neat, functional hotel is worth a try. Inner rooms are boxy so ask for one with a street view.

Noblehouse Hotel (Map p147; ☎ 512 8264; www .sanandresnoblehouse.com; Av Colón No 3-80; s/d US$35/50; ☒ ▣) This Italian-run operation has 15 large, comfortable rooms in the center of town, one block from the beach. Breakfast and free Internet are included.

Apartahotel Tres Casitas (Map p147; ☎ 512 5873; 3casitas@sol.net.co; Av Colombia No 1-60; r per person US$32; ☒ ▣) Tres Casitas is a reasonable option facing the sea. Spacious rooms have kitchenette and prices include breakfast and dinner.

RESPONSIBLE DIVING

Please consider the following tips when diving and help preserve the ecology and beauty of the reefs.

- Never use anchors on the reef and take care not to ground boats on coral.

- Avoid touching or standing on living marine organisms or dragging equipment across the reef. If you must hold on to the reef, touch only exposed rock or dead coral.

- Practice and maintain proper buoyancy control. Major damage can be done by divers descending too fast and colliding with the reef.

- Spend as little time as possible within caves, as your air bubbles may be caught in the roof, leaving organisms high and dry.

- Don't collect or buy corals or shells or loot shipwrecks.

- Take home all your rubbish and any litter you may find.

- Do not feed the fish.

Hotel Portobelo (Map p147; ☎ 512 7008; www
.portobelohotel.com; Av Colombia No 5A-69; d US$32-55;
🅿 🛅) This unassuming beachside prop-
erty has pleasant rooms (some with sea
views) with cable TV and minibar.

Hotel Tiuna (Map p147; ☎ 512 3235; www.tiuna.com;
Av Colombia No 5A-69; s/d US$40/60; 🅿 🛅) Located
in the center of town, this well-equipped
hotel overlooks the sea. Amenities include a
nightclub, restaurant and movie theater.

Sunrise Beach Hotel (Map p147; ☎ 512 3977; www
.sunrisehotel.com; Av Newball; s/d with full board
US$89/116; 🅿 🛅) Sunrise Beach is the largest
facility, offering 170 rooms overlooking the
ocean, two restaurants, three bars, a disco,
gym, sauna and tennis court.

Hotel Aquarium Decameron (Map p147; ☎ 512
9030; www.decameron.com; Av Colombia; s/d US$92/124;
🅿 🛅 🛅) This attractive complex of round
cabañas (cabins) is built on and off the
shore. Prices are all inclusive.

SAN LUIS
This hamlet is a 10-minute drive south of
San Andrés Town; bus connections are fre-
quent. If you have a group of four, contact
Karibik Diver (p148); it has an apartment
rental (US$40) opposite the Cocoplum.

Cocoplum Hotel (Map p146; ☎ 513 2121; www.coco
plumhotel.com; Carretera a San Luis No 43-39; s/d US$44/60;
🅿 🛅 🛅) On a private beach shaded with
palm trees, this 44 room low-key beach resort sports Caribbean architecture and represents a good midrange alternative to the
swanky hotels in San Andrés Town. There's
a restaurant that serves fresh meals all day,
and is open to nonguests. Rocky Cay, a
good spot for snorkeling, is nearby.

Ocean Beach Resort (Map p146; ☎ 513 2866; San
Luis; s/d incl 3 meals US$68/95; 🅿 🛅) Less than
five minutes' walk north of Cocoplum is
this all-inclusive resort with a fine location
on the beach. Feel free to bargain here – if
you pass on the meals you might be able to
get a double room for less than US$50.

Eating
There are a number of simple restaurants
in San Andrés Town which serve the usual
set lunches and dinners for US$2 to US$3.

Fisherman Place (Map p147; ☎ 512 2774; Av Colombia; 🕑 noon-4pm) This open-air, beachside
restaurant offers some of the best seafood in
town, including crab soup (US$3), fried fish
(US$3) and seafood stew (US$7).

Restaurante La Regatta (Map p147; ☎ 512 0437;
Av Newball; dishes US$11-26; 🕑 noon-10pm) One of
the islands' best restaurants, offering patrons excellent seafood and sweeping views
of the Caribbean.

Sea Watch Café (Map p147; ☎ 512 4115; Av Colombia; 🕑 7am-11pm) Travelers in the mood
for a hearty meal of pizza, pasta or crepes
should find a seat at this modern restaurant
attached to the Casablanca.

Niko's Restaurant (Map p147; ☎ 512 7535; Av Colombia No 1-93; 🕑 11am-11pm) This upscale seafood restaurant is decked out in relics heisted
from a shipyard, with fishing nets, ropes and
turtle shells scattered across the walls and
ceiling. Fresh lobsters are US$19 a pop.

Restaurante Aquarius (Map p147; ☎ 512 5933;
Av Colombia; 🕑 noon-9pm) One of several seafood restaurants along the promenade. It's
also a popular meeting place for locals who
come to shoot the breeze.

Entertainment
There are several nightspots in San Andrés
Town on Av Colombia between Hotel Lord
Pierre and Hotel Aquarium Decameron.
Your best bet is to head to this area and
see what's most popular.

Wet (Map p147; ☎ 512 3287; Edificio Big Point, Av
Colombia; 🕑 4pm-midnight) This flashy place has
a dance floor, video screens and blaring
music. It also serves food and expensive
margaritas (US$5).

Casa de la Cultura (Map p147; ☎ 512 3403; Av
Newball) Organizes 'Caribbean Evenings' on
Friday, which are folklore shows featuring
live music, dance and local food.

Some of the upmarket hotels have disco-
theques, the most trendy (and expensive)
of which is **Blue Deep** (Map p147; Av Newball) in
Sunrise Beach Hotel, followed by **Éxtasis** (Map
p147; Av Colón) in Hotel Sol Caribe San Andrés.

Getting There & Away
AIR
The airport is in San Andrés Town, a 10-
minute walk northwest of the center, or US$3
by taxi. Colombian airlines that service San
Andrés include **Avianca/SAM** (Map p147; ☎ 512
3211; cnr Avs Colombia & Duarte Blum) and **AeroRepública** (Map p147; ☎ 512 7334; Av Colón 3-64); there are
direct connections to Bogotá (US$140), Cali
(US$140), Cartagena (US$128) and Medellín (US$140). At the time of research there
were no direct flights between San Andrés

and Central America, but Avianca does offer a flight three times a week to Panama City via Bogotá (one way US$207).

The airport tax on international departures from San Andrés is the same as elsewhere in Colombia: US$30 if you have stayed in the country fewer than 60 days and US$50 if you've stayed longer. You can pay in pesos or US dollars.

Satena Airways (☎ 512 6867; satenaadz@yahoo.com; Aeropuerto Internacional Sesquicentenario) operates two or three flights per day between San Andrés and Providencia (return US$124), serviced by a 19-seater plane. Note that West Caribbean Airways had formerly flown this route but had suspended operations at the time of research.

BOAT
There are no ferries to the Colombian mainland or elsewhere. Cargo boats to Cartagena and Providencia might take passengers, but are only of interest to those who can stomach a long and rough sea journey.

Getting Around
Local buses circle a large part of the island; they also ply the inland road to El Cove. They are the cheapest way to get around (per ride US$0.50) unless you want to walk. They can drop you off close to all the major attractions.

A bus marked 'San Luis' travels along the east-coast road to the southern tip of the island; take this bus to San Luis and the Hoyo Soplador (catch it from the corner next to the Hotel Hernando Henry). The bus marked 'El Cove' runs along the inner road to El Cove, passing through La Loma. You can flag it down anywhere on Av 20 de Juliop; it'll drop you in front of the Baptist church, within easy walking distance of Cueva de Morgan and La Piscinita.

You can travel more comfortably by taxi, which can take you for a trip around the island. Otherwise, hire a bicycle (from US$1.50 per hour or US$5 a day). Cycling around San Andrés is a great way to get a feel for the island. Roads are paved and there is little traffic to contend with. The coastal route is flat, and a little windy on the eastern side. Getting up the hills to La Loma requires more leg power. You can also hire a motorcycle (from US$5 per hour or US$20 a day), scooter, car or jeep. They can be hired at various locations

throughout the town; many of the rental businesses are on Av Colombia. Shop around as prices and conditions vary.

PROVIDENCIA

☎ 8 / pop 4500 / temp 27°C

Providencia will fulfil your every expectation of paradise. Quiet, laid-back hamlets nestle against white-sand beaches shaded by palm trees. The sea is warm, the locals are friendly and the topography is gorgeous. If you're looking to get away from it all, Providencia is about as far as you can get.

Traditionally known as Old Providence, the island lies 90km north of San Andrés and covers an area of 17 sq km. It is the second-largest island of the archipelago. A mountainous island of volcanic origin, it is much older than San Andrés.

Santa Isabel, a village at the island's northern tip, is the local administrative headquarters. Santa Catalina, a small island facing Santa Isabel, is separated from Providencia by the shallow Canal Aury, spanned by a pedestrian bridge.

Despite its beauty, the ravages of tourism have not yet tainted Providencia, and strict zoning laws will probably keep out large-scale development. Unlike San Andrés, English is still widely spoken and there's much English-Caribbean–style architecture.

What tourist industry does exist can be found in the tiny hamlet of Aguadulce on the west coast, a 15-minute ride by *colectivo* (shared minibus or taxi) from the airport. Here you'll find a dozen small cottages and hotels strung along the road, and a handful of restaurants. While you can see virtually the whole island in a day, travelers end up staying longer than they expected, scuba diving, hiking or just combing the beach.

Information
There aren't any *casas de cambio* (money-exchange offices) on Providencia, but some businesses (including a couple of supermarkets in Santa Isabel and Body Contact in Aguadulce) may change your dollars although rates will be poor. It's best to bring enough pesos with you from San Andrés.

Banco Agrario de Colombia (Santa Isabel; ☯ 8am-1.30pm Mon-Thu, 8am-2pm Fri) Gives cash advances on Visa cards; the ATM next door to the bank services MasterCard.

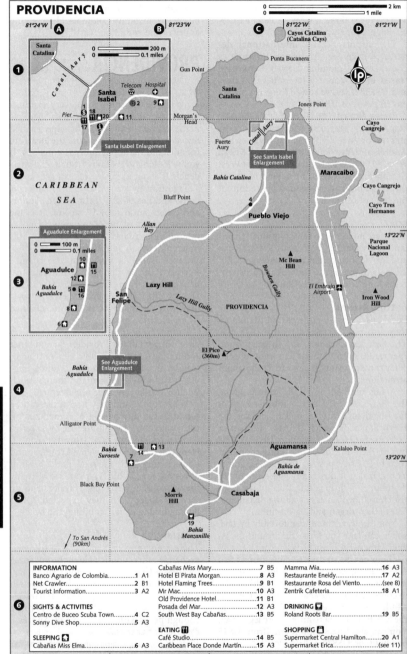

SAN ANDRÉS
& PROVIDENCIA

et Crawler (☎ 514 8956; Santa Isabel; ✆ 8:30am-
)on & 2:30-9pm) Internet café.

ourist Information (☎ 514 8054;
ovidencia2004@yahoo.com; Santa Isabel) Located in the
uilding of the Gobernación.

ights & Activities
rovidencia's beaches are pleasant, but rela-
ively small and narrow. The main ones
re at Bahía Aguadulce, Bahía Suroeste
nd (the best) at Bahía Manzanillo at the
outhern end of the island.

ARQUE NACIONAL MCBEAN LAGOON
'o protect the habitat, a 10-sq-km area in
he island's northeast was declared Parque
Nacional McBean Lagoon in 1995. About
0% of the park's area covers a coastal man-
rove system east of the airport; the remain-
ng 90% is an offshore belt including the
slets of Cayo Cangrejo and Cayo Tres Her-
nanos. An 800m-long ecopath helps you
dentify different species of mangroves and
he fauna that inhabits them. Access is from
he sector known as Maracaibo.

ANTA CATALINA
ome tiny, deserted beaches are on the is-
and of Santa Catalina, worth a look if only
o see Morgan's Head, a rocky cliff in the
hape of a human face, best seen from the
vater. An underwater cave is at the base of
he cliff. The shoreline changes considerably
vith the tides; beaches during high tide get
rery narrow and some totally disappear.

IIKING
The mountainous interior of the island,
with its vegetation and small animal life,
s attractive and provides pleasant walks.
Probably nowhere else in Colombia can
rou see so many colorful lizards scamper-
ng through bushes. Beware of a common
shrub with spectacular hornlike thorns;
ants living inside have a painful bite. Mosquitoes also abound on the island.

Don't miss a trip to the top of **El Pico**. The
most popular trail begins in Casabaja. Ask
for directions as several paths crisscross on
the lower part (further up there are no prob-
ems), or ask in Casabaja for a guide. Some
locals will take you up for a small charge,
or take a tour (see right). It is a steady 1½-
hour walk to the top. Carry drinking water
because there is none along the way.

SNORKELING & DIVING
Snorkeling and diving are the island's other
big attractions. The coral reefs around Providencia are more extensive than those around
San Andrés and the turquoise sea is beautiful. You can rent snorkeling gear in Aguadulce (or better, buy some in San Andrés
and bring it along). Diving trips and courses
can be arranged with local operators.

Recommended dive schools include **Centro de Buceo Scuba Town** (☎ 514 8481) in Pueblo
Viejo and **Sonny Dive Shop** (☎ 514 8231) in Aguadulce. Each offers an open-water or advanced course for about US$180 to US$200.
Most of the diving is done along the west
side of the island.

Tours
Body Contact (☎ 514 8283; www.oldprovidence.com.co
in Spanish; Aguadulce) This small agency offers tours and
a range of other services including bicycle rental (per day
US$9), snorkel gear rental (per day US$5), flight booking and
ticketing, Internet access and money exchange. Tours include
a hike to El Pico (per person US$8 to US$12), horseback-rides
(US$11), kayak trips (US$11) and boat excursions around the
island (per person US$8). Boats normally call at the Canal
Aury, Morgan's Head and Cayo Cangrejo.

Rodolfo (☎ 514 8626; 2hr ride per person US$7) Horseback
tours are organized by Rodolfo at Bahía Suroeste. A two-hour
trip includes rides in the mountain and on the beach.

Festivals & Events
Cultural Festival (June) Providencia's major event is in the
last week of June. It includes music and dance, a parade of
motorcycles and, just for kicks, an iguana beauty pageant.

Crab migration (May to June) An annual event of a quite
different nature is this one, which lasts for about a week or
two. There may be many crabs on the move then, particularly in Aguadulce and Bahía Suroeste, and even roads can
be closed to provide safe crossing for them.

Sleeping & Eating
Generally speaking, accommodations and
food are expensive on Providencia, even
more so than on San Andrés. Most travelers stay in Aguadulce, but there are also
some lodging and eating facilities in other
areas of the island, including Santa Isabel
and Bahía Suroeste.

AGUADULCE
This 20-house hamlet offers peace, quiet
and little else. There are more than a dozen
places to stay, some have their own restaurants and offer a bed-and-board package.

Cabañas Miss Elma (☎ 514 8229; s/d/ste US$16/32/68; 🐾) Miss Elma has both fan-cooled rooms and spacious air-conditioned suites. It's right on the beach and has its own restaurant, which is fine but not cheap.

Posada del Mar (☎ 514 8168; inforeservas@posadadelmarprovidencia.com; s/d incl breakfast US$32/46; 🐾) Next to Mr Mac is this midrange option with well-maintained rooms. All rooms have bathrooms and balconies with hammocks, and face the beach.

Hotel El Pirata Morgan (☎ 514 8067; www.hotelpirata morgan.com in Spanish; s/d incl breakfast US$46/69; 🐾 🍴) One of the island's better hotels, this place offers sea views from the rooms. There is also a handy minimarket downstairs.

Mr Mac (☎ 514 8366; jujentay@hotmail.com; s/d US$11/19) Right in the middle of the hamlet, Mr Mac is one of the cheapest hotels, mostly because it's unkempt and neglected. Rooms do have private bathroom and some overlook the beach.

Mamma Mia (breakfast/lunch US$3/5) Eating is generally pricey in Aguadulce, though there are some basic eateries such as Mamma Mia, which offers budget meals and beer (US$0.50 a bottle).

Restaurante Rosa del Viento (☎ 514 8067; 🕐 7am-7pm) Located behind the Hotel El Pirata Morgan, Rosa del Viento is a somewhat better option. You can get a platter of fish here for US$9 to US$18.

Caribbean Place Donde Martín (☎ 514 8698) Another charming address for seafood which serves excellent lobster (US$21).

SANTA ISABEL

Hotel Flaming Trees (☎ 514 8049; s/d US$13.50/23; 🐾) The best choice in this part of the island; offers nine spacious air-con rooms with bathroom, fridge and TV.

Old Providence Hotel (☎ 514 8691; r per person US$13.50; 🐾) This hotel offers bland but clean rooms, right over the Erika supermarket in the center of town.

The best place to eat in town is the open air **Restaurante Eneidy** (☎ 514 8758; seafood US$5-10; 🕐 7-9am, noon-3pm & 6-9pm). Alternatively, try the **Zentrik Cafeteria** (dishes US$3; 🕐 8am-8pm) across the street. There are several supermarkets where you can stock up on supplies.

BAHÍA SUROESTE

This is the second tourist destination after Aguadulce, but there are few facilities.

Cabañas Miss Mary (☎ 514 8454, 514 8206; US$30; 🐾) Miss Mary provides seven air con rooms right on the beach, plus a res taurant next door.

South West Bay Cabañas (☎ 514 8221; ste p person US$15) On the main road, 400m bac from the sea, this place has 16 large suite and a restaurant, and a variety of package for up to eight days.

Café Studio (☎ 514 9076; meals US$5-20; 🕐 11am 9pm Mon-Sat) On the main road is this pleas ant place that's run by a Canadian womar It has excellent espresso and cakes, plus full restaurant menu with some of the bes food on the island (traditional local cuis ine), and it's not that expensive.

Entertainment

Roland Roots Bar (☎ 514 8417; Bahía Manzanillo A charming open-air place amid coco nut palms that serves grilled fish (US$6) beer and reggae rhythms. Roland, a livin legend on the island for his late-night par ties, was planning to build basic bungalow in the forest behind his bar.

Getting There & Away

Satena Airways flies between San André and Providencia (return US$124) two o three times per day. You are most likely t buy a return in San Andrés before arriving but buy your ticket in advance in the hig season and be sure to reconfirm the retur trip at Providencia's airport.

Getting Around

Getting around the island is easy, as *colec tivos* and pick-up trucks run along the roa in both directions; it's US$1 for a ride of an distance. There may be only one or two pe hour, but locals will usually give you a rid on the back of their motorcycle.

Pick-ups congregate at the airport wait ing for incoming flights and ask as much as US$2.50 for any distance. To avoid over charging, walk a bit further from the airpor and wave down a *colectivo* or pick-up pas sing along the road for the usual US$1 fare.

A taxi from the airport will cost US$5 to Santa Isabel and US$7 to Aguadulce.

A pleasant way to get around is by bicycle which can be rented from Body Contact (see Tours, p153). You can also rent a motorcycle (per day US$15) from a few small operators in Aguadulce and Santa Isabel.

Northwest Colombia

For the people of northwest Colombia, the Andes provide more than gorgeous views. Their rugged, emerald-green peaks divide the region into two distinct geographies, which in turn define the warp and weave of daily life.

To the west of the Andes lies the Chocó department, occupying the lowlands along the Pacific coast. One of the world's wettest places, Chocó logs annual rainfalls of up to 10m – three times more than the Amazon. Such conditions complicate everything from farming to road maintenance, so it's no surprise that the Chocó department is one of the poorest in Colombia. Unfortunately, this isolation has also made Chocó an ideal base for both leftist rebels and paramilitaries. Conditions are improving, but the region still poses risks for travelers.

About 100km inland from the coast, the land rises quickly, the climate grows cooler and drier, and social conditions change dramatically as well. Consisting of Antioquia as well as the Zona Cafetera, this mountainous region has an economic and cultural dynamism that is in many ways the envy of the rest of Colombia. It's also the heartland for Colombian coffee growing – the valuable bean remains a mainstay of both the culture and the economy.

You can move easily between big cities as well as around the surrounding countryside, which is stunning, with terraced farms and colonial-style towns. There are also opportunities to trek through Andean cloud forests to the snow-capped peaks of Parque de los Nevados.

HIGHLIGHTS

- Crane your neck to see the tops of the majestic wax palms in the cloud forest of the **Valle de Cocora** (p185)

- Do shots of *aguardiente* (anise-flavored liquor) with surgically enhanced locals in **Medellín's Zona Rosa (p165)**

- Wander the colonial streets of **Santa Fe de Antioquia** (p169) while chewing on tamarind paste, the mouth-puckering local treat

- Gawk at the Andes from atop **El Peñol** (p168), Colombia's answer to Rio's Sugar Loaf

- Get buzzed on the history and science of coffee at the **Parque Nacional del Café** (p184)

- POPULATION: 7,012,200
- AREA: 124,015 SQ KM

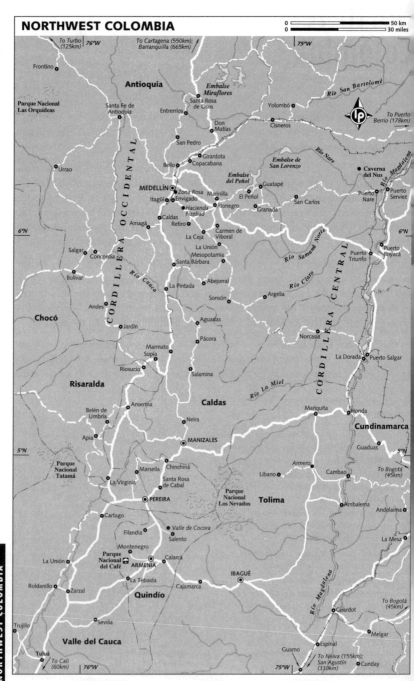

NORTHWEST COLOMBIA

| 0 | 50 km |
| 0 | 30 miles |

ANTIOQUIA

Paisas, as Antioquia natives are known, are the Texans of Colombia. They love their region more than their country. They're extremely affable but also harbor killer business instincts. And they possess a cowboy swagger even if they've never been on a horse. Welcome to Antioquia, y'all.

Granted, *paisas* have a lot to be proud of. Thanks to their dynamism, both the region's agricultural and industrial sectors are strong performers. Its mines produce 80% of Colombian gold. And Medellín, once synonymous with drugs and violence, is now one of the safest big cities in Latin America. Because the Andes shelter it from the intense heat and rain that plagues the coast, the climate is temperate year-round. And good roads make it easy to explore the small towns that dot *país paisa* (*paisa* country), where the windows and doors of the whitewashed colonial houses are typically decked out with rich wood carvings.

Note that while safety conditions have improved, you should still exercise caution in rural areas, particularly in the eastern part of the department.

MEDELLÍN

☎ 4 / pop 2.5 million / elevation 1540m / temp 23°C

Forget everything you've read about Medellín – it's probably old news by now. Yes, the city was the headquarters and principal killing grounds for Colombia's cocaine cartels. But the world press forgot to report Medellín's remarkable turnaround. Today, it's one of Latin America's safest big cities, and also one of its most pleasant.

Although Medellín may lack the sophisticated edge of Bogotá or the sumptuous languor of Cartagena, it has its own unique set of guiles to win over the traveler. Surrounded on all four sides by rugged peaks, there seem to be stunning views wherever you look. With mild temperatures year-round, Medellín deserves the nickname 'City of Eternal Spring.' A dynamic economy, driven by the huge textile industry as well as very brisk business in cut flowers, helps support a lively cultural scene. The narrow streets of downtown, safe once again, are supercharged with pedestrian life. Above all, it's the people who will win you over. Even in ultra-friendly Colombia, they are known for their graciousness and warmth.

Life isn't perfect by any means. The slopes around the city are crowded with makeshift slums, a constant reminder of the inequality that plagues not just Medellín but all of Latin America. Still, the city's residents have a special knack for enjoying themselves, and they're more than happy to have you join in. Medellín is rivaled only by Cali as the capital of Colombian nightlife. And like Cali, plastic surgery carries no stigma whatsoever. Some say all the fake boobs are a lingering reminder of the profound influence drug lords long exerted on Medellín's culture and aesthetic.

Note that there are no distinct wet or dry seasons, though there does tend to be more rain from March to May and September to November.

History

Spaniards first arrived in the Aburrá Valley in the 1540s, but Medellín itself was not founded until 1616; early development started in the southern part of the city now known as El Poblado. Historians believe that many early settlers were Spanish Jews fleeing the Inquisition. They divided the land into small haciendas which they farmed themselves – very different from the slave-based plantation culture that dominated much of Colombia. With their focus on self-reliance, these early *paisas* had little interest in commercial contact with neighboring regions. For these reasons, they came to be known as hard workers with a fierce independent streak – traits that you can still observe today on Medellín's bustling Pasaje Junín.

Though Medellín became the departmental capital in 1826, it long remained a

MEDELLÍN

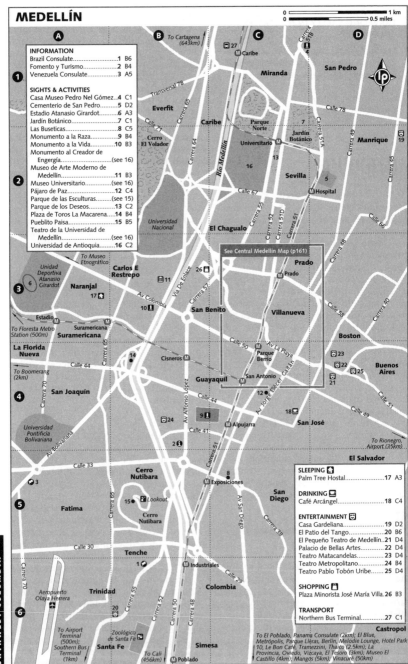

0 — 1 km
0 — 0.5 miles

INFORMATION
Brazil Consulate.................................1 B6
Fomento y Turismo.........................2 B4
Venezuela Consulate.....................3 A5

SIGHTS & ACTIVITIES
Casa Museo Pedro Nel Gómez..4 C1
Cementerio de San Pedro.........5 D2
Estadio Atanasio Girardot.........6 A3
Jardín Botánico.............................7 C1
Las Buseticas...............................8 C5
Monumento a la Raza.................9 B4
Monumento a la Vida.............10 B3
Monumento al Creador de
  Energía.................................(see 16)
Museo de Arte Moderno de
  Medellín.................................11 B3
Museo Universitario...............(see 16)
Pájaro de Paz...........................12 C4
Parque de las Esculturas.......(see 15)
Parque de los Deseos.............13 C2
Plaza de Toros La Macarena....14 B4
Pueblito Paisa.........................15 B5
Teatro de la Universidad de
  Medellín...............................(see 16)
Universidad de Antioquia........16 C2

To Cartagena
(643km)

To Museo
Etnográfico

See Central Medellín Map (p161)

To Floresta Metro
Station (500m)

To Boomerang
(2km)

To Rionegro,
Airport (35km)

SLEEPING
Palm Tree Hostal......................17 A3

DRINKING
Café Arcángel..........................18 C4

ENTERTAINMENT
Casa Gardeliana......................19 D2
El Patio del Tango....................20 B6
El Pequeño Teatro de Medellín..21 D4
Palacio de Bellas Artes...........22 D4
Teatro Matacandelas...............23 D4
Teatro Metropolitano...............24 B4
Teatro Pablo Tobón Uribe.......25 D4

SHOPPING
Plaza Minorista José María Villa.26 B3

TRANSPORT
Northern Bus Terminal............27 C1

To El Poblado, Panama Consulate (2km); El Blue,
Metrópolis, Parque Lleras, Berlin, Melodie Lounge, Hotel Park
10, Le Bon Café, Tramezzini, Thaico (2.5km); La
Provincia, Oviedo, Vizcaya, El Tesoro (3km); Museo El
Castillo (4km); Mangos (5km); Vinacure (50km)

To Airport
Terminal
(500m);
Southern Bus
Terminal
(1km)

To Cali
(456km)

provincial backwater, which explains why its colonial buildings are neither sumptuous nor particularly numerous. The city's rapid growth began only at the beginning of the 20th century, when the arrival of the railroad together with a highly profitable boom in coffee production quickly transformed the city. Mine owners and coffee barons invested their profits in a nascent textile industry, and their gamble paid off big. Within a few decades, Medellín had become a large metropolitan city.

By the 1980s, the city's entrepreneurial spirit was showing its dark side. Under the violent but ingenious leadership of Pablo Escobar, Medellín became the capital of the world's cocaine business. Gun battles were common, and the city's homicide rate was among the highest on the planet. The beginning of the end of the violence came with Escobar's death in 1993, and today Medellín is among the safest cities in Latin America, with rates of violent crime akin to many US cities.

Orientation

The city center consists of a compact grid ranged around Parque de Bolívar. The narrow, bustling streets are home to office buildings, a range of hotels, old-fashioned restaurants, museums and some reasonably priced shops. About 4km south of the center lies El Poblado, an upmarket residential and commercial suburb that continues to grow rapidly as businesses abandon the center for more modern digs. Here you'll find high-end restaurants and shopping malls as well as kicking nightlife around Calle 10.

Many of Medellín's tourist sights are scattered outside the central city area, so you'll need to use local transport (see p167). In contrast to all other Colombian cities, Medellín has two bus terminals and two airports. Make sure you know which terminal you depart from (see p166 for details).

Different from most other cities in Colombia, Medellín's central streets bear their proper names (not just their numbers) and are commonly known as such by the locals, especially in spoken language. In written language, in phone books or on business cards, the numerical system prevails, except for main thoroughfares that only have proper names.

Information

INTERNET ACCESS

There are plenty of Internet cafés through the center. Most charge around US$1 per hour for high-speed connections.

Café Internet Doble-Click (Map p161; ☎ 511 4183; Calle 50 No 43-135; ◷ 7am-9pm Mon-Fri, 7am-7pm Sat, 10am-4pm Sun) The largest downtown facility, and the only one open early mornings, evenings and Sundays.

Interphone.com (Map p161; ☎ 251 4853; Carrera 51, No 48-64)

Llámame (Map p161; ☎ 231 9090; Carrera 45 No 52-49)

Rapinet (Map p161; ☎ 239 8435; Av La Playa No 43-51)

MONEY

Cash advances on credit cards are available at most of the major banks; most of them also have ATMs that accept foreign Visa and debit cards. The banks may also change cash, but you will probably get similar or even better rates (and will save time) at *casas de cambio* (currency-exchange offices).

Bancolombia (Map p161; cnr Avs Colombia & Carabobo) Banks that are likely to change traveler's checks at reasonable rates include this one, in the center.

Banco Santander (Map p161; cnr Avs Oriental & La Playa) Also likely to change traveler's checks at reasonable rates and it's also in the center.

Centro Comercial Villanueva (Map p161; Calle 57 No 49-44) There are several *casas de cambio* located here.

Giros & Finanzas (Map p161; Local 241) In the Centro Comercial Villanueva, this *casa de cambio* is the agent of Western Union.

TOURIST INFORMATION

Fomento y Turismo (Map p158; ☎ 232 4022; Av Alfonso López; ◷ 7:30am-12:30pm & 1:30-5:30pm Mon-Fri) The tourist office is in the Palacio de Exposiciones, about 1km southwest of the center.

Dangers & Annoyances

The security situation in Medellín has dramatically improved. The poor outer suburbs can still be dangerous, but the city center and El Poblado are safe during the day. Exercise caution after dark in the city center, and rely on taxis for late-night outings.

Sights

CENTRAL MEDELLÍN

In the grand art deco Palacio Municipal, the **Museo de Antioquia** (Map p161; ☎ 251 3636; www.museodeantioquia.org in Spanish; Carrera 52 No 52-43; adult/student US$3/1.50; ◷ 9:30am-5pm Mon-Sat,

PAISA COUNTRY

Even other Colombians will tell you: *paisas,* as the Antioquia natives call themselves, are different from their fellow countrymen. Travelers will appreciate their remarkable hospitality, which consists of three-parts warmth and one-part old-fashioned formality. Founded by small farmers rather than slave-owning plantation owners, Antioquia is renowned for its hard-working, entrepreneurial spirit. Other Colombians accuse them of being resistant to change, a result perhaps of the region's historical isolation – and economic self-sufficiency. At the same time, *paisas* have also earned a reputation for straight dealing, even if they always seem to get the better end of the bargain.

President Uribe, himself a *paisa,* is believed to possess all these traits, including the chutzpah to negotiate for a second term even if it requires constitutional changes. Painter Fernando Botero is the city's other favorite native son – and another typical *paisa*. Prodigiously productive, he combines old-fashioned realism with incisive irony to create works that are at once naive and startlingly new.

10am-4pm Sun) is Colombia's second-oldest museum and one of its finest. The collection includes pre-Columbian, colonial, independence and modern art collections, but the real prize is a recent donation by native son Fernando Botero. The wildly prolific artist has donated 92 of his own works as well as 22 works by some of the world's leading modernist and contemporary artists, from Picasso to Jeff Koontz. For more Botero, just head across the street to the **Plazoleta de las Esculturas** (Map p161), home to a more than 20 of Botero's sculptures.

Standing guard over Parque Berrío is **Basílica de la Candelaria** (Map p161; cnr Carrera 50 & Calle 51), Medellín's most important church. Built in the 1770s, it served as the city's cathedral from 1868 to 1931. Inside is a beautiful coffered ceiling, a much venerated figure of the Señor Caido (Fallen Christ) in the left aisle, and an interesting main retable.

Overlooking Parque de Bolívar, the vast **Catedral Metropolitana** (Map p161; cnr Calle 8 & Carrera 48) is formed by some 1.2 million bricks arrayed in an attractive neo-Romanesque design. Designed by various architects, including Frenchman Charles Carré, construction began in 1875 and was completed only in 1931. Its spacious but dim interior boasts Spanish stained-glass windows, a German-made organ featuring 3478 pipes and paintings by Gregorio Vásquez de Arce y Ceballos. Don't be misled if the cathedral's front door is locked – check the side doors.

Ermita de la Veracruz (Map p161; cnr Calle 51 & Carrera 52) is regarded as the city's oldest church. Its construction was reputedly begun in 1682, but it wasn't inaugurated until 1803. It has a fine stone facade and a charming, white-and-gold interior.

Thanks to a local law requiring major new buildings to include public art, central Medellín can seem like a vast, outdoor art gallery. Besides the Plazoleta de las Esculturas, you can see Botero's massive bronze woman's torso, **La Gorda**, in front of the Banco de la República in Parque Berrío. There are three more Botero sculptures in Parque San Antonio, including the **Pájaro de Paz** (Bird of Peace; Map p158). Ironically, this work was seriously damaged by a bomb placed by guerrillas. As a vivid reminder of the city's hyper-violent episode, the damaged bird has been left untouched, though a new version now stands alongside it.

Rodrigo Arenas Betancur (1919–95), Colombia's favorite designer of monuments, is also well-represented in Medellín. His sinuous, 14m-high **Monumento a la Vida** (Monument to Life; Map p158; Centro Suramericana, cnr Av Colombia & Carrera 64B) was unveiled in 1974. Even more impressive is **Monumento a la Raza** (Map p158; Centro Administrativo La Alpujarra, Calle 44), which tells the story of Antioquia in dramatically twisting metal. Fans should also head to the Universidad de Antioquia campus 2km north of the city center to see his Monumento al Creador de Energía (below).

For another take on Medellín's history, check out the Social Realist–inspired murals by Pedro Nel Gómez displayed in two long showcases on the corner of Carrera 51 and Calle 51, just off Parque Berrío.

NORTH OF DOWNTOWN

For insight into the way *paisas* live and die, head to the fascinating **Cementerio de San Pedro** (Map p158; Carrera 51 No 68-68; 7:30am-5:30pm). Established in 1842, it has a collection of ornate tombstones, sepulchral

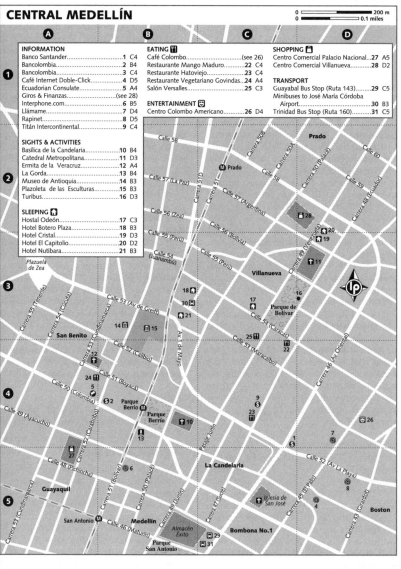

CENTRAL MEDELLÍN

0 — 200 m
0 — 0.1 miles

chapels and mausoleums. Many recent graves are decked out with paraphernalia related to passions of the deceased, from cars to football to tango music. Take the metro to Estación Hospital.

The **Casa Museo Pedro Nel Gómez** (Map p158; ☎ 233 2633; Carrera 51B No 85-24; adult/student US$2/1.25; ☒ 9am-noon & 2-5pm Mon-Fri, 9am-noon Sat) is dedicated to another beloved son of Medellín, Pedro Nel Gómez (1899–1984), and set in the house where the artist lived and worked. The museum has an extensive collection (nearly 2000 pieces) of his watercolors, oil paintings, drawings, sculptures and murals. Pedro Nel Gómez is said to have been Colombia's most prolific artist.

NORTHWEST COLOMBIA

The museum is 3km north of the city center. The Aranjuez bus from the center will drop you off at the museum's door.

Not far from the museum and across from the Universidad de Antioquia is the city's **Jardín Botánico** (Map p158; Carrera 52 No 73-182; metro Estación Universidad; admission US$1; 9am-5pm). Opened in 1978, the garden has 600 species of trees and plants, a lake, herbarium, auditorium and the Orquideorama where an orchid display is held in March and April. Just across the street is the sleek, all-concrete **Parque de los Deseos**, a favorite hangout of the area's college students.

On the Universidad de Antioquia campus itself, check out the **Museo Universitario** (Map p158; 210 5180; http://museo.udea.edu.co in Spanish; Calle 67 No 53-108; admission free; 8am-6pm Mon-Thu, 8am-4pm Fri, 9am-1pm Sat). It has an interesting collection of pre-Columbian pottery, as well as galleries devoted to art and the natural sciences. Out front is the **Monumento al Creador de la Energía** (Map p158), another trippy, grandiose sculpture by Rodrigo Arenas Betancur (see p160).

Located in what looks like an unassuming apartment building in a leafy suburb west of the city center, **Museo de Arte Moderno de Medellín** (MAMM; Map p158; 230 2622; Carrera 64B No 51-64; adults/students US$2/1; 10am-1pm & 2-6pm Mon-Fri, 10am-5pm Sat) stages changing exhibitions of contemporary art. To get there from the city center take any bus going west along Av Colombia from Parque Berrío, or walk for 15 minutes.

SOUTH OF DOWNTOWN

Occupying a mock-Gothic castle built in 1930 in El Poblado, the **Museo El Castillo** (266 0900; Calle 9 Sur No 32-269; adult/student US$2/1; 9-11am & 2-5pm Mon-Fri, 9-11:30am Sat) was once home to a wealthy Antioquian landowner. Inside are the family's belongings, including furniture and artwork from around the world. Outside, there are pleasant, French-style formal gardens. All visits are guided and take about half an hour. There may be recitals on some days in the castle's auditorium.

The museum is 5km south of the city center. Take the El Poblado–San Lucas bus from Parque Berrío, get off at Loma de Los Balsos and follow the side street downhill for five minutes to the museum. Instead of returning the same way, you can walk

further down to Carrera 43A where there are plenty of buses going to the center.

On top of the 80m-tall hill known as Cerro Nutibara, 2km southwest of the city center, sits the kitschy **Pueblito Paisa** (Map p158), a miniature version of typical Antioquian township. Views from an adjacent platform across the city are stunning. On the slopes of the Cerro Nutibara is the **Parque de las Esculturas** (Sculpture Park; Map p158), which contains modern abstract sculptures by South American artists, including such prominent names as Edgar Negret, Jesús Soto and Carlos Cruz Díez. The Guayabal bus from Av Oriental in the city center passes by the foot of Cerro Nutibara, or go by taxi (US$2.50).

Activities
PARAGLIDING
With optimum wind currents and stunning topography, Medellín has become Colombia's premier destination for paragliding. **Boomerang** (254 5943, 311-774 1175; piloto_x@hotmail.com; Calle 38B No 79-16, Barrio Laureles) is one of the best local gliding schools, with highly experienced pilots and good equipment. It offers courses (about US$300 for a week-long course), equipment rental and tandem flights over the city (spectacular views) with a skilled pilot (US$25). No previous gliding experience is necessary for tandem flights.

CYCLING
Paisas tend to be avid cyclists, and on weekends the mountain roads around the city fill

---

DETOUR: RÍO CLARO

Thanks to Colombia's improving security situation, it is again safe to visit the Río Claro valley in eastern Antioquia, where a crystal-clear river has carved stunning shapes into its marble bed. It's a favorite spot for bird-watchers, who come to see everything from hummingbirds to herons to vultures.

You can stay in the lodge known as El Refugio, which is about 1km from the river and near the town of Puerto Triunfo. Río Claro is just off the main road that connects Bogotá (US$14, five hours) and Medellín (US$10, three hours). Most buses that connect the two cities will drop you off in Puerto Triunfo. Note: nighttime travel in this area remains risky; check current conditions.

up with bikers. Contact the tourist office, **Fomento y Turismo** (Map p158; ☎ 232 4022; Av Alfonso López; ⏱ 7:30am-12:30pm & 1:30-5:30pm Mon-Fri) for current information about opportunities to join local groups.

HIKING
The mountains around Medellín offer plenty of hiking opportunities. For information or to join an organized outing, contact **Patianchos** (☎ 413 7705; lospatianchos@hotmail .com), a group devoted to ecologically sensitive hiking.

Tours
Las Buseticas (☎ 262 7444; www.lasbuseticas .com in Spanish; Carrera 43A No 34-95) For a guided, three-hour city tour try Las Buseticas. Prices for tours range from US$10 to US$20 per person, depending on the size of the group. Las Buseticas, as well as other operators, also organizes tours along the so-called Circuito de Oriente (p167) to the southeast of Medellín, which includes a variety of cultural and natural attractions. There are several standard routes, or operators can put together a tour to suit your interests. It's commonly a half- or full-day trip, with lunch en route, and can be done by car or minibus. Depending on the itinerary and size of the group, prices range from US$25 to US$50 per person, including lunch.
Turibus (Map p158; ☎ 285 1978; adult/child US$4/3; ⏱ 9am-5pm Tue-Sat) For a self-service tour of the city, consider Turibus. It connects all the city's major sites and lets you get on and off all day for the price of a single ticket. The main stop is on Parque de Bolívar.

Festivals & Events
Feria Taurina de la Macarena (January and February) The bullfighting season takes place at the Plaza de Toros La Macarena (Map p158), the 11,000-seat, Moorish-style bullring built between 1927 and 1944. It's on Autopista Sur on the corner of Calle 44.
Feria Nacional de Artesanías (late July or early August) A huge craft fair held at the sports complex Estadio Atanasio Girardot (Map p158). It attracts artisans from around the country and is a good opportunity to buy crafts at bargain prices.
Feria de las Flores (early August) Medellín's most spectacular event is this weeklong feria. Its highlight is the Desfile de Silleteros, when up to 400 *campesinos* (peasants) come down from the mountains and parade along the streets carrying flowers on their backs.
Alumbrado Navideño (December) A colorful Christmas illumination of the city, with thousands of lights strung across the streets and parks. The lights stay on from December 7 to January 6.

Sleeping
Thanks to stiff competition, accommodations are reasonably priced. For decent budget options head for the center.

Hotel Nutibara (Map p161; ☎ 511 5111; www.hotel nutibara.com in Spanish; Calle 52A No 50-46; s/d US$40/45; ⊠ ⌨) Once the city's top hotel, this 1940s art deco palace still has plenty of character inside and out. The large rooms are air-conditioned, though many are looking a little threadbare these days; angle for a higher floor for lower noise levels and better views. There's a gym and a large, outdoor pool. Buffet breakfast is included in the rates.

Palm Tree Hostal (Map p158; ☎ 260 2805; www.palm treemedellin.com; Carrera 67 No 48D-63; dm/d US$5/8; ⌨) Hidden in the Suramericana neighborhood west of the city center, the Palm Tree has become the backpacker's choice in Medellín. It offers six four-bed dorms as well as several private rooms, all without bathrooms. There's also a range of services, including laundry, Internet access, bicycle rental, book exchange and the use of the kitchen, plus free coffee. A taxi from either bus terminal to the hostel costs about US$2.50, or take the metro to Estación Suramericana.

Hotel El Capitolio (Map p161; ☎ 512 0012; fax 511 5631; Carrera 49 No 57-24; s/d US$13/15; ℗) Located just up from the cathedral, this place is great value with simple but spotless rooms above an attractive lobby. It retains some of its original art deco contours, and there's an open-air bar next to a tiny swimming pool.

Hotel Park 10 (☎ 266 8811; www.hotelpark10.com .co; Carrera 36B No 11-12; s/d US$85/105; ℗ ⊠ ⌨) Though it's crawling distance from the Zona Rosa, this new, postmodernist luxury hotel caters mostly to business people; expect steep weekend discounts. Rooms are large and plush, with everything from faux antiques to wireless Internet.

Hotel Botero Plaza (Map p161; ☎ 511 2155; hotelboteroplaza@epm.net.co; Carrera 50A No 53-45; s/d/tr US$29/31/37; ℗ ⊠ ⌨) Despite its location on a slightly sinister street in the center, the Botero Plaza has a remarkably swish reception. Rooms are less up-to-date but are comfortable enough, and those on higher floors afford excellent views.

Hotel Cristal (Map p161; ☎ 511 5631; Carrera 49 No 57-12; s/d US$11/15) This simple but clean establishment just up from Parque de Bolívar offers small, basic rooms. Note that many rooms have windows that open onto corridors rather than the outside. This makes them quiet if a little claustrophobic. All have private bathrooms.

Hostal Odeón (Map p161; ☎ 513 1404; Calle 54 No 49-38; s/d/tr US$9/14/19; 🐱) Another decent cheapie near Parque de Bolívar, this place has large if lugubrious rooms with OK beds and private bathrooms.

Eating

For hearty *paisa* food at great prices, head to central Medellín. For fine dining or ethnic food, your best bet is El Poblado, including the so-called Zona Rosa area.

CENTRAL MEDELLÍN

Salón Versalles (Map p161; ☎ 251 7416; Pasaje Junín No 53-39; mains from US$5; 🕑 7am-9pm Mon-Sat, 8am-6pm Sun) Famous for its scrumptious, Argentine-style empanadas (US$1), this Medellín classic may appear unassuming, but regularly attracts the city's movers and shakers. Meals are good if a little pricey for what you get.

Café Colombo (Map p161; ☎ 513 4444, ext 183; Carrera 45 No 53-24, piso 10; mains US$12-20; 🕑 noon-2:30pm & 5:30-11pm Mon-Sat) On the top floor of the building also housing the Centro Colombo Americano, this bright, stylishly minimalist spot serves up light meals with stunning views of the city and mountains.

Restaurante Mango Maduro (Map p161; ☎ 512 3671; Calle 54 No 47-5; meals US$2.50; 🕑 lunch Mon-Sat) Up an unassuming flight of stairs you'll find this festive little restaurant, which is popular with artists and intellectuals. Works by local painters adorn the orange walls, and the food, while simple, generally has an imaginative twist on *paisa* classics.

Restaurante Hatoviejo (Map p161; ☎ 251 2196; Carrera 47 No 52-17; mains US$6-8; 🕑 11:30am-11pm Mon-Sat) A favorite of Medellín's carnivores, this is the best place in the center for regional dishes such as *plato montañero*, an artery-clogging conglomeration of ground beef, eggs and fried pork skin.

Restaurante Vegetarian Govinda's (Map p161; ☎ 512 9481, ext 105; Calle 51 No 52-17; meals US$2; 🕑 lunch Mon-Sat) For decent vegetarian cuisine served by friendly Hari Krishnas, try this bright, upstairs restaurant near the Museo de Antioquia.

EL POBLADO

La Provincia (☎ 311 9630; Calle 4 Sur, No 43A-179; mains US$4-6; 🕑 lunch & dinner Mon-Fri, dinner Sat)

Located inside the Ovieda shopping mall, this upscale restaurant looks bland but it's regularly rated one of the city's top choices, with a menu inspired by both Mediterranean and classic French cuisines.

Thaico (☎ 311 5639; Calle 9A No 37-40; mains around US$10; 🕑 noon-1am Mon-Sat, noon-9pm Sun) Just across from Parque Lleras at the heart of Zona Rosa, this restaurant is popular with the city's party people for its large outdoor patio as much as its solid Thai cuisine.

Tramezzini (☎ 311 5617; Calle 9A No 37-56; mains around US$10; 🕑 noon-midnight Mon-Sat) This place looks like all the other casual, upmarket joints around Parque Lleras, but it is often cited as the best Italian restaurant in Medellín.

Drinking

While there is not much of a café scene in Medellín, you're never far from a cocktail. In the evening, action is most highly concentrated around Parque Lleras in El Poblado. If funds are low, buy a bottle of hooch and hang out in the small park itself – there are no open container laws and you'll find plenty of company.

Le Bon Café (☎ 266 8872; Parque Lleras; 🕑 9am-1am Mon-Sat, 9am-11pm Sun) If you prefer coffee to *aguardiente*, grab a table at this sophisticated café. It sits on the south side of Parque Lleras.

Café Arcángel (Map p158; ☎ 239 8755; Calle 47 No 42-64; 🕑 2-10pm Mon-Wed, 2pm-midnight Thu-Sun) A favorite of the alternative crowd, this place serves up beer, espresso, and even pierced poets reading their own works.

Melodie Lounge (☎ 268 1190; Carrera 37 No 10-29) This slick cocktail joint attracts high-end hipsters with its glowing walls and chill ambient music.

Berlín (☎ 266 2905; Calle 10 No 41-65) A lively bar with pool tables, rock classics and reasonably priced beer.

Entertainment

For entertainment listings, check out *El Colombiano*; the Thursday edition includes a special weekend supplement. Or buy *Opción Hoy* (US$1), a monthly publication that lists art exhibitions, theater, concerts, art-house cinema, and sports and cultural events.

CINEMA

Medellín has more than a dozen commercial cinemas (some of them multiplexes) screening the usual Hollywood repertoire. For more thought-provoking fare, check the programs of the *cinematecas*, the best known of which is the **Museo de Arte Moderno de Medellín** (Map p158; ☎ 230 2622; Carrera 64B No 51-64). In addition, **Museo de Antioquia** (Map p161; ☎ 251 3636; www.museodeantioquia.org in Spanish; Carrera 52 No 52-43) offers free films every Tuesday at 4pm. For interesting English-language films, check out the **Centro Colombo Americano** (Map p161; ☎ 513 4444; www.colomboworld.com in Spanish; Carrera 45 No 53-24).

THEATER
Medellín has a lively theater scene that ranges from the classical to the experimental, with more than 10 theaters and even more groups that work without a permanent home.

Teatro Matacandelas (Map p158; ☎ 215 1010; www.matacandelas.com in Spanish; Carrera 47 No 43-47) Matacandelas is one of the best experimental groups in town.

Teatro Pablo Tobón Uribe (Map p158; ☎ 239 7500; Carrera 40 No 51-24) This is Medellín's major mainstream theater.

El Pequeño Teatro de Medellín (Map p158; ☎ 269 9418; Carrera 42 No 50A-12) With a varied repertoire, this theater combines the traditional with the contemporary.

Teatro Metropolitano (Map p158; ☎ 232 4597; Calle 41 No 57-30) Inaugurated in 1987, Medellín's largest and most modern theater hosts concerts, opera and ballet and is home to Medellín's Philharmonic Orchestra.

CLASSICAL MUSIC
Both Teatro Metropolitano and Teatro de la Universidad de Medellín (Map p158) present concerts of classical and contemporary music. Another regular stage for concerts and recitals is the 300-seat Sala Beethoven in the **Palacio de Bellas Artes** (Map p158; ☎ 239 4820; Carrera 42 No 52-33).

TANGO
When tango singer Carlos Gardel's plane went down in Medellín in 1935, the city's love affair with the tango was sealed.

Casa Gardeliana (Map p158; ☎ 212 0968; Carrera 45 No 76-50) Located in Barrio Manrique, the Casa Gardeliana was the main tango venue for years, hosting tango bands and dance shows. It still has them from time to time, though now it's basically a small tango

museum, featuring memorabilia related to tango and Carlos Gardel.

El Patio del Tango (Map p158; ☎ 351 2856; Calle 23 No 58-38) Now the tango's major stage, El Patio del Tango is decorated like a typical Buenos Aires tango dive. There are often shows on Friday and Saturday nights.

NIGHTLIFE
To truly understand Medellín, you have to see its people in party mode. *Paisas* love to dress up, show off, throw some money around, and have a good time while they're at it.

The center of the action is around Parque Lleras in El Poblado, also known as the Zona Rosa. Roughly between Calles 9 and 10A, and Carreras 36 and 42, it draws the young, the beautiful, the rich, the surgically augmented and the merely enthusiastic. The area is packed with restaurants, bars and discos, many of which have large outdoor patios. Bars and clubs come in and out of fashion very quickly, so head to Parque Lleras and confer with locals. Cover charges vary by day, season and occasional special events; typically they charge US$5 to US$10. A taxi ride from the center to El Poblado costs about US$2 to US$3. Note that two of the best places – Mango's and Vinacuré – are located in suburbs south of the city.

If you don't want to explore Medellín by night on your own, you can go on a *chiva* (traditional bus) tour, which can be a convenient and reasonably safe way of visiting several hot nightspots in one go. A few drinks of *aguardiente* and some local snacks are included. The tours are run mostly on Friday and Saturday. They cost roughly US$10 to US$15 per person; you can get information at any local travel agency.

Mango's (☎ 277 6123; Carrera 42 No 67A-151) For raucous, *paisa*-style partying, head to the crown jewel of Medellín's nightlife. Mango's looks like the set of 'Urban Cowboy' and can shelter more than a thousand partiers. The music pumps, but if you need additional inspiration there are often shows with picture-perfect exotic dancers of both sexes.

Vinacuré (☎ 278 1633; Carrera 50 No 100D Sur-7) A piece of SoHo seems to have broken off and floated all the way to the hills south of Medellín. This outrageously imaginative place looks like a Frida Kahlo painting on acid, with choreography by the Cirque de Soleil. Give yourself over to the experience as you are greeted by honking geese, served by sexually ambiguous waitrons, and wowed by the circuslike live shows. It is a long and expensive cab ride (about US$8) but worth every penny.

Metrópolis (☎ 268 9404; Calle 10A No 40-37) With perhaps the best music and lighting infrastructure in the city, this place inside the Monterrey shopping mall serves up trance, techno and electronica to an adoring crowd of regulars.

El Blue (☎ 266 3047; Calle 10 No 40-20) Just off Parque Lleras, this place is devoted to rock, often hosting live bands. It has a large outdoor patio and a mostly laid-back crowd.

Shopping

Medellín is Colombia's major textile producer so there are plenty of clothes to choose from, and sometimes you can get good deals on surplus goods.

Centro Comercial Palacio Nacional (Map p161; ☎ 381 8144; cnr Carrera 52 & Calle 48) A palatial building from 1925 in the center, it has been transformed into a shopping mall with more than 200 budget shops (most with clothing and footwear). The area around the Palacio, nicknamed El Hueco (The Hole) by the locals, features plenty of bargain stores.

Plaza Minorista José María Villa (Map p158; cnr Carrera 57 & Calle 55) Home to a huge, bustling under-cover market with more than 2500 stalls, selling mostly food. It was established in 1984 to remove hawkers from the streets. It's open daily.

Mercado de San Alejo (Parque de Bolívar; ☉ 1st Sun each month) A colorful craft that's good for cheap buys or simply to stroll around.

For some finer shopping, head to the upscale malls of El Poblado, including **El Tesoro** (☎ 321 1010; Carrera 25A No 1AS-45), **Vizcaya** (☎ 268 4822; Calle 9 No 30-382) and **Oviedo** (☎ 321 6116; Carrera 43A No 6S-15). All of them have a variety of European and American fashion stores.

Getting There & Away
AIR
Medellín has two airports. The new José María Córdoba airport, 35km southeast of the city, near the town of Rionegro, takes all international and most domestic flights, except for some flights on light planes which use the old Olaya Herrera airport right inside the city.

At the time of writing, there were direct flights to Cali and Cartagena with SAM and to San Andres with Avianca. For other destinations you will likely have to change planes in Bogotá. Fortunately, connections are frequent. Avianca alone has more than a dozen Bogotá–Medellín flights daily.

BUS
Medellín has two bus terminals. The Northern Bus Terminal (Terminal del Norte), 3km north of the city center, handles buses to the north, east and southeast, including Santa Fe de Antioquia (US$4, three hours), Cartagena (US$39, 13 hours), Barranquilla (US$32, 14 hours), Santa Marta (US$35, 16 hours) and Bogotá (US$20, nine hours). It is easily reached from the center by metro in seven minutes (Estación Caribe), or by taxi (US$2).

The Southern Bus Terminal (Terminal del Sur), 4km southwest of the center, handles all traffic to the west and south, including Quibdó (US$17, 10 hours), Manizales (US$11, five hours), Pereira (US$11, five hours), Armenia (US$12, six hours), Cali (US$18, nine hours), Popayán (US$22, 12 hours) and Pasto (US$30, 18 hours). It's accessible from the center by the Guayabal bus (Ruta No 143) and the Trinidad bus (Ruta No 160). Alternatively, go by taxi (US$2).

Getting Around
TO/FROM THE AIRPORT
Minibuses shuttle between the city center and the new airport every half-hour from 4:30am to 7:30pm from the corner of Carrera 50A and Calle 53 (US$2, one hour); taxis cost about US$18. The old airport's terminal is next to the Southern Bus Terminal.

BUS
Apart from the metro, urban transport is serviced by buses and *busetas* (small buses), and is quite well organized. All buses are numbered and display their destination point. There are bus stops on most routes, though sometimes buses will also stop in-between. The majority of routes originate on Av Oriental and Parque Berrío, from where you can get to almost anywhere within the metropolitan area. Public transport stops around 10pm to 11pm however, leaving only taxis plying the streets at night.

DETOUR: CHOCÓ & THE PACIFIC COAST

While difficult to access, Colombia's Pacific coast is rich in rewards for the intrepid traveler. The people, most of whom are descendants of African slaves, are famously friendly. The few foreigners they meet they tend to treat as special guests rather than tourists. Warm temperatures and a year-round deluge of moisture – the region regularly receives more than 6m of rain a year – support a jungle of stunning biodiversity. There are beaches to enjoy – when it's not raining – and from August and September great schools of whales and dolphins sport in the coastal waters.

From Medellín or Pereira, you can travel by land to Quibdó, the departmental capital, though the rewards are few – it's neither an attractive nor a particularly interesting city. The roads in and out are rough going and remain potentially dangerous. Better to fly to the tiny coastal town of Nuquí. Satena Airlines has regularly scheduled flights from Medellín. From here, you can travel by boat to a number of remote, ecoresorts, perhaps the best of which is the award-winning Cabañas Pijiba, with rustic cabins set between jungle and sea, a 40-minute boat ride from the Nuquí airport.

METRO

Medellín is Colombia's first (and for the foreseeable future the only) city to have the metro, or fast metropolitan train. It is clean, cheap, safe and efficient, and has become the pride of the *paisas*. Its construction began in 1985 and after a series of setbacks it eventually opened in 1995.

The metro consists of a 23km north–south line (Línea 1) and a 6km east–west line (Línea 2). Trains run at ground level except for 5km through the central area where they go on viaducts above streets, providing good views. There's a new leg called Metrocable that consists of cable cars that climb up into the poor hillside communities north of the center. The ride itself is safe, and affords magnificent views.

The metro operates from 4:30am to 11pm Monday to Saturday, and from 5am to 10pm Sunday and holidays, with trains running every five to 10 minutes. Tickets can be bought at any metro station and cost US$0.45/0.80 for a single/double ride, or you can buy a 10-ride *multiviaje* for US$4. Learn more at www.metrodemedellin.org.co (in Spanish).

CIRCUITO DE ORIENTE

With rambling haciendas and lovely *pueblos paisas* (*paisa* towns), the mountainous region southeast of Medellín seems to have opted out of the struggles of the modern world. The steep slopes of the Cordillera Central are lush with vegetation, thanks to a year-round combination of moderate temperatures and regular rainfall. Along the winding mountain roads, the Andes range from picturesque to stunning.

With well-policed roads and a developed tourist infrastructure, this region, known as Circuito de Oriente, makes a great day trip from Medellín, as well as a fine place to wander and relax if you are interested in a longer introduction to the *paisa* way of life. If you really want to be wowed, head on your own to El Peñol, a dramatic volcanic outcropping that overlooks a gorgeous artificial lake.

The standard, one-day loop usually includes Marinilla, Rionegro, Carmen de Viboral, La Ceja, Salto de Tequendamita, Retiro and the Hacienda Fizebad. Several companies offer day tours, including **Las Buseticas** (Map p158; ☎ 262 7444; www.lasbuseticas.com in Spanish; Carrera 43A No 34-95, Medellín). Depending on the itinerary and size of the group, prices range from US$25 to US$50 per person, including lunch.

Food and accommodations are easy to come by throughout the region, and bus transport is frequent (all buses depart from Medellín's Terminal del Norte).

Marinilla
☎ 4

Some 46km southeast of Medellín on the road to Bogotá, Marinilla is a well-preserved example of Antioquian architecture and city planning, with a pleasant main plaza and adjacent streets. Dating from the first half of the 18th century, it's one of the oldest towns in the region. Stroll around the central streets and call at the **Capilla de Jesús Nazareno** (cnr Carrera 29 & Calle 32), a fine, whitewashed gem of a church erected in the 1750s.

Marinilla's Semana Santa celebration is one of the most elaborate in Antioquia, with processions and concerts of religious music held in the Capilla. Marinilla is also known for manufacturing top-quality stringed instruments.

There are half-a-dozen budget hotels in town, all of which are on or just off the main plaza. Buses to Medellín depart frequently from the plaza (US$1, one hour), as do *colectivos* to Rionegro (US$0.40, 15 minutes).

El Peñol

Reminiscent of the famous Sugar Loaf of Rio de Janeiro, El Peñol (literally 'the Stone') is a 200m-high granite monolith rising from the banks of Embalse del Peñol, an artificial lake about 30km east of Marinilla. An ascent up the 649 steps will reward you with magnificent bird's-eye views of the entire region, including the beautiful lake at your feet. There's a snack bar at the top.

The lake has become a popular weekend getaway for Medellín's dwellers, and a number of *estaderos* (roadside restaurants) have sprung up on the road and the lakeside. They provide accommodation in rooms and/or *cabañas* (cabins) and food in their own restaurants. Some of the cheapest *estaderos* are found at the foot of the rock, on the Peñol–Guatapé road.

Buses to and from Medellín run every one to two hours (US$3, 2½ hours) and they all pass through Marinilla (US$2, 1¼ hours).

Rionegro

☎ 4 / pop 40,000

Founded in 1663, Rionegro is the oldest and most populous town of the Circuito de Oriente. Surrounded by a patchwork of farms and lush orchards, it has a number of a number of classic, *paisa*-style buildings. It is also the town nearest to Medellín's main airport.

The town's main plaza boasts the **Monumento a José María Córdoba**, a statue of a local hero of the War of Independence. The allegoric figure of the naked general is one of many unconventional works by Rodrigo Arenas Betancur. The massive 200-year-old **Catedral de San Nicolás**, overlooking the plaza, has an impressive silver *sagrario* (tabernacle) in the high altar. Behind the altar is a small **museum** of religious art.

In 1863 politicians convened in the **Casa de la Convención** (Calle 51 No 47-67) to write the most liberal constitution in the country's history. The house is now a museum featuring a collection of documents and period exhibits related to the event. One block from the Casa is the 1740 **Capilla de San Francisco** (cnr Calle 51 & Carrera 48), the town's oldest existing church.

Located 48km southeast of Medellín and 7km southwest of Marinilla, Rionegro has many budget hotels and restaurants around the central streets. The town is also a busy transport hub, with frequent buses to Medellín (US$1.50, 1¼ hours) and *colectivos* to Marinilla (US$0.50, 15 minutes), Carmen de Viboral (US$0.75, 20 minutes) and La Ceja (US$0.75, 25 minutes).

Carmen de Viboral

☎ 4 / pop 15,000

This small town 9km southeast of Rionegro, is known nationwide as a producer of hand-painted ceramics. There are a few large factories on the outskirts of the town – including Continental, Capiro and Triunfo – and several small workshops that are still largely unmechanised. Almost all tours from Medellín include a visit to one of the factories.

Several *hospedajes* (budget hotels) are in the main plaza, as well as several restaurants. Frequent *colectivos* run to Rionegro from the plaza (US$0.75, 20 minutes).

La Ceja

☎ 4 / pop 25,000

Founded in 1789, La Ceja has developed into a handsome *pueblo paisa*. It has a pleasant, spacious main plaza lined with balconied houses, a number of which have preserved their delicate door and window decorations. There are two churches on the plaza, the smaller of which has a remarkably elaborate interior, complete with an extraordinary baroque retable carved in wood.

Like other towns on the route, La Ceja has a choice of budget hotels and restaurants. Buses to Medellín depart frequently from the main plaza (US$1.25, 1¼ hours), as do *colectivos* to Rionegro (US$0.70, 25 minutes). The road to Medellín winds spectacularly through pine forests.

Note that 9km northwest of La Ceja on the road to Medellín is the **Salto de Tequendamita waterfall**. A pleasant restaurant is ideally located at the foot of the falls. Many tours organized from Medellín stop here for lunch.

Retiro

☎ 4 / pop 6000

Founded around 1800, this tiny town remains one of the most picturesque in the region. It's set amid verdant hills 33km southeast of Medellín, 4km off the road to La Ceja. The main plaza is a good example of Antioquian architecture, as are many houses lining the surrounding streets.

The **Fiesta de Los Negritos** is held annually in late December to commemorate the abolition of slavery in the region. It was here, in Retiro, that 126 slaves were liberated in the early 1810s, possibly the first case of its kind in the country's history.

Small as it is, Retiro has a choice of cheap hotels and restaurants. Buses to Medellín run every half an hour (US$1.25, one hour) along a spectacular road dotted with lovely haciendas.

Hacienda Fizebad

Fizebad is an old hacienda, 27km southeast of Medellín on the road to La Ceja. The main house dates from 1825 and has its original furniture and other period objects. There's also a replica of a *pueblo paisa*, complete with chapel and shops, and about 150 species of orchids are grown on the grounds. One of the houses features a collection of pre-Columbian ceramics. Many buses from Medellín to La Ceja and Retiro pass by the hacienda and will let you off at the entrance.

SANTA FE DE ANTIOQUIA

☎ 4 / pop 12,500 / elevation 550m / temp 27°C

Set in a lush, low-lying and steaming hot valley near the banks of the Río Cauca, Santa Fe de Antioquia is the region's oldest settlement – and its best preserved. Founded in 1541 by Jorge Robledo, it served as the capital of Antioquia until 1826, when the government moved to Medellín.

Because it was eclipsed for so long by its neighbor 80km to the southwest, its colonial center never fell to the wrecking ball and today it looks very much like it did in the 18th century. The narrow streets are lined with whitewashed houses, all single-storey construction and many ranged around beautiful courtyards. You'll also see elaborately carved – and typically Antioquian – woodwork around windows and doorways. And don't miss *pulpa de tamarindo*, the

beloved sour-sweet candy made with tamarind from the surrounding valley. Pick up a pack from one of the vendors on Plaza Mayor, the town's sleepy main square.

Information

Oficina de Fomento y Turismo (☎ 853 2314; Plaza Mayor; ⏱ 8am-noon & 2-6pm Mon-Fri) The tourist office is in the Palacio Municipal on the main plaza.

Sights

Of the town's four churches, the **Iglesia de Santa Bárbara** (cnr Calle 11 & Carrera 8; ⏱ 5-6:30pm, plus Sun morning Mass) is the most interesting. Built by Jesuits in the second half of the 18th century, the church has a fine, baroque facade. The interior boasts an interesting, if time-worn, retable over the high altar. The **Museo de Arte Religioso** (☎ 853 2345; Calle 11 No 8-12; admission US$1; ⏱ 10am-5pm Sat, Sun & holidays), next door to Santa Bárbara church, has a collection of religious objects, including paintings by Gregorio Vásquez de Arce y Ceballos.

The **Catedral** (Plaza Mayor; ⏱ morning & evening Mass, plus 11am Sun service) is sometimes referred to as the Catedral Madre, as it was the first church built in the region. However, the original church was destroyed by fire, and the large building you see today was not completed until 1837. Until that year, Iglesia de Santa Bárbara did the honors as the cathedral. Once inside, have a look at the *Last Supper* in the right transept and at an image of San Francisco de Borja with a skull in the opposite transept.

The two remaining churches, the mid-17th-century **Iglesia de Chiquinquirá** (cnr Carrera 13 & Calle 10), also known as La Chinca, and the 1828 **Iglesia de Jesús Nazareno** (cnr Carrera 5 & Calle 10), are generally open only for evening Mass at 7pm daily. Admirers of funerary art may want to visit the local **cemetery** at the southeastern end of Calle 10, which has a collection of historic tombstones and a 150-year-old cemetery chapel.

While you are in Santa Fe, consider a short trip to the unusual bridge, the Puente de Occidente (p171).

Festivals & Events

Semana Santa (Easter Week) Like most traditional towns dating from the early days of the Spanish Conquest, Santa Fe celebrates this with pomp and solemnity. Book rooms in advance.

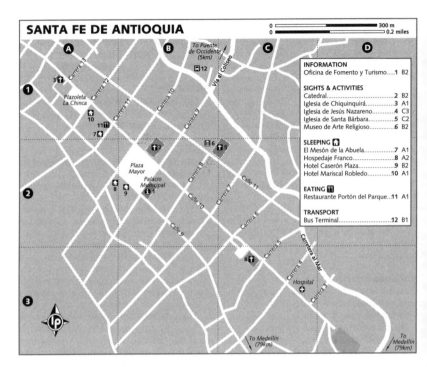

SANTA FE DE ANTIOQUIA

0 ——————— 300 m
0 ——————— 0.2 miles

INFORMATION
Oficina de Fomento y Turismo.....**1** B2

SIGHTS & ACTIVITIES
Catedral...**2** B2
Iglesia de Chiquinquirá..................**3** A1
Iglesia de Jesús Nazareno..............**4** C3
Iglesia de Santa Bárbara................**5** C2
Museo de Arte Religioso................**6** B2

SLEEPING ⌂
El Mesón de la Abuela...................**7** A1
Hospedaje Franco..........................**8** A2
Hotel Caserón Plaza.......................**9** B2
Hotel Mariscal Robledo.............**10** A1

EATING ⌘
Restaurante Portón del Parque...**11** A1

TRANSPORT
Bus Terminal.................................**12** B1

Fiesta de los Diablitos (December) The town's main popular festival is held annually over the last four days of the year. It includes music, dance and a craft fair, and – like almost every feast in the country – a beauty contest and bullfights.

Sleeping & Eating

Most people come to Santa Fe as a day trip, but the town also has about a dozen hotels catering to all budgets. They're usually empty except for weekends, so you may be able to negotiate better prices during the week. While there are few stand-alone restaurants, most hotels also have dining rooms serving simple meals of rice, beans, grilled meat or fish, and fried plantains.

Hotel Mariscal Robledo (☎ 352 3300; lagotours@epm.net.co; Carrera 12 No 9-70; r with full board adult/child US$40/24; P ⌘ ⌐) Hands down the best place in town, this elegant hotel is a bargain when you consider the price includes three delicious meals a day. Rooms are simply but elegantly appointed with beautiful mint-green tiles, and there is a large swimming pool in a gardenlike courtyard.

Hotel Caserón Plaza (☎ 853 2040; halcaraz@edatel.net.co; Plaza Mayor; d from US$33; ⌐) On the town's

main square, this inn was once home to a member of the local gentry. Rooms are ranged around an attractive courtyard, and there is a nice pool and garden in the back, plus a decent restaurant. Meals are extra.

El Mesón de la Abuela (☎ 853 1053; Carrera 11 No 9-31; s/d US$13/22) Basic rooms with fans and private bathrooms open onto an attractive, plant-filled courtyard. Hearty breakfasts ($2), lunches and dinners (both $5) are served in the open-air dining room.

Hospedaje Franco (☎ 853 1654; Carrera 10 No 8A-14; r per person US$6) This family-run place offers very basic rooms around a small courtyard. Mattresses are thin, and rooms lack cross-ventilation and sometimes working fans, but some do have private bathrooms at no extra cost. Still, it's clean and the low price even includes breakfast.

Restaurante Portón del Parque (☎ 853 3207; Calle 10 No 11-03; mains $10-15; ⌚ noon-2:30pm & 7-10pm) Occupying an elegant colonial house with high ceilings and a flowery courtyard, this restaurant is widely considered the best restaurant in town. The kitchen prepares regional cuisine with care and finesse.

Getting There & Away
There are at least half-a-dozen buses daily (US$4, three hours) and another half-dozen minibuses (US$5, 2½ hours) to and from Medellín's Northern Bus Terminal. There are also *colectivos* if there's a demand (US$5, two hours).

PUENTE DE OCCIDENTE
The Puente de Occidente, or the West Bridge, is a peculiar pearl of 19th-century engineering. This 291m-long bridge over the Río Cauca was designed by José María Villa and constructed in 1887–95. When built, it was one of the first suspension bridges in the Americas. It carried general traffic until 1978, when it was declared a national monument. Buses are now banned, though cars can still use it.

The bridge is 5km east of Santa Fe on the road to Sopetrán. Buses are not allowed to cross the bridge so you have two options: negotiate a return trip with a taxi driver in Santa Fe or walk (one hour), though be sure to avoid the unbearable midday heat.

ZONA CAFETERA

With just the brew of altitude and precipitation, the terraced slopes of the Zona Cafetera yield nearly half of Colombia's coffee crop on just over 1% of the country's total area. The conjunction of agreeable temperatures, lush green valleys, and impressive snow-capped peaks make it perfectly adapted for curious travelers as well.

The region wasn't settled by the Spanish until the mid-19th century, when Antioquia began expanding southwards during the so-called *colonización antioqueña*. By 1905, the area had developed enough to become a department in its own right, which was called Caldas. In 1966 conflicting economic interests within Caldas led to its split into three smaller units: Caldas, Risaralda and Quindío.

The region's *paisa* roots are evident in everything from its architecture to its hearty, meat-based cuisine. It has three cities, each of which is a departmental capital: Manizales, Pereira and Armenia. None is beautiful or particularly interesting in its own right, but all make good bases from which to explore the surrounding region. Their

lack of charm is due in large part to the region's seismic instability. The most recent catastrophic quake struck in 1999, severely damaging both Pereira and Armenia.

Nature is the real reason you come here, whether it's to explore the lush coffee plantations, which cover nearly every slope between 1300m and 1700m, or to trek through the spectacular High Andes.

MANIZALES
☎ 6 / pop 420,000 / elevation 2150m / temp 18°C

The capital of the Caldas department, Manizales has long been an important center of the region's coffee trade. Its prosperity is evidenced both in its bustling streets and its scattering of deluxe, modern high-rises. Unfortunately the city has, from its inception, suffered a punishing series of earthquakes as well as a devastating fire in 1925. As a result, little remains of historical interest. But because it's perched along a ridge of the Central Cordillera, its hilly streets have a certain charm.

The city was founded in 1849 by a group of Antioquian colonists searching for a tranquil place to escape the civil wars that plagued the country during that time. According to local legend, the original settlement consisted of 20 families, including the family of Manuel Grisales, after whom the new city was named. Manizales' early development was painfully slow, hindered by two serious earthquakes in 1875 and 1878. It wasn't until the beginning of the 20th century that the town began its rapid expansion, partly because it became the capital of the newly created Caldas department and a center of the region's coffee trade.

Temperatures are cool year-round, though the rainy seasons, from March to May and September to November, can be slightly depressing.

Information
INTERNET ACCESS
There is no shortage of Internet cafés in the center. Most charge around US$1 per hour.

Café Internet Fundadores (☎ 884 2538; Carrera 23 No 30-59)

Internet Café Tamanaco (☎ 889 6290; cnr Calle 23 & Carrera 21; ⏱ 8am-8pm) A pleasant ambience and decent espresso drinks, but slow connections.

NORTHWEST COLOMBIA

MANIZALES

0 ────── 400 m
0 ────── 0.2 miles

INFORMATION
Banco Unión Colombiano....1 B4
Bancolombia.........................2 B3
Café Internet Fundadores....3 F4
Cambios Country..................4 C3
Centro de Información
Turística de Caldas...........5 C3
Giros & Finanzas..................6 B3
Internet Café Tamanaco......7 C3

SIGHTS & ACTIVITIES
Bioturismo Arte y Café........8 F3
Catedral de Manizales........9 C4
Iglesia de la Inmaculada
Concepción........................10 F3
Museo del Oro...................11 C4
Palacio de Gobierno...........12 C3
Tesoro Tours Manizales....13 B3

SLEEPING
California Hotel...................14 B1
Hotel Fundadores..............15 F4
Hotel La Terminal.........(see 23)
Hotel Las Colinas..............16 B4

EATING
El Mural......................(see 16)
Punto Rojo........................17 C4
Restaurante El Pilón..........18 B3
Restaurante Zaguán
Caldense.........................19 F4

ENTERTAINMENT
Café La Cigarra..................20 C4
Las Faroles........................21 D4
Reminiscencias...................22 C3

TRANSPORT
Bus Terminal......................23 A1

MONEY

Banco Unión Colombiano (cnr Calle 21 & Carrera 22) Changes cash and traveler's checks.

Bancolombia (cnr Calle 21 & Carrera 22)

Cambios Country (Calle 22 No 21-44) Changing cash may be more favorable and quicker in a *casa de cambio*. There are plenty of these across the center, including this one.

Giros & Finanzas (Calle 19 No 21-30) This *casa de cambio* is the agent of Western Union.

TOURIST INFORMATION

Centro de Información Turística de Caldas (☎ 884 2400, ext 153; ☯ 8am-6pm Mon-Sat, 9am-1pm Sun) The tourist office is located on the bottom floor of the Palacio de Gobierno at the end furthest from Plaza de Bolívar.

Sights

The Plaza de Bolívar is the city's main square, with the mandatory statue of Bolívar by Rodrigo Arenas Betacur. It is known as Bolívar-Cóndor, since the sculptor endows Colombia's founder with distinctly birdlike features. The **Palacio de Gobierno**, a pretty neoclassical confection built in 1927, stands on the northern side of the plaza.

The square's south side is dominated by the odd but impressive **Catedral de Manizales**; it was the third church erected on this site. The first, built in 1854, was destroyed by an earthquake in 1878. The next, a handsome wooden church, went up in flames during the fire of 1925. Begun in 1929, the present church is an imposing piece of neo-Gothic architecture. Built of reinforced concrete, it is among the first churches of its kind in Latin America, and its main tower is 106m high, making it the highest church tower in the country. Be sure to check out the three front bronze doors. Covered with bas-reliefs that tell the history of Manizales as well as its cathedral, they seem more civic than holy. Don't be misled if these doors are locked (they are usually open only for Sunday Mass); you can enter the cathedral by either of the side doors. The spacious interior is decorated with richly colored stained-glass windows in a hodgepodge of styles.

The **Museo del Oro** (Gold Museum; ☎ 884 3851; Carrera 23 No 23-6, Piso 2; admission free; ☯ 8-11:30am & 2-6pm Mon-Fri) is located a block south of the Plaza de Bolívar in the Banco de la República building. It has a lovely if small collection of Quimbaya gold and ceramic artifacts.

A short walk east of Plaza de Bolívar is the **Iglesia de la Inmaculada Concepción**. Built

at the beginning of the 20th century, it has a beautiful, carved-wood interior reminiscent of a ship's hull.

Tours

Manizales sits on the northwestern outskirts of the Parque Nacional Los Nevados, which is the focus of local tour activity. The most popular tour is a full-day trip to the foot of Nevado del Ruiz, the highest volcano in the park. The standard package (about US$30 per person) includes transport from Manizales, a guide, a snack, a walk up the volcano slope (but not to the top) and a bath in the hot springs of the Hotel Termales del Ruiz. The tour can be organized through some of the city's major tour agencies.

Bioturismo Arte y Café (☎ 884 4037; Centro Comercial Parque Caldas) The best specialist company is managed by Omar Vargas. The agency also offers other tours in the park (Laguna del Otún, Laguna Verde) and beyond (Valle de Cocora, Parque del Café). It can also arrange a licensed guide to the park, should you prefer a tailor-made route or wish to go mountaineering.

Ecoturismo (☎ 880 8300; www.aventurascolombia .com in Spanish; Carrera 11 No 63-05) A tour company worth trying.

Tesoro Tours Manizales (☎ 883 7040; Hotel Escorial, Calle 21 No 21-11) Another reputable tour company.

Festivals & Events

Feria de Manizales (January) The city's annual blowout during the first weeks of the year. There are parades, craft fairs, nightly poetry meetings and, of course, a beauty pageant in which the Coffee Queen is elected. The most important corridas (bullfights) take place during this period.

Festival Latinoamericano de Teatro (late September) Held since 1968, this is one of two important theater festivals in Colombia (the other is in Bogotá). The festival lasts for about a week and includes free concerts in Plaza de Bolívar.

Sleeping

California Hotel (☎ 884 7720; fax 880 0906; Calle 19 No 16-37; s/d US$13/19) Just across from the bus station, this brand-new option has pleasant common areas and small but decent rooms at attractive prices.

Hotel Fundadores (☎ 884 6490; www.hotelfunda dores.com in Spanish; Carrera 23 No 29-54; s/d incl breakfast US$44/48) This small but attractive hotel occupies what looks like a traditional *paisa*-style building, though if you look closely you'll see it's made from poured concrete. Rooms are large and well-appointed, including very comfy beds.

Hotel Las Colinas (☎ 884 2009; www.hotellascolinas.com in Spanish; Carrera 22 No 20-20; r US$64) The poshest place in town, this modern glass-and-concrete hotel isn't pretty to look at but it has the largest, most comfortable rooms in town, plus a good restaurant. Prices include a generous breakfast buffet.

Hotel La Terminal (☎ 880 1800; fax 884 9516; d US$9, with bathroom US$13) Rooms here are lugubrious and very basic, but the price is right. And you won't find a more convenient location on the top floor of the city's bus station.

Eating

El Murál (☎ 884 2009; Carrera 22 No 20-20; mains US$7-12; ☼ 7am-9pm) The best option in the center of town, El Murál serves up classic continental dishes inside the Hotel Las Colinas. During the week, there's also a lunch buffet (US$6).

Restaurante Zaguán Caldense (☎ 883 6360; Carrera 23 No 30-64; set meals US$2.50, mains US$3-4) A local classic, this place serves typical *bandeja paisa* (regional cuisine) – including *mondongo* (tripe) and frijoles – that is only OK. The interior of the restaurant, which is covered entirely in *guadua* (a sort of local bamboo), is interesting.

Restaurante El Pilón (☎ 883 2021; Calle 21 No 21-21; mains US$4-5) This is another bamboo-lined restaurant serving hearty local dishes.

Punto Rojo (Carrera 23 No 21-39; mains US$2-3; ☼ 24hr) This 24-hour cafeteria serves dishes of varying quality, but the convenience factor is high.

Entertainment

Teatro Los Fundadores (☎ 884 5633; cnr Carrera 22 & Calle 33) Manizales' leading theater, and it also has a cinema.

Most nightlife takes place outside the center. One area noted for bars and discos is around the bullring on Av Centenario, 1km southwest of the center. In the center, there are two adjacent tango bars – **Reminiscencias** (Calle 24 No 22-40) and **Los Faroles** (Calle 24 No 22-46). Or you can watch Manizales' coffee traders and good old boys who gather day and night at **Café La Cigarra** (Carrera 23 near Calle 22).

Getting There & Away

AIR

La Nubia airport is about 8km southeast of the city center, off the road to Bogotá; take the urban bus to La Enea, then walk

for five minutes the rest of the way. Avianca operates around a half-dozen flights a day to Bogotá, with connections to other destinations.

BUS

The bus terminal is on Av 19 between Carreras 14 and 17, a short walk northwest of Plaza de Bolívar. Buses depart regularly to Bogotá (US$16, eight hours), Medellín (US$10, five hours) and Cali (US$12, five hours). Minibuses to Pereira (US$3, 1¼ hours) and Armenia (US$5, 2¼ hours) run every 15 minutes or so. To Salamina, there are minibuses (US$4, 2½ hours) and *colectivos* (US$5, 2¼ hours).

PARQUE NACIONAL LOS NEVADOS

Following a spine of snow-covered volcanic peaks, this 583-sq-km national park provides access to some of the most stunning – and safest – stretches of the Colombian Andes. With altitudes ranging from 2600m to 5325m, it encompasses everything from humid cloud forests and *páramos* (open highlands) to the perpetual snows of the highest peaks. The main peaks, from north to south, are: El Ruiz (5325m), El Cisne (4750m), Santa Isabel (4950m), El Quindío (4750m) and El Tolima (5215m).

The Nevado del Ruiz is the largest and the highest volcano of the chain. Its eruption on November 13, 1985 killed more than 20,000 people. Hot gases melted a part of the snow cap and swollen rivers of mud cascaded down the eastern slopes, sweeping away everything in their path. Armero, a town of about 25,000 inhabitants on the Río Lagunillas, disappeared entirely under the mud.

El Ruiz had previously erupted in 1845, but the results were far less catastrophic. Today, it seems that the volcano has returned to its slumber, and its activity is limited to the occasional puff of smoke hovering over the crater. It can wake up, however, at any time and several alerts have been raised over the past decade when the volcano's plume grew bigger than usual.

The Nevado del Tolima, the second-highest volcano in the chain, is the most handsome of all with its classic symmetrical cone. On a clear day it can be seen from as far away as Bogotá. Its last eruption took place in 1943, but today it is considered almost extinct.

Orientation

The only road access into the park is from the north. This road branches off from the Manizales–Bogotá road in La Esperanza, 31km from Manizales, and winds its way up to the snowline at about 4800m at the foot of Nevado del Ruiz.

The entrance to the park is at Las Brisas (4050m) where foreign visitors pay a US$8 admission fee (if you come with a tour group it's normally included in the tour price). About 4km uphill from Las Brisas is the Chalet Arenales and 10km further up the road is a shelter known as Refugio (4800m).

The volcano actually has three craters: Arenas, Olleta and Piraña. The main one, Arenas (5325m), responsible for the 1985 disaster, has a diameter of 800m and is about 200m deep. It's a three-hour hike from the Refugio up to the top. You walk on snow, but the ascent is relatively easy and no special mountaineering equipment is necessary.

The extinct Olleta crater (4850m), on the opposite side of the road, is covered with multicolored layers of sandy soil and normally has no snow. The walk to the top will take about 1¼ hours from the road, and it's possible to descend into the crater.

The road continues for another 38km along El Cisne and Santa Isabel down to the Laguna del Otún, a large, beautiful lake at 3950m.

The southern part of the park is accessible only by foot. From Refugio La Pastora in the Parque Ucumarí (p180) a 15km trail goes uphill to the Laguna del Otún. Another access route begins from Cocora, from where a path heads uphill to the *páramo* and on to the extinct Nevado del Quindío. Neither of these routes is popular with hikers and in the past there have been occasional instances of guerrilla activity on both trails. Be sure to check current conditions.

When to Go

The best months to trek in Los Nevados are January and February. December, March, July and August can be relatively good but more unpredictable in terms of weather. The rest of the year is quite rainy and the volcanoes are usually hidden in the clouds, showing themselves only on occasional mornings.

Tours

The northern access road is by far the park's most popular gateway, through which most tourists come on a day tour from Manizales (see p173). It's a 10-hour tour, which gives a glimpse of high-mountain scenery up to 5100m.

From the Refugio, tour participants take a walk uphill (up to two hours return), but don't go as far as the crater. On the way back the tours call at the Hotel Termales del Ruiz for a bath in the hot springs.

Individual visitors can only enter the park with a registered park guide. In Manizales, contact **Bioturismo Arte y Café** (☎ 884 4037; Centro Comercial Parque Caldas).

Sleeping & Eating

The park has some basic accommodations and food facilities, which allow for longer stays in the area. Information and bookings are available through Bogotá's Parques Nacionales Naturales de Colombia (p54).

Hotel Termales del Ruiz (☎ 851 7069, 870 0944; s/d US$32/38) Park facilities apart, there's a comfortable hotel just outside the northern boundary of the park. Set at 3500m, this is the highest hotel in the country. It has a restaurant and thermal pools, and is on the itineraries of most organized tours. There's no public transport on the access road to the hotel.

Cabaña Las Brisas, at the entrance to the park (4050m), provides basic accommodations for US$3, but you'll need a good sleeping bag. No food is available here. Chalet Arenales (4150m) offers dorm beds for about US$5 per night. Food is available, but you need to order in advance. Refugio (4800m) has no accommodations but sometimes sells snacks and hot drinks. Check whether it's open at the park's entrance.

Getting There & Away

There's no public transport to the park. Bioturismo Arte y Café in Manizales can provide transport in a car, jeep, minibus or *buseta,* but it can be costly if you are on your own or in a small party.

NORTHWEST COLOMBIA

THE BUZZ ON COLOMBIAN COFFEE

Need a quick shot of energy but unwilling to mess around with Colombia's number two agricultural export? Try coffee. It's legal, and you're almost never more than a few steps from a fresh pot. It is served everywhere, all day long: bus stations, hotel lobbies, restaurants, cafés and even on the street from vendors who will pour a splash of brown gold into a little plastic cup for about US$0.10. It's not always good, but it sure is ubiquitous.

Coffee snobs can be hard on Colombian beans. It's true that large cooperatives have imposed uniform conditions on growers, promoting consistency of price and quality at the price of excellence or innovation. In recent years, though, more and more small growers are producing winningly upmarket varietals. Here are a few Colombia coffee facts:

- Coffee plants were first introduced to Colombia around 1830.
- Coffee is brewed on a daily basis in an estimated 88% of all Colombian households.
- By the 1940s, coffee accounted for as much as 80% of Colombia's export income.
- Colombia, long-time second only to Brazil, is now rivaled by Vietnam in total production.
- Colombian coffee is prized for its brightness (balanced acidity), full flavors, clean finish, and remarkable consistency. All these qualities make it good for industrial use as well as a blend with more distinctive beans.
- Colombia grows the noble arabica plants as opposed to the less desirable robusta plants. Varietals include Typica, Caturra, and Maragogype.
- In Colombia (and countries at similar latitudes), the best coffee grows at between 1200m and 1700m.

SALAMINA

☎ 6 / pop 19,000 / elevation 1775m / temp 19°C

Founded in 1825, Salamina is one of the oldest towns in the Zona Cafetera and, thanks to its relative isolation, it has managed to retain the feel of a typical *pueblo paisa*. A number of houses still have doors and windows decked out elaborately with carved wood in typical *paisa* style.

Designed by an English architect and built between 1865 and 1875, the town's unusual **cathedral** consists of a single nave. The wide-open space is crowned with a flat ceiling of carved wood. There is also a fine wooden altar from the early 20th century, as well as a pretty cemetery chapel.

Most people visit Salamina as a half- or full-day trip from Manizales, although if you prefer to stay longer there are some budget hotels in the market area on Carrera 6 and around the main plaza. Regular minibuses (US$4, 2½ hours) and *colectivos* (US$5, 2¼ hours) operate between Manizales and Salamina, and all pass through Neira, another historic town that's worth a gander if you're a devotee of colonial-style *paisa* architecture.

PEREIRA

☎ 6 / pop 455,000 / elevation 1410m / temp 21°C

The capital of Risaralda and the Zona Cafetera's largest city, Pereira has a coffee-based prosperity and caffeine-driven bustle; it's a fine base to explore the region. The town was founded in 1863, though a series of destructive earthquakes have damaged or destroyed its historic center again and again. Even its **Catetral de Nuestra Señora de la Pobreza** has been repaired or rebuilt so many times that it has a distinctly patchwork look. Indeed, powerful tremblers affected the city as recently as 1995 and 1999.

While the city itself may be a bit thin on attractions, Marsella (p179), Termales de Santa Rosa (p179) and Ecotermales San Vicente (p180) are nearby. And Pereira is also a good launching pad for the Parque Ucumarí (p180) and Santuario Otún Quimbaya (p181).

While you're in Pereira, be sure to check out Arenas Betancur's **Bolívar Desnudo**, an 8.5m-high, 11-ton bronze sculpture of the naked Bolívar on horseback, in the Plaza de Bolívar – one of Colombia's most unusual monuments to El Libertador.

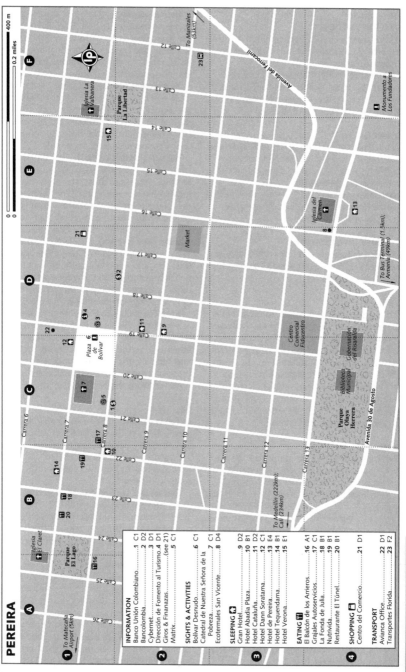

PEREIRA

Information
INTERNET ACCESS
There are Internet cafés throughout central Pereira. Access costs about US$1 per hour in most places.

Cybernet (☎ 335 0554; Plaza de Bolívar, Calle 19 No 7-49; ⏰ 8am-9:30pm Mon-Sat, 10am-8pm Sun) Large, centrally located and open evenings and Sundays.

Matrix (☎ 335 5708; Carrera 8 No 20-58)

MONEY
Banco Unión Colombiano (Carrera 8 No 20-61) Reliable banks changing traveler's checks include this one. Other banks may also cash your traveler's checks, and give cash advances on Visa and MasterCard.

Bancolombia (Carrera 8 No 17-56) Also a reliable bank.

Giros & Finanzas (Centro del Comercio, Carrera 7 No 16-50) The agent of Western Union.

TOURIST INFORMATION
Dirección de Fomento al Turismo (☎ 324 8030; Carrera 7 No 18-55, Piso 6; ⏰ 8-11:30am & 2-4pm Mon-Fri) In the Palacio Municipal.

Tours
The office of San Vicente thermal baths, **Ecotermales San Vicente** (☎ 333 6157; www.sanvicente.com.co; cnr Calle 16 & Carerra 13) sells day packages to the springs (US$16), which include return transport, admission to the baths, lunch and two short walks. The office also provides information, books accommodations and runs transport to the springs (US$5 return). See Ecotermales San Vicente (p180) for more information.

Sleeping
Pereira has plenty of accommodations in all price categories. Rates are reasonable. All prices listed include private bathroom.

Gran Hotel (☎ 335 9500; www.granhotelpereira.com in Spanish; Calle 19 No 9-19; s/d US$44/50) Once the city's top hotel, this grandly proportioned art deco mammoth is looking a bit threadbare these days. The good news is that the original architectural details are still intact, and it is slowly undergoing restoration. Rooms are spacious, with huge windows and high ceilings; some have balconies.

Hotel Cataluña (☎ 335 4527; fax 333 0791; Calle 19 No 8-61; s/d US$14/18) With clean, spacious rooms just a half block from Plaza de Bolívar, this place offers excellent value. Rooms facing the street are brighter and some have balconies, though they're also subject to street noise.

Hotel Abadia Plaza (☎ 335 8398; hotelabadiaplaza@etp.net.co; Carrera 8 No 21-67; s/d US$58/70) This stylish new place is as close as Pereira comes to a boutique hotel, with original art on the walls, plush rooms with marble bathrooms and noise-resistant windows.

Hotel Verona (☎ 333 5525; Carrera 7 No 14-19; s/d US$10/17) This place is slightly removed from the center in a rather seedy area around Parque La Libertad. Rooms are basic, and front rooms are bright but also loud. Internal rooms are quieter but dark.

Hotel Tequendama (☎ 335 7986; fax 334 3079; Carrera 7 No 22-34; s/d US$21/34) With large rooms around a pleasant courtyard, this centrally located hotel is a bargain. The problem is, the place is noisy thanks to an adjacent casino. Still, beds are good, service is friendly; a good option for heavy sleepers.

Hotel Dann Soratama (☎ 335 8650; Carrera 7 No 19-20; s/d US$30/45; ✺) On the main square, this glass-and-concrete monolith is not particularly beautiful to look at, but it offers the most upmarket rooms in the center of the city. Some upper floors have fine views.

Hotel de Pereira (☎ 335 0770; www.hoteldepereira.com in Spanish; Carrera 13 No 15-73; s/d US$74/95; ✺ ▣) The city's poshest hotel has every amenity, including a pool, extra security and huge rooms ranged around a spacious internal courtyard. Note that it's slightly removed from the heart of the city.

Eating
La Fonda de Julia (☎ 333 7848; Carrera 7 No 23-15; mains US$4-8; ⏰ 9:30am-10:30pm) Set around an airy, brightly painted courtyard, this place serves up good meat dishes, an excellent *cazuela* (fish in coconut sauce) and other seafood dishes.

Restaurante El Túnel (☎ 335 0226; Carrera 7 No 23-41; set meals US$2.50, mains US$3-7; ⏰ 7:30am-10pm) This traditional eatery serves a variety of plates from different regions (including *lechona* or suckling pig) and serves a generous set-menu lunch for US$2.50.

Grajales Autoservicios (Carrera 8 No 21-60; meals US$3-6; ⏰ 24hr) At this large, self-service 24-hour restaurant-cum-bakery you can put together your own lunch or dinner. It's also good for breakfast.

Nutrivida (☎ 335 0187; Calle 22 No 7-24; meals US$2; ⏰ noon-2:30pm Mon-Sat) This health-food store serves decent vegetarian lunches, including soup, main course, salad, juice and dessert.

NORTHWEST COLOMBIA

El Balcón de los Arrieros (☎ 335 3633; Carrera 8 No 24-65; mains US$4-6; ☽ noon-9pm) Decent *paisa*-style fare like *lengua* (tongue), chorizo (sausage) and *churrasco* (grilled meats), served around a wooden courtyard that is slightly sagging these days but pleasant enough.

Getting There & Away

AIR
The Matecaña airport is 5km west of the city center, 20 minutes by urban bus, or US$2 by taxi. Avianca operates eight flights a day to Bogotá, from where you can make connections to other destinations.

BUS
The bus terminal is about 1.5km south of the city center, at Calle 17 No 23-157. Many urban buses will take you there in less than 10 minutes.

There are regular departures to Bogotá (US$15, nine hours); all buses go via Armenia, not Manizales. A number of buses go to Medellín (US$12, five hours) and Cali (US$9, four hours). Minibuses run every 15 minutes to Armenia (US$2.50, one hour), Manizales (US$3, 1¼ hours) and Marsella (US$1.50, one hour). Minibuses to Manizales pass via Santa Rosa de Cabal (US$1).

For Parque Ucumarí (p180), you need to go to El Cedral. **Transportes Florida** (Calle 12 No 9-40) has *chivas* departing to El Cedral (US$1.25, 1½ hours) from its office (not from the bus terminal) at 9am and 3pm on weekdays, and at 7am, 9am, noon and 3pm on Saturday and Sunday.

MARSELLA
☎ 6 / pop 9000 / elevation 1600m / temp 20°C
Set amid verdant, coffee-growing country some 29km northwest of Pereira, Marsella is a pleasant, typically *paisa* town founded in 1860 by settlers from Antioquia. The main square and the streets just around it retain their original contours, though many buildings have been reconstructed in this quake-prone region. It's worth a stroll if this is the only *pueblo paisa* town you visit. However, the real reasons to come to Marsella are its quirky cemetery and its lovely botanical gardens.

Jardín Botánico Alejandro Humboldt
Created in 1979 to educate locals and tourists alike, the **botanical garden** (☎ 368 5233;

admission US$1.25; ☽ 8am-6pm) is a great introduction to the rich yet fragile ecosystems of the Zona Cafetera. An hour's walk along its cobblestone paths leads you through bamboo groves and past orchid-bearing trees to a museum devoted to local birds and insects. It also includes a series of simple mechanical devices that explain physical phenomena, as well as the **Museo de la Cauchera** (Slingshot Museum) – part of a campaign to protect birds from local kids, who had made sport killing birds with slingshots. Over the years they have deposited dozens of *caucheras* (slingshots) in exchange for free entrance to the park and other allurements.

Cementerio Jesús María Estrada
Designed by Julio César Vélez and constructed in 1927, Marsella's **cemetery** (admission free; ☽ 8am-6pm) is a masterpiece of funerary architecture. Built on a slope about a 10-minute walk from the town plaza, it is made up of a series of elaborate terraces. Bodies are buried for a period of four years in the *gradas* (the terraced area of the cemetery), the *bóvedas* (concrete boxlike constructions at the back) or *en tierra* (in the earth at the far right corner of the cemetery). After a time, the remains are permanently put to rest in family *osarios* (ossuaries) – openings in the cemetery's walls that are then sealed shut with cement. The remains of those who can't afford an *osario* are deposited after four years in the *templetes* – two towers on each side of the front wall of the cemetery.

Getting There & Away
Minibuses to and from Pereira run approximately every 15 minutes until about 7pm (US$1.50, one hour). The trip takes you through the spectacular coffee plantations.

TERMALES DE SANTA ROSA
☎ 6 / elevation 1950m / temp 18°C
Also known as Termales Arbeláez, these popular hot springs are 9km east of Santa Rosa de Cabal, on the Pereira–Manizales road. A tourist complex including thermal pools, a hotel, restaurant and bar, has been built near the springs amid splendid scenery at the foot of a 170m-high waterfall. The hot (70°C) water of the springs is cooled down to about 40°C in the main pool.

You can make a day trip to the **thermal baths** (admission US$6; ☽ 8am-midnight) or stay

NORTHWEST COLOMBIA

longer if you would like to. The springs are fairly quiet on weekdays, but tend to fill up with city-dwellers during weekends and holidays.

Sleeping & Eating

Hotel Termales (☎ 364 5500, 364 1322) This hotel at the springs is comprised of two parts. The Casa Vieja has rooms that accommodate two to seven guests (US$42 per person). The new part, La Montaña, offers *cabañas* with five to seven beds and costs US$52 per person. Both prices include full board and the use of the pools.

Getting There & Away

Santa Rosa de Cabal is on the main road between Pereira (15km) and Manizales (36km) and so is easily accessible. Transport from Santa Rosa de Cabal to the springs is operated by *chivas* from Calle 14 No 12-42 in the market area, usually with three departures daily: at 7am, noon and 3pm (US$0.80, 45 minutes). The *chivas* turn around and go back to Santa Rosa soon after their arrival at the springs. There are sometimes additional departures on weekends.

You can also go by jeep (they park in the same area), but they charge more. You can contract them to pick you up in the evening as well (US$8 each way).

ECOTERMALES SAN VICENTE

☎ 6 / elevation 2250m / temp 16°C
Very close to the Termales de Santa Rosa is the newer **Ecotermales San Vicente** (☎ 333 6157; www.sanvicente.com.co in Spanish). Located 18km east of the town of Santa Rosa de Cabal and linked by an unsurfaced road, the baths include a hotel, *cabañas*, a camp site, restaurant, car park and, of course, the thermal pools themselves. Paths have been traced into the scenic environs, allowing for pleasant walks and access to a few charming waterfalls. Trout tanks have been built for fishing. You can also treat yourself to a massage (US$10 per hour) and a bath in a mud pool.

The baths are operated from the office of Ecotermales San Vicente in Pereira (see p178), where you can make inquiries and bookings. There are various packages (day plan, week plan), or you can come independently for a day and just pay a US$4 entrance fee.

Sleeping & Eating

Stay in a double room without or with a bathroom (US$23/25 per person), in a six-bed *cabaña* (US$22 per person) or camp in their/your tent (US$14/12 per person). Prices include breakfast and the use of the pools. Breakfast, lunch and dinner (mains US$4 to US$7) are served in the dining room.

Getting There & Away

There's no public transport to the baths. The operator provides its own transport from Pereira. *Chivas*, minibuses or *busetas* are supposed to depart daily from the Pereira office at about 8:30am and return from the baths around 5pm. The trip takes 1¼ hours each way and costs US$4 return. The admission fee to the complex is not included; it's an extra US$4.

PARQUE UCUMARÍ

Established in 1984 just outside the western boundaries of the Parque Nacional Los Nevados, this reserve covers about 42 sq km of rugged, forested land around the middle course of the Río Otún, about 30km southeast of Pereira.

The reserve offers accommodations and food. It has ecological paths traced through verdant hills and you can see the lush vegetation and spot some of the park's rich wildlife. Birds are the reserve's most conspicuous inhabitants, with about 185 different species having been recorded here.

You can make some longer excursions. The hike up Río Otún, leading through a gorge to Parque Nacional Los Nevados, is the most popular. You can even get to Laguna del Otún (3950m) but it's a steady, six- to eight-hour walk uphill. It's possible to do the return trip within a day, though it's a strenuous hike. If you have camping gear, it's better to split the trek and do some side excursions up in the *páramo*.

The reserve offers a guide for US$20 per day, and also rents out mules and horses. Check the safety conditions with the rangers before setting off; there has been guerrilla activity here in the past.

Sleeping & Eating

The Refugio La Pastora (at 2400m) provides accommodation for 28 visitors in four- to eight-bed dorms for US$6 per person. You can also sleep on pillows around the lodge's open fireplace or camp for US$2 per person. The Refugio serves breakfast (US$1.50), lunch and dinner (US$2.50 each) for guests.

Accommodations have to be booked and paid for at **Grupos Ecológicos de Risaralda** (GER; ☎ 325 4781; grupos_ecologicos@yahoo.com) in Pereira. If you plan to make a day trip to the park, you still have to visit the GER office to get the free permit. At writing time, the office was in a transitional location and had yet to find a permanent home. Your best bet is to contact them via email.

Getting There & Away
The reserve is accessible from Pereira via a rough road. *Chivas* will take you up to El Cedral, 24km from Pereira. From El Cedral (at 1950m), it's a pleasant two-hour (6km) walk uphill along the path following the Río Otún to La Pastora. Sometimes locals will take you up on horseback (around US$8).

SANTUARIO OTÚN QUIMBAYA
The Santuario de Flora y Fauna Otún Quimbaya is a nature reserve 15km southeast of Pereira. It was created in 1996 to protect a 5-sq-km area of Andean forest between altitudes of 1800m and 2400m, characterized by high biodiversity. The reserve has a visitors center, La Suiza, and several ecological paths. The Santuario is close to Parque Ucumarí, so you can visit both reserves during one trip.

La Suiza (dm US$8-15) provides accommodations plus meals (US$2 to US$3 each). For reservations or more information, contact the Parques Nacionales Naturales de Colombia (p54) in Bogotá.

Chivas from Pereira to El Cedral pass by La Suiza and can drop you off at the entrance. Should you then want to visit Parque Ucumarí, it's a four-hour walk to La Pastora.

ARMENIA
☎ 6 / pop 245,000 / elevation 1550m / temp 22°C
Though not beautiful in itself, Armenia is set dramatically between a lush valley and one of the highest stretches of the Cordillera Central. Founded in 1889, the city quickly grew into the center for the region's coffee trade, and in 1966 it became the capital of the newly created Quindío department. Unfortunately, disaster struck in 1999 when a catastrophic earthquake destroyed almost a third of the city center.

The city rebuilt itself with remarkable speed and determination, and it's bustling and prosperous once again. Of course, the need to rebuild so quickly has given the city a rather makeshift feel. However, there are a few surprisingly slick new buildings, and the area around Plaza de Bolívar is a pleasant enough place for a stroll.

The city also makes a good base from which to explore the Quindío, Colombia's second-smallest department. It shares a part of the mighty Parque Nacional Los Nevados and has several smaller nature reserves. It is also a short drive from the Parque Nacional del Café – the Disneyland of the coffee bean.

Information
INTERNET ACCESS
There are many Internet cafés in the city center. Most charge around US$1 per hour and have fast connections.
Telefon (Carrera 14 No 20-26)
Valencia Comunicaciones (☎ 741 0609; Calle 21 No 15-53; ☉ 8am-10pm)

MONEY
Bancolombia (Calle 20 No 15-26) The most likely bank to change traveler's checks; it can also change cash.
Centro Comercial IBG (Carrera 14 No 18-56) Shelters half-a-dozen *casas de cambio*, including Giros & Finanzas, which represents Western Union.

TOURIST INFORMATION
Secretaría de Turismo (☎ 741 2991; Plaza de Bolívar; ☉ 8am-noon & 2-6pm Mon-Fri) The main office is situated on the ground floor of the Gobernación del Quindío building. There is also a kiosk in Plaza de Bolívar that is open weekends between 8am and noon, and between 2pm and 6:30pm.

Sights
The city's main square – called, not surprisingly, Plaza de Bolívar – sits atop a rise in the land and sports fine views of the Cordillera Central. The square is adorned by a traditional statue of its namesake as well as yet another Betancur extravaganza, called the Monumento al Esfuerzo. The square is also home to the **Catedral de la Inmaculada Concepción**, an oddly tentlike hunk of concrete that, if not beautiful, is at least a curious testament to the city's determination to rebuild itself.

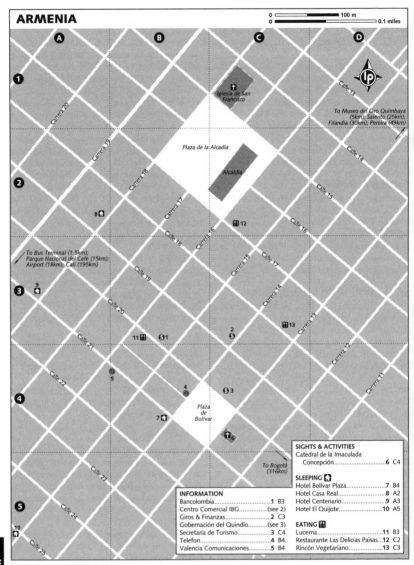

ARMENIA

0 — 100 m
0 — 0.1 miles

Iglesia de San
Francisco

To Museo del Oro Quimbaya
(5km); Salento (25km);
Filandia (30km); Pereira (49km)

Plaza de la Alcaldía

Alcaldía

To Bus Terminal (1.5km);
Parque Nacional del Café (15km);
Airport (18km); Cali (195km)

Plaza
de
Bolívar

To Bogotá
(316km)

INFORMATION
Bancolombia...........................1 B3
Centro Comercial IBG...........(see 2)
Giros & Finanzas.....................2 C3
Gobernación del Quindío.......(see 3)
Secretaría de Turismo.............3 C4
Telefon...................................4 B4
Valencia Comunicaciones........5 B4

SIGHTS & ACTIVITIES
Catedral de la Imaculada
  Concepción............................6 C4

SLEEPING
Hotel Bolívar Plaza.................7 B4
Hotel Casa Real......................8 A2
Hotel Centenario....................9 A3
Hotel El Quijote...................10 A5

EATING
Lucerna...............................11 B3
Restaurante Las Delicias Paisas..12 C2
Rincón Vegetariano...............13 C3

Museo del Oro Quimbaya (☎ 749 8433; cnr Av Bolívar & Calle 40N; admission free; ⏰ 10am-6pm Tues-Sun) has reopened in the wake of the 1999 earthquake and is once again one of Colombia's best gold museums, featuring an excellent collection of ceramics and gold artifacts of Quimbaya culture. It's in the Centro Cultural, 5km northeast of the center.

Sleeping

There are plenty of accommodations in the city center, and rates are competitive.

Hotel El Quijote (☎ 744 0663; Carrera 15 No 25-8; d US$17) This brand-new hotel offers small but comfortable rooms above a pleasant, plant-filled and almost stylish reception. It is slightly removed from the busiest part of the center, which is also a plus. Great value.

Hotel Centenario (☎ 744 3143; www.hotelcentenario.com in Spanish; Calle 21 No 18-20; s/d US$34/61) The first hotel to be built in the city center after the earthquake, the Centenario may have a poured-concrete facade, but inside you'll find rooms that are both tasteful and spotlessly clean. The top-floor restaurant serves simple, delicious and rigorously fresh regional and continental dishes.

Hotel Bolívar Plaza (☎ 741 0083; hotelbolivarplaza@telesat.com.co; Calle 21 No 14-17; s/d US$38/52) This new boutique hotel has a sleek, almost nautical facade that rises just across from Plaza de Bolívar. Rooms are smallish but shiny new, and many have small balconies that look out onto the Cordillera Central, making this place Armenia's most economical splurge. There's also an upper-floor restaurant that has good food and great views.

Hotel Casa Real (☎ 741 4550; Carrera 18 No 18-36; s/d with bathroom US$10/17) Rooms are small and basic at this central budget option, and not all of them have windows. Still they're also clean and have new beds, plus cable TV, all of which adds up to a good value.

Eating

The best places to eat in the city center are at the dining rooms of the Hotel Centenario and the Hotel Bolivar Plaza. In addition, there are plenty of budget restaurants in the center that serve set meals for around US$2.

Restaurante Las Delicias Paisas (☎ 745 5365; Calle 17 No 15-22; sandwiches US$2-3; 9am-7pm Mon-Sat) No-nonsense joint above a set of shops serving classic *paisa* cuisine at excellent prices, including a daily lunch special for US$2.

Lucerna (Calle 20 No 14-37; mains US$4; 7am-5pm) This classic *paisa* bakery-cum-café is a favorite that stays packed with locals who come more to socialize than for the food, though it's decent. The café has a brand-new home, thanks to the 1999 earthquake, but manages to retain a traditional feel.

Rincón Vegetariano (Calle 18 No 13-24) This is an all-vegetarian option in the center.

Getting There & Away
AIR

El Edén airport is 18km southwest of the city, near the town of La Tebaida on the road to Cali. Avianca has about five flights a day to Bogotá, with connections to other destinations.

BUS

All buses arrive at and leave from the bus terminal on the corner of Carrera 19 and Calle 35. It is 1.5km southwest of the center and can be reached by frequent city buses that run along Carrera 19.

There are plenty of buses to Bogotá (US$15, eight hours) and to Cali (US$8, four hours). Minibuses depart every 15 minutes or so to Pereira (US$2.50, one hour), Manizales (US$5, 2¼ hours), Filandia (US$1.50, one hour), Salento (US$1.50, 50 minutes) and Parque Nacional del Café (US$1, 25 minutes).

PARQUE NACIONAL DEL CAFÉ
☎ 6 / temp 21°C
Lacking an American-style theme park, the Colombian government decided to build the **Parque Nacional del Café** (☎ 753 6095; www.parquenacionaldelcafe.com in Spanish; basic admission

US$6; ⊗ 9am-4pm Wed-Sun) in honor of the be-loved bean. It provides an interesting and hassle-free – if slightly sanitized – introduction to the history, culture and science of coffee. Attractions include a small but well-organized museum, small coffee plantation and a number of amusement rides, including a roller coaster and water slide.

The park is near the small town of Pueblo Tapao, about 15km west of Armenia, and is easily accessible by frequent minibuses from the city. In the high season (mid-December to mid-January, Easter, mid-June to mid-July) the park may be open daily; check the official website. Don't bother to come if it's raining, as most attractions are outdoors.

Sights & Activities

At the entrance of the park is the **Torre Mirador**, an 18m timber tower that provides tremendous views across lush plains past Armenia to the rugged Cordillera Central. Just inside the entrance you arrive at the **Museo del Café**, housed in a rambling, *paisa*-style mansion. It has a number of interesting exhibits illustrating the history of coffee cultivation in Colombia as well as the biology of the plant itself.

Behind the museum, you'll find the **Sendero Ecológico**, an ecological path that zigzags downhill to the river, then doubles back uphill to the museum once again. It's a 4km loop that winds through a number of attractions, including a traditional coffee plantation, a Quimbaya Indian cemetery and the stunning **Bambusario** – a remarkable grove of enormous guadua bamboo trees.

Just behind the river is the **Pueblito Quindiano**, a recreation of a typical regional township, with its Plaza de Bolívar (actually, a replica of Armenia's main plaza from 1926) lined by houses built in traditional style. Inside one set of houses is a food court with various *paisa* specialties (mains US$3 to US$7). Beyond the Pueblito stretches the amusement park. The Pueblito is linked with the museum by the **Teleférico**, or a cable car, which provides some bird's-eye views.

FILANDIA

☎ 6 / pop 4500 / elevation 1930m / temp 18°C

A small town 30km north of Armenia, Filandia is perhaps the best-preserved *pueblo paisa* in Quindío. Uninterrupted rows of brightly painted houses from the beginning of the 20th century line many streets, with only the occasional intrusion of modern buildings. The town became famous when it was used as the backdrop of *Café*, a popular nighttime soap opera.

Several *residencias* (budget hotels/love hotels) are located on the main square, but most visitors just pop into town for a few hours. Minibuses to and from Armenia (US$1.50, one hour) run about every 15 minutes.

SALENTO

☎ 6 / pop 3500 / elevation 1900m / temp 18°C

Founded in 1850, Salento is one of the oldest town's in Quindío – and just about the smallest. One local sums it up this way: *el pueblo de calles cortas y recuerdos largos* (the town of short streets and long memories). It's less than an hour from Armenia, but it feels a hundred years away. The main square and streets around it retain the dimensions of a typical *pueblo paisa*, and Calle Real (Carrera 6) boasts plenty of fine old houses, many of which have been turned into shops, restaurants and hotels catering to weekend visitors.

Be sure not to miss Alto de la Cruz, a hill topped with a cross at the end of Calle Real. It's a bit of a climb, but from here you'll see the verdant Valle de Cocora as well as the high mountains that surround it. If the skies are clear (usually only early in the morning), you can spot the snow-capped tops of the volcanoes on the horizon.

Sleeping & Eating

Salento has half-a-dozen places to stay and many more to eat. The local specialty is trout from the nearby rivers; its flesh is pink, sweet and delicious. Most restaurants and inns are located on Calle Real (Carrera 6).

El Portal de Cocora (☎ 759 3075; anaisabel@telesat .com; cabañas from US$44) Located on the road toward Cocora about 500m from the main square, this restaurant has now also built two attractive *cabañas* with kitchenettes and extraordinary views of the Valle de Cocora. Alternatively, you can come for a meal or drink on the gardenlike terrace.

La Posada del Café (☎ 759 3012; malenacafé@ yahoo.com; Carrera 6 No 3-08; s/d US$18/30) A grander version of the Hostería Calle Real, this is the nicest place in the center. Rooms are spacious, and there is a carefully tended courtyard, which is a year-round riot of colorful blooms. The owner, who lived for many years in the US, speaks very good English and is most helpful.

Hostería Calle Real (☎ 759 3272; Carrera 6 No 2-20; r per person US$11) Housed in a typical *paisa* home with a pleasant, plant-filled courtyard, this place has small and rather basic rooms, but it's friendly and pleasant – and the price is right. Optional breakfast costs US$1.75.

Getting There & Away

Minibuses to and from Armenia (US$1, 50 minutes) run roughly every 15 minutes. Two jeeps a day, normally around 7:30am and 4pm, depart from Salento's plaza and go up the rough 11km road to Cocora (US$1, 35 minutes). There may be more departures if there's a demand, but you either have to wait until six passengers have been collected or pay for the empty seats (US$1 each). On weekends, when tourists come, there are usually at least four departures daily. Otherwise, it's a pleasant two-hour walk to Cocora.

VALLE DE COCORA

Stretching from Salento eastwards to the tiny hamlet of Cocora and beyond, the stunning Valle de Cocora is like a lush version of Switzerland, with a broad, green valley floor framed by rugged peaks. However, you'll remember you're a few degrees from the equator when, a short walk past Cocora, you suddenly encounter hills covered with the *palma de cera,* or wax palm. The trees tower above the cloud forests in which they thrive. It is an astonishing site.

The most spectacular part is east of Cocora. Take the rough road heading downhill to the bridge over the Río Quindío (just a five-minute walk from the restaurants) and you will see the strange palms. Walk further uphill and enjoy the scenery – you won't find this kind of landscape anywhere else.

The town of Cocora consists of a few houses, three restaurants serving delicious trout, and a trout-breeding station. The palms have made Cocora a tourist destination, with visitors mainly arriving on the weekends. On these days locals gather around the three restaurants to rent out horses (US$2.50 per hour).

Southwest Colombia

From the sultry, palm-filled Valle del Cauca to the barren grandeur of the Andes, southwest Colombia encompasses an astonishing variety of natural beauty. Along the coast, mangrove swamps and long sand beaches give way almost immediately to dense jungle. Yet a little over 100km inland stand the snowy slopes of the towering Nevado de Huila (5750m). From its peak, you can by turns look down onto the sweltering Tatacoa Desert and the rolling green hills of Tierradentro and San Agustín, home to some of the most important pre-Columbian sites in the Americas. Heading south to the Ecuadorian border, dry, rugged highlands suddenly give way to lush, volcanic valleys around the High Andean cities of Pasto and Ipiales. All these contrasts will wow you, just as the variations in altitudes may leave you feeling a little dizzy.

The people of southwest Colombia are nearly as diverse as the landscape. In coastal towns such as Buenaventura and Tumaco, the population is almost exclusively of African descent. Along the Andes, there are a series of indigenous communities that are only partially integrated with the rest of Colombia. There is the small but surprisingly sophisticated Popayán, which is both a university town as well as one of Colombia's best-preserved colonial cities. And, finally, there's Cali with its pleasantly tropical climate and stunning mix of races and cultures, all of whom have embraced a love of salsa – the city's unofficial religion and favorite pastime.

HIGHLIGHTS

- Test-drive the dance floors at the sweaty, sexy salsa joints in Cali's **Juanchito district** (p193)

- Discover hidden ruins by horseback in the emerald-green hills around **San Agustín** (p199)

- Admire the understated colonial splendor of **Popayán's** (p195) remarkably preserved historic center

- Descend into the elaborate, pre-Columbian tombs carved out of the volcanic hills of **Tierradentro** (p202)

- Gawk at the deep valleys and dizzying volcanic peaks that line the road from **Pasto to Ipiales (p206)**

- POPULATION: 5,587,039 | - AREA: 83,708 SQ KM

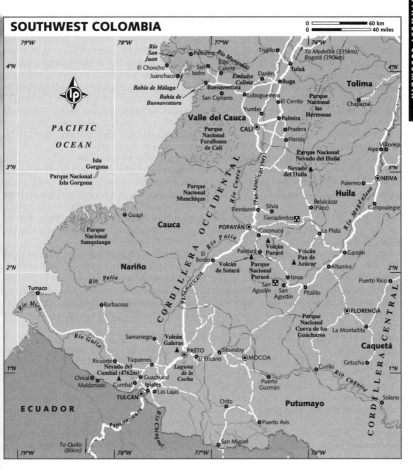

VALLE DEL CAUCA

The department of Valle del Cauca takes its name from the remarkably fertile valley of the same name. Local barons first made their fortune on sugarcane, and the region is still the biggest producer in Colombia, though the lush climate also supports bumper crops of tobacco, cotton, maize, grapes and, in uplands areas, coffee. Cali is the department's vibrant capital and largest city – and also Colombia's salsa headquarters.

The Valle del Cauca is flanked on each side by the Cordillera Occidental and Cordillera Central. Down its western slopes you will find the combination of jungle, swamps and beaches that make up the Atlantic coast. Here too is the colorful city of Buenaventura, Colombia's most important Pacific port.

CALI

☎ 2 / pop 2,250,000 / elevation 1005m / temp 24°C

In Colombia altitude defines attitude. While Bogotá (2650m) is perpetually chilly and Medellín (1485m) enjoys eternal spring, Cali (1005m) remains sultry 12 months of the year. And that's why Colombia's third-largest city wears less and parties more than its rivals. In their relentless pursuit of a good time, *caleños* have adopted salsa

---

TRAVELING SAFELY IN SOUTHWEST COLOMBIA

At the time of writing, the security situation in the southwest had improved significantly in many areas. The cities, including Cali, require only normal precautions. Travel along the Panamericana is safe during the day, though night travel is not recommended, particularly south of Popayán. Small roads and rural areas still pose potential risks. Double-check current conditions before overland travel to Buenaventura, Tumaco, San Agustín and Tierradentro.

---

music as their own, and in the Juanchito district you can dance until dawn seven nights of the week, no questions asked.

While largely modern and industrial, the city does have some interesting colonial buildings, and the tree-lined banks of the Río Cali make for a fine stroll. A hidden gem is the city's excellent zoo, which is devoted almost exclusively to Colombian wildlife. If you were a caged mammal in South America, this is where you'd want to be.

While the city itself isn't breathtaking, Cali famously claims to produce the most beautiful women in Colombia. If it's true, it's thanks in no small part to a remarkable mixture of African, European and indigenous gene pools. However, wealthy *caleñas* don't hesitate to get considerable help from Dr Lookgood – breast implants are a form of highly conspicuous consumption. Augmented or not, the city's residents take to the streets when remarkably reliable breezes dissipate the heat of the day and usher in soft, tropical evenings.

History

After helping Francisco Pizarro conquer the Incas, Sebastián de Belalcázar quarreled with his former boss and moved north to strike out on his own. After founding Quito and Popayán, he arrived in the Valle del Cauca in 1536, where he dubbed his new settlement Santiago de Cali. At the time of his arrival, the fertile valley was inhabited by various indigenous groups, of which the Calima community was the most advanced.

They initially offered stiff resistance to the Spanish presence, though in the long run the real impediment to growth was Cali's proximity to Popayán, which was the political and economic center of the region until the end of the 19th century. That said, much of Popayán's wealth actually came from the sugar plantations in the region around Cali. To work the fields, the Spaniards shipped in thousands of African slaves over the centuries, and the African legacy is still very much in evidence today; a significant portion of the population is of African or mixed African and European descent.

It was the arrival of the railroad at the beginning of the 20th century that sealed Cali's fate. Suddenly cash crops could reach world markets, and the newly rich sugar and coffee barons, needing to reinvest their earnings, built a thriving industrial base. This in turn led to explosive economic growth, especially after the 1940s.

Today, Cali is the capital of Valle del Cauca and is home to half of the department's population. As well as being the third-largest city after Bogotá and Medellín, it's the dominant industrial, agricultural and commercial center of the southwest.

Orientation

The city center is split in two by the Río Cali. To the south is the historic heart, laid out on a grid plan and centered on the Plaza de Caycedo. This is where you'll find most of the historic churches and museums.

To the north of the river is the new center, whose main axis is Av Sexta (Av 6N). This sector is modern, with trendy shops and restaurants, and it comes alive in the evening when a refreshing breeze tempers the daytime heat. For the city's best *salsotecas*, you'll have to head east about 12km to the Juanchito district.

Information

INTERNET ACCESS

There are lots of Internet cafés along Av Sexta as well as throughout the city. Most cost US$1 to US$1.50 per hour.

Cy@ncopias (☎ 668 8395; Av 6N No 13N-23)
Sc@nner (☎ 664 4119; Av 6N No 15N-37)
SCI Sala de Internet (☎ 661 5886; Av 6N No 13N-66) Large, fast connections and central location.

MONEY

There are plenty of banks with ATMs that accept Visa and debit cards on both Av Sexta and around Plaza de Caycedo.

CALI

0 —————— 400 m
0 —————— 0.2 miles

Bancolombia (cnr Calle 15N & Av 8N) Changes foreign cash and traveler's checks.

Giros & Finanzas (Carrera 4 No 10-12) Changes cash and is also a Western Union agent.

TOURIST OFFICES

Secretaría de Cultura y Turismo (☎ 886 0000 ext 2400; Carrera 7 btwn Calle 9 & Calle 10; ☽ 8am-12:30pm & 2:30-6pm Mon-Fri) On the 1st floor of the Gobernación del Valle del Cauca building.

Dangers & Annoyances

Though central Cali has a distinctly less urban feel than Bogotá or Medellín, don't be deceived. Muggers and thieves aren't inactive here, nor are they less clever or violent than elsewhere. Be careful while wandering around the streets at night. Even busy Av Sexta has its share of muggings. Avoid the park along Río Cali in the evening, and don't walk east of Calle 13 after dark.

Sights & Activities

With parklike grounds, humane exhibits and an excellent collection of species native to Colombia, the **Zoológico de Cali** (☎ 892 7474; cnr Carrera 2A Oeste & Calle 14 Oeste; admission US$2.50; ☽ 9am-5pm) is hands down the country's best zoo. The Río Cali runs picturesquely through the zoo's grounds, which are located about 2km west of the center in the Santa Teresita neighborhood. Its 10 hectares are home to about 1200 animals representing some 180 species, ranging from lemurs to condors.

The **Museo Arqueológico La Merced** (☎ 88 3434; Carrera 4 No 6-59; admission US$1; ☽ 9am-1pm & 2-6pm Mon-Sat) is housed in the former La Merced convent, Cali's oldest building dating back to the city's earliest days. In its five rooms, you'll find a collection of pre-Columbian pottery left behind by the major cultures from central and southern Colombia, including Quimbaya, Tolima, Calima, Tierradentro, San Agustín, Nariño and Tumaco.

In the same complex you'll find the **Iglesia de la Merced** (cnr Carrera 4 & Calle 7). Begun around 1545, it remains the city's oldest church. It' a lovely whitewashed building in the Spanish colonial style, with a long, narrow nave and humble wood and stucco construction. Inside, a heavily gilded baroque high altar is topped by the Virgen de las Mercedes, the patron saint of the city. Hours vary, but the church is generally open from 6:30am to 10am and from 4pm to 7pm.

The **Museo del Oro** (☎ 684 7754; Calle 7 No 4-69 admission free; ☽ 10am-5pm Mon-Sat), one block away from La Merced, has a small but fine collection of gold and pottery of the Calima culture.

Iglesia de San Francisco (cnr Carrera 6 & Calle 10 is a neoclassical construction dating from the 18th century. Next to the church are the Convento de San Francisco and the Capilla de la Inmaculada with the adjacent **Torre Mudéjar** (cnr Carrera 6 & Calle 9), an unusual brick bell tower, which is one of the best examples of Mudejar art in Colombia.

ONE WORD: PLASTICS

Colombia has some of the most innovative – and prolific – plastic surgeons in the world. Just head to a high-end nightclub in Cali or Medellín to see their prodigious results. The boobs may not be real, but they sure are big. Throw in a little rhinoplasty, a dash of liposuction, some light dermal abrasion, and just a hint of dental reconstruction, and suddenly an evening at the mall starts to look like a Miss Universe pageant.

Because procedures in Colombia often cost about a third what they would in the US or Europe, Colombia's plastic surgeons are attracting a small flood of vanity tourists who come not to admire the Andes or Amazon but their own refurbished beauty. Many clinics even offer package deals, including hotels and airfare, sending visitors home with a fresh outlook on life, especially those who get Lasik (laser-assisted in situ keratomileusis). Pioneered by Colombian eye surgeon Jose Barrequer beginning in the 1940s, Lasik cures poor eyesight by reshaping the cornea with lasers. The country is still considered a leader in the field.

Business has grown so quickly that the US State Department has issued advice specifically for Americans considering elective surgery in Colombia. They don't discourage the practice, but they do suggest that you thoroughly research who you surgeon will be – sound advice anywhere, of course.

Overlooking the Río Cali, the neo-Gothic **Iglesia de la Ermita** (cnr Av Colombia & Calle 13), constructed between 1930 and 1948, houses the 18th-century painting of *El Señor de la Caña* (Lord of the Sugarcane); many miracles are attributed to the image.

The small 1757 **Iglesia de San Antonio** is set atop a hill, the Colina de San Antonio, west of the old center. It shelters valuable *tallas quiteñas*, 17th-century carved-wood statues of the saints, representing the style known as the Quito School. The church also affords a good view of the city; it's just a 10-minute walk west of the Torre Mudéjar.

Museo de Arte Moderno La Tertulia (☎ 893 3942; Av Colombia No 5 Oeste-105; admission US$1; ☼ 10am-6pm) presents temporary exhibitions of contemporary painting, sculpture and photography. It's a 15-minute walk from the city center along the Río Cali.

Tours

There are plenty of travel agencies in Cali. Tours both within and outside the department (El Paraíso–Piedechinche, Popayán–Silvia) are offered, as well as city tours.

Ecocolombia Tours (☎ 557 1957, 514 0829; www.eco colombiatours.com in Spanish; Carrera 37A No 6-18) Arguably Cali's best specialist for tours to Isla Gorgona (US$250 to US$300).

Viajes Oganesoff (☎ 892 2840, 892 0656; www.via jesoganesoff.com in Spanish; Hotel Intercontinental, Av Colombia No 2-72) Organizes night tours in traditional buses called *chivas* (US$16). Tours go on weekends if there are enough people to fill up a *chiva*.

Festivals & Events

The main city event is the **Feria de Cali** (http://elpais-cali.terra.com.co/feriadecali in Spanish). It lasts from Christmas to New Year's, with parades, masquerades, music, theatre, bullfights and general citywide revelry. Given the city's staunch faith in the beauty of its women, it's no surprise that the beauty pageant also draws in hordes of spectators.

Sleeping

Cali has accommodations in all price ranges, though prices tend to be slightly higher than in Bogotá or Medellín.

BUDGET

Guest House Iguana (☎ 661 3522; iguana_cali@yahoo .com; Calle 21N No 9N-22; s/d with shared bathroom US$9/12) Run by a Swiss woman who is both welcoming and fluent in English, Iguana is one of the most reasonable places in town and also an ideal base for independent travelers. Located on a quiet street but near the action on Av Sexta, it boasts large, well-maintained rooms, kitchen and laundry facilities and Internet access. The owner even organizes salsa and Spanish lessons.

Calidad House (☎ 661 2338; Calle 17N No 9AN-39; dm US$6, s with shared bathroom US$10) Slightly more basic than Iguana, Calidad is still a fine option, with small four-bed dorms without bathrooms. It provides a range of facilities, including laundry and kitchen facilities, and luggage storage.

MIDRANGE

Hotel Pensión Stein (☎ 661 4999; www.hotelstein .com.co; Av 4N No 3-33; s/d with fan US$27/45, with air-con US$38/52; P ✷) Run by a Swiss couple, this small hotel offers spotlessly clean rooms in a castlelike stone mansion on a leafy street south of Av Sexta. All prices include breakfast. Reservations recommended.

Hotel Royal Plaza (☎ 883 9243; Carrera 4 No 11-69; s/d US$28/32) Located on pleasant Plaza Caycedo just across from the cathedral, this reasonably priced, modern hotel has threadbare but decent rooms with huge windows. Ask for a room on a high floor, both for the views as well as the quiet.

Hotel Don Jaime (☎ 667 2828; www.hoteldonjaime .com in Spanish; Av 6N No 15N-25; s/d US$40/50; ✷) This modern hotel may lack character, but it's comfortable, air-conditioned and located in the heart of the action on Av Sexta.

TOP END

Casa de Alférez (☎ 661 8111; www.sofitel.com; Av 9N No 9-24; d from US$90; P ✷ 🖳) On a lovely, tree-lined street, this Sofitel property has large, luxuriously appointed rooms with hardwood floors and huge French windows that open onto small balconies.

Hotel Intercontinental (☎ 882 3225; www.inter conti.com; Av Colombia No 2-72; d from US$100; P ✷ 🖳 🌊) It may not be a beautiful hotel to look at, but Cali's Intercontinental certainly offers all the creature comforts, including a swimming pool, gym and tennis courts.

Eating

The are plenty of places in Cali to get a solid meal of beans, rice and grilled meats for US$2 to US$4. If you have cash to spare, there are

THE AUTHOR'S CHOICE

Platillos Voladores (☎ 668 7588; www.platil losvoladores.com in Spanish; Calle 14N No 9N-32; mains US$9-16; ☯ noon-3pm & 7-11:30pm Mon-Fri, 7-11:30pm Sat) The food at Platillos Voladores (literally 'flying saucers') is out of this world, combining spicy, sweet, sour and savory in novel ways. A mecca for the city's foodies, the chef takes fusion to new heights, borrowing inspiration from Asian, European and indigenous Colombian cuisines. The decor is colorful and eclectic. There's also a small store on the premises that sells bottled versions of the restaurant's complex sauces and chutneys, many of which feature exotic produce from the surrounding Cauca valley.

some excellent restaurants in the city's gourmet ghetto along the Av 8N corridor.

Restaurante Carambolo (☎ 667 5656; Calle 14N No 9N-18; mains US$8-14; ☯ noon-3pm & 7-11:30pm Mon-Fri, 7-11:30pm Sat) This chic bar-restaurant attracts the city's movers and shakers with its nouvelle Mediterranean cuisine, upscale Bohemian dining area, and slick bar.

Restaurante M (☎ 660 1785; Av 9N No 15N-39; mains US$8-12; ☯ noon-11pm Mon-Fri, 6-11:30pm Sat) Set inside a small but stately home, this all-white extravaganza serves up fine Asian fusion cuisine, from classic beef teriyaki to salmon stuffed with plantains.

Archie's (☎ 653 5383; Av 9N No 14N-22; mains US$5-8; ☯ noon-10pm) Gourmet pizzas and salads are made with the freshest ingredients at this casual, upscale option.

Restaurante Balocco (Av 6N No 14N-04; set meals US$2; ☯ noon-9pm) This small, family-run restaurant serves up hearty, if basic, set meals right in the heart of the action on Av Sexta.

Restaurante Comfandi (Carrera 6 No 8-22; set lunches US$2; ☯ noon-2pm Mon-Fri) For a cheap, filling lunch, try this self-service restaurant. It's a downtown institution. Upstairs there is an exhibition space for contemporary art that is free to the public

Restaurante Vegetariano Sol de la India (Carrera 6 No 8-48; set meals US$2; ☯ noon-2pm Mon-Fri) Decent vegetarian near the La Merced complex.

Entertainment

Check the entertainment columns of *El País*, or consult the entertainment listings at www .terra.com.co/cali in Spanish.

CINEMA

Cali has a number of commercial cinemas including **Multiplex Chipichape** (☎ 644 2463; Centro Comercial Chipichape, Av 6N No 39N-25).

For more thought-provoking fare, check the program of the **Cinemateca La Tertulia** (☎ 893 2939; Museo de Arte Moderno La Tertulia, Av Colombia No 5 Oeste-105), which generally has two shows daily from Tuesday to Sunday.

THEATER

Teatro Experimental de Cali (TEC; ☎ 884 3820; Calle 7 No 8-61) Founded by Enrique Buenaventura, considered the father of Colombian theater, this continues to be one of the city's most innovative theater companies.

Teatro Municipal (☎ 684 3578; Carrera 5 No 6-64) The city's oldest existing theater, completed in 1918. Today it's used for various artistic forms, including musical concerts, theater and ballet.

NIGHTCLUBS

No doubt about it: *caleños* love to party and they've developed *la rumba* (partying into a fine art. The climate is remarkably conducive to good times – nights are warm enough to invite flesh-baring, yet evening breezes also freshen and re-animate.

A typical evening begins at the **Centro Comercial de Chipichape** (☎ 659 2199; www.chi ichape.com in Spanish; Calle 38N No 6N-35), an upscale mall just north of the main drag along Av Sexta. *Caleños* of all ages come to launch their evening with a *cerveza* (beer) or two at one of the many outdoor cafés.

From here you might head to a bar or lounge along the Av Sexta corridor. Regardless of whether your taste runs to sleaze discos or sleek cocktail lounges, you'll find what you're looking for. You can try **Lotu** (☎ 681 5906; Calle 15 No 9N-27; ☯ 7pm-2am Thu-Sat) an ultra-lounge with ambient music, glowing plastic walls, cocktail-swilling cuties. Otherwise, just wander up and down Av Sexta and listen for the kind of music that puts you in the mood – disco, classic salsa, hip-hop and Latin dance are all represented. **Las Brisas de la Sexta** (☎ 661 2996; Av 6N No 15N-9) is one of the largest, and a perennial favorite. A little to the north, **Kukuramakara** (☎ 653 5389; Calle 28N No 2 Bis-97; ☯ 9pm-4am Thu-Sat) is a simple, one-room affair, but locals say it attracts the most beautiful women in Cali.

DETOUR: BUENAVENTURA

It may not be Colombia's most beautiful city, but with some 6m of rainfall a year, Buenaventura is by far the wettest. It's also the country's principal Pacific port, handling as much as 80% of the country's coffee exports. With a population largely made up of descendants of African slaves, its culture remains distinct from the rest of Colombia. The region's isolation has enabled the people to retain much of their African heritage, though at a price. Poverty is rampant, and much of the city consists of unpaved streets and wooden shacks. Isolation has also made the region a bastion for both paramilitaries and leftist rebels, though the situation has improved in recent years.

There are some fine beaches a short water taxi–ride from the city. In addition, the mouth of the nearby Río San Juan attracts humpback whales and dolphins from August to October. There are a number of places to stay, but the real stand-out is the **Hotel Estación** (☎ 2-243 4070; www .hotelestacion.com; Calle 2 No 1A-08; d from US$70), a neoclassical confection with deluxe rooms, a good restaurant and three-day, all-inclusive whale-watching packages from $300 per person.

At the time of writing, the Cali–Buenaventura highway was heavily patrolled and considered safe, though be sure to check current conditions before setting out. Buses and *colectivos* leave frequently from Cali's bus station (US$4 to US$5, three hours).

An alternative Zona Rosa is around Calle in southern Cali. **Tin Tin Deo** (☎ 514 1537; alle 5 No 38-71; ☻ 7:30pm-4am Thu-Sat) pumps ut salsa and *musica del pacifico* (African-nfluenced music from Colombia's Pacific oast) for a mixed crowd that includes a lot f intellectuals from the nearby university.

By 2am, it's time to head to the *salsatecas* f the Juanchito district, 12km east of the enter. A taxi should be about US$5. *Salsate-as* generally don't charge admission; you rder drinks by the bottle – a fifth of *aguar-iente* generally runs between US$15 and JS$25. **Changó** (☎ 662 9701; Vía Cavasa; ☻ 8pm-am) is a Juanchito classic, and boasts cushy ooths around a smoking dance floor. Next oor is the humbler but no less sexy **Agapito** Vía Cavasa; ☻ 8pm-6am Mon-Sat, 2pm-6am Sun), with *viejoteca* on Sunday afternoon, when older lks take over the dance floor. Just down e street is **Sambacaramba** (☎ 663 0023; Vía avasa; ☻ 9pm-6am Wed-Sun). The newest Juan-hito hot spot, it attracts a sexy, younger rowd with a rocking sound system and lush, terraced seating.

If you're wary of setting off on your own, onsider a nighttime *chiva* tour. One of the est is organized by **Viajes Oganesoff** (☎ 892 40, 892 0656; www.viajesoganesoff.com in Spanish; Hotel tercontinental, Av Colombia No 2-72) Its *chiva*, with ve music aboard, departs from the hotel on riday and Saturday at 8pm. The five-hour ur calls at several music spots (usually one Juanchito and one on Av Sexta), includes alf a bottle of *aguardiente* per head and a nack, and costs US$16 per person.

Getting There & Away

AIR

The Palmaseca airport is 16km northeast of the city, off the road to Palmira. Minibuses between the airport and the bus terminal run every 10 minutes until about 8pm (US$1, 30 minutes), or take a taxi (US$12).

Avianca has more than half-a-dozen non-stop daily flights to Bogotá for national and international connections. SAM has non-stop flights to many other major Colombian cities, including Cartagena, Medellín, Pasto and San Andrés.

BUS

The bus terminal is around a 25-minute walk northeast of the center, 10 minutes by a frequent city bus and about US$1.50 by taxi. Buses run regularly to Bogotá (US$25, 12 hours), Medellín (US$18, nine hours) and Pasto (US$14, nine hours). Pasto buses will drop you off in Popayán (US$5, three hours) and there are also hourly minibuses to Popayán (US$6, 2½ hours). There are regular departures to Armenia (US$8, four hours), Pereira (US$9, four hours) and Manizales (US$12, five hours).

HACIENDAS EL PARAÍSO & PIEDECHINCHE

The old sugarcane plantations north of Cali make pleasant getaways from the city while providing insight into Cauca life in the 18th and 19th centuries. The two most famous, El Paraíso and Piedechinche, both about 40km north of Cali, have been converted into museums that document plantation life as well as the history of sugarcane production. Together, they make a lovely day trip from the big city.

El Paraíso

Built in 1815, **El Paraíso** (☎ 256 2378; admission US$1.75; ☺ 9am-5pm Tue-Sun) still provides insight into the way Colombia's elite lived in the 19th century. The quaint manor house, also known as Casa de la Sierra, is most famous as the setting of Jorge Isaacs' novel *María,* a classic, 19th-century tear-jerker. Besides all the romantic drama, Isaacs' novel provides a fine portrait both of upper-class manners as well as the Valle del Cauca itself. The house has been lovingly restored, and period furnishings makes it look the way it is described in the novel.

Piedechinche

Begun in the first half of the 18th century, **Piedechinche** (☎ 550 6076; admission US$1.25; ☺ 9am-4pm) consists of a rustic but elegant tile-and-stucco mansion. The mansion has been decked out with period furniture, while the surrounding gardens look largely as they did when it was still a working plantation. Nearby you can still see the hacienda's original *trapiche* (traditional sugarcane mill).

Piedechinche is also home to the **Museo de la Caña de Azúcar**, which does a good job documenting the natural, scientific and commercial history of the sugarcane.

All the visitors are guided in groups. The tour takes about 1½ hours and includes visits to both the original mansion and the museum.

Getting There & Away

The haciendas are near one another, so it's convenient to visit both of them in one trip. However, there's no regular public transport all the way to the haciendas; unless you come on a tour or by taxi, the trip will involve quite a bit of walking.

Many buses run along the Cali–Palmira–Buga road; get off on the outskirts of the town of Amaime (the drivers know where to drop you) and walk to Piedechinche (5.5km) or negotiate a taxi. El Paraíso is still further off the road.

Tours from Cali are run mostly on weekends (see p191).

SAN CIPRIANO

Hidden deep in the tropical forest near Colombia's Pacific coast, this town of fewer than 1000 souls is a traveler's delight. About 15km from the nearest road and rarely served by the local railway, residents have come up with an ingenious transportation solution: they've rigged up their own train cars, which they power with a combination of mopeds and their own strength. Don't ask about safety measures, because there are none, though you may wish there were on the downhill sections when the train achieves startling speeds.

The town itself is rustic, but the locals are infectiously friendly, and there is a great river in which to swim.

Getting There & Away

To get to San Cipriano from Cali, take a bus or *colectivo* to Buenaventura, get off at the village of Córdoba (US$3, two hours) and walk down the hill into the village and ask where the railway track begins. From here, the locals will take you to San Cipriano in their rail cars, a really great journey through the rainforest for US$1.

Make sure you check the safety conditions before setting off from Cali. At the time of writing, the Cali–Buenaventura highway had improved significantly, but was still potentially unsafe.

ISLA GORGONA

A volcanic island with a peak over 300m high, this former penal colony is blanketed with lush tropical rainforest that shelters a stunning diversity of flora and fauna. The eastern coast, facing the continent, is calmer than the west, with several beaches (some of them white, which is uncommon on the Pacific coast) and coral reefs along the shore. The Isla Gorgonilla, a smaller island off the southwestern tip of Gorgona and a few rocky islets, the Rocas del Horno on the northern end, complete the scene.

Gorgona is noted for a large number of endemic species resulting from the island's long separation from the continent. There are no large mammals, but there are a variety of smaller animals, such as monkeys, lizards, bats, birds and snakes. Two species of freshwater turtles and a colony of *babillas* (spectacled caimans) live at the Laguna Ayatuna. Dolphins as well as humpback and sperm whales visit its waters seasonally, and sea turtles come for their breeding period and lay eggs on the beaches.

Gorgona is hot and wet throughout the year, with a mean temperature of about 27°C, relative humidity close to 90%, and an annual rainfall that regularly exceeds 4000mm. There's no dry season, but there are significant monthly differences in the amount of precipitation: September and October are the wettest months, whereas rainfall is lowest February and March.

Visiting the Island

All visits to Gorgona must be booked with a private tour operator or in advance at the Parques Nacionales Naturales de Colombia (p54) in Bogotá. You need to pay the park's admission fee (US$5) and accommodation (US$12 a night per person) in the park's visitor center. Book well in advance, especially for Colombian holiday periods. There may be a waiting time of up to two months in the tourist peaks. When you book, the office should give you information about the island and how exactly to get there.

Once on the island you'll be in the hands of park rangers and guides who will organize your stay and take you on excursions to the most interesting parts of the island. All the walks are accompanied by guides. The program allows you time for recreational activities such as swimming, sunbathing and snorkeling. The local cafeteria serves meals (US$12 for full board which consists of three set meals per day), fast food, snacks, fruit juices and nonalcoholic drinks.

Bring boots, a long-sleeved shirt, some long trousers, rain gear, a swimsuit, hat and sunscreen. If you plan on snorkeling, bring along your gear. A flashlight is recommended; the use of candles is not permitted.

Getting There & Away

The usual departure point for Gorgona has been the port of Buenaventura (a three-hour bus trip from Cali), where you catch a (usually overcrowded) cargo boat for a 10- to 12-hour night trip to the island (about US$30). It can be a hellish experience if the sea is rough. The boats depart daily from Muelle El Piñal, in the late afternoon or early evening. Information and reservations are available from the **Bodega Liscano** (☎ 2-244 6089, 244 6106), near the wharf.

Since the access road to Buenaventura was targeted by the guerrillas on various occasions in the past and may not be 100% safe, some independent tourists and most tours have begun to use Guapí as a launching pad for Gorgona. Guapí is a seaside village in Cauca, just opposite Gorgona, 56km away. Guapí is not connected by road with the rest of the country but can be reached by air on daily flights from Cali via Satena. From Guapí, boats take tourists to Gorgona in less than two hours (about US$200 per boat; up to 10 passengers). For information and reservations, call ☎ 2-825 7137 or 2-825 7136.

If you desire more comfort, tour operators in Cali, including Ecolombia Tours (p191), offer all-inclusive tours, including air travel to Guapí and boat transfer to/from the island.

CAUCA & HUILA

Home to Colombia's most important archeological sites, as well as one of its loveliest colonial cities, these two departments have long been a must-see for any traveler to Colombia. A strong rebel presence made it dangerous for years, but at the time of writing the situation had significantly improved and travelers were starting again to tread the once-famous triangle that connects the pre-Colombian wonders of San Agustín and Tierradentro with Popayán and its remarkably intact colonial heart.

While Popayán has long been safe, you should check current conditions before leaving the Panamericana, especially the very rough roads to San Agustín and Tierradentro.

POPAYÁN

☎ 2 / pop 240,000 / elevation 1740m / temp 19°C

Amid rolling foothills at the southern end of the Valle del Cauca, Popayán is a small gem. Known as the 'Ciudad Blanca' for the stunning uniformity of its chalk-white facades, it is second only to Cartagena as Colombia's most impressive colonial city.

Founded in 1537 by Sebastián de Belalcázar, Popayán became the most important stopping point on the road between Cartagena and Quito. Its mild climate also attracted wealthy Spanish families from the

POPAYÁN

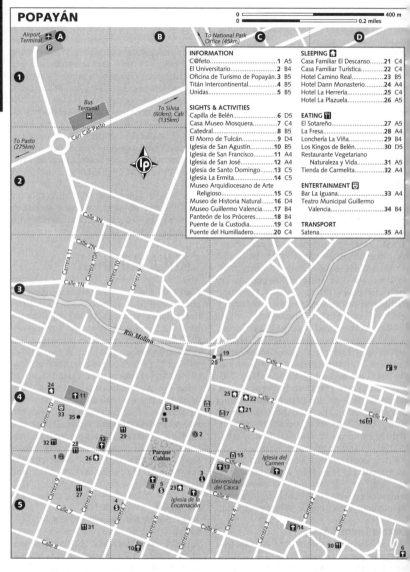

INFORMATION		
C@feto	1	A5
El Universitario	2	B4
Oficina de Turismo de Popayán	3	B5
Titán Intercontinental	4	B5
Unidas	5	B5

SIGHTS & ACTIVITIES		
Capilla de Belén	6	D5
Casa Museo Mosquera	7	C4
Catedral	8	B5
El Morro de Tulcán	9	D4
Iglesia de San Agustín	10	B5
Iglesia de San Francisco	11	A4
Iglesia de San José	12	A4
Iglesia de Santo Domingo	13	C5
Iglesia La Ermita	14	C5
Museo Arquidiocesano de Arte Religioso	15	C5
Museo de Historia Natural	16	D4
Museo Guillermo Valencia	17	B4
Panteón de los Próceres	18	B4
Puente de la Custodia	19	C4
Puente del Humilladero	20	C4

SLEEPING		
Casa Familiar El Descanso	21	C4
Casa Familiar Turística	22	C4
Hotel Camino Real	23	B5
Hotel Dann Monasterio	24	A4
Hotel La Herrería	25	C4
Hotel La Plazuela	26	A5

EATING		
El Sotareño	27	A5
La Fresa	28	A4
Lonchería La Viña	29	B4
Los Kingos de Belén	30	D5
Restaurante Vegetariano Naturaleza y Vida	31	A5
Tienda de Carmelita	32	A4

ENTERTAINMENT		
Bar La Iguana	33	A4
Teatro Municipal Guillermo Valencia	34	B4

TRANSPORT		
Satena	35	A4

sugar haciendas of the hot Cali region. In the 17th century they began building mansions, schools and several imposing churches and monasteries. Fortunately Cali overtook Popayán as the region's capital in the early 20th century, so the Ciudad Blanca was never bulldozed to make way for modernity like so many other Colombian cities.

Much of the city's historic fabric was seriously damaged by a violent earthquake in March 1983, moments before the much-celebrated Maundy Thursday religious procession was set to depart. The difficult and costly restoration was carried out over the next two decades, and the results are truly admirable – little damage is visible today.

Apart from its beauty, Popayán is a clean, tranquil and reasonably priced city. It has good food in all price categories, as well as a lively café culture, thanks to the city's universities. The weather is pleasant most of the year, although the best time to visit is from November to February, when the rainfall is lowest. The wettest months are June to September.

Information

Few of Popayán's banks change cash or traveler's checks, but there are plenty of ATMs that accept foreign Visa and debit cards. Internet cafés are plentiful and cost about US$1 per hour.

C@feto (Carrera 9 No 5-42) Internet access.

El Universitario (Carrera 6 No 3-47) Internet access.

Oficina de Turismo de Popayán (☎ 824 2251; Carrera 5 No 4-68; ⏰ 8am-noon & 2-6pm Mon-Fri, 9am-noon Sat) Helpful and knowledgeable.

Parques Nacionales Naturales de Colombia (☎ 823 1212, 823 1279; www.parquesnacionales.gov.co in Spanish; Carrera 9 No 25N-6)

Titán Intercontinental (Centro Comercial Luis Martínez, Carrera 7 No 6-40, Interior 106) Will change cash.

Unidas (Carrera 6 No 5-44) Will change cash.

Sights & Activities

Virtually all of Popayán's sites are concentrated in the compact colonial center, which is about 10 blocks long and as many wide, so it is easy to see all the sites in a single day. Note that churches are often open only during Mass (generally around 8am and again at 5pm).

The **Iglesia de San Francisco** (cnr Carrera 9 & Calle 4) is the city's largest colonial church and arguably the most beautiful. Inside are a fine high altar and a collection of seven unique side altars. Other colonial churches include the **Iglesia de Santo Domingo** (cnr Carrera 5 & Calle 4), **Iglesia de San José** (cnr Calle 5 & Carrera 5) and the **Iglesia de San Agustín** (cnr Calle 7 & Carrera 6). **Iglesia La Ermita** (cnr Calle 5 & Carrera 2) is Popayán's oldest church (1546), worth seeing for its fine main retable and for the fragments of old frescoes, which were only discovered after the earthquake.

Casa Museo Mosquera (☎ 824 0683; Calle 3 No 5-38; admission US$1; ⏰ 8am-noon & 2-5pm) is housed in an 18th-century mansion that was once home to General Tomás Cipriano de Mosquera, a politician and historian who was Colombia's president on four occasions

between 1845 and 1867. The museum contains personal memorabilia and a collection of colonial art. Note the urn in the wall containing Mosquera's heart.

Museo Arquidiocesano de Arte Religioso (☎ 824 2759; Calle 4 No 4-56; admission US$1; ⏰ 9am-12:30pm & 2-5pm Mon-Fri, 9am-2pm Sat) has a good collection of religious art, including paintings, statues, altarpieces, silverware and liturgical vessels, most of which date from the 17th to 19th century.

The neoclassical **catedral** (Parque Caldas) is the youngest church in the center, built between 1859 and 1906 on the site of a previous cathedral, which had been completely destroyed by an earthquake.

Museo Guillermo Valencia (☎ 824 2081; Carrera 6 No 2-65; admission US$1; ⏰ 10am-noon & 2-5pm Tue-Sun) is dedicated to the Popayán-born poet who once lived here. The spacious late-18th-century building is full of period furniture, paintings, old photos and documents related to the poet and his son, Guillermo León Valencia, who was Colombia's president from 1962 to 1966.

It is worth strolling past the early-20th-century eclectic **Teatro Municipal Guillermo Valencia** (cnr Calle 3 & Carrera 7). Located just next door to the theater is the neoclassical **Panteón de los Próceres**, which shelters the remains of Popayán's most illustrious sons, including General Tomás Cipriano de Mosquera and botanist Francisco José de Caldas (1770–1816).

Just north of the historic center, two unusual bridges cross the small Río Molino. The small one, the **Puente de la Custodia**, was constructed in 1713 to allow priests to cross the river to bring the holy orders to the sick of this poor northern suburb. About 160 years later, the solid 178m-long 12-arch **Puente del Humilladero** was built alongside the old bridge, and is still in use.

Just east from the historic center you'll find the **Museo de Historia Natural** (☎ 820 1952; Carrera 2 No 1A-25; admission US$1.50; ☽ 8am-noon & 2-5pm Tue-Sun). One of the best of its kind in the country, it's noted for its extensive collection of insects, butterflies and, in particular, stuffed birds.

The **Capilla de Belén**, a chapel set on a hill just east of the city center, offers good views over the town. **El Morro de Tulcán**, a hill topped with an equestrian statue of the town's founder, provides even better vistas. Note that in the past, tourists have been attacked and robbed in the environs. These areas are considered safe now, but it's best to double-check before heading here.

Festivals & Events

The **Semana Santa** (Holy Week) in Popayán is famous around Colombia, especially the nighttime processions on Maundy Thursday and Good Friday. Thousands of believers and tourists from all over Colombia come to take part in this religious ceremony and the accompanying festival of religious music. Book rooms in advance at this time.

Sleeping

Popayán has accommodations in all price ranges right in the historic center. A number of colonial mansions have been converted into elegant hotels.

Hotel Dann Monasterio (☎ 824 2191; www.hotelesdann.com in Spanish; Calle 4 No 10-14; s/d US$54/70; ⓟ ⌧ ▯ ⌦) The top choice in town, this Franciscan monastery-turned-hotel offers large, elegantly appointed rooms around a vast, arcaded courtyard. Breakfast is included, and there's even a pool in the back garden. It's rare to get this much class at these prices.

Hotel La Herrería (☎ 839 2740; laherreriahotel@yahoo.com; Carrera 5 No 2-208; s/d US$26/38) This spruce little hotel occupies one of the few noncolonial buildings in the center. Outside it resembles a Swiss chalet. Inside it's a homey affair, with a friendly little restaurant-café downstairs and cozy, well-maintained rooms upstairs.

Casa Familiar El Descanso (☎ 824 0019; Carrera 5 No 2-41; r per person US$6) The owner of El Descanso

rents out small but neat rooms in her rather grand house. It's not ideal if you crave anonymity, but the beds are decent, the water is hot, and the price is right.

Casa Familiar Turística (☎ 824 4853; Carrera 5 N 2-07; dm US$4, s/d US$6/9) Popayán's backpacker classic is not beautiful to look at but plenty practical. Rooms are basic, but there is hot water, and access to kitchen and laundry facilities. It's also a good place to meet travelers and get tips about current conditions in Tierradentro and San Agustín.

Hotel La Plazuela (☎ 824 1084; hotellaplazuela@hotmail.com; Calle 5 No 8-13; s/d US$35/50) In a beautiful, whitewashed mansion complete with a lovely arcaded courtyard, this small but classy hotel is definitely worth the splurge if you get one of the light-filled rooms that face the street.

Hotel Camino Real (☎ 824 3595; www.hotelcaminoreal.com.co in Spanish; Calle 5 No 5-59; s/d US$46/62) Occupying an even grander spread than La Plazuela, this place has exquisite, colonial-style common areas. Street-facing rooms are large and comfortable, though they could use a little refurbishing. Internal rooms are a bit cheaper but smaller and darker.

Eating

Restaurants in the historic center are plentiful, inexpensive, and generally quite good. Be sure to try *empanadas de pipián*, a local variation of empanadas stuffed with potato and peanut.

La Fresa (Calle 5 No 8-89; ☽ 8am-8pm Mon-Sat) This humble little place may have no sign on the door but serves up exquisite *empanadas de pipián* for about US$0.25 each.

Tienda de Carmelita (☎ 824 4862; Calle 5 No 9-4; ☽ 8:30am-12:30pm & 2:30-6:30pm Mon-Fri, 8:30am-1pm Sat) Another place for delicious *empanadas de pipián* (US$0.25), and they also have an interesting collection of before-and-after photos of the 1983 earthquake.

Lonchería La Viña (☎ 824 0602; Calle 4 No 7-79; set meals US$2.50, mains US$5-6; ☽ 9am-midnight) Has reliable cooking, bargain set menus and long hours; this place is a standby with locals.

Restaurante Vegetariano Naturaleza y Vida (☎ 822 1118; Carrera 8 No 7-19; meals US$1.25; ☽ 7:30am-8pm Mon-Sat) It may look a little ramshackle, but this place serves up dependable freshly prepared vegetarian dishes.

Los Kingos de Belén (Calle 4 No 0-55; mains US$4-) Good regional specialties. Try the *bandeja* *típica* and wash it down with *champús* (a cold drink made from rice and *lulo* fruit).

It's hard to imagine getting a six-course French meal for US$14, but at the Hotel Camino Real it's possible. Not all courses are uniformly excellent, but the beef is outstanding. So is the upper-class, colonial ambience. The elegant dining room at the Hotel Dann Monasterio (mains US$6 to US$10) is another relative bargain, considering the grandeur of the place.

Entertainment

El Sotareño (Calle 6 No 8-05) With its 40-year history, this legendary and impossibly old-fashioned bar plays tango, bolero and ranchera from scratched vinyls probably as old as the place itself.

Bar La Iguana (Calle 4 No 9-67) Has excellent salsa and Cuban *son* music at high volume.

Getting There & Away

AIR

The airport is situated just behind the bus terminal, a 15-minute walk north of the city center. At present, Avianca no longer flies to Popayán. Satena may have flights.

BUS

The bus terminal is a short walk north of the city center. Be sure to check conditions on all routes out of Popayán. At the time of writing, travel along the Panamericana was considered safe, but conditions can change quickly so check ahead. Avoid travel after dark. Also be sure to check conditions on any roads off the main highway, particularly to Tierradentro and San Agustín.

Plenty of buses run to Cali (US$5, three hours), and there are also minibuses and *colectivos* every hour or so. Buses to Bogotá run every hour or two (US$26, 15 hours). Likewise, there are buses to Pasto at least every hour (US$10, six hours).

Buses to Tierradentro (US$7, five to six hours) and Agustín (US$10 to US$12, six to eight hours) tend to leave in the mornings only; try to check timetables a day ahead if you're on a tight schedule.

SILVIA

☎ 2 / pop 5000 / elevation 2620m / temp 15°C

A picturesque mountain town 53km northeast of Popayán, Silvia is the center of the Guambiano region. The Guambiano people don't live in Silvia itself, but in the small mountain villages such as Pueblito, La Campana, Guambia and Caciques, scattered throughout the area. The whole community numbers about 12,000.

The Guambianos are considered one of the most traditional indigenous groups in Colombia. They have preserved their culture remarkably well given their proximity to, and contact with, the 'civilized' world. They speak their own language, dress traditionally and still use rudimentary farming techniques. They're also excellent weavers.

On Tuesday, market day, they come to Silvia to sell their fruit, vegetables and handicrafts. This is the best time to visit the town. Almost all the Guambianos come in traditional dress, the women in hand-woven garments and beaded necklaces, busily spinning wool. They come in *chivas* and tend to congregate around the main plaza. They don't like cameras, so try to respect this.

The market begins at dawn and goes until the early afternoon. You can purchase *ruanas* (ponchos), shawls, blankets, scarves and sweaters, as well as an amazing variety of fruit and vegetables. Don't forget to bring a sweater (or buy one at the market) – it can be pretty cold if the weather is cloudy.

Virtually all travelers visit Silvia as a one-day trip from Popayán, but if you feel like staying longer, there are at least half a dozen cheap *residencias*.

There are regular minibuses to Silvia from Popayán (US$2, 1½ hours). On Tuesday, there are also direct *colectivos*. Be sure to double-check safety conditions before setting off – the area around Silvia has seen significant guerrilla activity in the past.

SAN AGUSTÍN

☎ 8 / pop 2000 / elevation 1695m / temp 18°C

Centuries before Columbus dreamed of the new world, the rolling and remarkably green hills around San Agustín were home to an enigmatic civilization that congregated here to bury their dead and honor their memory with monumental stone statues. It's easy to understand why they chose to consecrate this lush, mountainous land of dramatic canyons and ethereal mists.

Little is known about the peoples of San Agustín. They didn't have a written language and had disappeared or dispersed several centuries before the Europeans arrived on the scene. Yet they have left behind at least 500 statues that still enthrall the visitor. Many of them are anthropomorphic figures – some realistic, others resembling masked monsters. Still others depict sacred animals such as the eagle, jaguar and frog. The largest is 7m high. Archeologists have also uncovered pottery and gold objects in the tombs of what is believed to be the tribal leaders.

Give yourself three days for leisurely visits to the most interesting places, preferably by horseback – a great way to see the scattered statues as well as the humble farms of this remote land. Note that this is the one place in the Colombian Andes where you're likely to receive a hard sell from tourist operators. The weather is varied, with the driest period from December to February and the wettest from April to June.

Before setting out, check current conditions on roads in and out, especially the rough journey from Popayán.

Orientation

The statues and tombs are scattered in groups over a wide area on both sides of the gorge formed by the upper Río Magdalena. The most important sight is the Parque Arqueológico, which boasts the largest number of statues and a museum. The second most important is the Alto de los Ídolos, 4km southwest of San José de Isnos on the other side of Río Magdalena from San Agustín town. You buy one admission ticket (adult/student US$3/1.50), which is valid for two consecutive days for entry to both parks. There's no admission fee to other archeological sites.

The region is centered on the town of San Agustín, which harbors most of the accommodations and restaurants. From there, you can explore the region on foot, horseback or by jeep.

Information

Banco Agrario (cnr Carrera 13 & Calle 4) Gives peso advances on Visa, but not on MasterCard; the closest places that accept MasterCard are in Pitalito.
Banco Ultrahuilca (Calle 3 No 12-73) It's best to bring as much cash as you're likely to need, since this is the only ATM in town. No-one reliably accepts traveler's checks, and rates for cash tend to be poor.
Internet Galería Cafe (Calle 3 No 12-16; ☼ 8am-10pm) Right across from the tourist office you'll find Internet service; connections can be sluggish.

Tourist office (☎ 837 3062 ext 15; cnr Calle 3 & Carrera 12; ☼ 8am-noon & 2-5pm Mon-Fri) The town recently opened this new office.

Sights
PARQUE ARQUEOLÓGICO
The 78-hectare **archeological park** (☼ 8am-4pm) is 2.5km west of the town of San Agustín, a pleasant half-hour's walk along a paved road. There are in total about 130 statues in the park, either found *in situ* or collected from other areas, and including some of the best examples of San Agustín statuary. Plan on spending at least three hours in the park. Guides, who congregate in the museum's outdoor café, will accompany you for a fixed rate (around US$12).

At the entrance to the park is the **Museo Arqueológico** (☼ 8am-5pm Tue-Sun), which features smaller statues, pottery, utensils, jewelry and other objects, along with interesting background information about the culture.

Besides the various clusters of statues (called *mesitas*), is the **Fuente de Lavapatas**. Carved in the rocky bed of the stream, it is a complex labyrinth of ducts and small terraced pools decorated with images of serpents, lizards and human figures. Archeologists believe the baths were used for ritual ablutions and the worship of aquatic deities.

From here, the path winds uphill to the **Alto de Lavapatas**, the oldest archeological site in San Agustín. You'll find a few tombs guarded by statues, and get a panoramic view over the surrounding countryside.

ALTO DE LOS ÍDOLOS
Located across the Río Magdalena 4km southwest of San José de Isnos, this is the second-most important **archeological park** (☼ 8am-4pm) in the region. It's home to the largest statue in the San Agustín area – it measures 7m high. You can get here on foot from San Agustín by crossing the deep Magdalena Gorge, a spectacular three-hour walk. Some travelers have been attacked and robbed on this route in the past, so check current safety conditions. You can also walk from San José de Isnos, which is connected to San Agustín by road.

ALTO DE LAS PIEDRAS
This site is 7km north of Isnos and contains tombs lined with stone slabs painted red,

black and yellow. One of the most famous statues, known as Doble Yo, is here; look carefully as there are actually four figures carved in this statue. You'll also find an intriguing statue representing a female figure in an advanced state of pregnancy.

EL TABLÓN, LA CHAQUIRA, LA PELOTA & EL PURUTAL

These four sites are relatively close to each other, so they can be seen in one trip. You can seem them all on a pleasant five-hour hike from San Agustín town, or you can travel by horseback. Don't miss La Chaquira – divinities carved into the mountain face and overlooking the stunning gorge of the Río Magdalena.

OTHER ATTRACTIONS

There are several more archeological sites to see if you are not in a hurry, including **La Parada**, **Quinchana**, **El Jabón**, **Naranjos** and **Quebradillas**.

Apart from its archeological wealth, the region is also noted for its natural beauty, and features two spectacular waterfalls, **Salto de Bordones** and **Salto de Mortiño**. It's also worth a walk or ride to **El Estrecho**, where the Río Magdalena passes through 2m narrows. All these sights are accessible by road.

Tours

Walk down the street in San Agustín and someone will offer you a tour of the archeological sites and surrounding countryside. Don't be shy about comparison shopping.

The best way to see the sites is by horseback. It will be about US$2 to US$3 per hour or US$12 for a whole day. A guide will accompany you for another US$2 to US$3 per hour. One of the most popular routes takes in El Tablón, La Chaquira, La Pelota and El Purutal, which lasts about four hours.

There are also a number of standard jeep tours that will take you to El Estrecho, Alto de los Ídolos, Alto de las Piedras, Salto de Bordones and Salto de Mortiño. You can see all of them in seven to eight hours. Expect to pay around around US$12 per person for groups of up to six people.

Sleeping

Casa de Nelly (☎ 837 3221; r per person with/without bathroom US$6/4) A tranquil inn with rustic but attractive rooms set around a lovely garden

about 1km west of the town, off the dirt road to La Estrella. Rooms can be musty, but that is hard to avoid in this damp climate.

Hotel Yalconia (☎ 837 3001; Vía al Parque Arqueológico; hyalconia@hotmail.com; s/d US$24/32) Currently the only upscale option in town, the Yalconia is not pretty to look at, though its gardens are pleasant. It has clean, comfortable, modern rooms – the only ones of their kind in town. It's located about 1km from the center of town.

Camping San Agustín (☎ 837 3192) Camping is available here, about 1km outside town on the way to the archeological park.

In town, there are a number of cheap if uninspired options near where buses stop. They all charge around US$3 to US$4 per person for very basic rooms with bathrooms. You'll save about US$1 on rooms with shared bathrooms.

Hotel Colonial (☎ 837 3159; Calle 3 No 11-54)

Residencias El Jardin (☎ 837 3159; Carrera 11 No 4-10)

Hotel Central (☎ 837 3027; Calle 3 No 10-54)

Eating

There are plenty of standard cheapies in town that serve set meals for around US$2. In addition, there a number of good grill restaurants clustered around the Hotel Yalconia on the road to the archeological park.

Donde Richard (☎ 311-809 3180; Via al Parque Arqueológico; mains US$5-6) Specializing in grilled meats, including the restaurant's signature marinated pork, this is hands down the best place in town. Ingredients are smacking fresh, and you can watch the smooth operations of the open kitchen from your table. Don't miss the homemade sausages.

Restaurante Brahama (Calle 5 No 15-11; ☺ 8am-9pm) Serves hearty set meals (US$2) and will fix vegetarian dishes on request.

Getting There & Away

The bus offices are clustered on Calle 3 near the corner of Carrera 11. There are regular minibuses to Neiva (US$5, four hours) and several buses a day to Bogotá (US$16, 12 hours). It is best to book ahead for buses to Popayán (US$6, six to eight hours), since some only stop if there are reservations.

There are no direct buses to Tierradentro; go to La Plata (US$8, five hours) and change for the bus to El Cruce de San Andrés (US$4, 2½ hours). From here it's a 20-minute walk to the Tierradentro museum.

DETOUR: TATACOA DESERT

Squeezed between the cloud forests of the Cordillera Central and the dense jungle of the Amazon basin, the Tatacoa Desert is a geographical anomaly that is intriguing for its very smallness. Thanks to the particularly effective combination of cloud-blocking peaks around Nevado de Huila (5750m), the dry scrublands of the Magdalena river valley give way to an all-out desert of cracked, red soil and prickly cacti. Tatacoa may only measure 300 sq km – smaller than metro Bogotá – yet it manages to support a mix of plant and animal life unlike anywhere else in Colombia, from scorpions and weasels to fruit-bearing cacti. Framed by the peaks of the Cordillera Central and Cordillera Oriental, it is a beautiful sight to behold.

Plan to visit Tatacoa in the early morning or late afternoon, since midday temperatures can reach 40°C year-round. The nearest town is the sleepy Villavieja, located on the banks of the Río Magdalena about 4km west of the desert proper. You must pass through the city of Neiva to reach Villavieja, which is 38km south along a poorly maintained road. There are regular buses between Neiva and Bogotá (US$14, eight hours) and minibuses to San Agustín (US$8, 4½ hours). From Neiva, there are buses to Villavieja (US$2.50, 1½ hours). Alternately, you can make arrangements with a taxi driver. If you plan to stay in Neiva, try the **Hotel Luna Verde** (☎ 8-871 1924; Carrera 3 No 9-59; d US$16, with air-con US$22; ✷).

The roads to both Popayán and Tierradentro are very rough going and have also seen lots of guerrilla activity in the past. Double-check current safety conditions.

TIERRADENTRO

☎ 2 / elevation 1750m / temp 18°

Like San Agustín, Tierradentro is a remote and enchanted place where green, mist-shrouded hills hold the remains of a civilization that disappeared centuries before Europeans first arrived here. Whereas San Agustín is noted for its statuary, Tierradentro is remarkable for its elaborate underground tombs. So far, archeologists have discovered about a hundred of these unusual funeral temples – the only examples of their kind in the Americas.

Measuring 2m to 7m in diameter, the tombs are scooped out of the soft volcanic rock that forms the region's undulating hillsides. They vary widely in depth; some of them are just below ground level, while others are as deep as 9m. The domed ceilings of the largest tombs are supported by massive pillars. Many are painted with red and black geometric motifs on white background. In addition, figures are carved into the columns and walls of many chambers.

Little is known about the people who built the tombs and the statues. Most likely they were of different cultures, and the people who scooped out the tombs preceded those who carved the statues. Some researchers place the 'tomb' civilization somewhere between the 7th and 9th centuries AD, while the 'statue' culture appears to be related to the later phase of San Agustín development, which is estimated to have taken place some 500 years later.

While conditions have improved, the Tierradentro region has been notorious for a strong guerrilla presence over the years. Check safety conditions carefully before heading out.

Orientation & Information

Scattered across the hills around the town of San Andrés de Pisimbalá, Tierradentro consists of five separate sites – four with tombs and one with aboveground statuary – plus two adjacent museums. The museums are a 25-minute walk from the town. Except for the burial site of El Aguacate, all the sights are relatively close to each other, so they can be visited on foot. Alternately, you can rent horses near the museums and in San Andrés (US$8 per day). A torch is necessary for many tombs – make sure to bring one with you.

There are no tourist offices or money-changing facilities in Tierradentro. General information is available from the museum staff and hotel managers.

Sights
MUSEUMS

Begin your visit from the two museums, across the road from one another; you buy one combined ticket (US$2.50), valid for two consecutive days to all archeological sites and the museums themselves. The museums are open 8am to 4:30pm daily.

Museo Arqueológico contains pottery urns used to keep the ashes of the tribal elders. Some of the urns are decorated with dotted patterns and, in some cases, with representations of animals. The **Museo Etnográfico** has utensils and artifacts of the Páez Indians.

BURIAL SITES & STATUES

A 20-minute walk up the hill north of the museums lies **Segovia**, the most important burial site. There are 28 tombs here, some with well-preserved decorations. It is forbidden to take photos with a flash as it affects the paintings. The tombs are open 8am to 5pm daily.

A 15-minute walk uphill from Segovia brings you to **El Duende**, where there are four tombs, though their decoration hasn't been preserved. More interesting is **Alto de San Andrés**, with five tombs; two have remarkably well-preserved paintings. Nearby is **El Tablón** with 10 stone statues, similar to those of San Agustín, excavated in the area and now thrown together under a single roof.

El Aguacate is the only remote burial site, located high on a mountain ridge that's about a two-hour walk from the museum (plus a two-hour walk back). There are a few dozen tombs, but most have been destroyed by *guaqueros* (tomb raiders). Only a few vaults still bear the remains of the original decoration. It's still worth taking this walk, if only for the sweeping views.

SAN ANDRÉS DE PISIMBALÁ

A 25-minute walk west of the museums, this little town has a few budget hotels and restaurants. It's particularly noted for its thatched **church**. If it's locked, peak at its simple interior through the gap in the entrance doors.

Sleeping & Eating

There are places to stay both in San Andrés de Pisimbalá and near the museums. Accommodations and food are simple but cheap – expect to pay US$2 to US$3 per person in rooms without bathrooms, and around US$1 to US$2 for meals.

About 200m up from the museums is **Hospedaje Pisimbalá**, one of the best budget places. Up another 200m is the **Hotel El**

Refugio (r per person US$16; 🐾). The top option in Tierradentro, it's got basic but comfortable rooms, plus a pool, sauna, restaurant and attractive grounds. For reservations or information, contact the **office** (☎ 2-824 0220; Calle 2 No 3-75) in Popayán.

For budget accommodations in San Andrés de Pisimbalá, check out **Los Lagos de Tierradentro**, which is friendly, serves meals and rents out horses.

Getting There & Away

Most buses stop at El Cruce de San Andrés, which is about a 20-minute walk from the museums. Three or four buses daily pass via El Cruce on their way to Popayán (US$6, five to six hours), and the same number to La Plata (US$2.50, 2½ hours). From La Plata, two direct buses go to Bogotá and two to San Agustín. Alternately, you can take a *colectivo* to Pitalito, then transfer to more regular buses to Bogotá or San Agustín.

NARIÑO

Nariño is Colombia's most southwesterly department; it's closer in many ways to neighboring Ecuador than the rest of Colombia. The Andes turn drier and more forbidding, with towering volcanic peaks. At the same time, the mountains around Pasto, the departmental capital, get enough moisture from the Pacific to turn the slopes into a patchwork of farms. Indigenous cultures exert a strong influence; the locals, known as the *pastusos,* are fine artisans known for their skill and their originality.

The lowlands along the Pacific coast are a very different story. Blanketed in jungle and sparsely populated except around the coastal city Tumaco, the region is populated almost exclusively by descendants of African slaves. While the people are famously friendly, guerrilla and paramilitary activity continue to make this region risky for travelers.

While daytime travel on the highway from Popayán to Ipiales is now considered safe, many rural areas are still in rebel hands. There are mixed reports about the road to Tumaco – get up-to-date information before setting out. In fact, if you plan to take any detours off the Panamerican, except to Laguna de la Cocha and Las Lajas, be sure to check conditions on the ground.

SOUTHWEST COLOMBIA

Pasto and Ipiales tend to be coldest and wettest from July to September. December and January are the sunniest months.

PASTO

☎ 2 / pop 420,000 / elevation 2530m / temp 13°C
Set at the foot of the Volcán Galeras in the fertile Atriz Valley, Pasto is the cultural and political capital of Nariño. Though not a beautiful city in itself, it has several fine colonial buildings as well as a bustling downtown area. Pack a sweater because days can be cool and nights are downright chilly.

The town was founded by Lorenzo de Aldana in 1537 and was an important cultural and religious center in colonial and republican times. Earthquakes have unfortunately destroyed much of its historic character; a handful of churches and palaces have been rebuilt in the original style. The city is also known nationwide for *barniz de Pasto,* a processed vegetable resin used to decorate wooden objects in colorful patterns.

You may be surprised at the prosperity of this remote city. Some say the economy gets a big boost from drug traffickers in neighboring Putamayo and Caquete who come to make their big-ticket purchases. That said, it feels quite safe, with streets that bustle until well after dark.

Information

Most of the major banks are around Plaza de Nariño. They pay advances on Visa and/ or MasterCard, and some, including the Banco Santander and Bancolombia, also change cash and traveler's checks. Lots of Internet cafés are in central Pasto, though access is relatively slow. Expect to pay US$1 to US$2 per hour in any listed cafés.
Ciber C@fe PC Rent (Calle 18A No 25-36)
Giros & Finanzas (Centro Comercial El Liceo, Carrera 26 No 17-12) Changes cash and is the Western Union agent.
Global System (Calle 18A No 25-51)
Infonet (Calle 18 No 29-15)
Oficina Departamental de Turismo de Nariño (☎ 723 4962; Calle 18 No 25-25; ☼ 8am-noon & 2-6pm Mon-Fri) Just off Plaza de Nariño (the main square).

Sights & Activities

On Pasto's main square, **Iglesia de San Juan Bautista** dates from the city's first days; it was rebuilt in the mid-17th century. Grand outside and gold-encrusted inside, it is a fine example of colonial baroque architecture.

For insight into the pre-Columbian cultures of Nariño, check out the **Museo del Oro** (☎ 721 9108; Calle 19 No 21-27; admission free; ☼ 8:30am-noon Mon, 8:30am-noon & 2-6pm Tue-Fri), which has a small but interesting collection of indigenous gold and pottery.

The **Museo Taminango de Artes y Tradiciones** (☎ 723 5539; Calle 13 No 27-67; admission US$0.50; ☼ 8am-noon & 2-6pm Mon-Fri, 9am-1pm Sat) has a hodgepodge of antiques but is worth seeing since it's housed in a meticulously restored *casona* (large house) from 1623 – reputedly the oldest surviving house in town.

Festivals & Events

The city's major event is **Carnaval de Blancos y Negros** held on January 5 and 6. Its origins go back to the times of Spanish rule, when slaves were allowed to celebrate on January 5 and their masters showed approval by painting their faces black. On the following day, the slaves painted their faces white.

The tradition is faithfully maintained. On these two days the city goes wild, with everybody painting or dusting one another with grease, chalk, talc, flour and any other available substance even vaguely black or white in tone. It's a serious affair – wear the worst clothes you have and buy an *antifaz,* a sort of mask to protect the face, widely sold for this occasion.

Sleeping

There are plenty of hotels throughout the central area.

Koala Inn (☎ 722 1101; Calle 18 No 22-37; r with/ without bathroom per person US$5/4) Huge rooms around a spacious internal courtyard; the backpacker's choice in Pasto. There are laundry facilities, a book exchange, a budget restaurant and a satellite TV in the patio.

Hotel Rey del Sur (☎ 720 7909; Carrera 9 No 15A-10; r US$5-7) Within view of the bus station, this brand-new hotel is simple but pleasant, and all rooms have a bathroom and cable TV. Tough to beat for price and convenience.

Hotel Agualongo (☎ 723 5216; fax 723 0604; Carrera 25 No 17-83; s/d US$46/58) Modern, 12-storey hotel; the highest-end option in the center. Rooms are large, with very nice bathrooms. Ask for a room on a higher floor, preferably with a view onto Plaza de Nariño.

Hotel Concorde (☎ 731 0658; Calle 19 No 29A-09, s/d US$12/16) Another decent budget choice a short walk from the Plaza de Nariño.

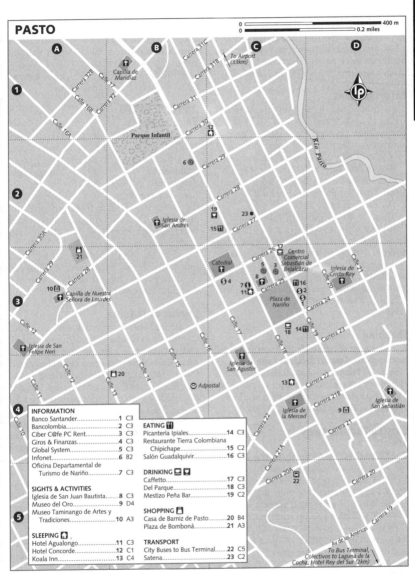

PASTO

Eating

Food here is fairly expensive by Colombian standards, but there are a number of interesting options in the center.

Salón Guadalquivir (☎ 723 9604; Plaza de Nariño; dishes US$2.50; ☺ 8am-12:30pm & 2:30-7:30pm Mon-Sat) This cozy café serves delicious, filling tamales and empanadas. The walls are lined with great posters from the annual Carnaval de Blancos y Negros.

Restaurante Tierra Colombiana Chipichape (☎ 772 8992; Calle 18 No 27-19; mains around US$3-4; ☺ 7am-9pm Mon-Fri, 7am-3pm Sat) Head here for simple but tasty dishes like grilled trout and *arroz con pollo* (chicken and rice), served in a bright, pleasant dining room.

Picantería Ipiales (Calle 19 No 23-37; 🕙 9:30am-9pm Mon-Sat, 10am-6pm Sun) Though it looks like a fast-food joint, this place serves delicious, made-to-order *lapingachos* (fried pancake made from mashed potato and cheese).

Entertainment

The local Zona Rosa, roughly between Calles 19 and 20 and Carreras 31C and 32, comes alive on weekend nights. There is another concentration of bars and discos on Calle 19 between Carreras 26 and 28.

Mestizo Peña Bar (☎ 729 3395; Calle 18 No 27-67; 🕙 4pm-1am Tue-Thu, 4pm-2am Fri & Sat) is a cozy, wood-lined bar that hosts live local Andean music on weekends.

There is also a growing café culture in Pasto. For superior coffee (not easy to come by in Colombia) head to **Del Parque** (Plaza del Nariño; 🕙 9am-8pm Mon-Sat), which roasts its own organic beans. Pasto society hobnobs at **Caffetto** (☎ 729 2720; Calle 19 No 25-62; 🕙 8am-9pm Mon-Sat), which has good sandwiches and salads (US$3 to US$4) and rich desserts (US$1.50).

Shopping

A wide range of *barniz de Pasto* artifacts can be bought in **Casa del Barniz de Pasto** (cnr Carrera 25 & Calle 13). **Plaza de Bombaná** (Calle 14 btwn Carreras 28 & 30) is a covered market with several craft shops. Pasto is also a good place to buy leathergoods (at Bombaná and nearby shops).

Getting There & Away

AIR

The airport is 33km north of the city on the road to Cali. *Colectivos* go there from Calle 18 at Carrera 25 (US$2.50, 45 minutes). Pay the day before your flight at the airline office or at a travel agency, and the *colectivo* will pick you up from your hotel.

Avianca and Satena currently service Pasto, with daily flights to Bogotá and Cali and connections to other cities.

BUS

The bus terminal is 2km south of the city center. Urban buses go there from different points in the central area, including Carrera 20A at Calle 17, or take a taxi (US$1.25).

Frequent buses, minibuses and *colectivos* go to Ipiales (US$2.50 to US$3.50, 1½ to two hours); sit on the left for better views. Plenty of buses ply the spectacular road to

Cali (US$14, nine hours). These buses will drop you off in Popayán in six hours. More than a dozen direct buses depart daily to Bogotá (US$35, 22 hours).

While security along the highway has improved, check current conditions.

AROUND PASTO
Volcán Galeras

The conical peak of Galeras volcano (4267m) looms over the city; its lower slopes are a patchwork of farms and bright green pastureland. The volcano's activity rose dangerously in 1989 putting the city and surrounding region in a state of emergency – the crater is only 8km from central Pasto. Since then, the volcano has erupted several times, though recently it has grown calm again. Tourists can again hike or ride to the top. The hike from Pasto to the top takes four to five hours. Pasto's tourist office can organize guides (around US$15) and transportation (around US$45 per vehicle).

Laguna de la Cocha

Located about 30 minutes east of Pasto, Laguna de la Cocha is beautiful to behold, and also offers a glimpse into a rare and remarkably well-preserved evergreen cloud forest. The lake's La Corota island is the best place to see the forest close-up. Located just offshore, it's a nature preserve run by the national park service.

To get to the island, head to the small town on the lake's shore, where you can rent a boat for up to six people for one hour for a fixed fee of US$7.50. Entrance to the reserve is US$0.25.

Colectivos for the lake (US$1.50, 30 minutes) leave from in front of Iglesia Santo Sepulcro, which is near the Hospital Departamental, at Calle 22 at Carrera 7, about 1.5km east of downtown. You can also negotiate a taxi to take you. Expect to pay around US$20 for the round-trip, including several hours at the lake.

IPIALES

☎ 2 / pop 75,000 / elevation 2900m / temp 11°C

Only 7km from the border with Ecuador, Ipiales is an uninspiring commercial town driven by trade across the frontier. There is little to see or do here, except for the colorful Saturday market, where the *campesinos* from surrounding villages come to buy and sell goods. A short side trip to the Santuario de las Lajas is the real draw, though the Panamerican from Pasto is also thrilling itself.

Information
IMMIGRATION
Passport formalities are processed in Rumichaca, not in Ipiales or Tulcán. The DAS office, on the Colombian side of the border, is open 24 hours; the Ecuadorian post, across the Río Rumichaca, is generally open from 5am to 10pm. Be sure to get stamps when coming and going in both directions.

Upon arrival from Ecuador, Colombian officials may require you to show an onward ticket. Some readers report that they will ignore the rule for a small 'fee' (around US$15). Alternately, you can travel to the bus station in Ipiales and purchase a oneway ticket back to Ecuador, then return to the border and show this as proof.

INTERNET ACCESS
There are several Internet cafés in town, but connections can be slow.
Internet (Calle 16 No 6-51)

MONEY
No bank in Ipiales changes cash or traveler's checks, but they're likely to give peso cash advances on credit cards. Several banks around Plaza La Pola, including Bancolombia, have ATMs.

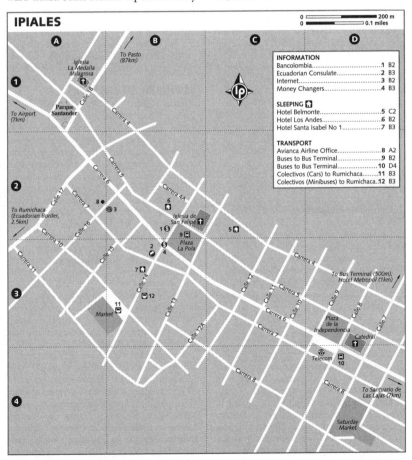

IPIALES

| 0 | 200 m |
| 0 | 0.1 miles |

INFORMATION
Bancolombia....................................**1** B2
Ecuadorian Consulate.....................**2** B3
Internet...**3** B2
Money Changers.............................**4** B3

SLEEPING
Hotel Belmonte...............................**5** C2
Hotel Los Andes...............................**6** B2
Hotel Santa Isabel No 1..................**7** B3

TRANSPORT
Avianca Airline Office......................**8** A2
Buses to Bus Terminal.....................**9** B2
Buses to Bus Terminal...................**10** D4
Colectivos (Cars) to Rumichaca.....**11** B3
Colectivos (Minibuses) to Rumichaca.**12** B3

Money changers on the Plaza La Pola (the main square) and a number of *casas de cambio* in the town's center will change US dollars, Colombian pesos and Ecuadorian sucres. There are also money changers at the border in Rumichaca.

Sleeping

Ipiales has plenty of hotels, and prices are extremely reasonable. Nights are cold, so check the number of blankets before you book a room in a rock-bottom *hospedaje*.

Hotel Los Andes (☎ 773 4338; fax 773 3255; Carrera 5 No 14-44; d US$20) It may be the top place in town, but prices are jaw-droppingly reasonable. It's a comfortable, modern place with neat, quiet rooms, plus a gym and sauna.

Hotel Belmonte (☎ 773 2771; Carrera 4 No 12-111; r per person with/without bathroom US$4.50/3.50) Small, friendly and family-run, this basic place is favored by local workers and backpackers alike. Note that there is no hot water.

Hotel Metropól (☎ 773 7976; Carrera 2A No 6-10; s/d US$8/11) Just across the street from the main bus station, this new hotel has acceptable rooms with bathroom.

Hotel Santa Isabel No 1 (☎ 773 3851; Calle 14 No 7-30; s/d US$10/15) This place offers basic but modern rooms, with windows that open onto a two-story internal courtyard.

Eating

There are plenty of budget restaurants on and around Plaza de la Independencia.

Restaurante Las Colinas (Carrera 5 No 14-42; mains US$4-7), attached to the Hotel Los Andes, is the top choice in town, with straightforward and pleasingly fresh international fare.

On the road to Santuario de Nuestra Señora de Las Lajas, several rustic *asaderos* serve *cuy* (spit-roasted guinea pig) in the suburb of El Charco, about 2km from central Ipiales.

Getting There & Away

AIR

The airport is 7km northwest of Ipiales, on the road to Cumbal, accessible by taxi (US$6). Avianca has flights to Bogotá, with onward connections to other cities.

There are no direct flights from Ipiales to Ecuador, but you can easily get to Tulcán, from where Tame has daily flights to Quito. Heading to Tulcán from the border, you pass the airport 2km before reaching town.

BUS

Ipiales has a new, large bus terminal, about 1km northeast of the center. It's linked to the center by urban buses (US$0.20) and taxis (US$1).

Expreso Bolivariano has frequent buses to Bogotá (US$35, 25 hours). Several companies run regular buses to Cali (US$14, 10 hours). All these buses will drop you in Popayán in eight hours. Don't travel at night on this route – see p206 for more information.

There are plenty of buses, minibuses and *colectivos* to Pasto (US$2 to US$3, 1½ to two hours). They all depart from the bus terminal. Sit on the right for better views.

Frequent *colectivos* (cars and minibuses) travel the 2.5km to the border at Rumichaca (US$0.50), leaving from the bus terminal and the market area near the corner of Calle 14 and Carrera 10. After crossing the border on foot, take another *colectivo* to Tulcán (6km). On both routes, Colombian and Ecuadorian currency is accepted.

SANTUARIO DE LAS LAJAS
elevation 2600m / temp 14°C

Built on a stone bridge spanning a deep gorge, the neo-Gothic Santuario de Las Lajas is a strange but spectacular site, as well as a hugely popular destination for pilgrims in need of a miracle. They place their faith in the Virgin Mary, whose image is believed to have emerged from an enormous vertical rock 45m above the river sometime in the mid-18th century. Plaques of thanksgiving line the walls of the canyon, many from prominent Colombian politicians.

The church is directly against the rocky wall of the gorge where the image appeared. A gilded painting of the Virgin, accompanied by Santo Domingo and San Francisco, has been painted directly on the rocks just to be sure there is no confusion. The first chapel was built in 1803; today's church, designed by Nariño architect Lucindo Espinoza, was built between 1926 and 1944.

The sanctuary is located just 7km southeast of Ipiales. *Colectivos* run regularly from Ipiales to Santuario de Las Lajas (US$0.50, 15 minutes), leaving from Carrera 6 at Calle 4. A taxi from Ipiales to Santuario de Las Lajas costs US$2.50. A return taxi (for up to four people), including an hour waiting in Santuario de Las Lajas, shouldn't cost more than US$6.

Amazon Basin

AMAZON BASIN

As you head southeast from the Andes, dry scrubland grows more lush, turning into almost impenetrable jungle long before you ever reach the Amazon. This huge, wild region, which Colombians call Amazonia, accounts for a third of the country's total area – it's about the size of California and larger than Germany. Biologists will probably never finish cataloging the region's dizzying array of flora and fauna. Likewise, visitors can never quite account for the strange exhilaration they feel when they come face-to-face with the rainforest for the first time.

With transportation largely limited to the rivers that crisscross the jungle, indigenous peoples have in many cases been able to preserve their cultures more or less intact. The region remains an ethnic and linguistic mosaic, with more than 50 languages (not counting dialects) belonging to some 10 linguistic families.

Unfortunately, isolation has made Amazonia a hotbed for cultivation of the coca plant, and the processing of its leaves into cocaine. It's an ideal base for leftist rebels. In many areas of the Caquete and Putumayo departments, they run what amounts to a state within a state supported by proceeds from the region's drug trade. These regions are off-limits to outsiders.

Fortunately, you can safely visit the Amazon itself by flying directly to Leticia, a town that sits on the banks of the great river – and is right at the borders with Brazil and Peru. It occupies a quirky strip of land that penetrates the territories of the other two countries, and that in fact was not part of Colombia until the three nations signed a treaty in 1922. From here you can venture up and down the river or strike out into the surrounding rainforest.

HIGHLIGHTS

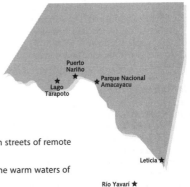

- Slip silently into the jungle as your canoe heads up one of the tributaries of the **Río Yavarí** (p217)
- Look out across the rainforest canopy from the observation deck in **Parque Nacional Amacayacu** (p216)
- Taste the tender flesh of the Amazonian fish known as the *pirarucú* in one of the pleasant outdoor restaurants in **Leticia** (p213)
- Stroll through the car-less and uncannily clean streets of remote **Puerto Nariño** (p216)
- Catch sight of pink dolphins slicing through the warm waters of the mighty **Lago Tarapoto** (p217)

- POPULATION: 403,348
- AREA: 643,000 SQ KM

> **TRAVELING SAFELY IN THE AMAZON BASIN**
>
> Leticia is very safe, as are all the points of interest along the Amazon River itself. Much of the rest of the Amazon Basin, however, is both difficult to access and unsafe for travelers.

LETICIA

☎ 8 / pop 35,000 / elevation 95m / temp 27°C

Despite its isolation and often oppressive heat, Leticia is a remarkably spruce little town, with brightly painted houses, pleasant outdoor cafés and restaurants, and a well-maintained grid of streets. It also has a complete infrastructure to support travelers, with hotels in all price categories, regularly scheduled flights between Leticia and Bogota, and a long-standing military presence that keeps the city and surrounding region safe. Note that all foreigners must pay US$5 tax upon arrival at Leticia's airport.

Founded in 1867 and christened San Antonio, Leticia remained part of Peru until a 1922 treaty ceded it to Colombia. The town's new masters renamed it Leticia and made it their gateway to the Amazon. Though it's the departmental capital – and the largest town for hundreds of miles – it feels very much like a small, frontier town.

With boat connections upriver to Iquitos, Peru and downriver to Manaus, Brazil, it can serve as a gateway to further Amazonian adventures. July and August are the only relatively dry months. The wettest period is from February to April. The Amazon River's highest level is reached between May and June, while the lowest is from August to October. The difference between low and high water can be as great as 15m.

Orientation

Leticia is on the banks of the Amazon right on the Colombia–Brazil border. Just across the frontier sits Tabatinga, a Brazilian town much the same size as Leticia, with its own port and airport. Leticia and Tabatinga are virtually merging; there are no border checkpoints between them. Frequent *colectivos* (shared taxis or minibuses) link the towns, or you can just walk.

On the island in the Amazon opposite Leticia/Tabatinga is Santa Rosa, a small Peruvian village. Boats head there from Leticia's Muelle Fluvial and the market, and Tabatinga's Porto da Feira.

On the opposite side of the Amazon from Leticia, about 25km downstream, is the Brazilian town of Benjamin Constant, the main port for boats downstream to Manaus. Boats shuttle regularly between Tabatinga and Benjamin Constant.

Information

IMMIGRATION

Locals and foreigners are allowed to come and go between Leticia and Tabatinga without visas or passport control, but if you plan on heading further into either country, you must get your passport stamped at both the DAS office at Leticia's airport and at **Policía Federal** (Av da Amizade 650; ☺ 7am-noon & 2-6pm), near the hospital in Tabatinga.

Citizens of some countries, including the USA, Canada, Australia and New Zealand, need a visa to enter Brazil and it may be costly (particularly for US nationals). Bring your photo and yellow-fever vaccination certificate. The Brazilian consulate (p226) is located in the northern end of Leticia and is open 8am to noon and 1pm to 4pm Monday to Friday.

If you're heading to or coming from Iquitos, you get your entry or exit stamp at the Policia Internacional Peruviano (PIP) office in Santa Rosa. The Peruvian consulate (p226) is also in Leticia's northern part and is open 9am to 2pm Monday to Friday.

Travelers coming here from Brazil may need the Colombian consulate (p226) in Tabatinga.

INTERNET ACCESS

Internet cafés cost US$1 to US$1.50 per hour. Connections are generally sluggish.

AMI (Carrera 10 No 11-119)

hispan@Internet (Calle 10 No 9-82)

Indio.net (Centro Comercial Acuarios, cnr Carrera 7 & Calle 8)

LAUNDRY

Lavandería Aseo Total (☎ 592 6051; Calle 9 No 9-85; wash & dry per kg US$1.50; ☺ 7am-8pm Mon-Sat, 8am-1pm Sun)

MONEY

Leticia has two banks, both on the corner of Carrera 10 and Calle 7. There are many

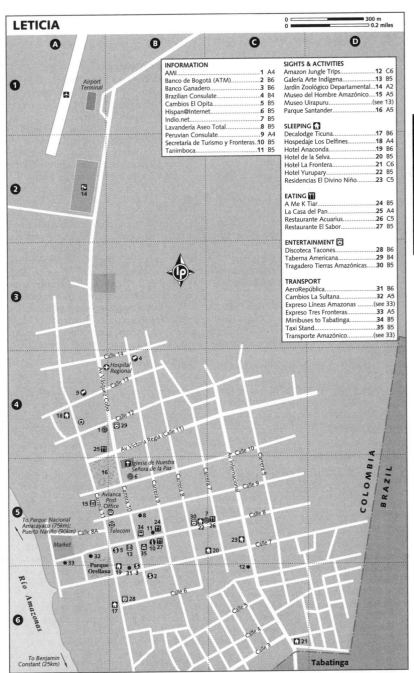

LETICIA

0   300 m
0   0.2 miles

INFORMATION
| | |
AMI......................................1 A4
Banco de Bogotá (ATM)..............2 B6
Banco Ganadero........................3 B6
Brazilian Consulate....................4 B4
Cambios El Opita.......................5 B5
Hispan@Internet.......................6 B5
Indio.net.................................7 B5
Lavandería Aseo Total.................8 B5
Peruvian Consulate.....................9 A4
Secretaría de Turismo y Fronteras.10 B5
Tanimboca..............................11 B5

SIGHTS & ACTIVITIES
Amazon Jungle Trips.................12 C6
Galería Arte Indígena................13 B5
Jardín Zoológico Departamental...14 A2
Museo del Hombre Amazónico...15 A5
Museo Uirapuru....................(see 13)
Parque Santander.....................16 A5

SLEEPING
Decalodge Ticuna.....................17 B6
Hospedaje Los Delfines.............18 A4
Hotel Anaconda......................19 B6
Hotel de la Selva.....................20 B5
Hotel La Frontera.....................21 C6
Hotel Yurupary........................22 B5
Residencias El Divino Niño........23 C5

EATING
A Me K Tiar............................24 B5
La Casa del Pan.......................25 A4
Restaurante Acuarius................26 C5
Restaurante El Sabor.................27 B5

ENTERTAINMENT
Discoteca Tacones....................28 B6
Taberna Americana...................29 B4
Tragadero Tierras Amazónicas.....30 B5

TRANSPORT
AeroRepública.........................31 B6
Cambios La Sultana...................32 A5
Expreso Líneas Amazonas ....(see 33)
Expreso Tres Fronteras...............33 A5
Minibuses to Tabatinga.............34 B5
Taxi Stand..............................35 B5
Transporte Amazónico.............(see 33)

AMAZON BASIN

casas de cambio on Calle 8 between Carrera 11 and the market. They change US dollars, Colombian pesos, Brazilian reais and Peruvian soles. They open around 8am or 9am until 5pm or 6pm weekdays and until around 2pm Saturday. Shop around, as rates vary. Check exchange rates on both sides of the border if these small differences are important to your budget or if you have a lot of money to change. Don't carry pesos any further into Brazil or Peru as it will be difficult to change them. By the same token, don't bring reais to Bogotá. Change all the money of the country you're leaving in Leticia/Tabatinga. Note that businesses in both Tabatinga and Leticia generally accept both reais and Colombian pesos.

Banco de Bogotá (cnr Carrera 10 & Calle 7) Won't touch your traveler's checks or cash dollars, but has an ATM that accepts Visa cards (but not MasterCard).

Banco Ganadero (cnr Carrera 10 & Calle 7) Changes American Express traveler's checks (but not cash) and provides peso advances on Visa (but not on MasterCard), either by teller or the bank's ATM.

Cambios El Opita (☎ 592 5134; Carrera 11 No 7-96) Changes traveler's checks.

There are also money-changing facilities in Tabatinga.

Banco do Brasil (Av da Amizade 60) Gives cash advances in reais on Visa.

CNM Câmbio e Turismo (☎ 412 3281; Av da Amizade 2017) About 500m from the actual border, it exchanges cash and traveler's checks, and pays in reais or pesos, but the rate may be a bit lower than in Leticia.

TOURIST INFORMATION

Secretaría de Turismo y Fronteras (☎ 592 7569; Calle 8 No 9-75; ☺ 7am-noon & 2pm-5:30pm Mon-Fri)

Sights & Activities

The **Jardín Zoológico Departamental** (Av Vásquez Cobo; admission US$1; ☺ 8am-noon & 2-5pm), near the airport, has animals typical of the region including anacondas, tapirs, monkeys, caimans, ocelots, eagles, macaws and a friendly manatee named Polo. The small lake at the far northern end of the zoo features the famous *Victoria amazonica*, a kind of water lily noted for its gigantic round leaves.

The small **Museo del Hombre Amazónico** (☎ 592 7729; Carrera 11 No 9-43; admission free; ☺ 9am-noon & 2:30-5pm Mon-Fri, 9am-1pm Sat) features artifacts and household implements of indigenous groups living in the region.

The **Galería Arte Indígena** (☎ 592 7056; Calle 8 No 10-35) is Leticia's largest craft shop selling artifacts of indigenous groups. At the back of the shop is **Museo Uirapuru** featuring an exhibition of historic crafts (not for sale).

Visit **Parque Santander** before sunset for an impressive spectacle as thousands of small screeching parrots (locally called *pericos*) arrive for their nightly rest in the park's trees.

Tours

The real wilderness begins well off the Amazon proper, along its small tributaries. The further you go, the more chance you have to observe wildlife in relatively undamaged habitats and to visit indigenous settlements.

FREE-FOR-ALL TRADE

When you first arrive in Leticia, you'll find yourself asking how a remote town 500 miles from the nearest Colombian highway and with virtually no visible industry – beyond fishing and a modicum of tourism – manages to have such bustling streets, well-stocked electronics shops, and a general air of prosperity. If history is any guide, you may not want to pry too deeply.

At the border of three countries in a region of dense jungle that is virtually impossible to patrol, it is an ideal conduit for contraband. During the civil wars of the 1940s and '50s, Leticia was a main entry point for illicit arms, and until a major government crackdown in the mid-1980s, cocaine trafficking was said to be both rampant and blatant. Indeed, an airstrip near Puerto Nariño was reputedly dubbed the 'International Airport' because of the constant comings and goings of cocaine traffickers. Even after the military intervention, an American entrepreneur named Mike Tsalickis, who had built a small tourism empire in Leticia, was caught in 1989 trying to bring more than 3000kg of cocaine into the US.

And what accounts for the current crackle in the local economy? Perhaps it's simply wise investment of previously ill-gotten gains, though there is no doubt that the Amazon remains a major highway as cocaine moves from Caquetá and Putumayo to the huge markets of Brazil, the US and beyond.

This involves time and money, but the experience can be rewarding. A three- to four-day tour is perhaps the best way to balance the cost of the trip with the insight it will give you into the workings of the jungle. Several companies also organize multiday tours to the small nature reserves that run along the lower reaches of the Río Yavarí, on the Brazil–Peru border. See p217 for information about the reserves and their lodges and tours. Whoever you decide to go with, always be sure to clearly fix the conditions, including duration, price and activities, and pay only a part of the cost of the trip before departure. There have been several reader reports of unscrupulous tour guide operators who wait at the airport to snag tourists. Be wary of anyone overly friendly or too forward; trust your instincts at all times.

Amazon Jungle Trips (☎ 592 7377; amazonjungletrips@ yahoo.com; Av Internacional No 6-25) There are plenty of tour operators in Leticia focusing on jungle trips, including this one. Most agencies offer standard one-day tours that go up the Amazon to Puerto Nariño and include lunch and visits to an indigenous village. These excursions are usually well organized, comfortable and trouble-free, but will hardly give you a real taste of the rainforest or its inhabitants.

Tanimboca (☎ 592 5973; tanimboca@yahoo.com; Calle 8 No 9-18) If you prefer setting up an independent tour of your own design, consider talking to the friendly guys here. Besides a rope-climbing tour to the top of the rainforest canopy, they can organize boat or hiking trips into the jungle outside Leticia, including trips to indigenous villages. The owner and several of the guides speak English.

Sleeping

There are plenty of places to stay in Leticia, and competition keeps prices moderate.

Hotel Yurupary (☎ 592 7983; www.hotelyurupary .col.nu in Spanish; Calle 8 No 7-26; s/d/tr US$18/27/35; 🅿) With large, spotless and recently refurbished rooms arranged around a bright if unbeautiful courtyard, this hotel offers good value for your money, especially if you're determined to have air-conditioning.

Decalodge Ticuna (☎ 592 6948; www.decameron .com; Carrera 11 No 6-11; s/d US$110/195; 🅿 🛏 🖥 🖨) Leticia's only luxury option, this place has plush, stylish *cabañas* that all open up onto a lush courtyard and pool. The hotel also has a huge open-air bar and restaurant that serves high-end Amazonian cuisine (mains cost US$8 to US$12).

Hospedaje Los Delfines (☎ 592 7388; losdelfineslet icia@hotmail.com; Carrera 11 No 12-81; s/d/tr US$14/18/22)

A 10-minute walk from the center, this small, family-run place has nine spacious if basic rooms around a courtyard that serves as a great introduction to Amazonian flora. Rooms are clean and have fans and private bathrooms.

Residencias El Divino Niño (☎ 592 5598; Av Internacional No 7-23; s/d US$8/11) There's nothing special about this basic place, except that it's very cheap. Located near the border with Brazil, the place is dog-eared but clean. All rooms have fan and private bathroom.

Hotel de la Selva (☎ /fax 592 76166; Calle 7 No 7-28; s/d US$12/20, with air-con US$16/24; 🛏) Rooms are small with basic furnishing, but the plant-filled common area makes this friendly place even more welcoming.

Hotel La Frontera (☎ 592 5600; fronterahotelet@ hotmail.com; Av Internacional No 1-04; s/d/tr US$16/25/36; 🛏) La Frontera is appropriately named as it's just 4m from the actual border. This new hotel offers 16 rooms with bath, fan, air-conditioning and cable TV.

Hotel Anaconda (☎ 592 7119; www.hotelanaconda .com.co; Carrera 11 No 7-34; s/d/tr US$40/60/75; 🛏 🖥) Located just across from Parque Orellana, Anaconda has large rooms, though they have a distinctly utilitarian feel. The courtyard, complete with pool and outdoor dining, is more pleasing to the eye. If you can get a room that looks out over the river, this place may be worth the premium.

Eating

Food in Leticia is generally good and prices reasonable. The local specialty is fish, including the delicious *gamitana* and *pirarucú*.

Restaurante El Sabor (☎ 592 4774; Calle 8 No 9-25; mains US$2-4; 🕒 24hr) On the main street, this is Leticia's best budget option. It serves good-value set meals (US$2 to US$3), vegetarian burgers, fruit salads, plus unlimited free fruit juices with your meal. The banana pancakes are excellent. Best of all, it's open 24 hours, except for one weekly closure from 6pm Tuesday until 6am Wednesday.

A Me K Tiar (☎ 592 6094; Carrera 9 No 8-15; mains US$3-5; 🕒 noon-11:30pm Mon-Sat, 5-11:30pm Sun) Serving good *parillas* (grilled meats) at great prices, this place is crowded with locals and tourists alike. The outdoor terrace is rustic but pleasant. Wash your meal down with cold beer or freshly blended juices.

Restaurante Acuarius (☎ 592 5025; Carrera 7 No 8-12; mains US$3-5; 🕒 7am-9pm) On a quiet corner slightly away from the center, this pleasant, outdoor restaurant is a cut above others; it's a good place to try meat and chicken, as well as local fish such as *pirarucú*.

La Casa del Pan (☎ 592 7660; Calle 11 No 10-20; ❧ 6:30am-11pm Mon-Sat) Facing Parque Santander, this bright, bustling bakery is great spot for breakfast (eggs, French bread, coffee and fruit juice for US$2) or a snack.

Drinking & Entertainment

There are a number of bars and cafés along Calle 8. Besides places that cater to locals (mostly men), there's **Tragadero Tierras Amazónicas** (Calle 8 No 7-50). It specializes in *aguardiente* and salsa music, but it can be pretty quiet outside tourist season (August, December and January).

For a big night on the town (for Leticia), there's **Discoteca Tacones** (Carrera 11 No 6-14), near Parque Orellana. It's nothing special once you get inside, but there's a dance floor and a mixed bag of Latin music and hip-hop. **Taberna Americana** (Carrera 10 No 11-108) is a cheap, rustic bar playing salsa music till late.

Getting There & Away

AIR

The only passenger airline servicing Leticia is **AeroRepública** (☎ 592 7666; www.aerorepublica.com .co in Spanish; Calle 7 No 10-36). It flies between Leticia and Bogotá three to four days a week. For travel in August, December and January, try to book as early as possible, as flights fill up.

Two airlines (Trip and Rico) fly from Tabatinga to Manaus; between them they fly every day except Wednesday. You can buy tickets from **Turamazon** (☎ 3412 2026; Av da Amizade 2271), or **CNM Câmbio e Turismo** (☎ 3412 3281; Av da Amizade 2017), both near the border. The airport is 2km south of Tabatinga; *colectivos* marked 'Comara' from Leticia will drop you off nearby. Remember to get your exit/entry stamps before departure.

A small Peruvian airline, **TANS** (www.tansp eru.com.pe in Spanish), flies its 15-seat hydroplane from Santa Rosa to Iquitos on Wednesday and Saturday (US$90). You may be able to find out information from **Cambios La Sultana** (☎ 592 7071; Calle 8 No 11-57) in Leticia.

BOAT

To Manaus (Brazil)

Boats down the Amazon to Manaus leave from Porto Fluvial de Tabatinga. There are generally three boats per week, departing from Tabatinga on Wednesday, Friday and Saturday around 2pm, with a stop at Benjamin Constant. Sometimes there are extra boats, so it's worth asking. Note that boats can be very crowded.

The trip to Manaus takes three days and four nights and costs around US$65 if you bring your own hammock, or around US$240 for two people in a double cabin. Food is included, but you're best advised to bring snacks and bottled water. There are a number of places to buy ordinary cloth hammocks (US$5 to US$10) along Rua Marechal Mallet. To negotiate your trip, head down to the Porto Fluvial a day or two in advance and ask which boat is headed to Manáus. Board the boat and let the crew know you want to join them.

Boats come to Tabatinga one or two days before their scheduled departure back down the river. You can string up your hammock or occupy the cabin as soon as you've paid the fare, saving on hotels. Food, however, is only served after departure. Beware of theft on board. Traveling upstream from Manaus to Tabatinga, the trip usually takes six days, and costs about US$110 in your hammock or US$330 for a double cabin.

To Iquitos (Peru)

Transtur (☎ 3412 2945; Rua Marechal Mallet 248) runs *rápidos* – high-powered passenger boats – between Tabatinga and Iquitos. Boats leave from Tabatinga's Porto da Feira at 4am Wednesday, Friday and Sunday and arrive in Iquitos about 10 hours later. The boats call at Santa Rosa's immigration post. The journey costs US$60 in either direction, including breakfast and lunch. Don't forget to get an exit stamp in your passport from DAS at Leticia's airport the day before departure.

Note that there are no roads out of Iquitos into Peru. You have to fly or continue by river to Pucallpa (five to seven days), from where you can go overland to Lima and elsewhere.

TABATINGA (BRAZIL)

☎ 8 / pop 35,000 / elevation 95m / temp 27°C

While distinctly less pleasant than Leticia, Tabatinga has a range of decent hotels and restaurants. You might want to consider staying here if the Colombian peso is outperforming the Brazilian real, or if you're

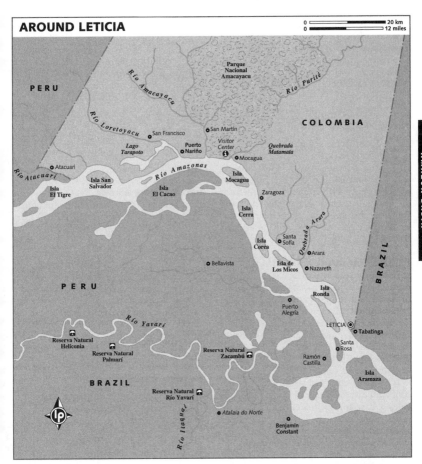

AROUND LETICIA

taking an early-morning boat to Iquitos. See Leticia for information about immigration (p210), banking (p210) and getting there and away (opposite).

Sleeping

Hotel Bela Vista (☎ 3412 3846; Rua Marechal Rondon 1806; d US$16; ✖) It may not be fancy, but this place packs a great combination – cheap, clean, air-conditioned and only steps from the morning boat to Iquitos. And it's friendly to boot.

Pousada Takaná's (☎ 3412 3557; Rua Oswaldo Cruz 970; s/d US$20/24; ✖ ▣) Tabatinga's most pleasant higher-end option, Takanás has a lush, open-air courtyard, including a restaurant and small pool. Rooms are air-conditioned

and newly if simply furnished. Note that it is a little removed from town, several blocks north of Av Amizade.

Pousada do Sol (☎ 3412 3987; fax 3412 5122; Rua General Sampaio 50; s/d/tr US$20/24/36; ✖ ▣) A 10-minute walk from the boats to Manaus and Iquitos, this place has seen some wear-and-tear but remains a decent choice. It offers seven large, air-conditioned rooms with bathroom and fridge, plus a courtyard with a small pool.

Eating

Restaurante Tres Fronteiras do Amazonas (☎ 3412 2341; Rua Rui Barbosa; mains US$4-7; ⏰ 9am-11pm) This attractive palm-thatched open-air restaurant offers a wide choice of fish and meat dishes, plus a selection of drinks, including *caipirinha* (the national cocktail made with limes, sugar and a Brazilian version of rum). The food is straightforward, but hearty and delicious.

Cozinha da Fazenda (☎ 3412 3406; Av da Amizade 1961; per kg US$6; ☯ 7am-11pm) This classic Brazilian *quilo* offers a buffet with cold and hot dishes, as well as grilled meats – all sold by weight. The food is decent, and the convenience factor is high.

Churrascaria Tia Helena (☎ 3412 2165; Rua Marechal Mallet 12; all-you-can-eat US$7; ☯ noon-11pm) At this delicious all-you-can-eat restaurant, waiters bring skewered meats directly from the grill, and carve it at the table in classic Brazilian fashion. The place may be no-frills (think cement floors and fluorescent lights), but it's highly convivial.

PARQUE NACIONAL AMACAYACU

Sprawling across almost 300,000 hectares, Amacayacu is ideal to observe the Amazonian rainforest up close at reasonable prices. About 75km upriver from Leticia, the park is home to a dizzying array of plant and animal life, including caimans, snakes (both boas and anacondas) and various species of monkey, not to mention a profusion of fish and some 450 bird species.

A recently renovated visitor centre at the confluence of the Quebrada Matamata provides a base for excursions into the park, whether by boat or by kayak. Local guides accompany visitors on set excursions, including visits to indigenous communities and nighttime camping (often the best way to see wildlife). Prices vary, but an all-day tour for up to three people is about $65. In the high-water period (May to June), much of the land turns into swamps and lagoons, significantly reducing walking options, but then trips in canoes are organized. Bring plenty of mosquito repellent, a flashlight, a long-sleeved shirt and waterproof gear. Plan on staying at least three days.

Sleeping & Eating

The visitor center offers large, mosquito-proofed dorms with beds and hammocks as well as communal showers and toilets. Three meals a day are served in the dining hall, and bedding is provided, so there is no need to bring a sleeping bag. Accommodation in a bed/hammock costs US$12/8 per

person, and three meals will run to about US$8. The park entry fee is US$8 for foreigners and US$3 for Colombians. Camping in the park is not permitted. You are allowed to bring in your own food provided you take the rubbish with you when you leave. However, you cannot use the cooking facilities at the center. Note that at the time of writing, there were plans for more comfortable accommodations, including a floating lodge, with prices to be determined.

In Leticia, the **Aviatur office** (Calle 7 near Carrera 11) handles bookings.

Getting There & Away

Passenger boats that run daily from Leticia to Puerto Nariño (see opposite) will drop you off at the visitor center (US$10, 1½ hours from Leticia). Boats are often full, so be sure to buy your tickets in advance.

Returning from the park to Leticia may occasionally involve a day (or even two) of unexpected waiting. Boats pass through from Puerto Nariño (normally passing by the visitor center around 12:30pm and 4:30pm), but can be full. If this is the case, they will simply pass by without stopping. Sometimes it's possible to wave down other boats, but they are mostly slow cargo vessels.

PUERTO NARIÑO

☎ 8 / pop 2000 / elevation 110m / temp 27°C
If you thought Leticia was small, wait till you see Puerto Nariño, about 90km upriver. The town has banned cars and mopeds, though they wouldn't be much use since the streets, which are really sidewalks, dead-end into the jungle after just a few hundred meters. A generator only provides electricity from dusk until about 11pm.

In addition to the eerie quiet, the town is pretty and neat as a pin. Houses are painted bright colors, and people take particular care of their yards and gardens. In fact, the town hall has organized citizen brigades that comb the town for trash each morning. With several rustic hotels and restaurants, the town makes a good base from which to explore the surrounding area.

Sights & Activities

Fundación Omacha, on the riverfront, is a conservation center working to save the dolphins and manatees of the Amazon, and includes a small exhibition space.

About 10km west of Puerto Nariño is the **Lago Tarapoto**, a beautiful lake only accessible by river, with varied flora including the famous *Victoria amazonica* lily. With luck you'll see pink dolphins. There are also some Indian settlements scattered around the lake. A half-day trip to the lake in a small motorized boat (locally called *pequepeque*) can be organized from Puerto Nariño (around US$25 per boat for up to four people). Locals can take you on boat excursions to many other places, including the Parque Nacional Amacayacu, or you can just rent a canoe (US$8 per day) and do your own tour.

Sleeping & Eating

Casa Selva (☎ 310 221 4379, 311 217 7758; s/d/tr US28/38/42) A tall, handsome building two blocks up from the boat landing. With simple but tasteful rooms surrounding a two-storey courtyard, this is the town's most luxurious option. Guests can also opt for a generous breakfast (US$3) as well as fixed-menu lunch and dinner (both US$5).

Eware Tourist Refuge (☎ 311 474 3466; zoraidaveloza@yahoo.com; dm US$10) One of several rustic inns about a 10-minute boat ride from town. Besides dorms with hammocks, amenities include hiking trails, use of a canoe, and a small tower with a view of the surrounding jungle.

Brisas del Amazonas (☎ 311 281 2473; dm US$6) Occupies what was once a grand home near the waterfront. It has seen better days, and rooms are rather dank, but it's still the best budget option in town.

There are two basic local restaurants (fixed meals about US$3) both within a block of the waterfront, Doña Francisca and Las Margaritas.

Getting There & Away

Puerto Nariño and Lago Tarapoto feature on the itineraries of Leticia tour operators. If you want to get there on your own, three small boat companies, Expreso Tres Fronteras, Transporte Amazónico and Expreso Líneas Amazonas (all with offices on Calle 8 near the riverfront in Leticia), operate scheduled fast passenger boats to Puerto Nariño, at 10am and 2pm weekdays (US$14, two hours). At times the boats are full, so buy your ticket in the morning or a day before, just in case.

RÍO YAVARÍ

Within reach of large stretches of virgin forest, the meandering Río Yavarí offers some of the best opportunities to see the Amazon up close and undisturbed. A few privately owned reserves provide more or less simple accommodations as well as guided tours and activities, including forest walks, fishing, nighttime alligator-spotting, bird-watching, dolphin-watching and visits to indigenous settlements. The lodges provide accommodation and food, and serve as bases for trips by boat or foot into the surrounding area.

Costs depend on the number of people in the party, length of the stay, season and number of guided tours; count on US$40 to US$80 per person per day. Note that there are no regularly scheduled boats, so you will have to arrange transportation with the reserves themselves or find a private boat operator in Leticia. Expect to pay up to $50 per person each way from Leticia or Tabatinga.

Note that because of increasing police patrols on the Yavarí, you must get a Brazilian entry stamp and, if necessary, a visa in Tabatinga (see p210).

Reserva Natural Zacambú

Zacambú is the reserve nearest to Leticia, about 70km by boat. Its lodge is on Lake Zacambú, just off Río Yavarí, on the Peruvian side of the river. The lodge is simple, with small rooms without bathrooms, and a total capacity of about 30 guests. Most excursions from here are by boat, since walking possibilities around the lodge are limited and, in the period of high water, almost nonexistent. Both the lodge and tours are run from Leticia by **Amazon Jungle Trips** (☎ 592 7377; amazonjungletrips@yahoo.com; Av Internacional No 6-25).

Reserva Natural Palmarí

About 105km by river from Leticia, Palmarí's rambling lodge sits on the high, south (Brazilian) bank of the river, overlooking a wide bend where pink and grey dolphins are often known to gather. The lodge itself features rooms with private bathrooms, a large round *maloca* (communal house) with hammocks and a viewing tower providing sweeping vistas. The lodge has good food and helpful guides, and offers a wide choice of walking trips and boat excursions. The reserve is managed from Bogotá by owner **Axel Antoine-Feill** (☎ 1-531 1404, 310 786 2770; www.palmari .org; Carrera 10 No 93-72), who can speak several languages including English. His representative in Leticia is **Francisco Avila** (☎ 8-592 4156, 310 596 0203), though he only speaks Spanish and Portuguese.

Prices include room and board (US$20 per day for a bed or US$15 per hammock). Overnight expeditions into the jungle cost around US$50 per day; all equipment is provided. Palmarí offers the best walking possibilities of the three reserves.

Reserva Natural Heliconia

About 110km from Leticia, Heliconia provides room and board in thatch-covered cabins, plus tours via boat or foot of the river, creeks and jungle. There are also organized visits to indigenous villages and special tours devoted to bird-watching and dolphin-watching. The reserve is managed from an **office** (☎ 311 508 5666; www.amazonhelico nia.com; Calle 13 No 11-74) in Leticia.

Directory

CONTENTS

ACCOMMODATIONS

Colombia has a reasonable range of accommodations suiting all budgets and most tastes. Most are straightforward Colombian hotels where you are unlikely to meet foreigners, but some budget traveler haunts in the main tourist areas reel in crowds of backpackers. These are often the best places for information about tours and local sights.

Where sections are broken down into price categories, budget accommodations includes anything costing less than about US$15 per double room, the midrange bracket covers hotels rated from approximately US$15 to US$45 per double, and anything over US$45 a double is top end.

PRACTICALITIES

- Colombians use the metric system for weights and measures, except for petrol, which is measured in US gallons. Food is often sold in *libras* (pounds), which is roughly equivalent to 500g.

- Electrical outlets accept US-type, flat, two-pin plugs. Electricity is 110V, 60 cycles AC.

- Colombia uses the NTSC system for video tapes, the same as in North America and Japan, but incompatible with the French SECAM system, and PAL, which is used in most of Europe and Australia.

- All major cities have daily newspapers. Bogotá's leading newspaper, *El Tiempo,* has reasonable coverage of national and international news, culture, sports and economics. The leading newspapers in other large cities include *El Mundo* and *El Colombiano* in Medellín, and *El País* and *El Occidente* in Cali. *Semana* is the biggest national weekly magazine. Another major weekly, *Cambio,* is an important opinion-forming magazine.

- Colombia has a variety of national and local TV stations. Bogotá TV is dominated by **City TV** (www.citytv.com.co in Spanish), **Caracol TV** (www.canalcaracol.com.co in Spanish) and **RCN TV** (www.canalrcn.com). Most hotels offer cable TV with English-language programming. Radio stations are likewise plentiful. College radio usually offers the best variety; try Universidad Javeriana (94.9 FM) or Universidad Nacional (106.9 FM).

Camping

Camping is not popular in Colombia, and there are only a handful of genuine camp sites in the country. Unofficial camping is theoretically possible almost anywhere outside the urban centers, but given the country's dangers you should be very careful. If you intend to camp, get permission to pitch your tent next to a peasant's house or in the grounds of a holiday center so that you have some protection.

Hotels

Accommodations appear under a variety of names including *hotel, residencias, hospedaje, pensión, hostería, hospedería* and *posada. Residencias* and *hospedaje* are the most common names for budget places. A hotel generally suggests a place of a higher standard, or at least a higher price, though the distinction is often academic.

BUDGET

Cheaper accommodations are usually clustered around markets, bus terminals and in the back streets of the city center. *Residencias* and *hospedajes* are generally unremarkable, without much style or atmosphere, but there are some pleasant exceptions.

Many cheapies have a private bathroom, which includes a toilet and shower. The bathroom is sometimes separated from the room by only a low partition. Note that cheap hotel plumbing can't cope with toilet paper, so throw it in the wastebasket that is normally provided.

In hot places (ie lowland areas), a fan is often provided. At altitudes above 2500m where nights can be chilly, hotels may offer hot water. Even the cheapest *residencias* provide a sheet and some sort of cover. Most will also give you a towel, a small piece of soap and a roll of toilet paper. These places cost US$3 to US$8 a single, US$5 to US$15 a double. Payment is almost exclusively upfront and by cash. Budget hotels rarely accept credit cards.

Many budget hotels have *matrimonios,* rooms with a double bed intended for couples. A *matrimonio* is usually cheaper than a double, sometimes only slightly more expensive than a single.

Always have a look at the room before booking. Check that the fan works and that the lock on the door is sufficiently secure. In hotels in the highlands check the hot water if the hotel claims to have it.

Many budget hotels provide TVs and since the insulation between the rooms is often flimsy, TV noise can be a nightmare. If there are no TVs in rooms, you can be sure that there's one around the reception area, and it's usually kept at top volume until late at night.

Hotels are reasonably safe places, but precautions and common sense are always advisable. Most budget places lock their doors at night, and some even keep them locked during the day, opening them only for guests. The biggest danger of being ripped off is most likely to come from other guests (and occasionally from staff). Hotels provide padlocks for doors, but it may be better to use your own lock instead.

Some budget hotels offer a deposit facility, meaning the management will guard your gear in their own room. This reduces the risk, but doesn't eliminate it completely. In most cheapies, the staff won't give any receipts for receiving your valuables, and if you insist on one they may simply refuse to guard them. Decide for yourself if it's safe.

MIDRANGE

Midrange hotels are usually in the city center; you can expect to find one or two right on Plaza de Bolívar or in its immediate vicinity. They provide more facilities than the cheapies, but often lack character. They almost always have private bathrooms and fan, sometimes even air-conditioning (but it can be noisy). Many are reasonably priced for what they offer, but some can be outrageously overpriced. It's a good idea to inspect the room in these hotels before you commit yourself. Some of the midrange hotels can be great value offering a spacious, comfortable double room in the heart of the city for US$25 to US$30.

TOP END

Top-end hotels usually offer more facilities and better standards than midrange establishments, including silent, central air-conditioning and a reception desk open round the clock with proper facilities to safeguard guests' valuables. There are usually some top-class hotels in the center, but most prefer quieter and greener locations in upmarket residential districts, sometimes far from the center. Prices vary greatly and don't always reflect quality. Most will accept payment by credit card. The best choice of top-end hotels is in Bogotá and Cartagena.

LOVE HOTELS

These places are designed for couples with an urgent need for privacy and togetherness. They have rooms with a double bed and private bathroom, rented by the hour. Many budget (and some midrange) hotels double as love hotels; it's often impossible to recognize them and to avoid staying in one from time to time. This shouldn't be a major problem, though, as love hotels are probably safer than some other places (the guests have more on their minds than stealing your belongings). Staff normally won't admit prostitutes and the sex section is separated from other hotel rooms so the sound of excited couples won't stop you sleeping. There are also upmarket love hotels, but these are well outside central areas, usually tucked away on the city outskirts.

Youth Hostels
Colombia is a member of the International Youth Hostel Federation, but there's only one youth hostel in the country, in Bogotá (p66).

ACTIVITIES
Colombia offers a range of activities from cycling to white-water rafting. Other possible activities include mountaineering, windsurfing, canoeing, fishing, caving and even bathing in a mud volcano; see Volcán de Lodo El Totumo (p139).

Cycling
Cycling is one of Colombia's favorite spectator sports, yet only in recent years have bicycle-rental agencies begun to appear. You can go cycling in San Andrés (p151), Providencia (p153) and Villa de Leyva (p89), among other places.

Diving & Snorkeling
Colombia's coral reefs provide good conditions for snorkeling and scuba diving. The main dive centers are San Andrés (p148), Providencia (p153), Santa Marta (p111), Taganga (p113) and Cartagena (p131), each of which has several diving schools offering courses and other diving services. Colombia is considered one of the world's cheapest countries for diving.

Hiking
Columbia's national parks (p41) offer walks ranging from easy, well-signposted trails to jungle paths where you might need a machete. Many parks are notorious for a guerrilla presence and may be unsafe for

visitors; those included in this book are generally OK for hiking. In Bogotá, contact the hiking associations (p63), which organize weekend walks in Bogotá's environs.

Horseback-Riding
Horseback-riding can be practiced in many places including Villa de Leyva (p88), San Agustín (p201), Valle de Cocora (p185), San Gil (p93) and Providencia (p153).

Paragliding
Colombia has also developed greatly as a center of paragliding. The main hub is Medellín (p162), but there are also gliding schools in Bogotá (p62) and elsewhere. Paragliding in Colombia is reasonably cheap.

Rock Climbing
Rock climbing is increasing in popularity. There are climbing walls in Bogotá (p62) and outdoor opportunities at Suesca (p79).

White-Water Rafting
White-water rafting is new in Colombia, but developing fast; its major base is in San Gil (p93). Like most other outdoor activities in Colombia, rafting is cheap.

BUSINESS HOURS
The office working day is, theoretically at least, eight hours long, usually from 8am to noon and 2pm to 6pm weekdays, but in practice offices tend to open later and close earlier. Many offices in Bogotá have adopted the so-called *jornada continua,* a working day without a lunch break, which finishes two hours earlier. It's nearly impossible to arrange anything between noon and 2pm though, as most of the staff are off for their lunch. Most tourist offices are closed Saturday and Sunday, and travel agencies usually only work on Saturday to noon. Post offices are not open for standard hours across the country. For example, in Bogotá the main post office opens from 9am to 5pm Monday to Friday, with some branches also open on Saturday morning, but on the Caribbean coast they close for lunch.

As a rough guide only, usual shopping hours are from 9am to 5pm Monday to Friday; some shops closing for lunch. On Saturdays most shops are open 9am to noon, or sometimes until 5pm. Large stores and supermarkets usually stay open till 8pm or

9pm Monday to Friday; some also open Sunday. Shopping hours vary considerably from shop to shop and from city to countryside. In remote places, opening hours are shorter and are often taken less seriously.

Restaurants opening for lunch open at noon. Those opening for breakfast open by 8am. Most of the better restaurants in larger cities, particularly in Bogotá, tend to stay open until 10pm or longer; restaurants in smaller towns often close by 9pm or earlier. Many don't open at all on Sunday. Most cafés are open from 8am until 10pm, while bars usually open around 6pm and close when the last customer leaves.

The opening hours of museums and other tourist sights vary greatly. Most museums are closed on Monday, but are open on Sunday. The opening hours of churches are even more difficult to pin down. Some are open all day, others for certain hours only, while the rest remain locked except during Mass, which in some villages may be only on Sunday morning.

CHILDREN

As with most Latin Americans, Colombians adore children. Due to a high rate of population growth, children are a significant proportion of the population, and they are omnipresent. Few foreigners travel with children in Colombia, but if you do plan on taking along your offspring, he or she will easily find plenty of local companions.

Basic supplies are usually no problem in the cities. There are quite a few shops devoted to kids' clothes, shoes and toys, and you can buy disposable diapers and baby food in supermarkets and pharmacies. Pick up a copy of Lonely Planet's *Traveling with Children* for general tips.

CLIMATE CHARTS

Colombia's proximity to the equator means its temperature varies little throughout the year. The temperature does change with altitude, creating various climatic zones from hot lowlands to freezing Andean peaks, so you can experience completely different climates within a couple of hours of travel.

As a general rule, the temperature falls about 6°C with every 1000m increase in altitude. If the average temperature at sea level is 30°C, it will be around 24°C at 1000m, 18°C at 2000m and 12°C at 3000m.

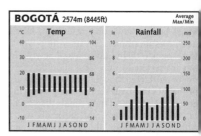

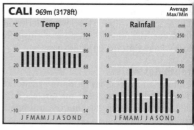

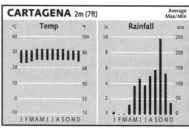

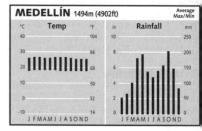

The altitude also affects the difference between daytime and nighttime temperatures. The higher the altitude, the greater the difference. Consequently, in the highlands there can be warm days but freezing nights, while in the lowlands days and nights are almost equally hot.

Colombia has two seasons: dry or *verano* (literally 'summer') and wet or *invierno* (winter). The pattern of seasons varies in different parts of the country, and has been greatly affected over recent years by El Niño and La Niña.

As a rough guideline only, in the Andean region there are two dry and two rainy seasons per year. The main dry season falls between December and March, with a shorter and less dry period between July and August. This general pattern has wide variations throughout the Andean zone.

The weather in Los Llanos has a more definite pattern: there is one dry season, between December and March, while the rest of the year is wet. The Amazon doesn't have a uniform climate but, in general, is quite wet year-round.

COURSES

Spanish-language courses are run by universities and language schools in some large cities, of which Bogotá (p63) has the widest choice. Try **Nueva Lengua** (www.nuevalengua.com/spanish), which has branches in Bogotá, Medellín and Cartagena. Many travelers opt for informal arrangements with the local tutors. Popular backpacker hotels are the best places to ask about independent teachers.

CUSTOMS

Customs procedures are usually a formality, both entering and leaving the country. However, thorough luggage checks can occur, more often at airports than at overland borders, and they can be very exhaustive, with a body search included. They aren't looking for your extra iPod, but for drugs. Trying to smuggle dope across the border is the best way to spend some years seeing what the inside of a Colombian jail looks like.

Customs regulations don't differ much from those in other South American countries. You can bring in personal belongings and presents you intend to give to Colombian residents. The quantity, kind and value of these items shouldn't arouse suspicion that they may have been imported for commercial purposes. You can bring with you cameras (still, video and movie), camping equipment, sports accessories, a laptop computer and the like without any problems.

On departure, you may be asked for receipts for any emeralds, antiques and articles of gold and platinum purchased in Colombia.

DANGERS & ANNOYANCES

Colombia definitely isn't the safest of countries, and you should be careful at all times. In fact, it was only a few years ago that Colombia was regarded as the 'world's most dangerous country' and the 'kidnapping capital of the world.' The situation has vastly improved over recent years but there are still inherent dangers. Whatever you do, don't let the rumors and urban legends scare you off. Within a day of arriving in Colombia you'll feel your confidence in the security situation quickly growing.

Theft & Robbery

Theft is the most common travelers' danger. In general, the problem is more serious in the largest cities. The more rural the area, the quieter and safer it is. The most common methods of theft are snatching your day-pack, camera or watch, pickpocketing, or taking advantage of a moment's inattention to pick up your gear and run away.

Distraction is often part of the thieves' strategy. Thieves often work in pairs or groups; one or more will distract you, while an accomplice does the deed. There are hundreds, if not thousands, of possible ways to distract you, and new scams are dreamt up every day. Some thieves are even more innovative and will set up an opportune situation to separate you from your belongings. They may begin by making friends with you, or pretend to be the police and demand to check your belongings.

If you can, leave your money and valuables somewhere safe before walking the streets. In practice, it's good to carry a decoy bundle of small notes, the equivalent of US$5 to US$10, ready to hand over in case of an assault; if you really don't have a peso, robbers can become frustrated and, as a consequence, unpredictable.

Armed hold-ups in the cities can occur even in some more upmarket suburbs. If you are accosted by robbers, it is best to give them what they are after, but try to play it cool and don't rush to hand them all your valuables at once – they may well be satisfied with just your decoy wad. Don't try to escape or struggle – your chances are slim. Don't count on any help from passers-by.

Be careful when drawing cash from an ATM as some robberies have been reported. Criminals may watch you drawing money,

---

SAFE TRAVEL

When traveling in Colombia, use common sense and don't get paranoid. Travelers do come to Colombia and few have any problems. Here are some basic rules of safe travel in Colombia.

For your own personal safety:

- Unless the rural area you plan to visit is regarded as safe, make cities the focus of your travel rather than the countryside.

- Don't accept any food, drink or cigarettes from strangers.

- Don't venture into poor suburbs, desolate streets or suspicious-looking surroundings, especially after dark.

- Before arriving in a new place, make sure you have a map or at least a rough idea about orientation.

- Behave confidently on the street; don't look lost or stand with a blank expression in the middle of the street.

- Use taxis if this seems the appropriate way to avoid walking through risky areas.

When traveling between cities:

- Consider air travel if the overland route is notorious for a lack of safety.

- Seek local advice about the safety of the region you are traveling in and the one you're heading for.

- If traveling by bus, do so during the daytime.

- Don't use a rented car (but if you insist on traveling this way we provide some guidelines under Car & Motorcycle, p241).

- Should you feel compelled to go off the beaten track, leave details about your planned whereabouts prior to departure.

To avoid the risk of theft:

- Keep your money and documents as secure as possible, preferably in a moneybelt next to your skin.

- Distribute your valuables about your person and luggage to avoid the risk of losing everything in one fell swoop.

- Wear casual and inexpensive clothes, preferably in plain, sober tones rather than in bright colors.

- Keep your camera out of sight as much as possible and only take it out to take a photo.

- Look around to see whether you're being observed or followed, especially while leaving a bank, *casa de cambio* (currency-exchange office) or ATM.

- Arrange comprehensive travel insurance just in case something goes wrong.

---

then assault you either at an ATM or a convenient place nearby. It may be safer to get an advance from the cashier inside the bank, even if this takes a while.

Police

Colombian police have a mixed reputation. Cases of police corruption, abuse of power and the use of undue authority have been known, so it's probably best to stay a safe distance from them if you don't need them. This, of course, doesn't mean that they will stay away from you.

On a more positive note, there's an increasing number of so-called tourist police. They are uniformed and easily recognizable by the Policía de Turismo labels on their arm bands. These forces have been formed and trained to attend to tourist needs and operate mainly in popular tourist destinations. They are usually friendlier and more helpful than ordinary police.

If your passport, valuables or other belongings are stolen, go to the police station and make a *denuncia* (report). The officer on duty will write a statement according to what you tell them. It should include the description of the events and the list of stolen articles. Pay attention to the wording you use, include every stolen item and document, and carefully check the statement before signing it to ensure it contains exactly what you've said. Your copy of the statement serves as a temporary identity document and you'll need to present it to your insurer to make a claim. Don't expect your things to be found, as the police are unlikely to even try to do anything about it.

If you happen to get involved with the police, keep calm and be polite, but not overly friendly. Don't get angry or hostile – it only works against you. Keep a sharp eye out when they check your gear because things sometimes 'disappear.'

Be wary of criminals masquerading as plainclothes police. They may stop you on the street, identify themselves with a fake ID, then ask to inspect your passport and money. Under no circumstances should you agree to a search. Call a uniformed police officer, if there happens to be one around, or decent-looking passers-by to witness the incident, and insist on phoning a bona fide police station. By that time, the 'officers' will probably walk discreetly away.

Drugs

Cocaine is essentially an export product but it is also available locally. More widespread is marijuana, and it's even more easily available. However, be careful about drugs – never carry them. The police and army can be very thorough in searching travelers.

Sometimes you may be offered dope on the street, in a bar or a disco, but never accept these offers. The vendors may well be setting you up for the police, or their accomplices will follow you and stop you later, show you false police documents and threaten you with jail unless you pay them off.

There have been reports of drugs being planted on travelers, so keep your eyes open. Always refuse if a stranger at an airport asks you to take their luggage on board as part of your luggage allowance. Needless to say, smuggling dope across borders is a crazy idea. Have you ever seen the inside of a Colombian prison?

BURUNDANGA

This is another security risk. Burundanga is a drug obtained from a species of tree widespread in Colombia and is used by thieves to render a victim unconscious. It can be put into sweets, cigarettes, chewing gum, spirits, beer – virtually any kind of food or drink – and it doesn't have any noticeable taste or odor.

The main effect after a 'normal' dose is the loss of will, even though you remain conscious. The thief can then ask you to hand over your valuables and you will obey without resistance. Cases of rape under the effect of burundanga are known. Other effects are loss of memory and sleepiness,

which can last from a few hours to several days. An overdose can be fatal.

Burundanga is not only used to trick foreigners – Colombians have been on the receiving end too, losing their cars, contents of their homes, and sometimes their life. Think twice before accepting a cigarette from a stranger or a drink from a new 'friend.'

Guerrillas & Paramilitaries

There's intense guerrilla and paramilitary activity in many regions; consequently the area of reasonably safe travel is limited. As a general rule, avoid any off-the-beaten-track travel. It's best to stick to main routes and travel during daytime only. Yet, even main routes can be risky. Among these, the Popayán–Pasto road has possibly the worst reputation, although routes between Bogotá and the Caribbean coast area are much safer than they were in the early 2000s.

Many regions may be unsafe for travel. The entire area east of the Andes (except Leticia and its environs) should be avoided as it's the guerrilla heartland. Parts of Cundinamarca, eastern Antioquia, Chocó, Córdoba, Magdalena, Bolívar, La Guajira, Cesar, southern Tolima, Valle del Cauca, Huila, Cauca and Nariño are considered high-risk areas due to the presence of guerrillas and paramilitaries.

Kidnapping for ransom has been part of guerrilla activity for quite a while, although actual incidents are on the decrease. What is important to note is that kidnappers are a very sophisticated group and acts of kidnapping are almost never random. The main targets are well-off locals and foreign executives and the ransoms start from US$1 million. Foreign tourists are not a target, mostly because they are not insured against kidnapping. From the kidnappers' point of view, Colombian, Japanese or European businessmen are more worthwhile, as they are likely to fetch a US$5 million ransom. Americans are not targeted – the US government does not deal with kidnappers and will freeze the bank accounts of the victim and the victim's family.

There's no need to be paranoid, but you should be aware of the potential risks, and avoid the regions notorious for guerrilla activity. Air travel may be worth considering as a way of skipping over some unsafe regions, even though it may eat into your pocket.

Monitor current guerrilla movements. It is not that easy because things change rapidly and unexpectedly, but the regional press and TV news can be useful. Possibly better and more specific is the advice of locals who best know what's going on in their region. Also, inquire at regional tourist offices, travel agents and bus terminals. Ask other travelers along the way and check online resources. The Platypus (p66) in Bogotá really has its finger on the pulse of the country, and is a good starting point for information.

DISABLED TRAVELERS
Colombia offers very little to people with disabilities. Wheelchair ramps are available only at a few upmarket hotels and restaurants, and public transport (with the exception of the TransMilenio) will be a challenge for any person with mobility problems. Few offices, museums or banks have special facilities for disabled travelers, and wheelchair-accessible toilets are virtually nonexistent.
Royal Association for Disability & Rehabilitation (RADAR; ☎ 020-7250 3222; www.radar.org.uk; 12 City Forum, 250 City Rd, London EC1V 8AF) In the UK, this is a useful contact.
Society for Accessible Travel & Hospitality (SATH; ☎ 212-447 7284; www.sath.org; 347 Fifth Ave, Suite 610, New York, NY 10016) Disabled travelers in the USA might like to contact this organization.

DISCOUNT CARDS
Student cards are handy in Colombia, and will get you a discount at museums and other tourist attractions. It will also get you a 25% discount on airplane tickets, but not bus tickets.

EMBASSIES & CONSULATES
Colombian Embassies & Consulates
Colombia has embassies and consulates in all neighboring countries, as well as around the world. The following is a selection.
Australia ACT (☎ 02-6257 2027; 101 Northbourne Ave, Turner, ACT 2601); NSW (☎ 02-9955 0311; 100 Walker St, North Sydney, NSW 2060)
Brazil (☎ 412 2104; Rua General Sampaio 623, Tabatinga; ☺ 8am-2pm Mon-Fri)
Canada Montréal (☎ 514-849 4852; 1010 Sherbrooke St West, Suite 420, Montréal, Quebec H3A 2R7); Toronto (☎ 416-977 0475; 1 Dundas St West, Suite 2108, Toronto, Ontario M5G 1Z3)
France (☎ 01 42 65 46 08; 12 rue de L'elysee, Paris 75008)

Germany (☎ 030-263 96 10; Kurfürsternstrasse 84, 10787 Berlin)
UK (☎ 020-7589 9177; www.colombianembassy.co.uk; 3 Hans Cres, London SW 1X OLN)
USA Washington DC (☎ 202-387 8338; www.colombiaemb .org; 2118 Leroy Place NW, Washington, DC 20008); Miami (☎ 305-441 1235; www.consuladodecolombia.com; 280 Aragon Ave, Coral Gables, Miami, FL 33134); New York (☎ 212-949 9898; 10 East 46th St, New York, NY 10017)

Embassies & Consulates in Colombia
Most countries that maintain diplomatic relations with Colombia have their embassies and consulates in Bogotá. Some countries also have consulates in other Colombian cities.
Argentina (Map p50; ☎ 1-288 0900; Av 40A No 13-09, Piso 16, Bogotá)
Australia (Map pp64-5; ☎ 1-636 5247; Carrera 18 No 90-38, Inter-Lingua Center, Bogotá)
Bolivia Bogotá (Map p50; ☎ 1-213 6308; Transversal 20 No 124-25, Bogotá); Cali (☎ 2-553 6386; Carrera 40 No 5C-102, Cali)
Brazil Bogotá (Map pp64-5; ☎ 1-218 0800; Calle 93 No 14-20, Piso 8, Bogotá); Cali (☎ 2-893 0615; Carrera 2 Oeste No 12-44, Cali); Leticia (Map p211; ☎ 8-592 7530; Carrera 9 No 13-84, Leticia); Medellín (Map p158; ☎ 4-265 7565; Calle 29D No 55-91, Medellín)
Canada (Map p50; ☎ 1-657 9800; Carrera 7 No 115-33, Piso 14, Bogotá)
Chile (Map pp64-5; ☎ 1-214 7990; Calle 100 No 11B-44, Bogotá)
Costa Rica Bogotá (Map pp64-5; ☎ 1-256 1105; Carrera 8 No 95-48, Bogotá); San Andrés (Map p146; ☎ 8-512 4938; Novedades Regina, Av Colombia, San Andrés)
Ecuador Bogotá (Map p50; ☎ 1-212 6512; Calle 72 No 6-30, Bogotá); Cali (Map p189; ☎ 2-661 2264; Av 5AN No 20N-13, L-103, Cali); Ipiales (Map p207; ☎ 2-773 2292; Carrera 7 No 14-10, Ipiales); Medellín (Map p161; ☎ 4-512 1303; Calle 50 No 52-22, Oficina 603, Medellín)
France (Map pp64-5; ☎ 1-638 1400; Carrera 11 No 93-12, Bogotá)
Germany (Map p50; ☎ 1-249 4911; Carrera 4 No 72-35, Bogotá)
Honduras Bogotá (Map p50; ☎ 1-213 0073; Calle 70 No 12-58, Bogotá); San Andrés (Map p146; ☎ 8-512 3235; Hotel Tiuna, Av Colombia, San Andrés)
Israel (Map p50; ☎ 1-327 7500; Calle 35 No 7-25, Piso 14, Bogotá)
Italy (Map pp64-5; ☎ 1-218 6680; Calle 93B No 9-92, Bogotá)
Japan (Map p50; ☎ 1-317 5001; Carrera 7 No 71-21, Torre B, Piso 11, Bogotá)
Mexico (Map p50; ☎ 1-629 5189; Calle 114 No 9-01, Torre A, Local 204, Bogotá)

Netherlands (Map pp64-5; ☎ 1-618 4299; Carrera 13 No 93-40, Piso 5, Bogotá)

Panama Barranquilla (Map p118; ☎ 5-360 1872; Carrera 54 No 64-245, Barranquilla); Bogotá (Map pp64-5; ☎ 1-257 4452; Calle 92 No 7-70, Bogotá); Cali (Map p189; ☎ 2-880 9590; Calle 11 No 4-42, Oficina 316, Cali); Cartagena (Map p128; ☎ 5-664 1433; Plaza de San Pedro Claver No 30-14, Cartagena); Medellín (☎ 4-268 1358; Carrera 43A No 7-50, Oficina 1607, Medellín)

Peru Bogotá (Map pp64-5; ☎ 1-257 0505; Calle 80A No 6-50, Bogotá); Bogotá (Map pp64-5; ☎ 1-257 6846; Calle 90 No 14-26, Bogotá); Cali (☎ 2-660 2052; Av 7N No 24N-57, Cali); Leticia (Map p211; ☎ 8-592 7204; Calle 13 No 5-32, Leticia)

Spain (Map pp64-5; ☎ 1-622 0090; Calle 92 No 12-68, Bogotá)

Switzerland (Map pp64-5; ☎ 1-255 3945; Carrera 9A No 74-08, Oficina 1101, Bogotá)

UK (Map pp64-5; ☎ 1-326 8301; fax 326 8303; www .britain.gov.co; Carrera 9 No 76-49, Piso 9, Bogotá)

USA (Map p50; ☎ 1-315 0811; Calle 22D Bis No 47-51, Bogotá)

Venezuela Barranquilla (Map p118; ☎ 5-358 0048; Carrera 52 No 69-96, Barranquilla); Bogotá (Map pp64-5; ☎ 1-640 1213; Carrera 13 No 87-51, Bogotá); Bogotá (Map p50; ☎ 1-636 4011; Av 13 No 103-16, Bogotá); Cartagena (☎ 5-665 0382; Carrera 3 No 8-129, Cartagena); Cúcuta (☎ 7-579 1956; Av Camilo Daza, Cúcuta); Medellín (Map p158; ☎ 4-351 1614; Calle 32B No 69-59, Medellín)

FESTIVALS & EVENTS

The Colombian calendar is full of festivals, carnivals, fairs and beauty pageants. Colombians love fiestas and they organize them at every opportunity. There are some 200 festivals and events annually, ranging from small one-day local affairs to international festivals lasting several days.

Given the strong Catholic character of Colombia, many feasts and celebrations follow the Church calendar. Accordingly, Christmas, Easter and Corpus Christi are often solemnly celebrated, particularly in more traditional rural communities. The religious calendar is dotted with saints' days, and every village and town has its own patron saint. In many cases, solemn religious ceremonies are accompanied by popular fiestas that may include beauty pageants and bullfights. Some events are celebrated throughout the country, but most are local, confined to a particular region or town. See Getting Started (p15) for Colombia's top 10 festivals and special events.

FOOD

You'll have no trouble finding a place to eat. For something fast, cities are well endowed with street stalls and serve-yourself cafeterias, although most of these only open for lunch (noon to 4pm). You might need to poke around a bit for a proper *desayuno* (breakfast), which is never anything special (usually just a fried egg, toast, bowl of meat soup and a coffee). Locals usually start their day with a pastry and cup of coffee. Most Colombians eat dinner at home, but you'll also find plenty of restaurants, the most common of which serve steak or roasted chicken. For the purposes of this guide, a budget meal will cost less than US$4, for a midrange meal you're looking at US$5 to US$9 and a meal at an 'expensive' top-end restaurant will go for US$10 and up.

GAY & LESBIAN TRAVELERS

The gay and lesbian movement is still very underdeveloped. Bogotá has the largest gay and lesbian community and the most open gay life, and therefore is the best place to make contacts and get to know what's going on. Check the website www.gaycolombia .com for more information.

Gay bars, discos and other venues are limited to the larger cities, but because of social pressures they come and go frequently. Again, Bogotá offers the largest choice. See p72 for some gay hangouts.

HOLIDAYS

The following days are observed as public holidays in Colombia.

Año Nuevo (New Year's Day) January 1
Los Reyes Magos (Epiphany) January 6*
San José (St Joseph) March 19*
Jueves Santo & Viernes Santo (Maundy Thursday and Good Friday) March/April (Easter)
Día del Trabajo (Labor Day) May 1
La Ascensión del Señor (Ascension) May*
Corpus Cristi (Corpus Christi) May/June*
Sagrado Corazón de Jesús (Sacred Heart) June*
San Pedro y San Pablo (St Peter and St Paul) June 29*
Día de la Independencia (Independence Day) July 20
Batalla de Boyacá (Battle of Boyacá) August 7
La Asunción de Nuestra Señora (Assumption) August 15*
Día de la Raza (Discovery of America) October 12*
Todos los Santos (All Saints' Day) November 1*
Independencia de Cartagena (Independence of Cartagena) November 11*

Inmaculada Concepción (Immaculate Conception) December 8
Navidad (Christmas Day) December 25

When the dates marked with an asterisk do not fall on a Monday, the holiday is moved to the following Monday to make a three-day long weekend, referred to as the *puente*.

INSURANCE
Ideally, all travelers should have a travel-insurance policy, which will provide some security in the case of a medical emergency, or the loss or theft of money or belongings. It may seem an expensive luxury, but if you can't afford a travel health insurance policy, you probably can't afford medical emergency charges abroad if something goes wrong.

If you do need to make a claim on your travel insurance, you must produce a police report detailing loss or theft (see p224). You also need proof of the value of any items lost or stolen. Receipts are the best bet, so if you buy a new camera for your trip, for example, hang on to the receipt.

INTERNET ACCESS
Virtually all large cities and many smaller urban centers have Internet cafés. These are usually open, without a lunch break, from 7am to 10pm weekdays, and many are also open all day Saturday. Some also open on Sunday. Most cafés provide a range of related services such as printing, scanning and faxing, and some offer cheap international calls. Internet connections are fastest in the major urban centers; they can be pretty slow in some remote places such as Providencia or Leticia. The access normally costs US$0.80 to US$2 per hour. The easiest way to keep up with email is to have an easily accessible inbox, using popular sites such as www.yahoo.com or www.hotmail.com.

Wireless fidelity is limited to a few places in the major cities, such as shopping malls and some hotels. However, using wi-fi means carrying your laptop around the city, something you should avoid for security reasons. Some upscale hotels in the biggest cities will have wall jacks to hook up to the Internet, if they don't already have wi-fi. But smaller hotels won't have usable jacks. Libraries aren't really an option for the Internet.

For Internet resources, see p16.

LEGAL MATTERS
If arrested you have the right to an attorney. If you don't have one, one will be appointed to you (and paid for by the government). There is a presumption of innocence.

As for drugs, you are legally allowed 20g of marijuana and 5g of cocaine. But it is illegal to buy or sell either. In any case, it's safest not to carry these. When approached by police, play it cool. If money is demanded, ask to go to the station and get a receipt for any fines due. Try not to pay bribes, but use your best judgment. Watch out for police imposters. Police have the right to confiscate weapons, including knives. The legal age for voting is 18 and the legal age for sex is 16.

MAPS
You'll probably find it difficult to buy anything other than general maps of Colombia outside the country itself. Check with good travel bookstores and map shops to see what is available. In the USA, **Maplink** (☎ 805-692 6777; www.maplink.com; 30 La Patera Lane, 5 Santa Barbara, CA 93117) has an excellent supply of maps. A similarly extensive selection of maps is available in the UK from **Stanfords** (☎ 020-7836 0189; www.stanfords.co.uk; 12-14 Long Acre, London WC2E 9LP).

Within Colombia, folded road maps of the country are produced by various publishers and are distributed through bookstores. They are of varied quality so check exactly what you're buying.

The widest selection of maps of Colombia is produced and sold by the **Instituto**

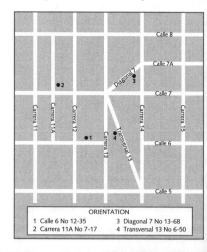

ORIENTATION			
1	Calle 6 No 12-35	3	Diagonal 7 No 13-68
2	Carrera 11A No 7-17	4	Transversal 13 No 6-50

ORIENTATION

Colombian cities, towns and villages have traditionally been laid out on a grid plan. The streets running north–south are called Carreras, often abbreviated on maps to Cra, Cr or K, whereas those running east–west are called Calles, labeled on maps as Cll, Cl or C. This simple pattern may be complicated by diagonal streets, called either Diagonales (more east–west and thus like Calles), or Transversales (more like Carreras).

All streets are numbered and the numerical system of addresses is used. Each address consists of a series of numbers, eg Calle 23 No 5-43 (which means that it's the building on Calle 23, 43m from the corner of Carrera 5 towards Carrera 6), or Carrera 17 No 31-05 (the house on Carrera 17, 5m from the corner of Calle 31 towards Calle 32). Refer to the Orientation map (see left) for examples.

The system is very practical and you will soon become familiar with it. It is usually easy to find an address. It's actually one of the most precise address systems in the world. If you have an address you can determine the location of the place with pinpoint accuracy.

In the larger cities the main streets are called Avenidas or Autopistas. They both have their own names and numbers, but are commonly known just by their names.

Cartagena's old town is the only Colombian city where centuries-old street names have withstood the modern numbering system. Streets in some other cities (eg Medellín) have both names and numbers, but elsewhere only numbers are used.

The Colombian system of designating floors is the same as that used in the USA; there is no 'ground floor' – it is the *primer piso* (1st floor). Thus, the European 1st floor will be the *segundo piso* (2nd floor) in Colombia.

Geográfico Agustín Codazzi (IGAC; Map pp64-5; ☎ 369 4075; www.igac.gov.co; Carrera 30 No 48-51, Bogotá), the government mapping body which has its head office in the Colombian capital and branch offices in departmental capitals.

IGAC produces general and specialist maps of the country, departmental maps, city maps, and 1:100,000 scale *planchas* (sheets), broken down into more detailed 1:25,000 scale maps. Unfortunately, most maps are long out of date. If the office runs out of color maps (usually the case) it makes a black-and-white copy of the original. Maps cost somewhere between US$2 and US$5 per sheet, depending on the type and size.

MONEY

Credit and debit cards are the safest and easiest way to access money in Colombia. Traveler's checks (Amex are by far the easiest to change) are safer than cash, though some US dollar bills may be useful.

Large amounts of counterfeit US dollars 'made in Cali' circulate on the market. According to rough estimates, about a quarter of all fake US dollars, virtually indistinguishable from the genuine article, circulating worldwide are printed in Colombia.

Generally, Bancolombia and the Banco Unión Colombiano are the banks to visit if you need to change money or do any over-the-counter transactions. However, you will find half-a-dozen other banks in most medium-sized towns that have ATMs.

ATMs

Almost all major banks have adjacent ATMs, and they usually work fine with cards issued outside Colombia. A debit card is usually best and will have the lowest fees. Check with your home bank and credit-card company before leaving. Ask about fees and inform them of your travel dates (if they suddenly see money extracted from Colombia they may freeze your account, assuming that your card has been stolen).

Credit Cards

Although the use of credit cards in Colombia is still not as common as it is in North America or Europe, they are becoming more widely accepted. They can be used for cash advances from banks and ATMs, and for purchases of goods and services in a variety of establishments.

The most useful card for cash advances is Visa, as it's accepted by most banks. Another possibility is MasterCard, which is honored by Bancolombia and Banco de Occidente. Other cards are of limited use.

You can get advance payments on cards from the cashier in the bank (it takes less time than changing traveler's checks) or from the bank's ATM.

Make sure you know the number to call if you lose your credit card, and be quick to cancel it if it's lost or stolen.

Currency

Colombia's official currency is the peso, although the prices in this book are provided in US dollars. There are 50, 100, 200, 500 and 1000 peso coins, and paper notes of 1000, 2000, 5000, 10,000, 20,000 and 50,000 pesos. Forged peso notes do exist, so watch exactly what you get. In contrast to perfect dollar fakes, peso forgeries are usually of poor quality and easy to recognize. There are also some fake 1000-peso coins in circulation. Many businesses don't accept 1000-peso coins and neither should you.

International Transfers

If you need money sent to you quickly, it's probably best to use Western Union, which has more than 80,000 agencies worldwide. Your sender pays the money at their nearest Western Union branch, along with a fee, and gives the details on who is to receive it and where. You can have the money within 15 minutes. When you pick it up, take along photo identification.

Western Union is represented in Colombia by Giros & Finanzas, which has offices in virtually all cities around the country and also in some smaller localities. There are about 20 offices in Bogotá alone. Call from anywhere in the country on ☎ 9800 111 999 toll-free for information. In the USA, call ☎ 1800 325 6000 toll-free. Or simply check the website at www.westernunion.com.

Money Changers

Some banks change cash and traveler's checks, but others don't. Some branches of a bank will change your money while other branches of the same bank will refuse. Banks that are most likely to exchange your cash and/or traveler's checks include: Banco Unión Colombiano and Bancolombia.

Banks (except for those in Bogotá) are open 8am to 11:30am and 2pm to 4pm Monday to Thursday, and 8am to 11:30am and 2pm to 4:30pm on Friday. However, they usually offer currency-exchange services within limited hours, which may mean only one or two hours daily; your best chances are in the morning. Banks close at noon on the last working day of the month; it may be difficult to change money on that day so plan ahead.

Your passport is required for any banking transaction. Banks are often crowded and there's much paperwork involved in changing money, so the process may prove time-consuming – set aside up to an hour.

You can also change cash (and sometimes traveler's checks) at *casas de cambio* (authorized money-exchange offices), found in virtually all major cities and border towns. They are open until 5pm or 6pm on weekdays, and usually until noon on Saturday. They deal mainly with US dollars, offering rates comparable to, or slightly lower than, banks. The whole operation takes five to 10 minutes.

Titán Intercontinental is one of the largest *casas de cambio,* with branch offices in most large cities. It changes both cash and traveler's checks, gives reasonable rates and charges no commission on cashing checks. You'll find many other *casas* that offer similar services, but shop around: the rate might be better at the *casa* next door.

You can change cash dollars on the street, but it's not recommended. The only street money markets worth considering are those at the borders, where there may be simply no alternative. There are money changers at every land border crossing.

LOST TRAVELER'S CHECKS

American Express (Amex) is by far the most useful brand of traveler's checks in Colombia, so stick to it. It is represented by **Expreso Viajes & Turismo** (☎ 1-593 4949; fax 1-611 3053; amexcosc@expresoviajes.com; Calle 85 No 20-32, Bogotá). The office doesn't cash checks but it's useful in case your checks or credit card are lost.

If your Amex checks are lost or stolen, the first thing you should do is call Amex toll-free in the USA on ☎ 1800 915 4458 to report and cancel the checks. Then contact Expreso Viajes for a replacement. Remember that you are likely to be asked details of where you bought the checks and date of purchase. Ideally, you should have the 'purchase record customer's copy' – your purchase receipt which you should have got when buying the checks.

Tipping & Bargaining

Tipping is essentially limited to upscale restaurants (leave about 10% of the bill) and posh hotels. As in most neighboring countries, bargaining is limited to informal trade and services, such as markets, street stalls, taxis and, sometimes, long-distance buses.

Traveler's Checks

Banks change traveler's checks at rates 2% to 5% lower than the official rate, and usually pay about a further 1% to 3% less for cash. Exchange rates vary from bank to bank, so shop around. Some banks charge a commission for changing checks.

POST

The postal service is operated by three companies, Avianca, Adpostal and Depris. All cover international post, but Avianca only deals with airmail; to ship a parcel overseas by surface mail, you'll need Adpostal. All are efficient and reliable. Avianca and Depris are much more expensive: a 10g letter sent with Avianca to Europe costs US$3 (and only US$1 with Adpostal). Depris prices can border on the outrageous (US$4 for a postcard to the US or Europe).

Avianca operates the poste restante system. You can receive poste restante letters in any city where Avianca has a post office, but not all provincial offices do a good job. The most reliable office is in Bogotá (Your Name, c/o Lista de Correos Avianca, Edificio Avianca, Carrera 7 No 16-36, Bogotá). Mail is kept for one month. Courier companies do not accept mail sent to Lista de Correos.

SHOPPING

Colombia is famous for its emeralds, but if you aren't knowledgeable about these gemstones you are unlikely to strike a good deal.

Colombian handicrafts vary region by region. Some areas and towns are famous for particular local crafts. Boyacá is the largest handicraft manufacturer, with excellent hand-woven items, basketry and pottery. The basketwork of the Pacific coast is also interesting; the best selection is in Cali. Pasto is noted for decorative items covered with the *barniz de Pasto*, a kind of vegetable resin. Ceramic miniatures of *chivas* (traditional buses) have become a popular souvenir.

Hammocks are another tempting buy and come in plenty of regional variations, from the simple, practical hammocks made in Los Llanos to the elaborate *chinchorros* of the Guajiro Indians. Another well-known Indian product is the *mola* (rectangular cloth with colored designs) made by the Cuna Indians, sold in plenty of craft shops.

Ruanas (Colombian woolen ponchos) are found in the colder parts of the Andean zone, where the climate justifies it. In many villages they are still made by hand with simple patterns and natural colors. Bogotá and Villa de Leyva are good places to buy them.

The best and most fashionable *mochilas* (a kind of woven handbag) are those of the Arhuaco Indians from the Sierra Nevada de Santa Marta. They are not cheap, but are beautiful and usually of good quality.

Leather goods (mostly boots and bags) are a better buy. They are relatively cheap and are among the best in South America; the best selection is in Bogotá.

Colombia publishes an assortment of both well-edited and illustrated coffee-table books about the country's flora and fauna, art and architecture. The best choice is in bookstores of large cities. If you're interested in local music, there are lots of CDs (US$10 to US$15). Bogotá has the widest selection.

SOLO TRAVELERS

Solo travel in Colombia is certainly doable, though you'll save a lot of money on hotels by finding a travel partner. Dorm rooms in backpacker haunts offer a cheap alternative for solo travelers, but these are only found in a few main tourist destinations. The other obvious benefit of a travel partner is security; you're more of a target in the eyes of a thief when walking by yourself. Women travelers have reported being hassled by men when walking alone, especially along the Caribbean coast. This problem is usually solved by having a male companion. See Women Travelers (p233) for more info.

TELEPHONE & FAX

The telephone system is largely automated for both domestic and international calls. Telecom is the most prominent company, with Orbitel and ETB not far behind.

Public telephones exist in cities and large towns but, except for the centers of the largest cities, they are few and far between, and many are out of order. As a rule, Telecom offices have some operable phones. Local calls are charged by timed rate (not flat rate). Public telephones use coins; newly installed telephones accept *tarjeta telefónica* (phonecards). Phonecards can be used for international, intercity and local calls, and can be bought at Telecom offices. For directory assistance or information call ☎ 1235.

Telephone offices are common in cities and towns, and often double as Internet cafés. Ask how much calls are per minute to avoid being overcharged at the end.

You can call direct to just about anywhere in Colombia. Phone numbers are seven digits countrywide. Area codes are single digits, and you'll find them included immediately under the headings of the relevant destinations throughout this book. However, before using them you need to dial the index of the provider you want to use – ☎ 05 for Orbitel, ☎ 07 for ETB and ☎ 09 for Telecom. As yet, Orbitel and ETB provide connections only between some of the major cities, so in most cases you'll be using Telecom.

All three companies provide an international service and may temporarily offer significant discounts – watch out for their advertisements in the electronic and print media. Calling abroad from Colombia, you dial ☎ 005, ☎ 007 or ☎ 009, respectively, then the country code etc.

Colombia's country code is ☎ 57. If you are dialing a Colombian number from abroad, drop the prefix of the provider (05, 07 or 09) and dial only the area code and the local number.

Larger Telecom offices offer fax services. You can also send faxes from Internet cafés.

INTERNATIONAL COLLECT CALLS

Reverse-charge or collect calls *(llamadas de pago revertido)* are possible to most major countries. Here are the international direct-dialing numbers of some countries.

Australia	☎ 01 800 961 0057
Canada	☎ 01 800 933 0057
France	☎ 01 800 933 0057
Germany	☎ 01 800 949 0057
UK	☎ 01 800 944 0057
USA	
AT&T	☎ 01 800 911 0010
MCI	☎ 01 800 916 0001
Sprint	☎ 01 800 913 0010

Cell Phones

The two major cell- (mobile-) phone companies are Movistar and Celcom. Both have branches in most towns and cities. It costs US$5 to US$10 to get a SIM card and then you buy units as needed. Chances are you'll end up with Celcom, which sells SIM cards on the spot. To subscribe to Movistar you'll need to show Colombian residency.

TIME

All of Colombia lies within the same time zone, five hours behind Greenwich Mean Time. There is no daylight-saving time.

TOILETS

There are virtually no self-contained public toilets in Colombia. If you are caught in need, use a restaurant's toilet. Choose better-looking establishments because basic eateries either have no toilets or, if they do, you're better off not witnessing them. Museums and large shopping malls usually have public toilets, as do bus and airport terminals. Toilets are usually sit-down style, but often lack a seat, so become the squat variety.

You'll rarely find toilet paper in toilets, so carry some at all times. Some toilets charge fees (normally not exceeding US$0.25), but in return you can receive some toilet paper. If it seems to be too little for your needs, do not hesitate to ask for more.

Except in some upmarket places, toilet plumbing might not be what you are used to. Pipes are narrow and water pressure weak, so toilets can't cope with toilet paper. A wastebasket is normally provided.

The most common word for toilet is *baño*. Men's toilets will usually bear a label saying *señores, hombres* or *caballeros,* while the women's toilets will be marked *señoras, mujeres* or *damas.*

TOURIST INFORMATION

The provision of tourist information is administered by municipal tourist information offices in departmental capitals and other tourist destinations. Some are better than others, but on the whole they lack city maps and brochures. Staff members may be friendly but rarely speak English. The practical information they provide sometimes leaves a bit to be desired and the quality of information largely depends on the person attending to you.

In some cities, tourist offices are supported by the Policía de Turismo, police officers specially trained to attend tourists.

Colombian consulates and embassies abroad may provide limited tourist information. Overseas offices of Colombian airlines occasionally have brochures.

VISAS

Nationals of some countries, including most of Western Europe, the Americas, Japan, Australia and New Zealand, don't need a visa to enter Colombia. It's a good idea to check this before your planned trip, because visa regulations change frequently.

All visitors get an entry stamp or print in their passport from Departamento Administrativo de Seguridad (DAS; the security police responsible for immigration) upon arrival at any international airport or land border crossing. The stamp says how many days you can stay in the country. The maximum allowed is 90 days, but DAS officials often stamp 60 or just 30 days.

Make sure you get an entry stamp or you'll have troubles later. Official money changers and banks will want to see your entry stamp, as will police if there are any problems. When departing the country, if you don't have a stamp you'll also have to pay a fine (around US$60) and get a *salvoconducto* (literally, 'safe conduct') from a DAS office. Similarly, make sure you have a departure stamp or there will be trouble the next time around.

Visa Extensions

You are entitled to a 30-day extension (costing US$25), which can be obtained from DAS in any departmental capital. The new 30 days begins from the end of the visa already stamped in your passport (so there's no need to wait to the last minute). Most travelers apply for an extension in Bogotá (see p55).

WOMEN TRAVELERS

Colombia is very much a man's country. Machismo and sexism are palpable throughout society. The dominant Catholic church with its conservative attitude to women doesn't help matters. In this context, it's not difficult to imagine how a gringa traveling by herself is regarded.

Women travelers will attract more curiosity, attention and advances from local men than they would from men in the West. Many Colombian men will stare at women, use endearing terms, make comments on their physical appearance and, in some cases, try to make physical contact. It is the Latin American way of life, and local males would not understand if someone told them that their behavior constituted sexual harassment. On the contrary, they would argue that they are just paying the woman a flattering compliment.

Men in large cities, especially in male-only groups, and particularly when drunk, will generally display more bravado and be more insistent than those in small villages. To balance things a little, some male travelers have reported that they themselves felt hassled by Colombian women, who are seen as being rather sexually aggressive.

The best way to deal with unwanted attention is simply to ignore it. Maintain your self-confidence and assertiveness and don't let macho behavior disrupt your holiday. Dressing modestly may lessen the chances of you being the object of macho interest, or at least make you less conspicuous to the local peacocks. Wearing a wedding band and carrying a photo of a make-believe spouse may minimize harassment.

Traveling with a man solves much of the problem because local men will see your male companion as a protector and a deterrent. Traveling with another woman will make things easier; the harassment is likely to continue, but you will at least have the emotional support of your companion.

Harassment aside, women traveling alone face more risks than men. Women are often targets for bag-snatchers and assault, and rape is a potential danger. However, female travelers need not walk around Colombia in a constant state of fear. Just be conscious of your surroundings and aware of situations that could be dangerous. Shabby barrios, solitary streets and beaches, and all places considered male territory, such as bars, sports matches, mines and construction sites should be considered risky.

There's not much in the way of women's support services in Colombia, let alone resources specifically for women travelers. Books which might be worth looking at include *Handbook for Women Travelers* by Maggie and Jemma Moss and *Women Travel – Adventures, Advice & Experience* by Natania Jansz and Miranda Davies.

Transportation

THINGS CHANGE...

The information in this chapter is particularly vulnerable to change. Check directly with the airline or a travel agent to make sure you understand how a fare (and ticket you may buy) works and be aware of the security requirements for international travel. Shop carefully. The details given in this chapter should be regarded as pointers and are not a substitute for your own careful, up-to-date research.

GETTING THERE & AWAY

ENTERING THE COUNTRY

A valid passport (with at least six more months of validity) is an essential document and it must be stamped with a visa if you need one. Entry into Colombia is fairly straightforward. You'll be asked to fill out a customs form, which will be stamped and handed back. Keep the form safe – you'll need it when leaving the country and will pay a lower departure tax if you return the form. Immigration procedures at both the airport and border crossings are fairly streamlined and won't take long, although lines tend to back up at the airport. For information on visas, see p233.

AIR
Airports & Airlines

Colombia's main entrepôt is **El Dorado airport** (BOG; ☎ 1-413 9053; www.bogota-dc.com/trans/aviones.htm) in Bogotá. Other airports servicing international flights include Cartagena's **Rafael Nuñez airport** (CTG; ☎ 5-359 6273; airportctg@sacsa.com.co), Barranquilla's **Ernesto Cortissoz airport** (BAQ; ☎ 5-334 8052; www.baq.aero/index.php in Spanish), **San Andrés airport** (ADZ; ☎ 8-512 6110), Medellín's **Jose Maria Codova airport** (MDE; ☎ 4-601 1212) and Cali's **Alfonso Bonilla Aragón airport** (CLO; ☎ 2-442 2624). Charter flights bringing international package tourists fly into Cartagena.

Avianca (AV; ☎ 1-404 7862; www.avianca.com), Colombia's flagship airline, connects Bogotá with Europe (Madrid), North America (New York, Los Angeles, Miami and Mexico City), Central America (San José and Panama City) and South America (Caracas, Quito, Guayaquil, Lima, Santiago, Buenos Aires, São Paulo and Rio de Janeiro). It has a well-serviced fleet and a reasonable safety record.

Other airlines flying to and from Colombia include the following. The address of airline offices in Bogotá can be found on p74.
Air France (AF; ☎ in Bogotá 1-413 0505; www.airfrance.com; hub Charles de Gaulle Airport, Paris)
American Airlines (AA; ☎ in Bogotá 1-343 2424; www.aa.com; hub Dallas-Fort Worth Airport)
British Airways (BA; ☎ 1-800 934 5700, 1-900 331 2777; www.britishairways.com; hub Heathrow Airport, London)
Continental (CO; ☎ 1-800 944 0219; www.continental airlines.com; hub George Bush Airport, Houston)
Copa (CM; in Bogotá ☎ 1-623 1566; www.copaair.com; hub Panama City)
Iberia (IB; in Bogotá ☎ 1-610 5066; www.iberia.com; hub Madrid Barajas Airport)
TACA (TA; in Bogotá ☎ 1-637 3900; www.taca.com; hub San Salvador Airport)

Tickets

Colombia requires, technically at least, that visitors have an onward ticket before they're allowed into the country. This is quite strictly

---

DEPARTURE TAX

The airport tax on international flights out of Colombia is US$30 if you have stayed in the country up to 60 days, and US$50 if you have stayed longer. The tax is payable either in US dollars or pesos at the exchange rate of the day, but can't be paid by credit card. Make sure you present your customs form or you may have to pay a higher departure tax.

---

enforced by airlines and travel agents, and probably none of them will sell you a one-way ticket unless you already have an onward ticket. Upon arrival in Colombia, however, hardly any immigration official will ask you to present your onward ticket.

Australia & New Zealand

Unless you already have an around-the-world ticket, the best way to get to Colombia is via Argentina or Chile.

The shortest route between Australasia and South America goes over the South Pole. Aerolíneas Argentinas flies three times a week between Auckland and Buenos Aires, and has arrangements with other carriers which cover the Auckland–Australia leg. Aerolíneas Argentinas can fly you to Bogotá, but the total fare will be pretty high; expect to pay between A$2500 and A$3000 for the Sydney–Bogotá return flight. The Auckland–Bogotá fare will be only marginally lower.

Another option is to fly right across the southern Pacific to Santiago de Chile. Lan Chile flies from Sydney via Auckland to Santiago, and has flights on to Bogotá. The Sydney–Bogotá return fares of Lan Chile cost much the same as those of Aerolíneas Argentinas.

It's worth asking your travel agent about flights via Europe (London or Paris) or the USA (Los Angeles or Miami) – ticket prices may not be that much more expensive than the direct route.

The following agents offer the cheapest fares, and have branches throughout Australia and New Zealand.

Flight Centre (☎ in Australia 133 133, ☎ in New Zealand 0800 243 544; www.fightcentre.com)

STA Travel (☎ in Australia 1300 733 035, ☎ in New Zealand 0508 782 872; www.statravel.com)

Canada

Most travelers from Canada end up flying to Colombia by connecting through a US gateway city, though Air Canada has direct flights three or four times per week from Toronto for US$850 return. A good choice for student, youth and budget airfares is **Travel Cuts** (☎ 866-246 9762; www.travelcuts.com).

Central America

Colombia has regular flight connections with most Central American capitals. Sample fares include: Guatemala City–Bogotá US$390 to US$410, San José–Bogotá US$370 to US$400 and Panama City–Bogotá US$200 to US$250.

It may work out cheaper to go via the Colombian island of San Andrés and then get a domestic flight to the Colombian mainland. See p150 for details.

Continental Europe

A number of airlines, including British Airways, Air France and Iberia, link Bogotá with European cities. Colombia is one of the cheapest South American destinations to reach from Europe, and many travel agents will offer flights to Bogotá. The cheapest return flight is with Iberia from Madrid to Bogotá (US$838 return). From Amsterdam, expect to pay US$1100 return on KLM and Air France. Some recommended agencies:

Anyway (☎ 0892 302 301; www.anyway.fr) French travel agent.

CTS Viaggi (☎ 06-462 0431; www.cts.it) Italian company that specializes in student and youth fares.

NBBS Reizen (☎ 0900 1020 300; www.nbbs.nl in Dutch) Branches in most Dutch cities.

Nouvelles Frontiéres (☎ 08 25 00 07 47; www .nouvelles-frontieres.fr in French) Many branches in Paris and throughout France.

STA (☎ in Paris 01 43 59 23 69, ☎ in Frankfurt 069-430 1910; www.statravel.com) Branch offices across Europe.

South America

There are a dozen flights a week between Quito and Bogotá (US$200 to US$250). Tame (an Ecuadorian carrier) has flights between Cali and Tulcán in Ecuador (US$95 one way) and between Cali and Quito (US$140 one way).

A one-way ticket to Lima on TACA, Avianca or LAN Peru will cost US$240 to US$300, or just US$174 for a student fare. A flight to Santiago, Chile on TACA is not too

TRANSPORTATION

bad if you can get a student fare (US$300 to US$350), but a regular-priced fare will cost around US$550. To Boliva, student fares run around US$250 to US$280 while regular tickets cost US$300 to US$450.

There are several flights daily between Caracas and Bogotá, with Avianca, Aeropostal and Servivensa. The regular one-way fare is US$200, but there may be some promotional fares that could bring the price down to US$150.

Fares to Brazil can be ridiculous. From Bogotá to Sao Paulo, you'll pay US$700 to US$800 with TACA or US$750 to US$900 to Rio de Janeiro. It will be cheaper to fly through Leticia in the Colombian Amazon. See Leticia (p214) for details.

UK

Compared with other European cities, London has reasonably priced fares to Bogotá. You'll find plenty of deals listed in the travel sections of weekend editions of London newspapers. Advertisements for many travel agents appear in the travel pages of the weekend broadsheets, such as the *Independent* on Saturday and the *Sunday Times*. Look out for free magazines, such as *TNT*, which are widely available in London.

Prices for discounted flights from London to Bogotá start at around UK£250 one way and UK£400 return. Bargain hunters may find lower prices, but make sure you use a travel agent affiliated with the ABTA (Association of British Travel Agents). If you have bought your ticket from an ABTA-registered agent who then goes out of business, ABTA will guarantee a refund or an alternative. Unregistered bucket shops are sometimes cheaper, but can be riskier. Travel agents include the following:

Flightbookers (☎ 0800 082 3000; www.ebookers.co.uk)
STA (☎ 08701-630 026; www.statravel.co.uk)
Travel Bag (☎ 0800 082 5000; www.travelbag.co.uk)

USA

The major US gateway for Colombia is Miami, from where several carriers, including American Airlines, Avianca and Aces, fly to Bogotá. A 90-day return ticket normally costs about US$400 to US$500 depending on the season.

Another important gateway to Colombia is New York, from where American Airlines and Avianca have flights to Bogotá. A 30-day return ticket is around US$550 to US$650 depending on the season.

On the West Coast, the major departure point is Los Angeles, but flights to Bogotá can be expensive. The cheapest 60-day return fares will be probably somewhere between US$700 and US$800. The cheapest flights are with TACA, which makes stops in El Salvador and Costa Rica. TACA is not recommended during the hurricane season (September to November) because almost daily bad weather in San José frequently causes planes to be diverted to other airports, and you'll miss your connection.

Venezuelan carriers (Aeropostal, Servivensa) may offer good fares for their Miami–Caracas–Bogotá route.

For discount travel agencies, check the Sunday travel sections in newspapers such as the *Los Angeles Times, San Francisco Examiner, Boston Globe, Chicago Tribune* and *New York Times*.

STA Travel and Council Travel are two of the most reputable discount travel agencies in the USA. Although they both specialize in student travel, they may offer discount tickets to nonstudents of all ages.

Cheap Tickets (www.cheaptickets.com)
Orbitz (☎ 888 656 4546; www.orbitz.com)
STA Travel (☎ 800 781 4040; www.sta-travel.com)

LAND

Colombia borders Panama, Venezuela, Brazil, Peru and Ecuador, but has road connections with Venezuela and Ecuador only. These are the easiest and the most popular border crossings. The only crossing completely out of the question is the Panamanian border. This stretches across the infamous Darien Gap, a hostile area of swamps, jungle and guerrilla fighters.

Border Crossings

BRAZIL & PERU

The only viable border crossing from these two countries into Colombia is via Leticia in the far southeastern corner of the Colombian Amazon. Leticia is reached from Iquitos (Peru) and Manaus (Brazil). See Leticia (p214) for details. The area around Leticia is safe.

ECUADOR

Virtually all travelers use the Carretera Panamericana border crossing through Tulcán

(Ecuador) and Ipiales (Colombia). See Ipiales (p208) for information. Parts of the Panamericana (particularly the section between Pasto and Popayán) may be at times unsafe to travel; check for news when you come. The province of Putumayo is another risky area, and best avoided. If you find the road too risky for travel, consider flying to Cali from Ipiales or Pasto.

VENEZUELA

There are four border crossings between Colombia and Venezuela. By far the most popular with travelers (and probably the safest) is the route via San Antonio del Táchira (Venezuela) and Cúcuta (Colombia), on the main Caracas–Bogotá road. See Cúcuta (p104) for details.

There is another reasonably popular border crossing at Paraguachón, on the Maracaibo (Venezuela) to Maicao (Colombia) road. Take this if you plan to head from Venezuela straight to Colombia's Caribbean coast. Buses and shared taxis run between Maracaibo and Maicao, and direct buses between Caracas/Maracaibo and Santa Marta/Cartagena. Your passport will be stamped by both Colombian and Venezuelan officials at the border. See Santa Marta (p112) and Cartagena (p136) for details.

Not so popular is the border crossing between Colombia's Puerto Carreño and either Puerto Páez or Puerto Ayacucho (both in Venezuela). Still less useful is the crossing from El Amparo de Apure (Venezuela) to Arauca (Colombia), a guerrilla-ridden region.

SEA

Sailboats operate between Colón in Panama and Cartagena in Colombia; see p136.

TOURS

Tours to South America have become popular, and there are plenty of companies in the USA, the UK and elsewhere that organize them.

UK

Following is a list of some overland operators offering tours in South America:

Dragoman (☎ 1728-861 133; www.dragoman.co.uk)
Exodus Travels (☎ 020-8673 0859; www.exodus.co.uk)
Guerba Expeditions (☎ 01373-826 611; www.guerba.co.uk)

Last Frontiers (☎ 01296-653 000; www.lastfrontiers.co.uk)
Top Deck (☎ 0208-8796 789; www.topdecktravel.co.uk)

USA

The USA has plenty of tour companies specializing in South America. They are advertised in travel and outdoor magazines such as *Outside, Escape* and *Ecotraveler*, as well as magazines of a more general nature, including *Natural History* and *Audubon*. Here is a list of some reputable operators:

Eco Voyager (☎ 305-629 3200, 800 326 7088; www.ecovoyager.com)
International Expeditions (☎ 205-428 1700, 800 633 4734; www.ietravel.com)
Lost World Adventures (☎ 404-373 5820, 800 999 0558; www.lostworldadventures.com)
Mountain Travel Sobek (☎ 510-594 6000, 888 687 6235; www.mtsobek.com)
Southwind Adventures (☎ 303-972 0701, 800 377 9463; www.southwindadventures.com)
Wilderness Travel (☎ 510-558 2488, 800 368 2794; www.wildernesstravel.com)
Wildland Adventures (☎ 206-365 0686, 800 345 4453; www.wildland.com)

GETTING AROUND

AIR

Flying is the fastest and arguably safest way to get around Colombia, but also the least interesting. For some destinations, such as Leticia, it may be your only option. Several domestic carriers share the load, including Avianca, SAM, Satena and AeroRepública, and most main cities are served by one of them. Prices are usually fixed between the airlines, but it's worth asking your agent if one airline has a special fare that could drop the price. If fares are the same, just look for the flight that best meets your schedule.

Tickets can be purchased directly from the airlines or from travel agents. Some small airlines operate from an office at the airport and may not accept credit-card payment. You'll need to show a passport and your entry stamp to buy a ticket. Ticket prices are usually the same whether you pay for it one month out or the day before, but discounts are sometimes given with an advance purchase so try to buy early. In any case, flights do fill up so get a ticket as early as possible to guarantee yourself a seat.

TRANSPORTATION

Check your ticket carefully to make sure that no mistakes have been made – errors are common. One way to minimize errors and make sure you get to the correct city is to show your agent a map of Colombia and point to where you want to fly to. If you plan to be in Colombia for a while, it's worth asking about discount air passes.

Airlines in Colombia

Colombia has more than half-a-dozen main passenger airlines and another dozen smaller carriers. Note that at the time of research West Caribbean (which at one time connected San Andrés and Providencia) was not operating and it was questionable as to whether the company would remain

MAIN DOMESTIC FLIGHTS

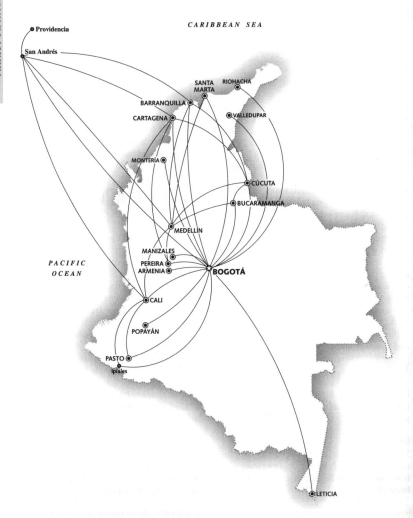

in business. The on-board service of the major carriers is OK. As flight time is usually not much longer than an hour, don't expect any gastronomic treats; on most flights you get no more than a snack. The following fly a variety of routes:

AeroRepública (☎ 1-320 9090; www.aerorepublica .com.co) The second-biggest airline covers much the same domestic territory as Avianca.

Aires (☎ 1-336 6039; www.aires.com.co) This smaller operation uses mostly turbo planes and travels to smaller localities.

Avianca/SAM (☎ 1-404 7862; www.avianca.com) Longtime principal domestic airline, with the widest network of both domestic and international routes. Avianca has merged with the Medellín-based SAM.

Satena (☎ 1-281 7071; www.satena.com) This is the commercial carrier of the FAC (Colombian Air Force) and services flights to the vast areas of the Amazon, Los Llanos and the Pacific coast; it lands at 50 small towns and villages that would be otherwise virtually inaccessible. It is also the only airline flying to Providencia.

BICYCLE
Colombia is not the easiest of countries for cyclists. Road rules favor drivers and you'll end up fighting traffic on main roadways. Never assume that a driver will give you right of way. On the plus side, most roads are paved and security is improving. Even the smallest towns will have a repair shop and you can get your bike fixed cheaply and easily. Bike rentals are uncommon but you can buy a bike almost anywhere. However, if you want something really reliable, bring your own bike and all your own kit.

It is also worth nothing that cities are becoming more bike friendly, with new bike tracks and *ciclovías* (the weekend closures for cars and buses of selected streets, making them tracks for bikers and skaters instead).

Bike shops in some towns may have a bike for you to rent, but don't count on it.

BOAT
With some 3000km of Pacific and Atlantic coastline, there is a considerable amount of shipping traffic, consisting almost exclusively of irregular cargo boats, which may also take passengers. They are of little interest to travelers except, perhaps, boats from Buenaventura to Isla de Gorgona.

Rivers are important transport routes in regions such as the Chocó and the Amazon where there is no other way of getting around. Unfortunately, both these regions are noted for guerrilla and paramilitary activities and are not recommended for tourists, except the area around Leticia.

The Río Magdalena was once the principal waterway of the central part of the country, but no longer has much importance as far as river transport goes. The only boats you are likely to use on the Magdalena are in the Mompós area.

BUS
As there are almost no passenger-train services in Colombia, buses are the main means of travel. The system is well developed and extensive, reaching even small villages.

All intercity buses depart from and arrive at a *terminal de pasajeros* (bus terminal). Every city has such a terminal, usually outside the city center, but always linked to it by local transport. Bogotá is the most important bus transport hub in Colombia, handling buses to just about every area of the country.

On the main roads buses run frequently, so there is no need to buy tickets in advance – just go to the terminal, find which company has the next bus due to depart, buy your ticket and board. On some minor routes, where there are only a few departures a day, it's worth considering buying your ticket several hours before the scheduled departure. The only times you really need to book well in advance are during and around Christmas and Easter, when Colombians rush to travel.

Classes
There are three principal classes of buses: ordinary (called *corriente, sencillo* or *ordinario*), 1st class (which go by a variety of names such as *pullman, metropolitano* or *directo*) and air-conditioned buses (known as *climatizado* or *ejecutivo*).

The *corriente* buses are usually old crates and mostly service side (back) roads. They often stop for every passenger on the road, which sometimes results in the bus being packed far beyond its capacity. The *pullmans* are more modern and comfortable. They ply both side roads and main routes.

Climatizados are the best. There's plenty of legroom, reclining seats and large luggage compartments; some have toilets. They are mainly long-distance buses covering main routes, and many travel at night. They are the fastest and most comfortable way of traveling. They normally depart and arrive on schedule, stop only in a few main towns en route and won't pick up passengers elsewhere. They almost never take more passengers than they have seats. They are the dominant means of intercity transport, but carry warm clothes – some drivers have the air-conditioning going full blast.

Smoking in buses is not allowed, although in *corrientes* people often smoke and nobody seems to care. The long-distance buses stop for meals, but not necessarily at mealtimes; it seems to depend on when the driver is hungry or when the bus gets to a restaurant that has an arrangement with the bus company. Don't leave any hand luggage in the bus when you get off for your meal.

The traditional bus entertainment is music (anything from vallenato to salsa) chosen according to the driver's taste. The volume is also at the whim of the driver and you may experience an entire night of blaring music – not necessarily great fun.

A newer form of entertainment is the video movie. Most buses, including some *corrientes*, are now equipped with video equipment. Hollywood action movies interlaced with sweet Mexican love stories – two Colombian favorites – played most of

---

TEN ROAD-TESTED GETTING-AROUND TIPS

- Check airfares as soon as you arrive in Colombia. Some tickets bought in advance or for weekend flights may be attractively cheap and a tempting alternative to long bus trips.

- Some airlines may offer packages to major tourist destinations (Cartagena, San Andrés), which can cost not much more than you'd pay for air tickets only. Check as soon as you can because good deals sell quickly.

- Flights do not always depart on time, and sometimes are rescheduled, suspended or cancelled. It's a good idea to call the airport and ask for your scheduled departure before going there. In any case, be prepared to spend some time at the airport and don't plan any immediate connections.

- Airfares tend to rise significantly in the holiday seasons, approximately from mid-December to late January and from mid-June to late July. Flights fill up fast during these periods and you may need to book well in advance.

- Avoid bus or air travel between Christmas and early January and during Semana Santa (Easter Week). Colombians get crazy about traveling in these periods so buses and flights are completely full and traffic is chaotic.

- Most long-distance buses are air-conditioned and some may be as cold as freezers. Have a sweater on hand, just in case.

- At the bus terminal, if several companies have buses to your destination departing around the same time, go and view the buses and select the best option before buying your ticket.

- Because of fierce competition between bus companies servicing main routes, some companies may offer discount fares, sometimes much lower than others. Be sure to shop around bus offices at the terminal before buying your ticket.

- If your budget is not completely rock bottom, always consider a *colectivo* (shared taxi), a faster and usually more comfortable means of road transport than a bus, especially an ordinary bus that usually makes many stops.

- Taxis are cheap in Colombia, so don't be afraid to use them in cities for safety, comfort and to save time.

the night and often at full volume can be a form of torture. The technical quality, too, often leaves a bit to be desired.

Costs

Bus travel is reasonably cheap in Colombia. As a rule of a thumb, the *climatizado* costs roughly US$4 for every 100km. *Pullmans* cost about 20% less than *climatizados* and the *corrientes* 20% less than the *pullmans*.

If various companies service the same route, the comparative fares are much the same (though some may offer temporary promotions). However, the condition of the buses varies and you almost always get what you pay for, so if one bus company is offering a lower fare than its competitor, you can bet there's something wrong with the bus. In general, you can count on Brasilia to offer the best service.

When you get on a bus out on the road, you pay the fare to the *ayudante* (driver's sidekick) and rarely get a ticket. *Ayudantes* have been known to charge gringos more than the actual fare or at least to round the price up. Ask other passengers beforehand to be sure of the correct fare.

CAR & MOTORCYCLE

Unfortunately, Colombia is not the best country for traveling by car or motorcycle. The major problem is security. Car theft is a well-established business and thieves usually steal accessories and anything of value left inside. More importantly, roads can be unsafe due to guerrillas, paramilitaries or common criminals – and cars are an obvious target. You may pass through unsafe regions undisturbed if you travel by public transport, but a nice jeep won't get through unnoticed.

In the cities, on the other hand, traffic is heavy, chaotic and mad. Driving 'manners' are wild and unpredictable. It takes some time to get used to the local style of driving, but even if you master it, the risk of an accident remains high.

Colombians drive on the right side of the road and there are seat belt requirements so buckle up or risk a fine.

If you do plan to drive in Colombia, bring your driver's license. The driver's license from your country will normally do, but if you want to be 100% sure, bring along an International Driving Permit as well.

Bring Your Own Vehicle

There's no way of bringing your vehicle to South America other than by sea or air, involving time, substantial costs and a lot of paperwork. You'll probably spend less on (and be safer) traveling in Colombia by air and using taxis. To sum up, driving in Colombia can be unsafe and is not recommended, and bringing in your own car or motorcycle is not a good idea at all.

If you really wish to bring your car from Central America to Colombia there are cargo boats between Colón (Panama) and Cartagena. There is no set schedule and no set price for shipping a car, so bargain hard. On arrival in Colombia the car is given a one- or two-month permit. You will require international insurance: local insurance policies are not expensive, but you cannot buy them for a car that has foreign plates.

Hire

Renting a car might be a better solution than bringing your own car, but it's still not recommended. It does save you the money you would spend on getting your own car to Colombia (but obviously adds car-rental costs). As well, your rental vehicle will have Colombian registration plates so it won't stand out from local vehicles as much and attract unwanted attention. But given the convenience of public transport, you may still be better off and safer using planes and taxis, rather than driving a rented car.

Should you still be determined to rent a car, it's best to contact major international rental companies such as **Avis** (www.avis.com), **Hertz** (www.hertz.com) or **Budget** (www.budget.com) at home before your trip to check what they can offer in Colombia (they all have offices in major Colombian cities and at El Dorado airport in Bogotá), and possibly to prebook, which is likely to be cheaper than renting a car after arrival.

Car rental is not cheap (expect to pay around US$50 a day) and there are seldom any discounts. Carefully check clauses pertaining to insurance and liability before you sign a rental contract. Pay close attention to any theft clause as it may load a large percentage of any loss on to the hirer.

Motorcycles

Some cities, especially in the north, use 'moto-taxis,' which are a quick way of getting around if you're on your own. These, however, are not the safest method of transport and are even illegal in some places, including Cartagena (though no one seems to stop them). There may be options of renting a motorcycle, especially in resort-type areas such as San Andrés.

HITCHHIKING

Predictably, hitchhiking in Colombia is uncommon and difficult. Given the complex internal situation, drivers don't want to take risks and simply don't stop on the road. As intercity buses are fast, efficient and relatively cheap, it's not worth wasting time on hitching and taking a potentially serious risk.

LOCAL TRANSPORTATION
Bus

Buses are the main means to get around the cities. Almost every urban centre of more than 100,000 inhabitants has a bus service, as do many smaller towns. The standard, speed and efficiency of local buses vary from place to place, but on the whole they are slow and crowded. City buses have a flat fare, so the distance of the ride makes no difference. You get on by the front door and pay the driver or his assistant. You never get a ticket.

In some cities or on some streets there are bus stops (paraderos or paradas), while in most others you just wave down the bus. To let the driver know that you intend to get off you simply say, or shout, por aquí, por favor (here, please), en la esquina, por favor (at the next street corner, please) or el paradero, por favor (at the coming bus stop, please).

There are lots of different types of local buses, ranging from old wrecks to modern air-conditioned vehicles. One common type is the buseta (small bus), a dominant means of urban transport in cities such as Bogotá and Cartagena. The bus fare is somewhere between US$0.25 and US$0.40, depending on the city and type of bus.

Some cities, such as Bogotá also have colectivos. These vehicles ply main city routes, are faster than buses and charge about US$0.40.

A bus or buseta trip, particularly in large cities such as Bogotá or Barranquilla, is not a smooth and silent ride but rather a sort of breathtaking adventure with a taste of local folklore thrown in. You'll have an opportunity to be saturated with loud tropical music, learn about the Colombian meaning of road rules, and observe your driver desperately trying to make his way through an ocean of vehicles.

A special, new kind of bus is the Trans-Milenio (p76), which was introduced to Bogotá in 2000. It's fast, clean and efficient, and has no musical entertainment.

BUSING ABOUT, CHIVA-STYLE

The chiva is a Disneyland-style vehicle that was Colombia's principal means of road transport several decades ago. Also called bus de escalera in some regions, the chiva is a piece of popular art on wheels. The body is made almost entirely of wood and has wooden benches rather than seats, with each bench accessible from the outside. The body of the bus is painted with colorful decorative patterns, each different, with a main painting on the back. There are homebred artists who specialize in painting chivas. Ceramic miniatures of chivas are found in just about every Colombian handicraft shop.

Today, chivas have almost disappeared from main roads, but they still play an important role on back roads between small towns and villages. There are still a few thousand of them and they are most common in Antioquia, Huila, Nariño and on the Caribbean coast. Chivas take both passengers and any kind of cargo, animals included. If the interior is already completely packed, the roof is used for everything and everybody that doesn't fit inside. Chivas usually gather around markets, from where they depart for their journeys along bumpy roads. They are rare guests at the bus terminals.

Night city tours in chivas are organized by travel agents in most large cities and have become a popular form of entertainment. There is normally a band on board playing local music, and a large stock of aguardiente (anise-flavored liquor) to create the proper atmosphere. The tour usually includes some popular nightspots and can be great fun.

Colectivo

Quite widespread in Colombia, the *colectivo* is a cross between a bus and a taxi. They are often Japanese-made cars, and occasionally vans, minibuses, jeeps or pick-up trucks. They ply fixed routes and depart when all the seats are filled rather than to a set schedule. The *colectivo* service came into being on roads where bus service was deficient and slow. Although *colectivos* mainly cover short-distance routes, there are some medium- and long-distance services.

Colectivos charge roughly 30% to 60% more than buses, but are faster and usually more comfortable. They are a good option if you have a long wait for a bus, and a savior if the last bus is gone. In some cities they depart from and arrive at the bus terminal, but in smaller towns they are usually found in the main square. The frequency of service varies largely from place to place. At some places there may be a *colectivo* every five minutes, but elsewhere you can wait an hour or longer until the necessary number of passengers has been collected.

Metro

Medellín began constructing its metro in 1985 and opened it in 1995. It was the first (and is currently the only) Colombian city to have a fast metropolitan train system.

Bogotá spent 30 years drawing up plans for a subway but eventually dumped the idea in favor of a fast bus system called TransMilenio. It may not be as fast as a subway, but its building costs were five times less than the Medellín subway, saving the public from an additional tax burden.

Taxi

Taxis are an inexpensive and convenient means of getting around, especially if you are traveling with a few companions. The price will usually be the same, regardless of the number of passengers, though some drivers may demand more if you have a lot of luggage.

A taxi may also be chartered for longer distances. This is convenient if you want to visit places near major cities that are outside local transport areas but too near to be covered by long-distance bus networks.

In major cities taxis have meters, though drivers are not always eager to switch them on, preferring to charge a gringo fare, obviously far higher than the normal metered fare. It's always advisable to ask a few people beforehand (eg a bus terminal official or hotel receptionist) what the usual taxi fare to your destination would be. Then, ask the taxi driver for the expected fare, and if they quote a significantly higher fare, bargain and agree on a price. If you are not satisfied, try another taxi.

While taxis are officially obliged to display the current legal tariff, due to regular price rises their meters are not always adjusted to the latest tariff amount and the driver can legitimately ask more than is shown on the meter. In provincial towns metered taxis are rare. Instead there are commonly accepted fares on given routes so always fix the price beforehand.

Don't use taxis with a driver and somebody else inside. Taxi drivers sometimes have a friend along for company or for security reasons, but it may be insecure for you; some cases of robbery have been reported.

TOURS

There are very few genuine tour companies in Colombia, so don't expect many adventure tours. Some travel agencies organize tours, but these are mostly conventional affairs such as city tours, one-day excursions to nearby attractions and night *chiva* trips around the city discos. Longer, more adventurous tours to remote regions are thin on the ground, due to both safety fears and a lack of demand. Information about tours has been included in relevant sections throughout the regional chapters in this book.

TRANSPORTATION

Health David Goldberg MD

CONTENTS

Most visitors travel to Colombia without incident, but there are certain medical conditions to be aware of and several things you can do to prevent sickness. Most illnesses are the result of Colombia's tropical-zone location. If traveling anywhere along the coast or jungle, you can bank on little tropical nuisances – infected bug bites, a spreading rash or heat exhaustion. Other, more dangerous afflictions, including malaria, dengue fever and yellow fever, can strike travelers who get further off the beaten track or spend a lot of time trekking through the national parks. Other problems can occur in the mountains, including altitude sickness. The good news is that Colombia has some of the best medical care in South America. Prices for treatment are usually reasonable and the local pharmacy network is developed and extensive: there are *droguerías* (pharmacies) even in small towns, and those in the cities are usually well stocked.

BEFORE YOU GO

If you require a particular medication take an adequate supply with you; it may not be available locally. Take the original prescription specifying the generic rather than the brand name; this makes getting replacements easier. It's also wise to have the prescription with you to prove you're using the medication legally. you can register online with the **International Association for Medical Assistance to Travelers** (IAMAT; www.iamat.org).

INSURANCE

Buying a travel insurance policy to cover medical problems is recommended. There is a wide variety of policies and your travel agent will have recommendations.

MEDICAL CHECKLIST

Colombian pharmacies stock all kinds of drugs, and medication can be cheaper than in Western countries. There are few restricted drugs; almost everything is sold over the counter. Many drugs are manufactured locally under foreign license. Be sure to check expiry dates.

- antibiotics
- antidiarrheal drugs (eg loperamide)
- acetaminophen (Tylenol) or aspirin
- anti-inflammatory drugs (eg ibuprofen)
- altitude sickness pills (acetazolamide or dexamethasone)
- antihistamines (for hay fever and allergic reactions)
- motion sickness pills (eg Dramamine)
- antibacterial ointment (eg Bactroban) for cuts and abrasions
- steroid cream or cortisone (for poison ivy and other allergic rashes)
- bandages, gauze, gauze rolls
- adhesive or paper tape
- scissors, safety pins, tweezers
- pocket knife
- DEET-containing insect repellent for the skin
- permethrin-containing insect spray for clothing, tents and bed nets
- sun block
- oral rehydration salts
- iodine tablets (for water purification)

INTERNET RESOURCES & BOOKS

A good place to start is **Lonely Planet.com** (www.lonelyplanet.com). The World Health Organization publishes a superb book, called *International Travel and Health,* which is revised annually and is available online at no cost at www.who.int/ith.

IMMUNIZATIONS

Yellow fever vaccine is required for visitors to the national parks along the Atlantic coast. No other vaccines are legally mandated, but the following are strongly recommended.

Vaccine	Recommended for	Dosage	Side effects
hepatitis A	all travelers	1 dose before trip; booster 6-12 months later	soreness at injection site; headaches; body aches
typhoid	all travelers	4 capsules by mouth, 1 taken every other day	abdominal pain; nausea; rash
yellow fever	all travelers, except for those limiting their trip to the western edge of the country	1 dose lasts 10 years	headaches; body aches; severe reactions are rare
hepatitis B	long-term travelers in close contact with the local population	3 doses over 6-month period	soreness at injection site; low-grade fever
rabies	travelers who may have contact with animals and may not have access to medical care	3 doses over 3-4 week period	soreness at injection site; headaches; body aches
tetanus-diphtheria	all travelers who haven't had booster within 10 years	1 dose lasts 10 years	soreness at injection site
measles	travelers born after 1956 who've had only one measles vaccination	1 dose	fever; rash; joint pains; allergic reactions
chickenpox	travelers who've never had chickenpox	2 doses 1 month apart	fever; mild case of chickenpox

HEALTH

If you plan to travel in remote areas, you might consider taking a health guide such as Lonely Planet's *Healthy Travel Central & South America* or *Staying Healthy in Asia, Africa & Latin America* by Dirk Schroeder.

IN TRANSIT

DEEP VEIN THROMBOSIS (DVT)

Blood clots may form in the legs during plane flights. Most are reabsorbed uneventfully, but some may break off and travel through the blood vessels to the lungs, where they could cause complications.

The chief symptom of DVT is swelling or pain of the foot, ankle or calf, usually but not always on just one side. When a blood clot travels to the lungs, it may cause chest pain and difficulty breathing.

To prevent the development of DVT on long flights you should walk about the cabin, perform isometric compressions of the leg muscles (ie contract the leg muscles while sitting), drink plenty of fluids and avoid alcohol.

JET LAG & MOTION SICKNESS

Jet lag is common when crossing more than five time zones resulting in insomnia, fatigue, malaise or nausea. To avoid jet lag try drinking plenty of fluids (nonalcoholic) and eating light meals. Upon arrival, get exposure to natural sunlight and readjust your schedule (for meals, sleep etc) as soon as possible.

Antihistamines such as dimenhydrinate (Dramamine) and meclizine (Antivert, Bonine) are usually the first choice for treating motion sickness. Their main side-effect is drowsiness. An herbal alternative is ginger, which works like a charm for some people.

FOLK REMEDIES

Problem	Treatment
altitude sickness	gingko
jet lag	melatonin
motion sickness	ginger
mosquito bite prevention	oil of eucalyptus, soybean oil

IN COLOMBIA

AVAILABILITY & COST OF HEALTH CARE

Adequate medical care is available in major cities, but may be difficult to find in rural areas. For an online guide to physicians, dentists, hospitals and pharmacies in Colombia, go to the US Embassy website at http://usembassy.state.gov/bogota/wwwfmedl.pdf. Most doctors and hospitals will expect payment in cash, regardless of whether you have travel health insurance.

If you develop a life-threatening medical problem, you'll probably want to be evacuated to a country with state-of-the-art medical care. For air ambulance service in Colombia, call **Aeromedicos** (Ambulancia Aerea, El Dorado International Airport, Entrance 2, Int 1, Of 105; ☎ 1-413 9160, 413 8915; fax 1-413 9550). Since this may cost tens of thousands of dollars, be sure you have insurance to cover this before you depart.

INFECTIOUS DISEASES

Cholera

Cholera is an intestinal infection acquired through ingestion of contaminated food or water. The main symptom is profuse, watery diarrhea, which may be so severe that it causes life-threatening dehydration. The key treatment is drinking oral rehydration solution. Antibiotics are also given, usually tetracycline or doxycycline, though quinolone antibiotics such as ciprofloxacin and levofloxacin are also effective. In recent years, only a small number of cholera cases have been identified and a cholera vaccine is no longer required.

Dengue Fever

Dengue fever is a viral infection and the number of cases reported from Colombia has risen sharply in recent years, especially in Santander, Tolima, Valle del Cauca, Norte de Santander, Meta and Huila. Dengue is transmitted by Aedes mosquitoes, which bite preferentially during the daytime and are usually found close to human habitations, often indoors. Dengue is especially common in densely populated, urban environments.

Dengue usually causes flulike symptoms, including fever, muscle aches, joint pains, headaches, nausea and vomiting, which are often followed by a rash. The body aches may be quite uncomfortable, but most cases resolve uneventfully in a few days.

There is no treatment for dengue fever. The only thing to do is take analgesics such as acetaminophen/paracetamol (Tylenol) and drink plenty of fluids. Severe cases may require hospitalization for intravenous fluids and supportive care. There is no vaccine. The cornerstone of prevention is insect protection measures.

Hepatitis A

Hepatitis A is the second most common travel-related infection (after traveler's diarrhea). It's a viral infection of the liver that is usually acquired by ingestion of contaminated water, food or ice, though it may also be acquired by direct contact with infected persons. The illness occurs throughout the world, but the incidence is higher in developing nations. Symptoms may include fever, malaise, jaundice, nausea, vomiting and abdominal pain. Most cases resolve without complications, though hepatitis A occasionally causes severe liver damage. There is no treatment.

The vaccine for hepatitis A is extremely safe and highly effective. And if you get a booster six to twelve months later, it lasts for at least 10 years. Because the safety of hepatitis A vaccine has not been established for pregnant women or children under age 2; they should instead be given a gamma-globulin injection.

Hepatitis B

Like hepatitis A, hepatitis B is a liver infection that occurs worldwide but is more common in developing nations. Unlike hepatitis A, the disease is usually acquired by sexual contact or by exposure to infected blood, generally through blood transfusion or contaminated needles. The vaccine is recommended only for long-term travelers (on the road more than six months) who expect to live in rural areas or have close physical contact with the local population. Hepatitis B vaccine is safe and highly effective. However, a total of three injections are necessary to establish full immunity. Several countries added hepatitis B vaccine to the list of routine childhood immunizations in the 1980s, so many young adults are already protected.

HIV & AIDS

Infection with the human immunodeficiency virus (HIV) may lead to acquired immune deficiency syndrome (AIDS), which is a fatal disease. Any exposure to blood, blood products or body fluids may put the individual at risk. The disease is often transmitted through sexual contact, and in Colombia it's primarily through contact between heterosexuals.

HIV and AIDS can also be contracted through infected blood transfusions, and you should be aware that not all the hospitals screen blood supplies. The virus may also be picked up through injection with an unsterilized needle. Acupuncture, tattooing and body piercing are other potential dangers.

Intestinal Worms

These parasites are common in humid, tropical areas. They can be present on unwashed vegetables or in undercooked meat, or you can pick them up through your skin by walking barefoot. Infestations may not show up for some time and, although they are generally not serious, can cause further health problems if left untreated. A stool test on your return home is not a bad idea if you think you may have contracted them. Medication is usually available over the counter and treatment is easy and short.

Malaria

Malaria is transmitted by mosquito bites, usually between dusk and dawn. The main symptom is high spiking fevers, which may be accompanied by chills, sweats, headache, body aches, weakness, vomiting or diarrhea. Severe cases of malaria may involve the central nervous system and lead to seizures, confusion, coma and death.

Taking malaria pills is strongly recommended for all rural areas below 800m. Risk is highest in the departments of Amazonas, Chóco, Córdoba, Guainía, Guaviare, Putumayo and Vichada. There is no malaria risk in or around Bogotá.

There is a choice of three malaria pills, all of which work about equally well. Mefloquine (Lariam) is taken once weekly, starting one to two weeks before arrival and continuing through the trip and for four weeks after return. The problem is that a certain percentage of people develop neuropsychiatric side effects, which may range from mild to severe.

Atovaquone/proguanil (Malarone) is a newly approved combination pill taken once daily with food starting two days before arrival and continuing through the trip and for seven days after departure. Side effects are typically mild. Doxycycline is a third alternative, but may cause an exaggerated sunburn reaction.

In general, Malarone seems to cause fewer side effects than mefloquine and is becoming more popular. The chief disadvantage is that it has to be taken daily.

Protecting yourself against mosquito bites is just as important as taking malaria pills, since none of the pills are 100% effective.

If you may not have access to medical care while traveling, you should bring along additional pills for emergency self-treatment, which you should take if you can't reach a doctor and you develop symptoms that suggest malaria, such as high spiking fevers. One option is to take four tablets of Malarone once daily for three days. However, Malarone should not be used for treatment if you're already taking it for prevention.

If you develop a fever after returning home, see a physician, as malaria symptoms may not occur for months.

Rabies

Rabies is a viral infection of the brain and spinal cord that is almost always fatal. The rabies virus is carried in the saliva of infected animals and is typically transmitted through an animal bite, though contamination of any break in the skin with infected saliva may result in rabies. In Colombia, a rabies outbreak caused by large numbers of bat bites was reported in May–June 2004 from Birrinchao, along the Purricha river in the Choco region.

Rabies vaccine is safe, but a full series requires three injections and is quite expensive. Those at high risk for rabies, such as animal handlers and spelunkers (cave explorers), should certainly get the vaccine.

All animal bites and scratches must be promptly and thoroughly cleansed with large amounts of soap and water and local health authorities contacted to determine whether or not further treatment is necessary.

Sexually Transmitted Diseases

Sexual contact with an infected partner can result in you contracting a number of diseases. While abstinence is the only 100%

effective prevention, the use of condoms lessens the risk of infection considerably.

The most common sexually transmitted diseases are gonorrhea and syphilis, which in men first appear as sores, blisters or rashes around the genitals and a discharge or pain when urinating. Symptoms may be less marked or not present at all in women. Syphilis symptoms eventually disappear, but the disease continues and may cause severe problems in later years. Gonorrhea and syphilis are treatable with antibiotics.

Typhoid Fever

Typhoid fever is caused by ingestion of food or water contaminated by a species of *Salmonella* known as *Salmonella typhi*. Fever occurs in virtually all cases. Other symptoms may include headache, malaise, muscle aches, dizziness, loss of appetite, nausea and abdominal pain. Either diarrhea or constipation may occur. Possible complications include intestinal perforation, intestinal bleeding, confusion, delirium or (rarely) coma. Unless you expect to take all your meals in major hotels and restaurants, typhoid vaccine is a good idea.

The drug of choice is usually a quinolone antibiotic such as ciprofloxacin (Cipro) or levofloxacin (Levaquin), which many travelers carry for treatment of traveler's diarrhea. However, if you self-treat for typhoid fever, you may also need to self-treat for malaria, since the symptoms of the two diseases may be indistinguishable.

Tetanus

This potentially fatal disease is difficult to treat, but is easily prevented by immunization. Tetanus occurs when a wound becomes infected by a germ that lives in soil in the feces of horses and other animals. It enters the body via breaks in the skin, so the best prevention is to clean all wounds promptly and thoroughly and use an antiseptic. Use antibiotics if the wound becomes hot or throbs or pus is seen. The first symptom may be discomfort in swallowing or stiffening of the jaw and neck; this can be followed by painful convulsions of the jaw and whole body.

Typhus

This is spread by ticks, mites and lice. It begins as a severe cold followed by a fever, chills, headaches, muscle pains and a body rash. There is often a large and painful sore at the site of the bite, and nearby lymph nodes become swollen and painful.

Yellow Fever

Yellow fever is a life-threatening viral infection transmitted by mosquitoes in forested areas. The illness begins with flu-like symptoms, which may include fever, chills, headache, muscle aches, backache, loss of appetite, nausea and vomiting. These symptoms usually subside in a few days, but one person in six enters a second, toxic phase characterized by recurrent fever, vomiting, listlessness, jaundice, kidney failure and hemorrhage, leading to death in up to half of the cases. There is no treatment except for supportive care. The vaccine is highly recommended for visitors to the country's national parks along the Atlantic coast.

The vaccine should be given at least 10 days before any potential exposure to yellow fever and remains effective for approximately ten years. Reactions to the vaccine are generally mild and may include headaches, muscle aches, low-grade fevers or discomfort at the injection site. Severe, life-threatening reactions have been described but are extremely rare.

TRAVELER'S DIARRHEA

To prevent diarrhea, avoid tap water unless it has been boiled, filtered or chemically disinfected (iodine tablets); only eat fresh fruits or vegetables if cooked or peeled; be wary of dairy products that might contain unpasteurized milk; and be highly selective when eating food from street vendors.

If you develop diarrhea, be sure to drink plenty of fluids, preferably an oral rehydration solution containing lots of salt and sugar. A few loose stools don't require treatment but, if you start having more than four or five stools a day, you should start taking an antibiotic (usually a quinolone drug) and an antidiarrheal agent (such as loperamide). If diarrhea is bloody or persists for more than 72 hours or is accompanied by fever, shaking chills or severe abdominal pain you should seek medical attention.

FUNGAL INFECTIONS

Fungal infections occur more commonly in hot weather and are most likely to be found between the toes or fingers or around the roin. The infections are spread by infected animals or humans; you may contract them by walking barefoot in damp areas, for example. Moisture encourages these infections.

To prevent fungal infections wear loose, comfortable clothes, avoid artificial fibers, wash frequently and dry thoroughly. Use flip-flops while taking a shower in bathrooms of cheap hotels. If you become infected, wash the infected area daily with a disinfectant or medicated soap, and rinse and dry well. Apply an antifungal cream or powder.

ENVIRONMENTAL HAZARDS
Mosquito & Tick Bites
Try to prevent mosquito bites by wearing long sleeves, long pants, hats and shoes (rather than sandals). Bring along a good insect repellent, preferably one containing DEET, which should be applied to exposed skin and clothing, but not to eyes, mouth, cuts, wounds or irritated skin. Use sparingly though – neurologic toxicity has been reported from DEET, but is extremely rare.

Insect repellents containing certain botanical products, including oil of eucalyptus and soybean oil, are effective but last only ½ to two hours. DEET-containing repellents are preferable for areas where there is high risk of malaria or yellow fever. Products based on citronella are not effective. For additional protection, you can apply permethrin to clothing, shoes, tents and bed nets, but not directly to your skin.

Don't sleep with the window open unless there is a screen. Use a bed net when available or at least a mosquito coil. Repellent-impregnated wristbands are not effective.

To protect yourself from tick bites, follow the same precautions as for mosquitoes, except that boots are preferable to shoes, with pants tucked in. Be sure to perform a thorough tick check at the end of each day. Ticks should be removed with tweezers, grasping them firmly by the head. Insect repellents based on botanical products, described above, have not been adequately studied for insects other than mosquitoes and cannot be recommended to prevent tick bites.

Altitude Sickness
Altitude sickness may develop in travelers who ascend rapidly to altitudes greater than 2500m, including those flying directly to Bogota. Being physically fit does not in any way lessen your risk of altitude sickness. Symptoms may include headaches, nausea, vomiting, dizziness, malaise, insomnia and loss of appetite. Severe cases may be complicated by fluid in the lungs (high-altitude pulmonary edema) or swelling of the brain (high-altitude cerebral edema). Most deaths are caused by high-altitude pulmonary edema.

The standard medication to prevent altitude sickness is a mild diuretic called acetazolamide (Diamox), which should be started 24 hours before ascent and continued for 48 hours after arrival at altitude. Possible side effects include numbness, increased urination, tingling, nausea, drowsiness, nearsightedness and temporary impotence. For those who cannot tolerate acetazolamide, most physicians prescribe dexamethasone, which is a type of steroid. A natural alternative is gingko, which some people find quite helpful. The usual dosage is 100mg twice daily.

To lessen the chance of altitude sickness, you should also be sure to ascend gradually or by increments to higher altitudes, avoid overexertion, eat light meals and avoid alcohol.

If you or any of your companions show any symptoms of altitude sickness, you should be sure not to ascend to a higher altitude until the symptoms have cleared. If the symptoms become worse, immediately descend to a lower altitude. Acetazolamide and dexamethasone may be used to treat altitude sickness as well as prevent it.

Water & Sun
Tap water in Bogotá and other big cities is safe to drink, but it's better to avoid it. Use bottled water instead. In very remote areas, boil water for one minute to purify. At altitudes greater than 2000m (6500ft), boil for three minutes. Another option is to disinfect water with iodine pills.

To protect yourself from excessive sun exposure, you should stay out of the midday sun, wear sunglasses and a wide-brimmed sun hat, and apply sunscreen with SPF 15 or higher, with both UVA and UVB protection. Travelers should also drink plenty of fluids and avoid strenuous exercise when the temperature is high.

HEALTH

Animal & Snake Bites

Do not attempt to pet, handle or feed any animal, with the exception of domestic animals known to be free of any infectious disease. Most animal injuries are directly related to a person's attempt to touch or feed the animal.

Any bite or scratch by a mammal, including bats, should be promptly and thoroughly cleansed with large amounts of soap and water, followed by application of an antiseptic such as iodine or alcohol. The local health authorities should be contacted immediately for possible post-exposure rabies treatment, whether or not you've been immunized against rabies. It may also be advisable to start an antibiotic, since wounds caused by animal bites and scratches frequently become infected. One of the newer quinolones, such as levofloxacin (Levaquin) which many travelers carry in case of diarrhea, would be an appropriate choice.

In the event of a venomous snake bite place the victim at rest, keep the bitten area immobilized, and move the victim immediately to the nearest medical facility. Avoid tourniquets, which are no longer recommended.

Language

CONTENTS

Colombia's official language is Spanish, and apart from some remote Indian groups, all inhabitants speak it. On San Andrés and, particularly, Providencia, English is still widely used. Many Indian groups use their native languages. There are about 65 indigenous languages and nearly 300 dialects spoken in the country.

English speakers can be found in large urban centers, but it's certainly not a widely spoken or commonly understood language, even though it's taught as a mandatory second language in the public school system. Once you leave urban areas, Spanish will virtually be the only medium of communication. You'll probably manage to travel without knowing a word of Spanish, but you'll miss out on a good part of the pleasure of meeting people, and your experience of the country will be limited.

Spanish is quite an easy language to learn and, as a bonus, it's useful in most other Latin American countries as well. It's well worth making some effort to learn at least the essentials before setting off. Colombians will offer much encouragement, so there's no need to feel self-conscious about vocabulary, grammar or pronunciation. To help you on your way, grab a copy of Lonely Planet's compact *Latin American Spanish Phrasebook*. Another quality resource is the University of Chicago *Spanish-English, English-Spanish Dictionary*. It's small and light, and has a thorough list of entries.

COLOMBIAN SPANISH

The Spanish spoken in Colombia is generally clear and easy to understand. There are regional variations, but these won't be noticeable to visitors, apart perhaps from the *costeños* from the Caribbean Coast, who tend to speak fast and may be difficult to understand.

The use of the forms *tu* ('you' informal) and *usted* ('you' polite) is flexible in Colombia, unlike Spain, where *tu* is generally only used among friends. Strangers can often use *tu*, while a husband and a wife may use *usted* when speaking to each other and to their children. While either form is OK, the best advice is to answer in the same form that you are addressed in – and always use *usted* when talking to the police.

Note that Colombians, like all Latin Americans, do not use *vosotros* (the plural of *tu*); *ustedes* is commonly used.

Local Lingo

Latin American Spanish vocabulary has lots of regional variations and differs noticeably from European Spanish. Colombian Spanish has altered the meaning of some words or taken their secondary meaning as the main one. Colombians have also created plenty of *colombianismos*, words or phrases used either nationally or regionally, but almost unknown outside Colombia.

Colombians and other South Americans normally refer to the Spanish language as *castellano* rather than *español* (as it is known in Spain).

PRONUNCIATION

Pronunciation of Spanish is not difficult. Many Spanish sounds are similar to their English counterparts, and the relationship between pronunciation and spelling is clear and consistent. Unless otherwise indicated, the following English examples take standard American pronunciation.

LANGUAGE

The most significant pronunciation differences between the Spanish of Colombia and that of Spain are: **ll** – as 'y' in Colombia, as 'ly' in Spain; **z** and **c** before **e** and **i** – as 's' in Colombia, not the lisped 'th' of Spain.

Vowels & Diphthongs

a	as in 'father'
e	as in 'met'
i	as the 'i' in 'police'
o	as in British English 'hot'
u	as the 'u' in 'rude'
ai	as in 'aisle'
au	as the 'ow' in 'how'
ei	as in 'vein'
ia	as the 'ya' in 'yard'
ie	as the 'ye' in 'yes'
oi	as in 'coin'
ua	as the 'wa' in 'wash'
ue	as the 'we' in 'well'

Consonants

Spanish consonants are generally the same as in English, with the exception of those listed below.

The consonants **ch**, **ll** and **ñ** are generally considered distinct letters, but in dictionaries **ch** and **ll** are now often listed alphabetically under **c** and **l** respectively. The letter **ñ** still has a separate entry after **n** in alphabetical listings.

b	similar to English 'b,' but softer; referred to as 'b larga'
c	as in 'celery' before **e** and **i**; elsewhere as the 'k' in 'king'
ch	as in 'choose'
d	as in 'dog'; between vowels and after **l** or **n**, it's closer to the 'th' in 'this'
g	as the 'ch' in the Scottish *loch* before **e** and **i** ('kh' in our pronunciation guides); elsewhere, as in 'go'
h	invariably silent
j	as the 'ch' in the Scottish *loch* ('kh' in our pronunciation guides)
ll	as the 'y' in 'yellow'
ñ	as the 'ni' in 'onion'
r	as in 'run,' but strongly rolled
rr	very strongly rolled
v	similar to English 'b,' but softer; referred to as 'b corta'
x	usually pronounced as **j** above; as in 'taxi' in other instances
z	as the 's' in 'sun'

Word Stress

In general, words ending in vowels or the letters **n** or **s** are stressed on the second-last syllable, while those with other endings have stress on the last syllable. Thus *vaca* (cow) and *caballos* (horses) are both stressed on the next-to-last syllable, while *ciudad* (city) and *infeliz* (unhappy) are stressed on the last syllable.

Written accents generally indicate words that don't follow the previous rules, eg *sótano* (basement), *América* and *porción* (portion).

GENDER & PLURALS

In Spanish, nouns are either masculine or feminine, and there are rules to help determine gender (there are of course some exceptions). Feminine nouns generally end with **-a** or with the groups **-ción**, **-sión** or **-dad**. Other endings typically signify a masculine noun. Endings for adjectives also change to agree with the gender of the noun they modify (masculine/feminine singular **-o**/**-a**). Where both masculine and feminine forms are included in this language guide, they are separated by a slash, with the masculine form first, eg *perdido/a* (lost).

If a noun or adjective ends in a vowel, the plural is formed by adding **s** to the end. If it ends in a consonant, the plural is formed by adding **es** to the end.

ACCOMMODATIONS

I'm looking for ...

Estoy buscando ...	e·stoy boos·kan·do ...	
a hotel	un hotel	oon o·*tel*
a boarding house	una pensión	oo·na pen·*syon*
a youth hostel	un albergue juvenil	oon al·*ber*·ge khoo·ve·*neel*

Are there any rooms available?

¿Hay habitaciones libres?	ay a·bee·ta·*syon*·es lee·bres

I'd like a ...	Quisiera una	kee·*sye*·ra oo·na
room.	habitación ...	a·bee·ta·*syon* ...
double	doble	do·ble
single	individual	een·dee·bee·*dwal*
twin	con dos camas	kon dos *ka*·mas

How much is it	¿Cuánto cuesta	*kwan*·to kwes·ta
per ...?	por ...?	por ...
night	noche	*no*·che
person	persona	per·*so*·na

MAKING A RESERVATION

(for phone or written requests)

To ...	A ...
From ...	De ...
Date	Fecha

I'd like to book ...	Quisiera reservar ...
	(see the list under
	'Accommodations' for bed
	and room options)
in the name of ...	en nombre de ...
for the nights of ...	para las noches del ...
credit card ...	tarjeta de crédito ...
number	número
expiry date	fecha de vencimiento

Please confirm ...	Puede confirmar ...
availability	la disponibilidad
price	el precio

private/shared bathroom	baño privado/ compartido	ba·nyo pree·va·do/ kom·par·tee·do
full board	pensión completa	pen·syon kom·ple·ta
too expensive	demasiado caro	de·ma·sya·do ka·ro
cheaper	más económico	mas e·ko·no·mee·ko
discount	descuento	des·kwen·to

Does it include breakfast?
    ¿Incluye el desayuno?   een·kloo·ye el de·sa·yoo·no
May I see the room?
    ¿Puedo ver la   pwe·do ver la
      habitación?   a·bee·ta·syon
I don't like it.
    No me gusta.   no me goos·ta
It's fine. I'll take it.
    OK. La alquilo.   o·kay la al·kee·lo
I'm leaving now.
    Me voy ahora.   me voy a·o·ra

CONVERSATION & ESSENTIALS

Greetings in Colombia have become an elaborate ritual; the short Spanish *hola* has given way to an incalculable number of expressions, all of them meaning something between 'hello' and 'how do you do'. Here are some examples:

¿Cómo está?
¿Cómo ha estado?
¿Qué ha hecho?
¿Cómo le va?
¿Cómo me lo han tratado?
¿Qué tal?
¿Q'hubo? or ¿Quiubo?
¿Qué me cuenta?
¿Cómo le acabó de ir?
¿Qué más (de nuevo, de su vida)?
¿Qué hay (de cosas, de bueno)?

This list could be continued for several more pages. When people meet or phone each other, they always begin the conversation with a long exchange of these and similar expressions.

You may find it funny, surprising, irritating, ridiculous, tiring, fascinating – but whatever you say about it, it is typically Colombian and you should learn some of these expressions to keep to the local style.

Hello.	Hola.	o·la
Good morning.	Buenos días.	bwe·nos dee·as
Good afternoon.	Buenas tardes.	bwe·nas tar·des
Good evening/ night.	Buenas noches.	bwe·nas no·ches
Bye/See you soon.	Hasta luego.	as·ta lwe·go
Yes.	Sí.	see
No.	No.	no
Please.	Por favor.	por fa·vor
Thank you.	Gracias.	gra·syas
Many thanks.	Muchas gracias.	moo·chas gra·syas
You're welcome.	De nada.	de na·da
Pardon me.	Perdón.	per·don
(used before asking for information, for example))		
Excuse me.	Permiso.	per·mee·so
(used when asking to get past, for example)		
Forgive me.	Disculpe.	dees·kool·pe
(used when apologizing)		

How are things?
    ¿Qué tal?   ke tal
What's your name?
    ¿Cómo se llama? (pol)   ko·mo se ya·ma
    ¿Cómo te llamas? (inf)   ko·mo te ya·mas
My name is ...
    Me llamo ...   me ya·mo ...
It's a pleasure to meet you.
    Mucho gusto.   moo·cho goos·to
The pleasure is mine.
    El gusto es mío.   el goos·to es mee·o
Where are you from?
    ¿De dónde es? (pol)   de don·de es
    ¿De dónde eres? (inf)   de don·de er·es
I'm from ...
    Soy de ...   soy de ...
Where are you staying?
    ¿Dónde está alojado/a? (pol)   don·de es·ta a·lo·kha·do/a
    ¿Dónde estás alojado/a? (inf)   don·de es·tas a·lo·kha·do/a

LANGUAGE

May I take a photo?
¿Puedo sacar una foto?   pwe·do sa·*kar* oo·na *fo*·to

DIRECTIONS
How do I get to ...?
¿Cómo puedo llegar a ...?   ko·mo pwe·do ye·*gar* a ...
Is it far?
¿Está lejos?   es·*ta le*·khos

Go straight ahead.
Siga derecho.   see·ga de·*re*·cho
Turn left.
Voltée a la izquierda.   vol·*te*·e a la ees·*kyer*·da
Turn right.
Voltée a la derecha.   vol·*te*·e a la de·*re*·cha
Can you show me (on the map)?
¿Me lo podría indicar   me lo po·*dree*·a een·dee·*kar*
(en el mapa)?   (en el *ma*·pa)

SIGNS	
Entrada	Entrance
Salida	Exit
Información	Information
Abierto	Open
Cerrado	Closed
Prohibido	Prohibited
Comisaria	Police Station
Servicios/Baños	Toilets
Hombres/Varones	Men
Mujeres/Damas	Women

north	*norte*	*nor*·te
south	*sur*	soor
east	*este*	*es*·te
west	*oeste*	o·*es*·te
here	*aquí*	a·*kee*
there	*allí*	a·*yee*
avenue	*avenida*	a·ve·*nee*·da
block	*cuadra*	*kwa*·dra
street	*calle*	*ka*·ye

HEALTH
I'm sick.
Estoy enfermo/a.   es·*toy* en·*fer*·mo/a
I need a doctor.
Necesito un médico.   ne·se·*see*·to oon *me*·dee·ko
Where's the hospital?
¿Dónde está el hospital?   don·de es·*ta* el os·pee·*tal*
I'm pregnant.
Estoy embarazada.   es·*toy* em·ba·ra·*sa*·da
I've been vaccinated.
Estoy vacunado/a.   es·*toy* va·koo·*na*·do/a

I'm allergic to ...	*Soy alérgico/a a ...*	soy a·*ler*·khee·ko/a a ...
antibiotics	*los antibióticos*	los an·tee·*byo*·tee·kos
nuts	*las fruta secas*	las *froo*·tas *se*·kas
penicillin	*la penicilina*	la pe·nee·see·*lee*·na

I'm ...	*Soy ...*	soy ...
asthmatic	*asmático/a*	as·*ma*·tee·ko/a
diabetic	*diabético/a*	dee·ya·*be*·tee·ko/a
epileptic	*epiléptico/a*	e·pee·*lep*·tee·ko/a

I have ...	*Tengo ...*	*ten*·go ...
a cough	*tos*	tos
diarrhea	*diarrea*	dya·*re*·a
a headache	*un dolor de cabeza*	oon do·*lor* de ka·*be*·sa
nausea	*náusea*	*now*·se·a

EMERGENCIES
Help!	*¡Socorro!*	so·*ko*·ro
Fire!	*¡Incendio!*	een·*sen*·dyo
I've been robbed.	*Me robaron.*	me ro·*ba*·ron
Go away!	*¡Déjeme!*	*de*·khe·me
Get lost!	*¡Váyase!*	*va*·ya·se

Call ...!	*¡Llame a ...!*	*ya*·me a ...
an ambulance	*una ambulancia*	oo·na am·boo·*lan*·sya
a doctor	*un médico*	oon *me*·dee·ko
the police	*la policía*	la po·lee·*see*·a

It's an emergency.
Es una emergencia.   es oo·na e·mer·*khen*·sya
Could you help me, please?
¿Me puede ayudar,   me pwe·de a·yoo·*dar*
por favor?   por fa·*vor*
I'm lost.
Estoy perdido/a. (m/f)   es·*toy* per·*dee*·do/a
Where are the toilets?
¿Dónde están los baños?   don·de es·*tan* los *ba*·nyos

LANGUAGE DIFFICULTIES
Do you speak (English)?
¿Habla/Hablas (inglés)?   a·bla/a·blas (een·*gles*) (pol/inf)
Does anyone here speak English?
¿Hay alguien que hable   ai al·*gyen* ke *a*·ble
inglés?   een·*gles*
I (don't) understand.
(No) Entiendo.   (no) en·*tyen*·do
How do you say ...?
¿Cómo se dice ...?   ko·mo se *dee*·se ...

What does ... mean?

	¿Qué quiere decir ...?	ke kye·re de·seer ...

Could you please ...?

	¿Puede ..., por favor?	pwe·de ... por fa·vor
repeat that	repetirlo	re·pe·teer·lo
speak more slowly	hablar más despacio	a·blar mas des·pa·syo
write it down	escribirlo	es·kree·beer·lo

NUMBERS

0	cero	ce·ro
1	uno/a	oo·no/a
2	dos	dos
3	tres	tres
4	cuatro	kwa·tro
5	cinco	seen·ko
6	seis	seys
7	siete	sye·te
8	ocho	o·cho
9	nueve	nwe·ve
10	diez	dyes
11	once	on·se
12	doce	do·se
13	trece	tre·se
14	catorce	ka·tor·se
15	quince	keen·se
16	dieciséis	dye·see·seys
17	diecisiete	dye·see·sye·te
18	dieciocho	dye·see·o·cho
19	diecinueve	dye·see·nwe·ve
20	veinte	vayn·te
21	veintiuno	vayn·tee·oo·no
30	treinta	trayn·ta
31	treinta y uno	trayn·tai oo·no
40	cuarenta	kwa·ren·ta
50	cincuenta	seen·kwen·ta
60	sesenta	se·sen·ta
70	setenta	se·ten·ta
80	ochenta	o·chen·ta
90	noventa	no·ven·ta
100	cien	syen
101	ciento uno	syen·to oo·no
200	doscientos	do·syen·tos
1000	mil	meel

SHOPPING & SERVICES

I'd like to buy ...

	Quisiera comprar ...	kee·sye·ra kom·prar ...

I'm just looking.

| | Sólo estoy mirando. | so·lo es·toy mee·ran·do |

May I look at it?

| | ¿Puedo mirarlo? | pwe·do mee·rar·lo |

How much is it?

| | ¿Cuánto cuesta? | kwan·to kwes·ta |

That's too expensive for me.

| | Es demasiado caro para mí. | es de·ma·sya·do ka·ro pa·ra mee |

Could you lower the price?

| | ¿Podría bajar un poco el precio? | po·dree·a ba·khar oon po·ko el pre·syo |

I don't like it.

| | No me gusta. | no me goos·ta |

I'll take it.

| | Lo llevo. | lo ye·vo |

Do you accept ...?

	¿Aceptan ...?	a·sep·tan ...
credit cards	tarjetas de crédito	tar·khe·tas de kre·dee·to
traveler's checks	cheques de viajero	che·kes de vya·khe·ro
less	menos	me·nos
more	más	mas
large	grande	gran·de
small	pequeño	pe·ke·nyo

I'm looking for (the) ...

	Estoy buscando ...	es·toy boos·kan·do
ATM	el cajero automático	el ka·khe·ro ow·to·ma·tee·ko
bank	el banco	el ban·ko
bookstore	la librería	la lee·bre·ree·a
embassy	la embajada	la em·ba·kha·da
exchange office	la casa de cambio	la ka·sa de kam·byo
general store	la tienda	la tyen·da
laundry	la lavandería	la la·van·de·ree·a
market	el mercado	el mer·ka·do
pharmacy	la farmacia/ la droguería	la far·ma·sya/ la dro·ge·ree·a
post office	los correos	los ko·re·os
supermarket	el supermercado	el soo·per·mer·ka·do
tourist office	la oficina de turismo	la o·fee·see·na de too·rees·mo

What time does it open/close?

| | ¿A qué hora abre/cierra? | a ke o·ra a·bre/sye·ra |

I want to change some money/traveler's cheques.

| | Quiero cambiar dinero/ cheques de viajero. | kye·ro kam·byar dee·ne·ro/ che·kes de vya·khe·ro |

What's the exchange rate?

| | ¿Cuál es el tipo de cambio? | kwal es el tee·po de kam·byo |

I want to call ...

| | Quiero llamar a ... | kye·ro ya·mar a ... |

airmail	correo aéreo	ko·re·o a·e·re·o
letter	carta	kar·ta
registered mail	certificado	ser·tee·fee·ka·do
stamps	estampillas	es·tam·pee·yas

TIME & DATES

What time is it?	¿Qué hora es?	ke o·ra es
It's (one) o'clock.	Es la (una).	es la (oo·na)
It's (seven) o'clock.	Son las (siete).	son las (sye·te)
midnight	medianoche	me·dya·no·che
noon	mediodía	me·dyo·dee·a
half past two	dos y media	dos ee me·dya

now	ahora	a·o·ra
today	hoy	oy
tonight	esta noche	es·ta no·che
tomorrow	mañana	ma·nya·na
yesterday	ayer	a·yer

Monday	lunes	loo·nes
Tuesday	martes	mar·tes
Wednesday	miércoles	myer·ko·les
Thursday	jueves	khwe·ves
Friday	viernes	vyer·nes
Saturday	sábado	sa·ba·do
Sunday	domingo	do·meen·go

January	enero	e·ne·ro
February	febrero	fe·bre·ro
March	marzo	mar·so
April	abril	a·breel
May	mayo	ma·yo
June	junio	khoo·nyo
July	julio	khoo·lyo
August	agosto	a·gos·to
September	septiembre	sep·tyem·bre
October	octubre	ok·too·bre
November	noviembre	no·vyem·bre
December	diciembre	dee·syem·bre

TRANSPORT
Public Transport

What time does	¿A qué hora ...	a ke o·ra ...
... leave/arrive?	sale/llega?	sa·le/ye·ga
the bus	el autobús	el ow·to·boos
the plane	el avión	el a·vyon
the ship	el barco	el bar·ko

airport	el aeropuerto	el a·e·ro·pwer·to
bus station	la estación de autobuses	la es·ta·syon de ow·to·boo·ses
bus stop	la parada de autobuses	la pa·ra·da de ow·to·boo·ses

| luggage check room | guardería/ equipaje | gwar·de·ree·a/ e·kee·pa·khe |
| ticket office | la boletería | la bo·le·te·ree·a |

I'd like a ticket to ...
Quiero un boleto a ...   kye·ro oon bo·le·to a ...
What's the fare to ...?
¿Cuánto cuesta hasta ...?   kwan·to kwes·ta a·sta ...

student's (fare)	de estudiante	de es·too·dyan·te
1st class	primera clase	pree·me·ra kla·se
2nd class	segunda clase	se·goon·da kla·se
one-way	ida	ee·da
return	ida y vuelta	ee·da ee vwel·ta
taxi	taxi	tak·see

Private Transport

pickup (truck)	camioneta	ka·myo·ne·ta
truck	camión	ka·myon
hitchhike	hacer dedo	a·ser de·do

I'd like to hire a/an ...	Quisiera alquilar ...	kee·sye·ra al·kee·lar ...
bicycle	una bicicleta	oo·na bee·see·kle·ta
car	un auto/ un coche	oon ow·to/ oon ko·che
4WD	un todo terreno	oon to·do te·re·no
motorbike	una moto	oo·na mo·to

Is this the road to ...?
¿Se va a ... por esta carretera?   se va a ... por es·ta ka·re·te·ra
Where's a gas/petrol station?
¿Dónde hay una gasolinera?   don·de ai oo·na ga·so·lee·ne·ra
Please fill it up.
Lleno, por favor.   ye·no por fa·vor
I'd like (20) liters.
Quiero (veinte) litros.   kye·ro (vayn·te) lee·tros

ROAD SIGNS	
Acceso	Entrance
Ceda el Paso	Give Way
Despacio	Slow
Dirección Única	One-Way
Mantenga Su Derecha	Keep to the Right
No Adelantar/ No Rebase	No Passing
Peligro	Danger
Prohibido Aparcar/ No Estacionar	No Parking
Prohibido el Paso	No Entry
Pare	Stop

LANGUAGE

diesel	diesel	dee·sel
leaded (regular)	gasolina con plomo	ga·so·lee·na kon plo·mo
gas/petrol	gasolina	ga·so·lee·na
unleaded	gasolina sin plomo	ga·so·lee·na seen plo·mo

(How long) Can I park here?
  ¿(Por cuánto tiempo) Puedo aparcar aquí?
  (por kwan·to tyem·po) pwe·do a·par·kar a·kee
Where do I pay?
  ¿Dónde se paga?
  don·de se pa·ga
I need a mechanic.
  Necesito un mecánico.
  ne·se·see·to oon me·ka·nee·ko
The car has broken down in ...
  El carro se ha averiado en ...
  el ka·ro se a a·ve·rya·do en ...
The motorbike won't start.
  No arranca la moto.
  no a·ran·ka la mo·to
I've run out of gas/petrol.
  Me quedé sin gasolina.
  me ke·de seen ga·so·lee·na
I've had an accident.
  Tuve un accidente.
  too·ve oon ak·see·den·te

TRAVEL WITH CHILDREN
I need ...
  Necesito ...   ne·se·see·to ...
Do you have ...?
  ¿Hay ...?   ai ...
    a car baby seat
    un asiento de seguridad para bebés
    oon a·syen·to de se·goo·ree·da pa·ra be·bes
    a child-minding service
    un servicio de cuidado de niños
    oon ser·vee·syo de kwee·da·do de nee·nyos
    (disposable) diapers/nappies
    pañales (de usar y tirar)
    pa·nya·les de oo·sar ee tee·rar
    an (English-speaking) babysitter
    una niñera (de habla inglesa)
    oo·na nee·nye·ra (de a·bla een·gle·sa)
    infant formula (milk)
    leche en polvo para bebés
    le·che en pol·vo pa·ra be·bes
    a highchair
    una trona
    oo·na tro·na
    a potty
    una pelela
    oo·na pe·le·la
    a stroller
    un cochecito
    oon ko·che·see·to

Also available from Lonely Planet:
Latin American Spanish Phrasebook

Glossary

The solidus (/) in some words in bold separates masculine and feminine forms.

arrecife – coral reef

asadero – place serving roasted or grilled meats

atarraya – circular fishing net widely used on the coast and rivers

AUC – Autodefensas Unidas de Colombia; a loose alliance of paramilitary squads known as *autodefensas*

autodefensas – right-wing squads created to combat guerrillas, also called *paramilitares* or just *paras*

ayudante – driver's assistant on intercity buses

azulejos – ornamental handmade tiles that were brought to South America from Spain and Portugal during colonial times

balneario – seaside, lakeside or riverside bathing place with facilities

bambuco – musical genre of the Andean region

bandola – an instrument derived from the mandolin that is used in the music of the Andean region; also an entirely different guitar-type instrument that is played in Los Llanos

bandolero – bandit, brigand; term used to refer to guerrillas to undermine their political aims, emphasising their criminal activities

baquiano – peasant who hires out horses or mules for horseback excursions, and usually accompanies the group as a guide

basuco or **bazuco** – base from which cocaine is refined; smoked in cigarettes

boleteo – the guerrilla practice of 'taxing' local landowners in exchange for leaving them in peace, 'a bourgeois contribution to the revolution;' people who refuse to pay are often hijacked or assassinated

bomba – petrol (gasoline) station

brujo – witch doctor, shaman

burundanga – drug extracted from a plant, used by thieves to render their victim unconscious

buseta – small bus that is a popular means of city transport

cabalgata – horseback ride

cabaña – cabin, usually found on beaches or up in the mountains

cachaco/a – person from Bogotá, although for the *costeños* anyone not from the coast is a *cachaco*

cacique – Indian tribal head; today the term is applied to provincial leaders from the two traditional political parties, also called *gamonales*

CAI – Centro de Atención Inmediata; the network of police posts that were established in the cities in order to upgrade public security

caipirinha – Brazilian cocktail based on sugarcane rum

caleño/a – person from Cali

caminata – trek, hike

camino de herradura – bridle path, commonly paved with stone; these were the early tracks built under Spanish rule by Indian labour

campero – jeep

campesino/a – rural dweller, usually of modest economic means; peasant

caneca – wastepaper basket or bin

carriel – typical Antioquian leather bag used by men

carro – car

casa de cambio – money-exchange office

caserío – hamlet

casona – big, rambling old house

caucheras – slingshots

cédula – ID of Colombian citizens and residents

ceiba – common tree of the tropics; can reach a huge size

celador – security guard (usually armed) at a public building or private house; a very common job these days – there are at least 100,000 of them in Bogotá alone

chalupa – small passenger boat powered by an outboard motor

chévere – good, nice (informal)

chichamaya – traditional dance of the Guajiro Indians

chigüiro – capybara; the world's large rodent common to Los Llanos

chimbo – false; of bad quality; not as good as expected (informal)

chinchorro – hammock woven of cotton threads or palm fibre like a fishing net; typical of many Indian groups; the best known are the decorative cotton hammocks of the Guajiros

chirimía – street band popular on the Pacific coast and in the Andean region

chiva – traditional bus with its body made of timber and painted with colourful patterns; still widely used in the countryside

ciénaga – shallow lake or lagoon

cinemateca – art-house cinema that screens quality films

climatizado – air-conditioned; term used for air-con buses

colectivo – shared taxi or minibus; a popular means of public transport

corraleja – dangerous kind of bullfight in which spectators can take their chances with the bull; popular mainly in the Sucre department, it originated in Pamplona, Spain

corrida – bullfight

corriente – ordinary bus

costeño/a – inhabitant of the Caribbean coast

criollo/a – Creole, a person of European (especially Spanish) blood, but born in the Americas

cuadrilla – kind of popular theatre group or play, always using disguises, usually accompanied by music and sometimes by dance

cuatro – small, four-stringed guitar, used in the music of Los Llanos

cumbia – one of the most popular musical rhythms (and corresponding dance) of the Caribbean coast; African in origin

currulao – popular dance of the Pacific coast, of mixed African-Spanish origin, usually accompanied by a *marimba*

danta – tapir; large, hoofed mammal of tropical and subtropical forests

dar papaya – to give someone the opportunity to take advantage of you (informal)

DAS – Departamento Administrativo de Seguridad; the security police, responsible for immigration

denuncia – official report/statement to the police

derrumbe – landslide; the main cause of blocked roads, particularly during the rainy season

(los) desechables – literally 'the disposables'; term referring to the underclass including the homeless, beggars, street urchins, prostitutes, homosexuals and the like, who are treated as human refuse and are the objects of an abhorrent process of 'social cleansing' by death squads known as *los limpiadores*, or 'the cleaners'

deslizador – term used in some regions for a high-powered boat

droguería – pharmacy

ELN – Ejército de Liberación Nacional; the second-largest guerrilla group after the FARC

esquina – street corner

estadero – roadside restaurant that often offers accommodation

FARC – Fuerzas Armadas Revolucionarias de Colombia; the largest guerrilla group in the country

finca – anything from a country house with a small garden to a huge country estate

fique – sisal obtained from the agave, widely used in handicrafts

flota – general term for intercity buses

frailejón – espeletia, a species of plant typical of the *páramo*

fresco – take it easy (informal)

fulano – so-and-so; a person whose name has been forgotten or is unknown

gallera – cockfight ring

gamín – street urchin; originated from the French *gamin*; the word was adopted in Colombia when the French media began reporting on the appalling conditions of street children in Bogotá

gamonales – see *cacique*

greca – large, cylindrical coffee-maker; the old ones, often lavishly decorated with engraved patterns, are reminiscent of Russian samovars

gringo/a – any white male/female foreigner; sometimes, not always, used in a derogatory sense

guacamaya – macaw

guacharaca – percussion instrument consisting of a stick-like wooden body with a row of cuts and a metal fork; used in *vallenato* music

guácharo – oilbird; a species of nocturnal bird living in caves

guadua – the largest variety of the bamboo family, common in many regions of moderate climate

guaquero – robber of pre-Columbian tombs

guardaequipaje – the left-luggage office, checkroom

guardaparque – national-park ranger

guayabera – men's embroidered shirt, popular throughout the Caribbean region

guayabo – hangover (informal); warranted after an *aguardiente* session

hacienda – country estate

hospedaje – budget hotel

indio – literally 'Indian'; in Colombia it has acquired a pejorative connotation and is used to insult someone, regardless of race; to refer respectfully to Indians, use *indígena*

invierno – literally 'winter'; refers to the rainy season

isleño/a – literally 'islander'; inhabitant of San Andrés and Providencia

IVA – *impuesto de valor agregado*, a value-added tax (VAT)

joropo – typical music of Los Llanos, also referred to as *música llanera*

lancha – launch, motorboat

ligre – cross of Bengal tiger and African lion, first bred in Colombia (in Pereira's zoo)

(los) limpiadores – see *los desechables*

liqui liqui – men's traditional costume, typical of most of the Caribbean; a white or beige suit comprising trousers and a blouse with a collar, usually accompanied by white hat and shoes

llanero/a – inhabitant of Los Llanos

(Los) Llanos – literally 'plains'; vast plains between the Andes and the Río Orinoco

mafioso – member of the mafia; big fish of the drug business

malecón – waterfront promenade

maloca – large, communal house of certain Indian groups; usually a wooden structure thatched with palm leaves

manta – long, loose dress worn by Guajiro Indian women; also a bedspread

maracas – gourd rattles; an accompanying instrument of the *joropo* and other rhythms

marimba – percussion instrument

matrimonio – literally 'wedding;' hotel room with a double bed intended for married couples

mecha – small triangular envelope with gunpowder, used in *tejo*

merengue – musical rhythm originating in the Dominican Republic, today widespread throughout the Caribbean and beyond

meseta – plateau

mestizo/a – person of mixed European-Indian blood

mirador – lookout, viewpoint

mochila – bucket-shaped shoulder bag, traditionally made by Indians, today produced commercially

mola – colourful, hand-stitched applique textile of the Cuna Indians; a rectangular piece of cloth made of several differently coloured, superimposed layers sewn together

mopa mopa – also known as *barniz de Pasto*; vegetable resin used for decorating wooden crafts, typical of Pasto

moriche – palm common in Los Llanos, used for construction, household items, handicrafts etc

motorista – boat driver

múcura – kind of traditional pottery jar

muelle – pier, wharf

mula – literally 'mule'; a person hired by drug traffickers to smuggle drugs overseas; also means 'big truck'

mulato/a – mulatto; a person of mixed Spanish-African blood

narcotraficante – drug dealer

Navidad – Christmas

nevado – snowcapped mountain peak

ñapa – a little bit extra for having bought something, eg buy six oranges and get one free

orquídea – orchid

oso hormiguero – anteater

paisa – person from Antioquia; *pueblo paisa* – a typical Antioquian town

palanca – literally 'lever'; a connection or person with influence to help out when the regular avenues don't work (informal); it's very important to have them in Colombia

papagayo – popular term for macaw

paradero – bus stop; in some areas called *parada*

paramilitares – see *autodefensas*

páramo – open highlands between about 3500m and 4500m, typical of Colombia, Venezuela and Ecuador

parapente – paragliding

parqueadero – car park

pasillo – type of music/dance played in the Andean region

pastuso/a – person from Pasto, but also anyone a bit slow or dumb; the *pastuso* is the butt of many jokes

perica – cocaine (informal)

pescadería – fish (seafood) restaurant

piso – storey, floor

pito – car horn; used indiscriminately in and outside the city

plaza de toros – bullfight ring

poporo – a vessel made from a small gourd, used by the Arhuacos and other Indian groups to carry lime; while chewing coca leaves, Indians add lime to help release the alkaloid from the leaves

porro – musical rhythm of the Caribbean coast

propina – tip (not a bribe)

puente – literally 'bridge'; also means a three-day-long weekend (including Monday)

refugio – rustic shelter in a remote area, mostly in the mountains

requinto – small 12-string guitar used as a melodic instrument

requisa – police document search, sometimes a body search

residencias – budget hotel, often love hotels with rooms rented by the hour.

retén – police checkpoint on the road

ruana – Colombian poncho

rumba – fiesta; private or public party with music and drinking

rumbeadero – discotheque or other place to go to drink and dance

rumbear – to party; a Colombian speciality

salinas – seaside saltpans or shallow lagoons used for extraction of salt

salsa – type of Caribbean dance music of Cuban origin, very popular in Colombia

salsoteca – disco playing salsa music

Semana Santa – Holy Week, the week before Easter Sunday

sicario – a paid killer hired to eliminate adversaries

SIDA – AIDS

soborno – bribe

sobrecargo – surcharge

son – one of the main rhythms of Afro-Cuban music

soroche – altitude sickness

sumercé – originated from Su Merced, old-fashioned, respectful form of address; used mostly in rural areas of the Andean region

taberna – pub/bar/tavern

tagua – hard ivory-coloured nut of a species of palm; used in handicrafts

tejo – traditional game, popular mainly in the Andean region; played with a heavy metal disk, which is thrown aiming to make a *mecha* (a sort of petard) explode

Telecom – state telephone company

teleférico – cable car

telenovela – TV soap opera

terminal de pasajeros – bus terminal

tiple – small 12-stringed guitar used as an accompanying instrument

tombos – common informal term for police

tonina – freshwater dolphin

torbellino – music/dance typical of the Andean region

totuma – cup-like vessel made from the hollowed-out dried fruit of a tree cut in half; used in some areas for drinking, washing etc

trapiche – traditional sugarcane mill

tugurios – shantytowns built of waste materials by the poor on invaded public or private land around big cities, particularly extensive in Bogotá and Medellín

tunjo – flat gold figurine, often depicting a warrior; typical artefact of the Muisca Indians

vacuna – literally 'vaccine'; term used to refer to the payments made to guerrillas by farmers to avoid being harassed

vaina – thing (informal); *qué vaina* – what a problem

vallenato – music typical of the Caribbean region, based on the accordion; it's now widespread in Colombia

vaquero – cowboy of Los Llanos

verano – literally 'summer'; refers to the dry season

(La) Violencia – bloody period of civil war (1948–57) between Colombia's two political parties

vivero – plant nursery

voladora – high-powered speedboat

yagé – plant with hallucinogenic properties used by traditional healers of some Indian groups

yanchana – bark paintings made by some Indian groups of the Amazon

zambo/a – person of mixed Indian-African ancestry

Behind the Scenes

THIS BOOK
This is the 4th edition of *Colombia*. Michael Kohn served as coordinating author, writing much of the front and back chapters as well as the Bogotá, North of Bogotá, Caribbean Coast and San Andrés & Providencia chapters. Robert Landon covered Northwest Colombia, Southwest Colombia and the Amazon Basin. Thomas Kohnstamm wrote the History, Culture, Environment and Food & Drink chapters. Dr David Goldberg MD contributed the Health chapter. The first three editions of this book were written by Krzysztof Dydyński.

THANKS FROM THE AUTHORS
Michael Kohn In Lonely Planet World, many thanks to Commissioning Editor Kathleen Munnelly, mapping expert Alison Lyall, and fellow authors Robert Landon and Thomas Kohnstamm. A big thanks to Baigalmaa 'Gail' Kohn and Justin 'Jurassic Norm' Anderson for making the trip with me down to Colombia. In Colombia, special thanks to Michael Forest, Pavel Toropov, Mark Baker, Chloe Rutter, Nick Morgan, Simone Bruno, German Escobar, Oscar Gilede, Arnon Yogev, Tomor and Chaim at L'Jaim restaurant, and Señor Manuel.

Robert Landon I must thank: Laura Anderson of Medellín and Juan Carlos Uribe of Cali for all their insider insights; Kathleen Munnelly for her trust and patience; Carlos Ponce for nourishing me while I wrote; Paulo Bellot for getting me to the airport and much more; and my father, whose final act was to replace my fried Mac. I miss him terribly.

Thomas Kohnstamm Thank you to Carolina Orozco Rincón, Kathleen Munnelly, Michael Kohn and Julia Taylor.

CREDITS
This title was commissioned in Lonely Planet's Oakland office and produced by:

Commissioning Editor Kathleen Munnelly
Coordinating Editors Julia Taylor, Kyla Gillzan
Coordinating Cartographer Owen Eszeki
Coordinating Layout Designer Jacqueline McLeod
Managing Cartographer Alison Lyall
Assisting Editors Kate Evans, Helen Koehne, Lauren Rollheiser
Assisting Cartographers Emma McNicol, Sophie Reed
Cover Designer Nic Lehman
Project Managers Ray Thomson, Nancy Ianni
Language Content Coordinator Quentin Frayne

Thanks to Jessa Boanas-Dewes, Melanie Dankel, Sally Darmody, Jennifer Garrett, Michala Green, Adriana Mammarella, Stephanie Pearson, Emily K Wolman, Celia Wood

OUR READERS
Many thanks to the hundreds of travelers who used the last edition and wrote to us with helpful hints, useful advice and interesting anecdotes.

A Francesca Alaimo, Erich Ammann, Rohan Ayres **B** Jonathan Barach, Sam Bass, Karen Bedlack, Jonathan Bird, Mette Bosmann Mortensen, Andres Botero, James G Botts, Jack Brewster, Fetz Brown

---

THE LONELY PLANET STORY
The story begins with a classic travel adventure: Tony and Maureen Wheeler's 1972 journey across Europe and Asia to Australia. There was no useful information about the overland trail then, so Tony and Maureen published the first Lonely Planet guidebook to meet a growing need.

From a kitchen table, Lonely Planet has grown to become the largest independent travel publisher in the world, with offices in Melbourne (Australia), Oakland (USA) and London (UK). Today Lonely Planet guidebooks cover the globe. There is an ever-growing list of books and information in a variety of media. Some things haven't changed. The main aim is still to make it possible for adventurous travelers to get out there – to explore and better understand the world.

At Lonely Planet we believe travelers can make a positive contribution to the countries they visit – if they respect their host communities and spend their money wisely. Every year 5% of company profit is donated to charities around the world.

C Carlos Arturo Camargo, Leah Caseley, Ana Castano, Olivier Cazenave **D** Eugénie Dumais **E** Brian Eaton, Miguel Escobar **F** Triston Farmer, Thomas Fassbender, Jonathan Fefer, Rolf Forster, Valery Fueg **G** Paola Garzon, Thomas Grimm, **H** Richard Hanson, Max Harris, Kate Hill, Paul Hofmann, Nafisa Hunedy, Magda Huwyler, Mike Huwyler **I** Hans Izeboud **J** Jan Jasiewicz, Richard Jenkins **K** Daniel J Kimmons, Lisa Knappich, Carsten Koebisch, Alexander Komm, Monica Kremer **L** Christy Lanal, Christy Lanzl, Stuart Leather, Kelvin Leeming, Dan Levin, Steve Lidgey, Adrian Lion, Lina Lopez, Lourdes Lopez **M** Sarah Mason, Michelangelo Mazzeo, Ben McCay, Jenny McHugh, Matthew Memberg, Kjell Mittag, Harald Moeller, Alejandro Moreno Saldarriaga, Maarten Munnik, Wim Muys **O** Héctor Ocampo **P** Maria Paola, Rob Pilkington

R Caccuri Roberto, Raul Rodriguez, Maria Rueda, Eliza Russell **S** Rania Salameh, Gavin Sexton, Yuval Shafir, Jonathan Sibtain, Ondrej Sklenar, Stefan Smedegaard Hansen, Kristi Sundberg, Judy & Ariana Svenson **T** Joshua Taylor Barnes, Gea Testi, Russ Turla **V** Matthieu Van Der Veldt, Matthew VanCleave, Oswaldo Vanegas, Francisco Vasquez, Danny Vermeersch, Christian von Allmen, Ulli Von Baggehufwudt **W** Douglas Webster, Ludwig Wirth, Uwe Wrenger **Y** Avi Yan, María Yanguas, **Z** Jacobo Zanella

ACKNOWLEDGMENTS

Many thanks to the following for the use of their content: Globe on back cover © Mountain High Maps 1993 Digital Wisdom, Inc.

Index

INDEX

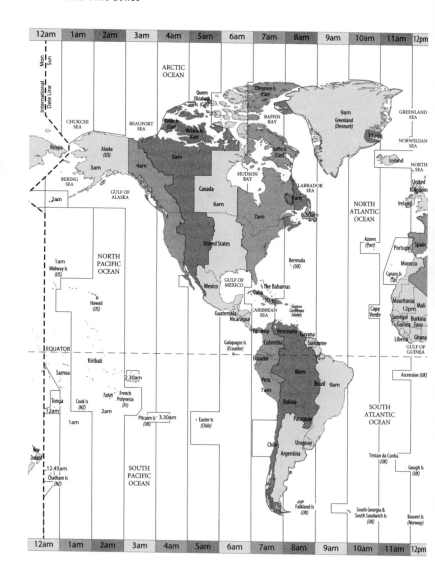

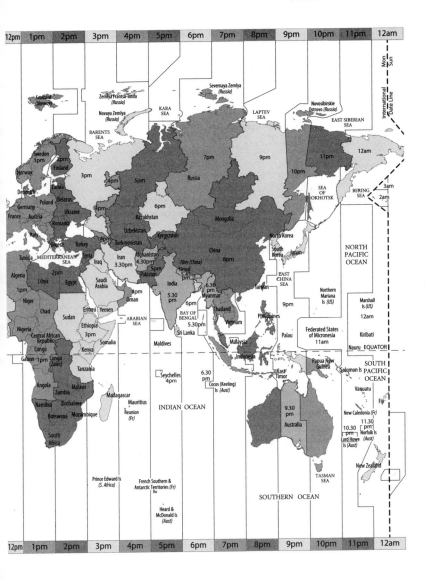

12pm	1pm	2pm	3pm	4pm	5pm	6pm	7pm	8pm	9pm	10pm	11pm	12am

Svalbard (Norway)
Zemlya Frantsa-Iosifa (Russia)
Severnaya Zemlya (Russia)
KARA SEA
Novaya Zemlya (Russia)
LAPTEV SEA
Novosibirskie Ostrovo (Russia)
EAST SIBERIAN SEA
BARENTS SEA
Sweden 1pm
2pm Finland
Norway
Denmark
3pm
4pm
5pm
7pm
9pm
11pm
12am
International Date Line
Mon/Sun
Latvia
Germany Poland Belarus
France Austria Ukraine
Italy Romania
Tunisia Greece Turkey
MEDITERRANEAN SEA
Algeria 2pm
Libya Egypt
Niger
1pm
Chad
Sudan
Nigeria
Central African Republic
Gabon 1pm Congo (Zaire)
Congo
Angola
Zambia
Namibia Zimbabwe
Botswana Mozambique
South Africa

Russia
Kazakhstan
Uzbekistan
Turkmenistan
4pm
5pm
6pm
Mongolia
Kyrgyzstan
China
8pm
North Korea
South Korea Japan
10pm
SEA OF OKHOTSK
BERING SEA
3am
2am
NORTH PACIFIC OCEAN

Syria
Iraq Iran 3.30pm
Afghanistan 4.30pm
5pm
Pakistan
Tibet (China)
Nepal 5.45
pm
India
5.30 pm
6pm
6.30
pm
Myanmar
Thailand
Taiwan
EAST CHINA SEA
9pm
Northern Mariana Is (US)
Marshall Is (US)
12am
Saudi Arabia
Oman
BAY OF BENGAL
5.30pm
Vietnam
Philippines
Palau
Federated States of Micronesia 11pm
Kiribati
Eritrea Yemen
ARABIAN SEA
Sri Lanka
Ethiopia 3pm
Somalia
Maldives
Malaysia
Indonesia
Nauru EQUATOR
Kenya
Tanzania
Seychelles
4pm
6.30 pm
Cocos (Keeling) Is (Aust)
East Timor
Papua New Guinea
Solomon Is SOUTH PACIFIC OCEAN
Vanuatu
Madagascar
Mauritius
Reunion (Fr)
INDIAN OCEAN
9.30 pm
Australia
New Caledonia (Fr)
10.30 pm
Lord Howe Is (Aust)
11.30 pm Norfolk Is (Aust)
Fiji
Prince Edward Is (S. Africa)
French Southern & Antarctic Territories (Fr)
New Zealand
Heard & McDonald Is (Aust)
TASMAN SEA
SOUTHERN OCEAN

12pm	1pm	2pm	3pm	4pm	5pm	6pm	7pm	8pm	9pm	10pm	11pm	12am

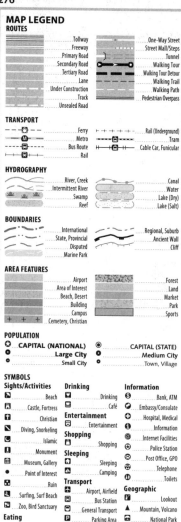

MAP LEGEND
ROUTES

Tollway
Freeway
Primary Road
Secondary Road
Tertiary Road
Lane
Under Construction
Track
Unsealed Road

One-Way Street
Street Mall/Steps
Tunnel
Walking Tour
Walking Tour Detour
Walking Trail
Walking Path
Pedestrian Overpass

TRANSPORT

Ferry
Metro
Bus Route
Rail

Rail (Underground)
Tram
Cable Car, Funicular

HYDROGRAPHY

River, Creek
Intermittent River
Swamp
Reef

Canal
Water
Lake (Dry)
Lake (Salt)

BOUNDARIES

International
State, Provincial
Disputed
Marine Park

Regional, Suburb
Ancient Wall
Cliff

AREA FEATURES

Airport
Area of Interest
Beach, Desert
Building
Campus
Cemetery, Christian

Forest
Land
Market
Park
Sports

POPULATION

CAPITAL (NATIONAL)
Large City
Small City

CAPITAL (STATE)
Medium City
Town, Village

SYMBOLS

Sights/Activities
Beach
Castle, Fortress
Christian
Diving, Snorkeling
Islamic
Monument
Museum, Gallery
Point of Interest
Ruin
Surfing, Surf Beach
Zoo, Bird Sanctuary

Eating
Eating

Drinking
Drinking
Café

Entertainment
Entertainment

Shopping
Shopping

Sleeping
Sleeping
Camping

Transport
Airport, Airfield
Bus Station
General Transport
Parking Area
Taxi Rank

Information
Bank, ATM
Embassy/Consulate
Hospital, Medical
Information
Internet Facilities
Police Station
Post Office, GPO
Telephone
Toilets

Geographic
Lookout
Mountain, Volcano
National Park
Waterfall

LONELY PLANET OFFICES

Australia
Head Office
Locked Bag 1, Footscray, Victoria 3011
☎ 03 8379 8000, fax 03 8379 8111
talk2us@lonelyplanet.com.au

USA
150 Linden St, Oakland, CA 94607
☎ 510 893 8555, toll free 800 275 8555
fax 510 893 8572
info@lonelyplanet.com

UK
72–82 Rosebery Ave,
Clerkenwell, London EC1R 4RW
☎ 020 7841 9000, fax 020 7841 9001
go@lonelyplanet.co.uk

Published by Lonely Planet Publications Pty Ltd
ABN 36 005 607 983

© Lonely Planet Publications Pty Ltd 2006

© photographers as indicated 2006

Cover photographs: Girl holding stick, Danny Lehman/Corbis/APL (front); Pedestrian timber bridge spanning Provencia and Santa Catalina over the shallow Canal Aury, Krzysztof Dydyński/Lonely Planet Images (back). Many of the images in this guide are available for licensing from Lonely Planet Images: www.lonelyplanetimages.com.

Printed by SNP Security Printing Pte Ltd, Singapore